AF608561

Degree Zero

in Architecture

Form, Value, Authorship

Degree Zero

Spector Books

in Architecture

Edited by
Lyna Bourouiba, Wouter Van Acker

Form, Value, Authorship

49-151

153-249

251-319

I
Ways for Architecture to Be Form

II
Ways for Knowledge to Be a Research Object

III
Ways for Research to Be a Form of Knowledge

Degree Zero

in Architecture

introduced by
Lyna Bourouiba

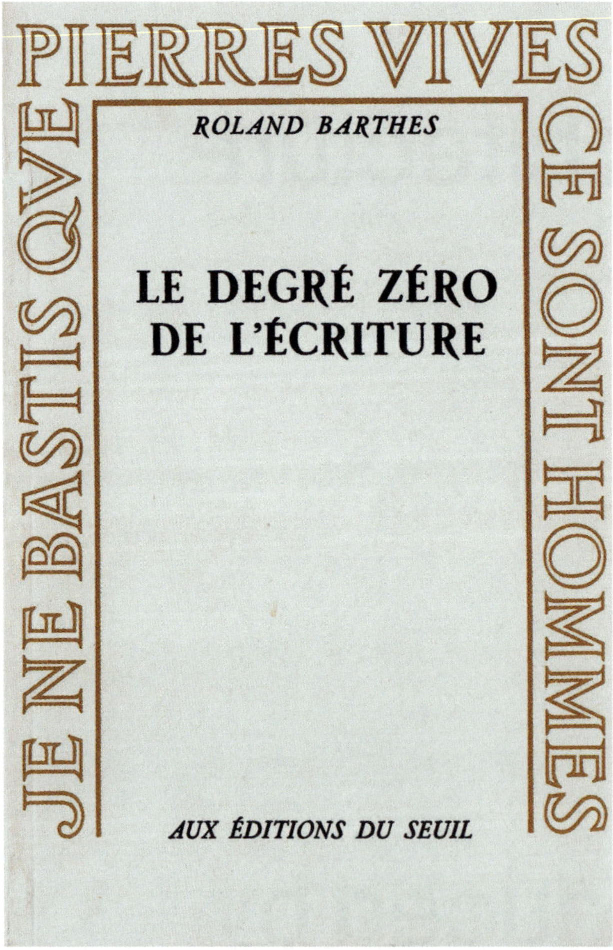

PIERRES VIVES

ROLAND BARTHES

LE DEGRÉ ZÉRO
DE L'ÉCRITURE

AUX ÉDITIONS DU SEUIL

JE NE BASTIS QVE

CE SONT HOMMES

Fig. 1 Cover of the first edition of *Le degré zéro de l'écriture* (Paris, Seuil, 1953).

Beginning in the second half of the twentieth century, the term "degree zero" began to punctuate architectural discourse. It has structured, fueled, thickened, and illustrated several intellectual positions, particularly from the 1960s to the 1980s, although interest in its applications continues today. Among those who theorize, review, and construct architecture, some refer metaphorically to a degree zero to illustrate a point while others believe that elements of the degree zero idea have the potential to respond the postmodern architectural crisis. It contains certain theoretical reference points by which architects can position themselves, allowing them to overcome the disciplinary crisis that constrains their practice—a crisis of language and form that is also a crisis of the social role of the architect-author.

LOST IN TRANSLATIONS

The manifestation of the idea of a degree zero in architecture testifies to an act of translation from literary studies by those who use and manipulate it, since it refers to the first book by Roland Barthes, *Le degré zéro de l'écriture*, published in 1953 (Fig. 1).[1] At the time of his death in 1980, for some two decades Barthes had been a leading intellectual figure in France, where he lived and taught at two prestigious academic institutions, École Pratique des Hautes Études (1962 to 1977) and Collège de France (1977 to 1980). With his ideas internationally known and translated, Barthes was recognized as a "master of modern times," as much a semiologist and structuralist as "a man of sentences," "literary historian," "mythologist," "critic," "polemicist," and "writer."[2]

While his work inspired and shaped reflections in fields of the arts, the idea of a degree zero in architecture began to be manipulated in the context of the crisis of modernity of the postwar period. It appeared in architectural publications of that time to feed the intellectual and speculative exercises of not only historians, theoreticians, and critics but also architects writing about their own work. The idea was also debated during conferences to evaluate its efficiency for the architectural discipline and to negotiate the meaning of its architectural transpositions. Often used without reference to Barthes's essay, the idea of degree zero has thus come to be part of the common vocabulary of the architecture field, with no apparent necessity to explain the notion's source. For Charles Jencks, the term covered a "rearguard discipline" that was led by Bruno Zevi, Vittorio Gregotti, Aldo van Eyck, and Kenneth Frampton.[3] Martin Steinmann associated it with the enigmatic idea of a "new presence" in the architectural production of northern Switzerland in the 1980s and 1990s.[4] The term continues to be used to characterize and analyze minimalist projects[5] or to name the absence of rhetoric and the refusal of mannerism in contemporary architecture.[6] Some authors attribute to an architectural degree zero the values of an anonymous architecture,[7] the cracking of prescriptive architectural codes,[8] or even the absence of architecture.[9] The idea of a degree zero is regularly brought into play to qualify the formal and aesthetic attributes of certain productions or to define some intellectual opposition to postmodernism.[10] Few architectural critics, however, have made it the subject of a continual reflection over time. Bruno Zevi is one of the notable exceptions.[11] In the 1970s and 1980s, Zevi wrote a number of texts that paraphrased Barthes's statements, replacing "literature" and "writing" with "architecture," a tempting exercise that others in different contexts, like Jean Attali in an article in *L'architecture d'aujourd'hui* in 2001, or Peter Eisenman when teaching at the Institute for Architecture and Urban Studies (IAUS) in 1982, have also tried.[12]

As president of the International Committee of Architectural Critics (CICA), Zevi invited members to discuss, at private meetings and public events, the possibility of an architectural degree zero. It came up, for example, in 1980 at a public roundtable introduced and moderated by Arthur Drexler at the New York Museum of Modern Art and in 1981 at an open working session of the UIA Congress in Warsaw, which, according to CICA, was their most convincing, and conflicting, event. In 1985, Zevi again proposed the degree zero as a theme, this time for the 1987 UIA Congress in Brighton. In 1997, he finally organized his own event, divided into a conference, an architecture competition, and a publication entitled *Landscape and the Zero Degree of Architectural Language* (Fig. 2–3).

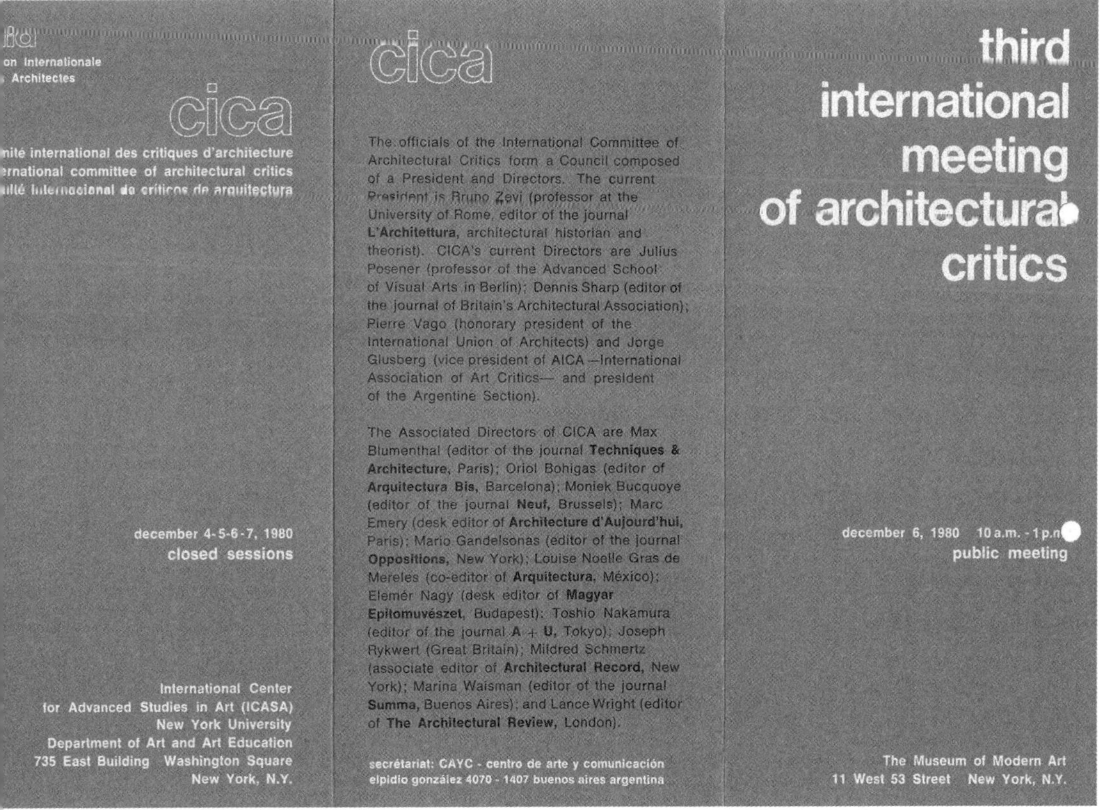

on Internationale
Architectes

cica

nité international des critiques d'architecture
ernational committee of architectural critics
ité internacional de criticos de arquitectura

december 4-5-6-7, 1980
closed sessions

International Center
for Advanced Studies in Art (ICASA)
New York University
Department of Art and Art Education
735 East Building Washington Square
New York, N.Y.

cica

The officials of the International Committee of Architectural Critics form a Council composed of a President and Directors. The current President is Bruno Zevi (professor at the University of Rome, editor of the journal **L'Architettura**, architectural historian and theorist). CICA's current Directors are Julius Posener (professor of the Advanced School of Visual Arts in Berlin); Dennis Sharp (editor of the journal of Britain's Architectural Association); Pierre Vago (honorary president of the International Union of Architects) and Jorge Glusberg (vice president of AICA—International Association of Art Critics— and president of the Argentine Section).

The Associated Directors of CICA are Max Blumenthal (editor of the journal **Techniques & Architecture**, Paris); Oriol Bohigas (editor of **Arquitectura Bis**, Barcelona); Moniek Bucquoye (editor of the journal **Neuf**, Brussels); Marc Emery (desk editor of **Architecture d'Aujourd'hui**, Paris); Mario Gandelsonas (editor of the journal **Oppositions**, New York); Louise Noelle Gras de Mereles (co-editor of **Arquitectura**, México); Elemér Nagy (desk editor of **Magyar Epitomuvészet**, Budapest); Toshio Nakamura (editor of the journal **A + U**, Tokyo); Joseph Rykwert (Great Britain); Mildred Schmertz (associate editor of **Architectural Record**, New York); Marina Waisman (editor of the journal **Summa**, Buenos Aires); and Lance Wright (editor of **The Architectural Review**, London).

secrétariat: CAYC - centro de arte y comunicación
elpidio gonzález 4070 - 1407 buenos aires argentina

third international meeting of architectural critics

december 6, 1980 10 a.m. - 1 p.m.
public meeting

The Museum of Modern Art
11 West 53 Street New York, N.Y.

Fig. 2 Leaflet of the third CICA meeting in New York where the possibility of an architectural degree zero was debated. (front)

Participants

Max Blumenthal (France)
Moniek Bucquoye (Belgium)
George Collins (U.S.A.)
Michèle Champenois (France)
Angiola Churchill (U.S.A.)
Marc Emery (France)
Mario Gandelsonas (U.S.A.)
Jorge Glusberg (Argentina)
Luis Grossman (Argentina)
Adam Kowalewski (Poland)
Louise Noelle Mereles (México)
Luciana Miotto (France)
Elemér Nagy (Hungary)
Toshio Nakamura (Japan)
Joseph Rykwert (England)
Mildred Schmertz (U.S.A.)
Dennis Sharp (England)
Pierre Vago (France)
Stanislaus von Moos (Switzerland)
Marina Waisman (Argentina)
Lance Wright (England)
Bruno Zevi (Italy)

Greetings by Arthur Drexler, Director, Department of Architecture and Design, Museum of Modern Art, New York.

Louis deMoll, President of the UIA (International Union of Architects), will open the Meeting.

The International Committee of Architectural Critics (CICA) will hold the Third International Meeting of Architectural Critics in New York, from December 4 through 7, 1980.

The gathering is sponsored by the International Union of Architects and is organized by the International Center for Advanced Studies in Art (ICASA), of New York University. It will be attended by the members of CICA and leading figures in the field of architecture.

The Third Meeting will encompass a public round table on the following subjects:
— The "Zero Degree" of architectural writing: mirage or challenge?
— The ten most controversial buildings of the last three years.
— Retro/pre/post/late/post post modernism.
— The five most controversial books of the last three years.
This debate will be held at the Museum of Modern Art of New York.

The closed sessions of the Third Meeting will take place at the Department of Art and Art Education of New York University, to which ICASA is attached.

The sessions of the Third Meeting are intended as preparatory work for the participation of CICA in the XIV World Congress of the International Union of Architects to be held in Warsaw, in June 1981.

CICA will organize at the XIV Congress a Working Group, open to all participants in the Congress, on June 17 and 18, 1981. CICA delegates will participate in the panel discussion of the plenary meeting (June 19-20) during which the working groups will present their findings.

It is planned, that CICA will participate in the exhibitions to be held in Warsaw within the framework of the Congress. Members of CICA will also debate in New York the draft of the XIV Congress final document, the "Warsaw Declaration" with a view to proposing amendments and additions.

At the same time, members of CICA will discuss new projects, exchange ideas about future International Meetings, examine the admission of new members and begin to consider entries for the three International Awards for Architectural Criticism, set up during the Second Meeting held in Buenos Aires last April.
The first of CICA's Annual Awards will be given to a book on architectural criticism and/or theory published between October 31, 1979 and October 31, 1980, which the Committee considers to be the most significant contribution to these subjects. The content of books and not their typographical qualities will be considered.

The second of CICA's Annual Awards will be made for the most significant article on architectural criticism and/or theory, published in journals, newspapers or any other kind of periodical publication, also between October 31, 1979 and October 31, 1980.

The third of CICA's Annual Awards will go to the author of the most significant catalog preface or introduction for an original architectural exhibition staged at a museum, cultural center or gallery between October 31, 1979 and October 31, 1980. This award reflects the fact that one of CICA's primary aims is the promotion of architectural exhibitions.

The date for submission of entries has been extended until March 15, 1981. The Annual Awards will be delivered on June 21, 1981, the last day of the XIV World Congress and will be included in the official ceremony of handing prizes, at Warsaw.

The works —in quintuplicate— should be addressed to CICA's Secretariat: CAYC, Elpidio González 4070, 1407 Buenos Aires, Argentina, or to International Center for Advanced Studies in Art, New York University, Department of Art and Art Education, 735 East Building, New York, N.Y., 10003.

The Jury who will decide on the three Annual Awards for Architectural Criticism will be composed by Bruno Zevi, George Collins, Dennis Sharp, Jorge Glusberg and Michèle Champenois, all members of CICA and nominated by the Council and the Associate Board, the two governing bodies of the Committee.

Fig. 2 (back)

Fig. 3 CICA private meetings and visits in Barcelona, 1979.

For some architects engaged in architectural projects and construction, a degree zero was a conceptual and formal ideal to which they aspired. While the idea has emerged predominantly in the work of historians, theorists, and critics from the European and American scene, many architects who worked with the notion seem to be of Sino-American origin. Hiromi Fujii from the 1960s (Fig. 5–11), Kazunari Sakamoto in the 1970s, and Kazuo Shinohara in the 1980s all associated a particular, though each a different, symbolism with the idea of degree zero.[13] During this period, the notion was rather prevalent in the visual arts of Japan after World War II. Nakahira Takuma, one of the founders of the three-issue photographic journal *Provoke*, states, for example, that one of the motivations for his work was to "reach the degree zero of language (with Roland Barthes)."[14] Kojii Taki, who photographed Shinohara's projects and who was also a co-founder of the journal, is credited with introducing structuralism and the work of Barthes into the Japanese image and architecture discourse. Eisenman befriended some of these architects, including Fujii and Arata Isozaki, with whom he shared an interest in the application of linguistic theories to architecture.[15] The name given to the famous journal Eisenman co-founded, *Oppositions*, was also understood by its editors to mean "0 positions," which is a well-known sign of Barthes's influence on Eisenman's work.[16] Later in the 1990s, Rem Koolhaas began a short essay on the homogeneity and repetition of Manhattan office buildings with the idea of degree zero (Fig. 12). He categorized their layout as that of a "Typical Plan," defining it as "zero-degree architecture, architecture stripped of all traces of uniqueness and specificity"; this type "threatens the myth of the architect as demiurge, source of unlimited supplies of uniqueness."[17] A few years earlier, concerned with another scale of projects and a completely distinct formal resolution, Lars Lerup criticized the typology of the single-family house using Barthes's 1977 book *Fragments d'un discours amoureux* and the idea of degree zero (Fig. 13-16).[18]

Many French and foreign architects, such as Diana Agrest and Mario Gandelsonas, who were also members of the IAUS, attended Barthes's seminars. Conceiving architecture as a language with a semantic and syntactic dimension, they proposed reflections on form and its meaning.[19] In Paris in 1973, at the first colloquium on the semiotics of space to be held in France, the Syntax Group established "certain analogies between the structure of the narrative and that of the architectural space," with the aim of "taking architecture, and in particular teaching, out of the professional ghetto both in terms of thought... and vocabulary."[20] The following year, "the Swiss journal *Archithèse* [saw] in architectural semiotics a possibility of renewing criticism on real criteria."[21] In addition to these more indirect interactions that testify to how semiology served the architectural debate, Barthes's expertise was often also directly solicited. In 1970, he was invited to give a lecture at the ETH Zurich and to judge the work of students who had analyzed buildings from the perspective of semiotic theories.[22] He wrote several short texts for the exhibition *MA. Espace-Temps du Japon*, initiated by Isozaki in 1978 in Paris, and was a jury member for architectural competitions, such as the counter-competition for Les Halles de Paris in 1980 (Fig. 4).

Fig. 4 Conversation between Kazuo Shinohara and Roland Barthes on architectural modernity and tradition after the counter competition of Les Halles de Paris in 1980.

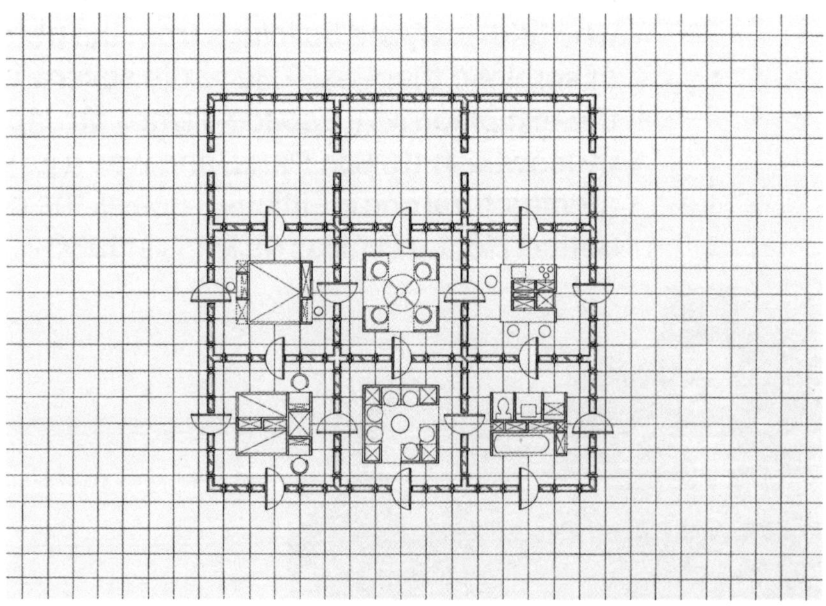

Fig. 5 Axonometric and plan view of E1 Project, by Hiromi Fujii, 1968–1971.

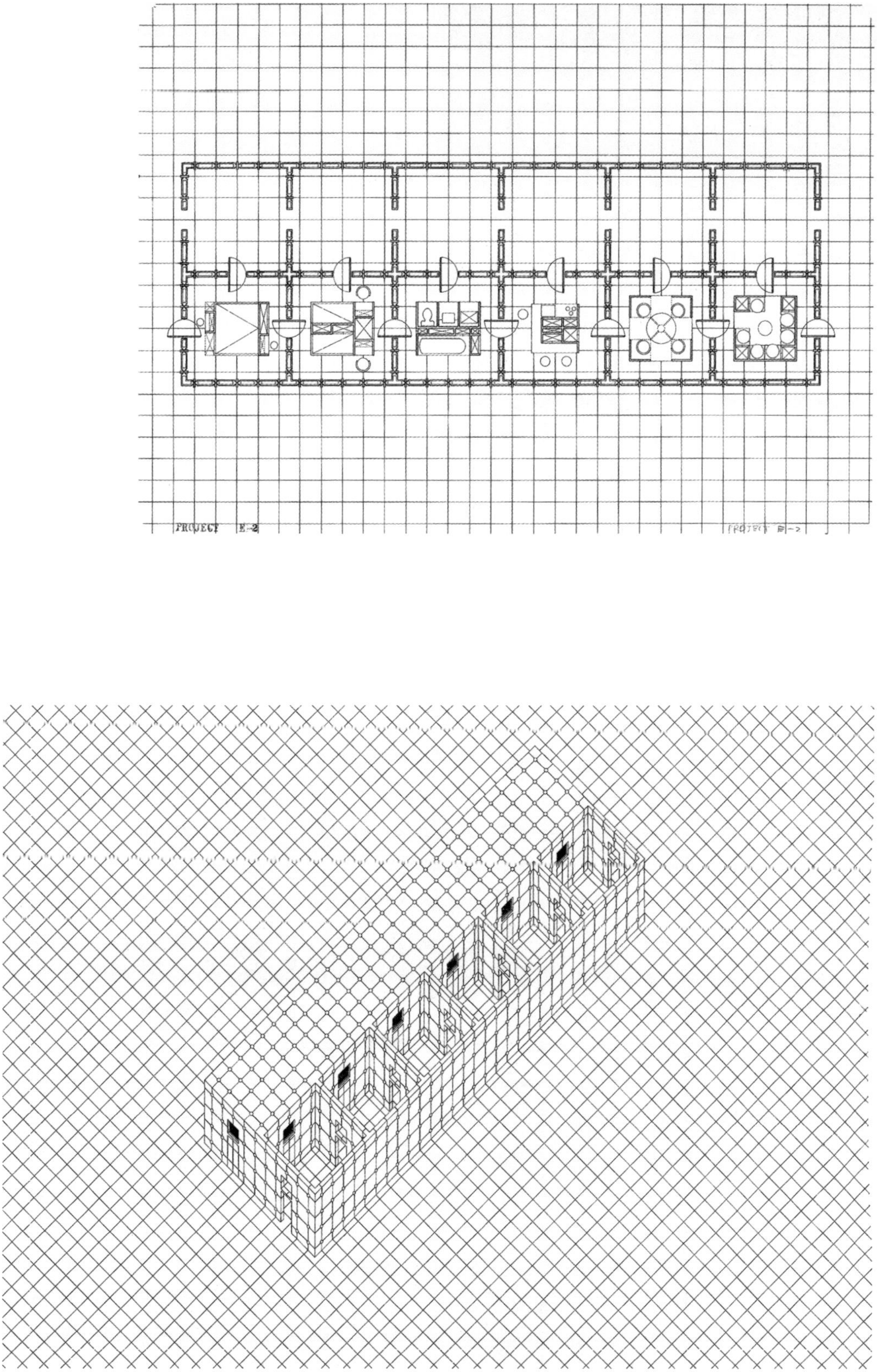

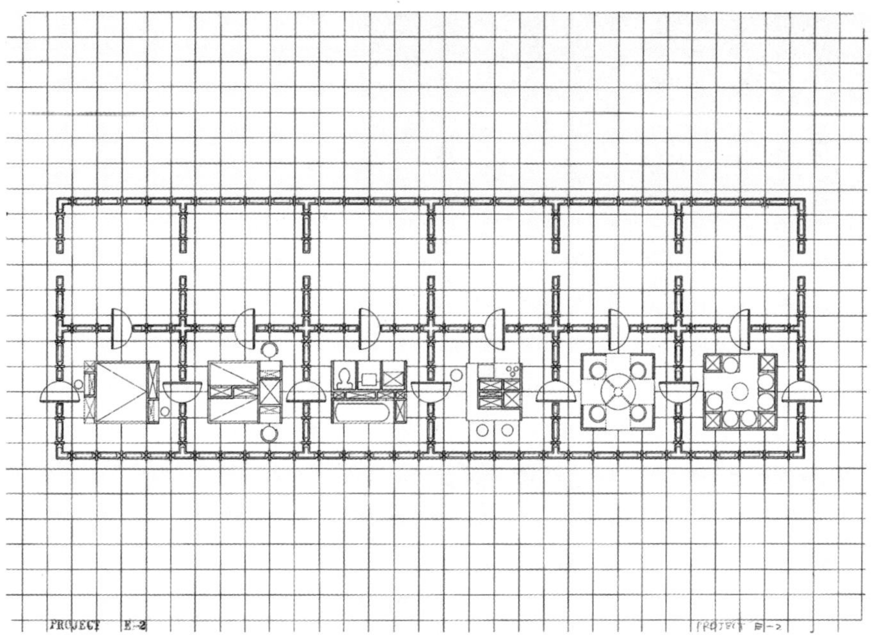

Fig. 6 Plan and axonometric view of E2 Project by Hiromi Fujii, 1968–1971.

Fig. 7 Exterior views of the Todoroki Residence by Hiromi Fujii.

Fig. 8 Interior view of the Todoroki Residence by Hiromi Fujii.

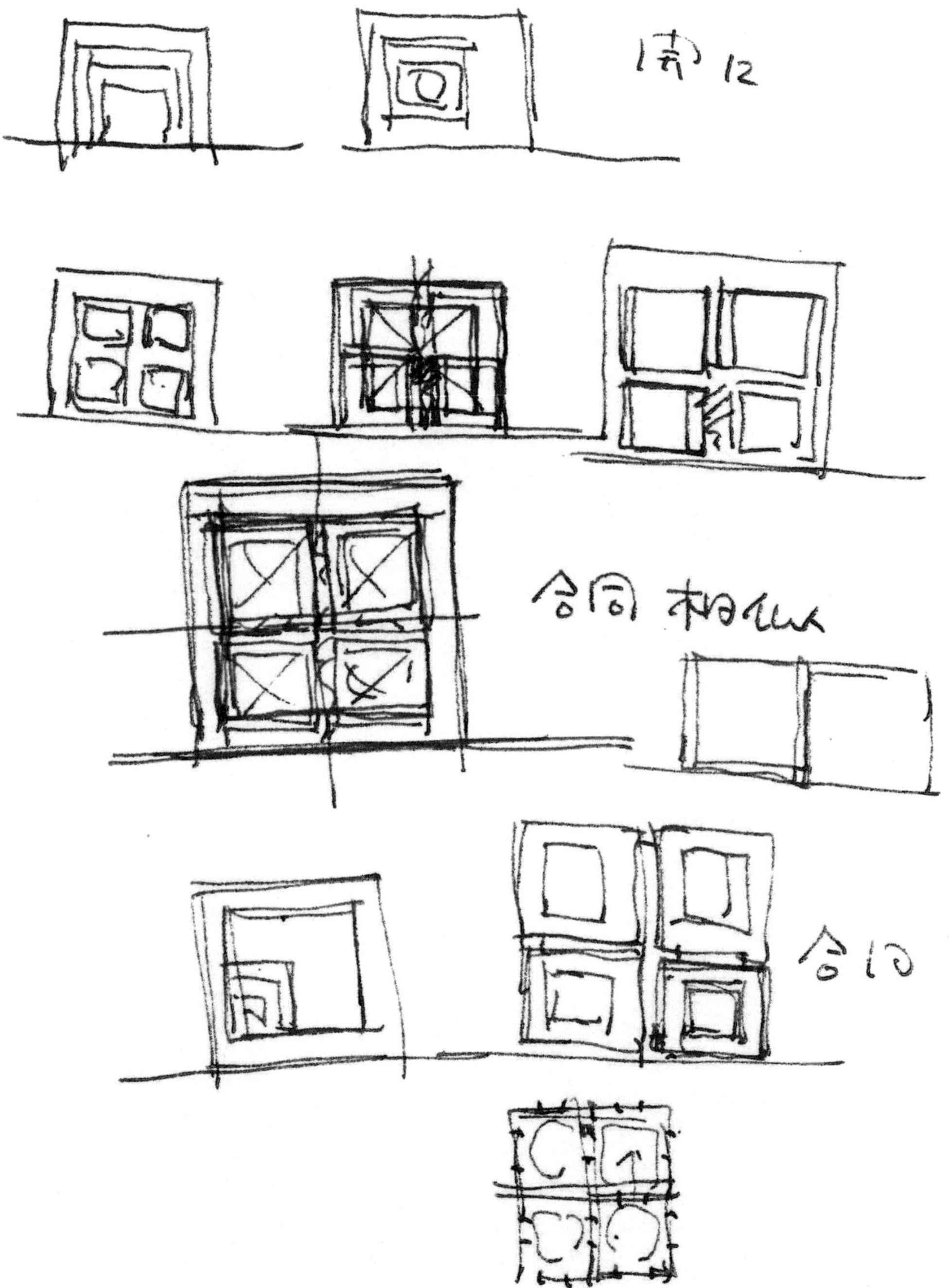

Fig. 9 Sketches of the Todoroki Residence by Hiromi Fujii.

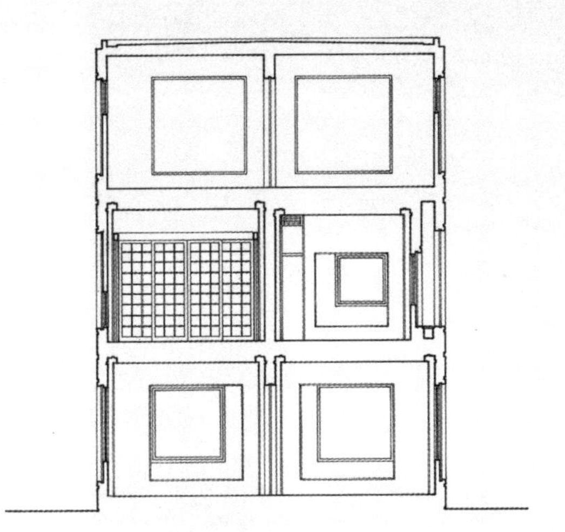

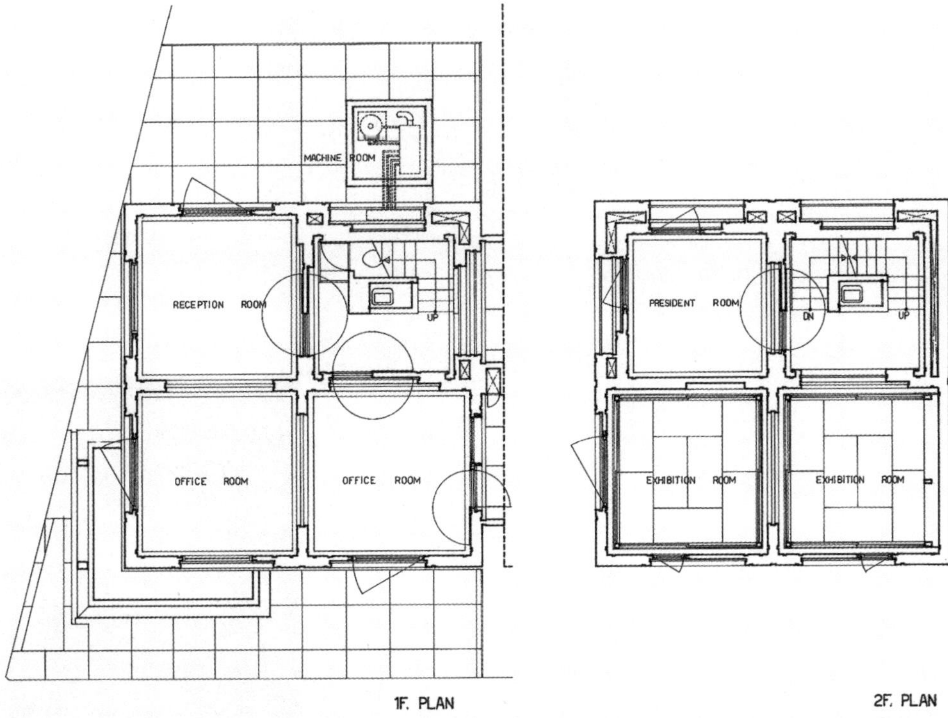

Fig. 10 Plans and section of the Marutake Building by Hiromi Fujii, 1976.

Fig. 11 Exterior and interior views of the Marutake Building by Hiromi Fujii, 1976.

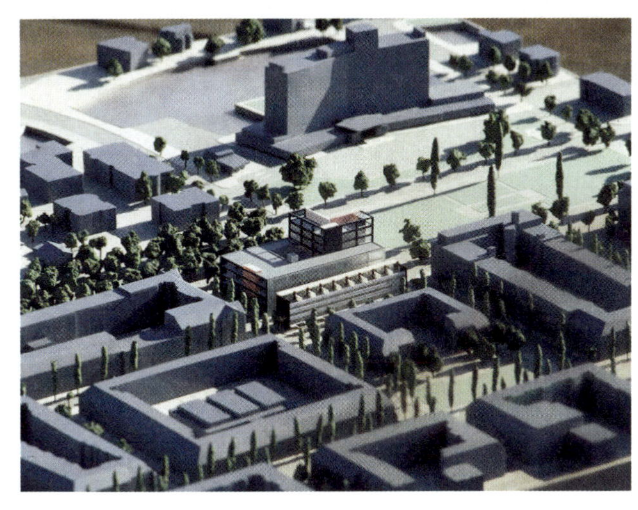

Fig. 12 Model and drawing for the Morgan Bank Competion by OMA, 1985.

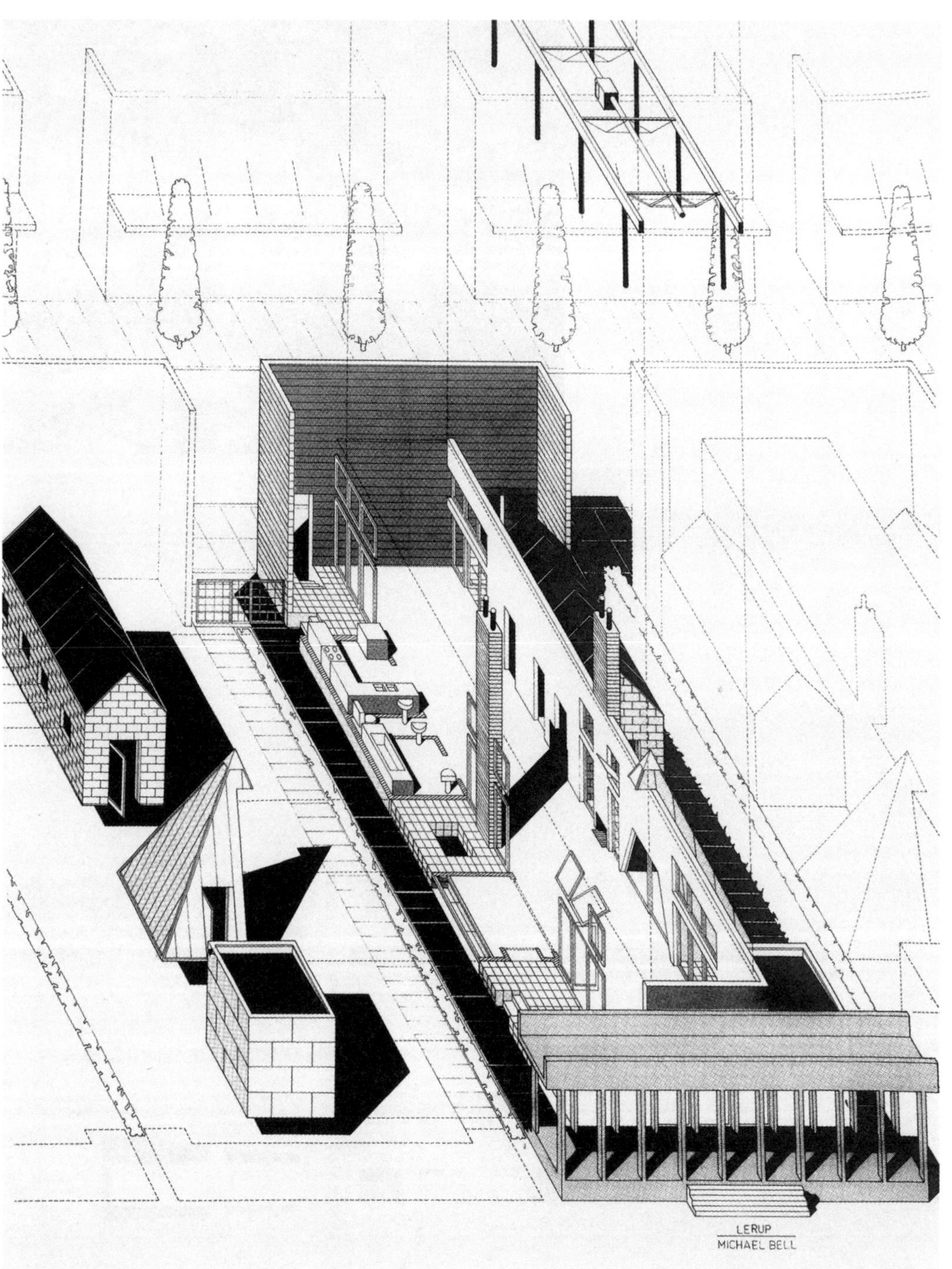

Fig. 13 Axonometric view of the New Zero House by Lars Lerup, 1986.

Fig. 14 Drawing of the New Zero House by Lars Lerup, 1986.
Fig. 15 Drawing of the Texas Zero House by Lars Lerup, 1984.

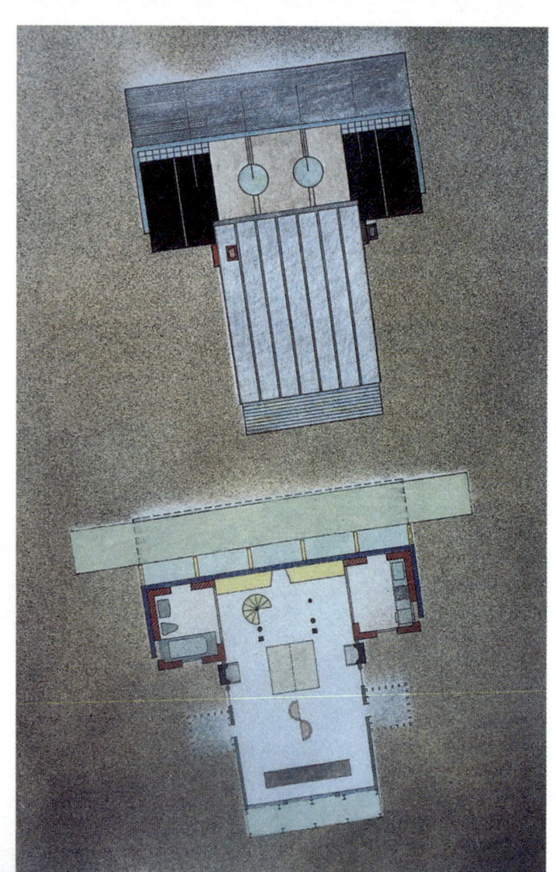

Fig. 16 Plans and axonometric view of the Texas Zero House by Lars Lerup, 1984.

Although Barthes wrote only two texts on architecture and urbanism, and otherwise did not write actively on the topic, the interactions outlined above illustrate that many actors within the international field of architecture saw how his work might intellectually affect their own and stimulate debates within and about the discipline.[23] However, the translation of the Barthesian idea of degree zero into architecture lacks the scholarly attention it has received in the (visual) arts: photography,[24] theatre,[25] drawing,[26] and visual culture.[27]

DZ: AUTHOR, AUTHORSHIP, AUTHORITY

Le degré zéro de l'écriture is an essay on the history and topicality of literary language in which Barthes takes a position on what literature should be. In this book he interprets the concept made by certain linguists, according to which "between the two terms of a polarity (singular-plural, preterit-present)" there exists "a third term, a neutral term or term-zero."[28] Binary oppositions and dualisms of thought have shaped much of Barthes's thinking. "The opposition is minted (like a coin), but we don't try to honor it. What purpose does it serve? Quite simply to say something," he wrote in 1975.[29] In *Le degré zéro de l'écriture*, Barthes thus uses a linguistic opposition to say something about literature. Also understood as neutral, white, or amodal writing, writing at its degree zero is both an observation and a claim, a partial state of literature at the time Barthes wrote his book and a wish he formulated for writers. Barthes observes degree zero in the works of some authors, defines its tendency, and advocates for it.

Nevertheless, Barthes does not favor one literary genre over another because of a genre's ability to affect the reader through its language or because of some assessment of it as pure literature. Degree zero actually refers to a raw and direct writing.

But Barthes's intention is inextricably linked to what the very form of this writing represents for the writer—to what it refers to socially, morally, and politically. Indeed, a tension of class conflict marks the idea of degree zero. More precisely, degree zero is a hypothesis of action regarding that conflict in positioning itself as a third party in the antagonistic relationship between popular and literary language. It aims to go beyond this paradigmatic view of the state and history of literature.

With the degree zero, Barthes accuses classical literature, as a bourgeois heritage, of governing the ways of saying in the act of writing and then codifying the form of written language. For him, classical literature is in a dominant position. He exposes it as "political authority" and "dogmatism of the Spirit."[30] Later in the book, he locates the death of the hegemony of bourgeois writing in the mid-nineteenth century. Correlated with the birth of modern capitalism, a multiplication of forms of literary writing appeared, "the worked, the populist, the neutral, the spoken," through which "the writer assumes or abhors his bourgeois condition."[31] In facing this class conflict, writers have to make a stand and negotiate with their side. What is the social significance of writing? What is the ethical responsibility of literary language? The degree zero comes into play precisely here: as a means by which writers can free themselves from this dualism of options—of using either popular or literary language while assuming the political weight of their choice. It is a way of not deciding upon one side or another but rather of moving beyond that situation—without disengaging—and finding in degree zero a third way, another way.

Thus, Barthes considers degree zero as a literary ideal in which class markers have disappeared.

Degree zero erases relations of domination and suspends social assignments. It strives to lift from the author their social authority in language. Free of this burden, Literature then leaves all the room for the *écriture* itself and any possible appropriations the reader might make. The literary object finds a multitude of existences and meanings in those who read it, enabled by the raw ideal of its form that is ready to be invested. Literature is no longer just the work of the writer, of the person who writes, but of all those who seize it. To refer to a later text by Barthes, *Le degré zéro de l'écriture* is also *La mort de l'auteur*.[32] The idea intends to be intellectually emancipatory and liberating from the social significance of language. It is a political ideal embodied in a literary form, an immediate writing, at the degree zero of its form.[33]

FORM, VALUE, AND AUTHORSHIP

The degree zero thus entangles form, value, and authorship. Through literary form, it aims to overturn the social relations of power that structure the history of literature and question an author's ethical responsibility towards their form. "All Form is also Value," Barthes writes, before adding that all writing is the site of "writers' reflection on the social use of their form and the choice they assume of it."[34]

This book, *Degree Zero in Architecture: Form, Value, and Authorship*, is concerned with the degree zero in architecture because of this interweaving of form, value, and authorship, according to Barthes's conceptualization of the term. He used it as a means by which to see how form implies value, which helped him consider the formalization of a social commitment—the materialization of an ethical position in the social world. This book thus engages with the degree zero because it invites us to ponder the inherent character of an ethical aim in all forms. It examines how the degree zero, in linking form, value, and authorship, has fueled, continues to feed, and may continue to serve reflections on how architecture is exercised and formalized, that is to say, how any form manifests the articulation of an authorial positioning with a set of values.

This book defends the idea tha t within the practices that compose this discipline—projectual, constructive, discursive, prospective, critical, academic, etc.—there is always a question of form—of formalization—for which a way of being an author, and therefore a way to position within that form a spectrum of values, is articulated. Through the prism of this triptych of form-value-authorship, one can analyze and thus (re)configure any practice in the field of architecture, because this triptych provides the structure for any act of creation that necessarily involves the author's commitment to an act of formalization, and because the need to reconfigure architectural practices is as urgent as it is topical, having tempered the spheres of practice, teaching, and academic research. Barthes's degree zero in the early 1950s and the following architectural translations bear witness to how the critics of modernity revisited this triptych of form-value-authorship. They questioned the writer's and the architect's authority of authorship and pointed out how literary and architectural forms embody this authority. They have made the status of the author political. Today, the ways of looking at this connection to authority that is inherent in the moral responsibility of being an author have multiplied and become more complex. It is no longer a simple question of social domination; it now also involves racial domination, domination specific to gender, to humans regarding their environment and resources, or to humans involving other species. The notion of authorship conveys a contemporary issue reflected in a desire to dispel the modern myth of the solitary author, by taking into account (through architectural practice or academic research) of the eminently collective and multi-author nature of architecture.[35] All these topics reconfigure our contemporary societies and the spectrum of values within which architects-authors must find their way through their practices and forms, which are, de facto, reevaluated.

The "tireless conquest of values replayed in every form," and carried by any author, thus sums up the ambitions of this book.[36] The interrelationship between form and value in literature mentioned by Barthes in his book on the degree zero has later found a new echo in the work of Marielle Macé, in *Styles: Critique nos formes de vie*.[37] Macé proposes re-engaging the notion of style because it intertwines form with value within all "forms-of-life."[38] Our book is equally contingent on this proposal to see every form—not just literary or architectural—as an expression of value (Fig. 17). Based on this broadened understanding of the field of forms, the formal categories analyzed by the different authors of our book expand to include architectural forms and urban forms, certainly, but also discursive forms, forms of writing, forms of the elaboration and restitution of knowledge, and forms of architectural practice. A spectrum of ways of doing, ways of saying, and ways of conceiving ideas and situations, engaged in forms.

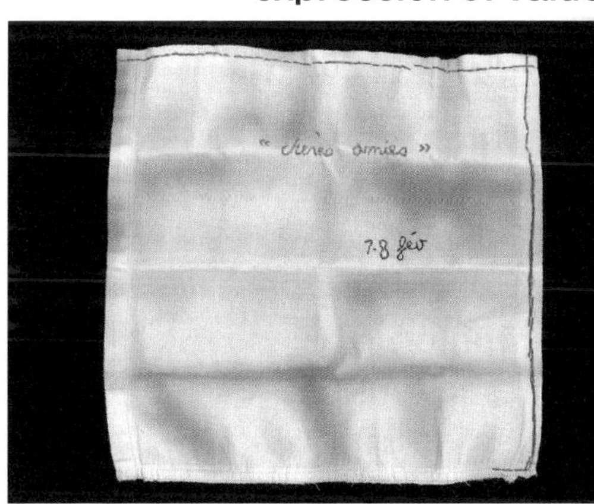

Macé adds in her introduction that style as a "word cannot be brandished like a slogan; it merely opens up, in its very inadequacy, a critical reflection on the meaning of the forms taken on by life."[39] A similar ambition can be attributed to the present

Fig. 17 Image of the seminar "Chères amies" organized by Anne-Laure Iger, Alice Paris, and Lyna Bourouiba at the faculty of architecture la Cambre Horta of the ULB on February 7-8, 2024.

book, that of taking the idea of degree zero in architecture out of its slogan-like attributes, out of how it has been used to label certain architectural productions for its formal attributes, to restore it, for the architectural field, to its critical and analytical force. The degree zero idea is not just an aesthetic issue but a set of relationships that not only links form to its moral and ethical values and its social and political commitment but also makes it possible to envisage the architectural translations of the idea of degree zero as a search for what characterizes some of the very foundations of architecture: an act of creation, a way of being an author through form in its broadest types, in and for the social world.

Considering the idea of degree zero from the perspective of the continuity of the questions it raises, also makes it possible to position this book as contributing to a critical history of architectural semiology. Some chapters focus specifically on the period when semiotics and semiology served as a means of conceiving architecture as a language. Some of the subjects covered in the chapters are therefore situated in the postmodern period, to observe not only the effects and limits of translations from linguistics to architecture but also to understand how the idea of degree zero, which came from semiology and literary studies, contributed to a social and critical understanding of architecture. Even though many architects, historians, theoreticians, and critics contributed to the exchanges between semiology, semiotics, and architecture, this history has scarcely been explored. Some of these exchanges have given rise to complex content and mathematical resolutions that are difficult to grasp, in which architecture became a system of meanings, with a signified and a signifier, as proposed by the language sciences. The distance of the present allows us to be easily tempted to discredit those reasonings for their absence of any tangible effects. Paradoxically, these attempts to translate notions from semiology and semiotics to architecture have often reinforced the autonomy of architecture, whereas the ambitions were frequently the opposite, oriented toward a desire to extricate architecture from the authority of its positions. By restoring degree zero to its ethical ambitions and critical force, this book hopes to renew the understanding of that period, in which the sciences of language led not only to an intellectual fog but also to a commitment to architectural theory that is devoted as much to building practices as to discursive ones. It aims to contribute to a way of envisaging how this history might serve the present, and it thus responds to the invitation made by André Loeckx and Hilde Heynen in their text of 2020, "Meaning and Effect: Revisiting Semiotics in Architecture":

It is our contention therefore that rather than dismissing successive paradigms out of hand—including both semiotics and postcriticality—architectural theory would do well to recognize, evaluate, and valorize its own recent history of thought and practice. In our opinion, our retrospective of semiotic paradigms and scenes did not unveil a collection of intellectual failures but rather a sequence of promising concepts, interrupted reasonings, unaccomplished adaptations, and semi-results. All this provides materials for critical evaluation, selective recycling, and further processing in the light of the actual condition of the discipline and its present challenges.[40]

The idea of a degree zero entangles form, value, and authorship, providing it a role in contemporary architectural issues. Because the form is always synonymous with the value conveyed by its author, investigating the degree zero in architecture—this moment in the history of architectural semiology—can enable us to address current questions that continue to be asked, just as Michel Foucault did in 1969: "What is an author?"[41]

WAYS FOR, WAYS OF

This book looks at form in terms of architectural forms and forms of architectural knowledge.[42] The first part of the book reflects what architecture can do as a form, as a distinct act of shaping that bears the ethical ambitions that the authors of a form project onto it. The rest of the book looks at how forms of architectural knowledge are modeled. In the second part, the authors discuss how methods and ways of conceiving situations construct specific forms of knowledge within their object of research. In the third part, in a self-reflexive process, authors put these approaches to the test within their own research and teaching practice to consider ways of assuming an authorial responsibility toward the forms of knowledge they produce.

Among these forms of knowledge, we also find ways of expressing ideas, which give rise to specific forms of discourse and ways of reporting and sharing that raise concerns about forms of restitution. The authors of each chapter examine gestures —"ways, modes, manners," to quote Macé again— to understand the author-value relationship within each of architectural forms and forms of knowledge they explore.[43] How are ways of being an author articulated within these architectural forms and forms of knowledge? What ability do these forms have, now understood as the morphological manifestation of an authorial gesture inseparable from its values?

WAYS FOR ARCHITECTURE TO BE FORM

The first part of the book opens with a text by Thomas Daniell. The author examines how an unbuilt project by Sei'ichi Shirai, the Temple of Atomic Catastrophes, or Genbakudo, testifies to the architect's ethical stance towards the post-traumatic context in Japan at the time. Daniell portrays Shirai as part of a specific generation of human architects who have experienced destruction and deprivation. This context, also marked by American cultural imperialism under the guise of security necessity, leads to an ambiguous but critical relationship with architecture as a human-architect-author. It makes Shirai's project a complex and singular approach in which the architectural form reflects both the a-cultural and the a-historic ambitions of its author as well as a way to refer to the catastrophe.

In a different time and geography, this first part continues with explorations written by Martin Steinmann on the degree zero. Likely produced in the late 1990s and early 2000s, they are published for the first time in this book. Introduced by Irina Davidovici and translated by Duncan Brown, these three essays demonstrate how the degree zero has served as a theoretical investigation into the reasons behind forms, an exploration of the decision-making processes that leads authors to arrive at certain forms rather than others. Looking at architectural, artistic, and industrial forms and translating the degree zero into architectural concerns, Steinmann asks how form must provide formal objectivity to be part of a common culture beyond the author's creative and subjective gesture.

The chapter by Carla Frick-Cloupet and myself addresses the same issues. It reports on conversations with the architect Éric Lapierre about some of his projects and concepts. By reconstructing these conversations alongside other authors, this chapter examines how authorship is negotiated between subjectivity and shared culture in both Lapierre's projects and the chapter's form itself. We observe how, in contemporary architecture, a desire to get as close as possible to the foundations of the discipline is emerging, a way to reconstruct a relationship between form, value, and authorship in architecture through architecture itself. Architects are invited to consider the political values of forms by investing the notion of style in the manner of Macé.

In a text published in 1980, here introduced and translated into English by Christophe Van Gerrewey, Geert Bekaert also raises the question of what architecture should and can do through its forms. Bekaert accuses architects of attributing ambitions to architecture that architecture cannot fulfill. He points to the impossibility of architecture as a form to assume the power of social action, despite the hope architects have that such a power inheres in architecture. Architects need to measure what form can honestly embody in terms of value. By pointing out what architecture cannot do, Bekaert invites them to see what it can and should be: specific forms in the cultural landscape of society, the right of every society to architecture.

In another chapter, Davidovici looks back at how the idea of the zero degree not only informed Steinmann's thinking but also her own, when faced with the task, twenty years ago, of assessing the Swiss architecture of the 1980s and 1990s. This past work is republished in that chapter and introduced by the author. Davidovici explains how she used the notion of degree zero to conceptualize these architectual forms for their aesthetic, material, and volumetric attributes. She demonstrates the out-dated nature of such an approach in light of the ethical and environmental questions posed by architecture today.

Finally, this first part closes with a contribution by Sunil Manghani, who co-authored, with Ryan Bishop, the 2019 book *Seeing Degree Zero: Barthes/ Burgin and Political Aesthetics*. Through a digression on the potential parallels between degree zero, architecture, and spatiality, Manghani builds a reflection on how visual practice engages with discourse cross different eras, authors, and subjects. By bringing together the idea of degree zero and spatiality, Manghani raises issues about the responsibility of form, the relationship between form and content—subject and object—and authorship, knowledge, and image through the lens of AI.

WAYS FOR KNOWLEDGE TO BE A RESEARCH OBJECT

This second part, devoted to ways in which knowledge itself can be an object of research, begins with a text by Andrew Leach that analyzes a significant academic event from 1967, when a large group of scholars gathered in Rome to discuss the work of the architect Francesco Borromini. For ten days, they investigated ways of portraying his work from different angles and through several means. Leach examines the effects of the form of the event, and the antagonistic approaches deployed by the speakers, on the type of knowledge they produce. The ambition to multiply the ways of approaching a topic characterizes the form of the academic event. But Leach demonstrates that it may lead to a form of knowledge that is as multi-authored as enigmatic.

Pablo Miranda and Ole Fischer both focus on translations from linguistic theories to architectural issues. They question the effects of this method on ways of considering architecture as a discipline and on the role of the architect-author regarding forms. Drawing on a symposium organized in 2000 by Stanford Anderson, entitled "Virtual Palladio: Two Views," Miranda explains how Eisenman and William Mitchell, who shared common interests, held distinct understandings of architecture as language even while they both supported an autonomist vision of the discipline. These two approaches lead to a conception of architecture focused on form that in turn leads to two distinct visions of how authorship and form are intertwined. While one leads to a strengthening of the figure of the architect-author of form, the other envisages replacing the author's subjectivity with a combinatorial mechanism. Fischer studies a reflexive back-and-forth between philosophy and architecture, between Jacques Derrida and Bernard Tschumi, on the occasion of Tschumi's winning of the Parc de La Villette project in 1983. Fischer questions how this act of disciplinary translation reinforced the myth of the architect-author-savant seeking to translate commendable values into architectural form that were nevertheless formalized behind complex concepts.

Finally, Gilles Malzac, Giulia Tellier, and Wouter Van Acker observe how ways of engaging with the practice of architectural history shape specific types of historical knowledge. Malzac and Tellier focus on the practices of Zevi and Manfredo Tafuri and their way of using the degree zero in their work. They demonstrate how the political divergences of the two led to distinct ways of conceiving the practice of architectural history and appropriating the same Barthesian idea. They show how a commitment to a spectrum of political values models ways of being authors of architectural history and generates different ways of manipulating and disseminating ideas. Van Acker also looks at Zevi's practice and the place he gives to the degree zero. He depicts how his specific conception of time shapes a history of architecture made up of exemplary models and temporal ruptures. Considering the practice of architectural history in this way led Zevi to instrumentalize the idea of degree zero to serve this logic and bolster his positions.

WAYS FOR RESEARCH TO BE A FORM OF KNOWLEDGE

In this last part, four chapters discuss ways of engaging with the forms of architectural knowledge produced by researchers. The contribution by Klaske Havik and Jorge Mejía Hernández first leads us to consider how two ways of conceiving of situations to study — the dialectical approach and the pluralist approach — give rise to two different forms of knowledge. These two methods differ in terms of what knowledge should and can do. By first analyzing authors and spaces where both these approaches and the degree zero are examined, the authors finally consider their practices under the lens of these methods to better understand how belief in one form of knowledge can be reconciled with modes of investigation and restitution.

The essays by Adil Mansure, B. Beril Kapusuz-Balcı, and myself postulate a renewed perspective on three objects widely studied by others before them. By focusing on type in architecture, Mansure shifts the focus on form, from which type is generally studied, to how type exists: the process of repeating and propagating the model. To this end, he draws a parallel between the architectural notion of type and the linguistic one of cliche to highlight the similarities between the dissemination mechanisms of these two authorless forms. My contribution also looks at the contexts and means of production, not of architectural forms but of forms of knowledge. I examine how the logic of domination and competition that characterizes the practice of architectural history, theory, and criticism also shapes the ideas we analyze and their discursive forms. Taking as its subject a long-running debate between Zevi and Kenneth Frampton, where the two historians discussed an architectural translation of the degree zero, this chapter draws on the Bourdieusian notion of the field to show how the notions of concept and context intertwine. Finally, based on a survey of the magazine *Spazio e Società*, Kapusuz-Balcı reveals the multi-author nature of a work hitherto attributed mainly to the architect Giancarlo De Carlo. Kapusuz-Balcı deconstructs the myth of the solitary author that structures the way we consider the elaboration of knowledge. She also points to the social commitment that an editorial form can carry by questioning the form of the language (a degree zero of scholarly writing) and how the nature of the images conveys a type of value.

VALUE AND AUTHORSHIP IN THE EDITORIAL FORM

This book results from a symposium we, Wouter Van Acker and myself, organized in November 2022 at the Faculty of Architecture la Cambre Horta in Brussels. We invited participants to contribute to a history of degree zero in architecture that enabled shape theories and designs. The idea of degree zero was presented as a third term—a way of overcoming certain dualisms of thought that have structured the postmodern architectural period. Our intent was also to examine the potential topicality of the idea of a degree zero from these angles. In another session, we linked the notion of the third term to that of the third space proposed by Homi K. Bhabha, who sees "the encounter of two social groups with different cultural traditions and potentials of power as a special kind of negotiation or translation that takes place in a Third Space of enunciation."[44] By bringing together researchers who were examining collective spaces as specific sites of conflictuality and knowledge production, we saw the event as a third space where contributors could debate the third term.

The two types of form that frame this book, architectural forms and forms of knowledge, result from how we conceived and named our symposium (Fig. 18).

Fig. 18 Call for paper's illustration for the symposium
The Zero Degree of Architectural Writing: Theorizing, Drawing, and Debating the Third Term.

The editorial work that followed this event has enabled us to gather the contributions under the fresh perspective of an entanglement of forms, values, and authorship. It now opens up several lines of thought. Some authors, for example, could tackle other angles of the issues and to thus explore a broader range of forms that could lead to other geographies and temporalities. They could also more diversely analyze forms already discussed in the book, such as discursive forms or forms of design practices and constructive practices, to delve into what is at stake or could be at play in the author-value correlation within those forms. All are ways by which architects might consider how to negotiate their way of being authors in the shape of their practice.

Like any editorial object, this book is also a form in itself. It explores how an editorial form can reflect a collective work and thus turn the notion of authorship into co-authorship or plural-authorship. It proposes a way of testifying, through form, to the collective knowledge specific to scientific events: sharing our thoughts and integrating those of others always engenders a reflexive permeability between us and others. This process produces a displacement —a disruption, as much as a clarification or reaffirmation, even slight, of our ideas. What we think and write is also the result of assimilating the thinking of others. It is the very essence of that collective construction that is knowledge. In scholarly spaces, as Christian Jacob would say, and in those of everyday life, as Fred Moten discusses, participating in the construction of knowledge "means being involved in a kind of shared intellectual practice."[45]

Some comments thus punctuate the reading of the chapters and reflect two additional intentions. The first is a tribute to the everyday tools that make the practice of scientific writing a collective one. When we authors write a text, our work is debated through commentary. We transmit a text on which others add their thoughts in the margins of a paper or through the comment tools of a digital medium. As part of the work process, one person annotates the thoughts of others to make them shareable with even more others. This method and these means are also characteristic of an editorial process, which puts each contribution up for the discussion of those who direct the work, the scientific committee, and the copyeditors. For these reasons, the comment are the tools, par excellence, for knowledge discussion on the page.

The second intention relies on the desire to augment each chapter by the reflections of someone else. Authors of the book, colleagues, and members of the scientific committee are all invited to contribute to the knowledge produced within each chapter. Each contributor has slid into the role of co-author throughout the volume. By seeking to distort the auctorial convention of single authorship, we aim to reaffirm the plural nature of knowledge in terms of its elaboration processes, always collective, and its receptions, always plural (Fig. 19).

Fig. 19 Speakers, organizers, and scientific committee around the table during the lunch break on November 3, 2022.

1 Roland Barthes, *Le degré zéro de l'écriture* (Paris: Seuil, 1953).

2 Jonathan Culler, *Roland Barthes* (Saint Denis: Presses Universiatires de Vincennes, 2015). In that book, Culler wonders how to define Roland Barthes's practice: a master of what? He organizes his book into different chapters cited here.

3 Charles Jencks, "La bataille des étiquettes—Modernisme tardif contre postmodernisme," in *Nouveaux plaisirs d'architectures*: Les pluralismes de la création en Europe et aux États-Unis depuis 1968 vus à travers les collections du Deutsches Architekturmuseum de Francfort (Paris: ed. Centre Georges Pompidou, 1985), 27.

4 Martin Steinmann, "The Presence of Things: Comments on Recent Architecture in Northern Switzerland," in *Construction Intention Detail: Five Projects from Five Swiss Architects*, ed. G. Mark and K. Alter (Zurich: Artemis, 1994), 24.

5 Ignasi De Solà-Morales, "Mies and the Degree Zero," *Lotus*, no. 81 (1994): 20-27; Irina Davidovici, "Degree Zero," in *Forms of Practice, German-Swiss Architecture, 1980-2000* (Zurich: gta Verlag, 2012), 285-291.

6 Jacques Lucan, "Au-delà des références: Des dispositifs sans rhétorique," in *Précisions sur un état présent de l'architecture* (Lausanne: Presses polytechniques et universitaires romandes, 2015), 246-251.

7 Stéphane Dawans, "Architecture et minimum : Quel degré zéro ?," *Intervalles*, no. 1 (2004): 74-82.

8 Ido Avissar, "Degré zéro," *San Rocco*, no. 8 (2013): 176-185. For a wider understanding of how the degree zero has been recently used to investigate contemporary architectural issues, see *Faces*, no. 78 (Autumn 2020), "Architecture Amodale."

9 Georges David Emmerich, "Le kitsch ou le degré zéro de l'architecture," *Le carré bleu*, no. 2 (1985): 15-18.

10 Charles Jencks, *The Language of Post-modern Architecture* (London: Academy Editions, 1977).

11 Some authors have studied the idea of degree zero in Zevi's work. Among them, see Paola Ardizzola, "History will teach us everything. Bruno Zevi and the innovative methodology for future design," *Esempi di Architettura -International Journal of Architecture and Engineering* 5, no. 1 (2018): 6-11; Franco De Faveri, "L'espressionismo come 'grado zero' dell'architettura," *Tra Passado e futuro, Assaggi di teoria dell'architettura* (Trente: Autem, 1995), 13-40; Guendalina Salimei, "Paesaggistica e linguaggio grado zero dell'architettura: Un progetto aperto," in *Bruno Zevi e la didattica dell'architettura*, ed. Piero Ostillo Rossi (Rome: Quodlibet, 2019), 363-369; Maria Sambo Marco, "Grado Zero: Dinamica Culturale. Architettura," and Luigi Prestinenza Puglisi, "L'ultimo Zevi," *AR Magazine*, no. 120 (2018): 30-39, 126-129; Tamar Zinguer, "Bruno Zevi's Architecture Degree Zero," in *Bruno Zevi, History, Criticism and Architecture after World War II*, ed. Elena Dellapiana and Matteo Cassani Simonetti (Milano: Franco Angeli: 2021), 195-208.

12 Jean Attali and Dominique Gonzalez-Foster, "Le degré zéro de l'architecture," *L'architecture d'aujourd'hui*, no. 336 (2001): 64-67. For Eisenman, see note 28 in my chapter in this volume, "The Presence of Myth in Contemporary Life: Bruno Zevi and Kenneth Frampton in the Field."

13 Hajime Yatsuka, "Architecture in the Urban Desert: A Critical Introduction to Japanese Architecture After Modernism," in *Oppositions Reader: Selected Readings from a Journal for Ideas and Criticism in Architecture, 1973-1984*, ed. K. M. Hays (New York: Princeton Architectural Press, 1998), 255-287.

14 Myriam Sas, *Experimental Arts in Postwar Japan: Moments of Encounter, Engagement, and Imagined Return* (Cambridge and London: Harvard University Asia Center, 2011), 183.

15 Thomas Daniell, *An Anatomy of Influence* (London: Architectural Association, 2018).

16 C. Greig Crysler, "From Zero Positions to 'Assemblage,'" in *Writing Spaces: Discourses of Architecture, Urbanism and the Built Environment, 1960-2000* (New-York: Routledge, 2003), 50-52. On Eisenman's architectural work, see Gevork

Hartoonian, "Peter Eisenman: In Search of Degree Zero Architecture," in *Architecture and Spectacle: A Critique*, ed. Gevork Hartoonian (London: Ashgate Publishing, 2012), 55–80.

17 Rem Koolhaas and Bruce Mau, "Typical Plan," in *S,M,L,XL* (New York: Monacelli Press, 1995), 335, 343.

18 Lars Lerup, *Planned Assaults* (Cambridge: MIT Press, 1987); see also Avissar, "Degré zero." Avissar invited Lerup to an online conference in 2020, during which he presented his work on the narrative of the Plan and his Plan Degree Zero. "Leçon du Mardi 17 novembre 2020—Lars Lerup," conference session, posted by Ensa de Paris-Est on Youtube, Dec. 17, 2020, https://www.youtube.com/watch?v=3YqcmjZsVBI.

19 Alain Colquhoun, "On Writing Architecture," *Progressive Architecture*, June (1983): 80–85.

20 Jean Castex and Philippe Panerai, "Structures de l'espace architectural," in *Sémiotique de l'espace. Architecture, urbanisme, sortir de l'impasse*, ed. Jean Zeitoun, Algirdas Julien Greimas, and Alain Renier (Paris: Denoël, 1979), 65.

21 Hélène Jannière, "*La critique architecturale, objet de recherche," La critique en temps et lieux: Les cahiers de la recherche architecturale et urbaine*, ed. Kenneth Frampton and Hélène Jannière (Paris: Éditions du patrimoine, 2009), 126.

22 Bruno Reichlin, "Interview with Émeline Curien," in *Pensées constructives: Architecture Suisse Alémanique, 1980–2000*, ed. Émeline Curien (Liège: Fourre-Tout, 2019), 58–60.

23 Roland Barthes, "Sémiologie et urbanisme," *L'architecture d'aujourd'hui*, no. 153 (1971): 11–13; Roland Barthes, *La Tour Eiffel* (Paris: André Delpire, 1964).

24 Geoffrey Batchen, *Photography Degree Zero: Reflections on Roland Barthes's Camera Lucida* (Cambridge: The MIT Press, 2011).

25 Timothy Scheie, *Performance Degree Zero: Roland Barthes and Theatre* (Toronto: University of Toronto Press, 2006).

26 Anna Lovatt, *Drawing Degree Zero: The Line from Minimal to Conceptual Art* (University Park: Pennsylvania State University Press, 2019).

27 Ryan Bishop and Sunil Manghani, *Seeing Degree Zero: Barthes/Burgin and Political Aesthetics* (Edinburgh: Edinburgh University Press, 2019).

28 Barthes, *Le degré zéro de l'écriture*, 59.

29 Culler, *Roland Barthes*, 17.

30 Ibid., 47.

31 Ibid., 48.

32 Roland Barthes, "La mort de l'auteur," in *Le bruissement de la langue: Essais critiques IV* (Paris: Seuil, 1984), 63–69.

33 The covers of some translations of *Le degré zéro de l'écriture* testify to the editor's reception of the book's content. For example, throughout the graphism and the choice to put the table of contents on the cover, the 1966 second edition of the Italian translation affirms a political presentation of the book. The 1977 Portuguese and 2008 Japanese editions both show images of writings that emphasize a formal and esthetic first reading.

34 Barthes, *Le degré zéro de l'écriture*, 25–26.

35 See, for example, issue 113 of *OASE*, "Authorship" (2023) and issue 54 of *Log*, "Coauthoring" (2022). In recent architectural history, the notion of a contact zone has been mobilized to build a collective and transcultural historiography. See Tom Avermaete and Nuijsink Cathelijne, "An Architecture Culture of 'Contact Zones': Prospects for an Alternative Historiography of Modernism," in *Global Modernism and the Postcolonial: New Perspectives on Architecture*, ed. Vikramaditya Prakash, Maristella Casciato, and Daniel E. Coslett (NY: Routledge, 2021), 103–119; Cathelijne Nuijsink and Jorge Mejía Hernández, "Architecture as Exchange: Framing the Architecture Competition as Contact Zone," *Footprint* 14, no. 1 (2020): 1–8. At the 2024 EAHN conference, Despina Stratigakos's lecture depicted the collaborative efforts of women architects to write architectural history. In 2018, Beatriz Colomina gave a lecture titled "The Secret Life of Modern Architecture or We Don't Need Another

Hero," in which she affirmed that the "deeply collaborative" nature of architecture "has been a secret carefully guarded." The recording is online at the Harvard University Graduate School of Design Website, March 28, 2018, at https://www.gsd.harvard.edu/event/beatriz-colomina-the-secret-life-of-modern-architecture-or-we-dont-need-another-hero/

36 Marielle Macé, *Styles: Critiques de nos formes de vie* (Paris: Gallimard, 2016), 20.

37 The work conducted with my colleagues and friends Anne-Laure Iger and Alice Paris is equally contingent on the ideas set out here and after. For a year, we shared the reading of *Styles*. We presented an account of this work during a two-day seminar at the Faculty of Architecture La Cambre Horta in Brussels in February 2024, entitled "Chères amies" (Dear Friends). Along with Macé's presence and participation, three sessions enriched the event: Warming Up, Reading Styles, and Writing as We Speak.

38 In *Styles*, the term "form-of-life" is a reference to Giorgio Agamben's work.

39 Macé, *Styles*, 14–15.

40 André Loeckx and Hilde Heynen, "Meaning and Effect: Revisiting Semiotics in Architecture," in *The Figure of Knowledge: Conditioning Architectural Theory, 1960s–1990s*, ed. Sebastiaan Loosen, Rajesh Heynickx, and Hilde Heynen (Leuven: Leuven University Press, 2020), 55.

41 Michel Foucault, "Qu'est-ce qu'un auteur?," in *Dits et écrits: 1954–1988*, vol. 1 (Paris: Gallimard, 2001), 789–821 (first published in 1969).

42 In the book edited for the 2016 4th Lisbon Architecture Triennale, the editors also discuss architecture as visual forms that convey "hidden values," architecture as a"type of knowledge," and architects as authors. André Tavares, Diogo Seixas Lopes, eds., *The Form of Form* (Zurich: Lars Müller Publishers, 2016), 8–13.

43 Macé, *Styles*, 27.

44 Karin Ikas and Gerhard Wagner, eds., *Communicating in the Third Space* (New York: Routledge, 2009), 2.

45 Stefano Harney and Fred Moten, *Les sous-communs: Planification fugitive et étude noire* (Montreuil: Brook, 2022), 132. Christian Jacob has edited two collective volumes that examine how knowledge is produced and disseminated through gestures, practices, or tools. The first volume focuses on the sites of scientific knowledge: Christian Jacob, *Lieux de savoir: Espaces et communautés* (Paris: Albin Michel, 2007).

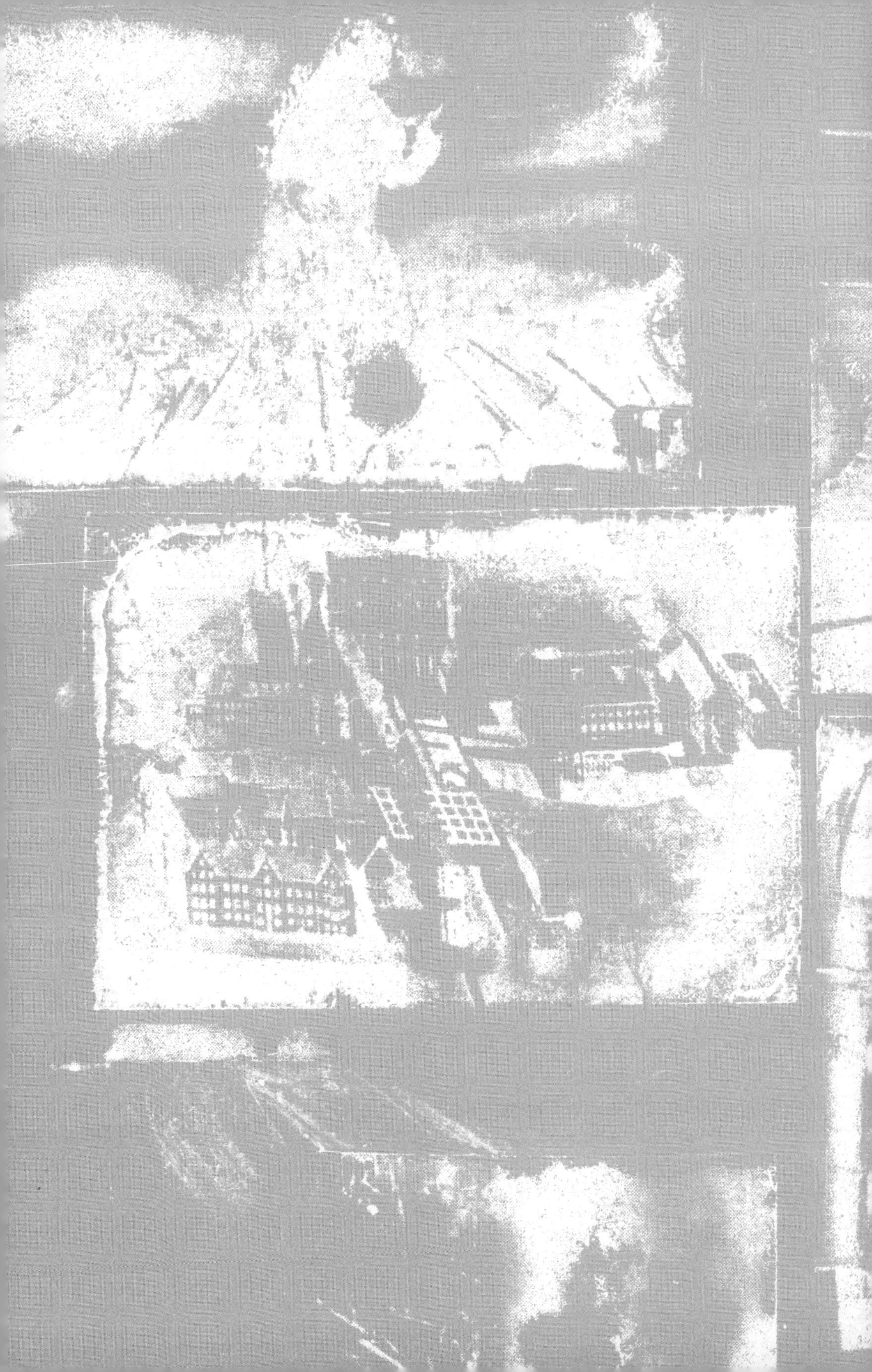

I

Ways for Archi-tecture to Be Form

51
GROUND ZERO
Thomas Daniell
comments by
Matthew Mullane

75
THE SIGNIFICANCE OF THE GENERAL FORM: REFLECTIONS ON THE DEGREE ZERO
Martin Steinmann
introduced and edited by
Irina Davidovici
translated by
Duncan Brown
comments by
Carla Frick-Cloupet

93
BUILDING ON CONVERSATIONS WITH ÉRIC LAPIERRE
Lyna Bourouiba,
Carla Frick-Cloupet
comments by
Victoire Chancel

109
THE RIGHT TO ARCHITECTURE
Geert Bekaert
translated and introduced by
Christophe Van Gerrewey
comments by
Pierre Chabard

121
DEGREE ZERO REVISITED. A LOOK BACK ON SWISS ARCHITECTURE AT THE TURN OF THE TWENTY-FIRST CENTURY
Irina Davidovici
comments by
Thomas Daniell

137
NOTES ON ARCHITECTURE, BARTHES'S ZERO DEGREE, AND AI IMAGING
Sunil Manghani
comments by
Adil Mansure

Ground Zero

Thomas Daniell

comments by
Matthew Mullane

Fig. 1 Still from *Godzilla*, 1954.
Fig. 2 Hiroshima, 1945.

The Romantic mindset tends to regard artistic genius as a type of madness, symptomatic of some primal psychic wound, and the production of artworks as part of a lifelong process of catharsis. From the true artist, then, one expects and accepts eccentricity, irascibility, perversion, substance abuse, self-mutilation, suicide, and so on. There is an essential truth to all such clichés, though Rudolf and Margot Wittkower's book *Born Under Saturn: The Character and Conduct of Artists* argues that the figure of the alienated, tortured artist was also fabricated, or at least exaggerated, by Renaissance artists trying to distinguish themselves from mere artisans. The artisan was seen as slick, happy, and commercially successful, whereas the true artist was brooding, struggling, and profound.

> Of all the intricate questions concerning the nature and personality of artists few have given rise to more consistent inquiry than that of the connection between genius and madness. First discussed in Greece almost twenty-five hundred years ago, the problem has lost none of its peculiar attraction and urgency. Admittedly, silence prevailed during the Middle Ages, at least so far as artists were concerned, but since post-medieval times the idea has never again been wholly abandoned that artistic talent and genius are dependent on a precariously balanced type of personality.[1]

For those Japanese who came of age in the immediate aftermath of the Second World War, known as the *yakeato* generation, the primary cause of their psychic wounds is obvious. The word *yakeato* literally means "remains of a fire" (more poetically, "charred ruins" or simply "ashes") and it refers to the apocalyptic scenes at the end of the war. Every major city in Japan was devastated by incendiary bombs, which were designed to cause widespread fires, and two had been the target of nuclear bombs. Between 1945 and 1952 Japan was governed by what was nominally a coalition of the Allied Powers but effectively an American administration, which initiated a program of national reform, purged wartime leaders and wrote an idealistic new constitution. Until that time, the Emperor had been considered literally to be a deity, but he was forced to admit he was not, in a radio broadcast now known as the "Declaration of Humanity." The *yakeato* generation experienced the destruction of their hometowns as children and became adults during the terrible deprivations of the immediate postwar period, simultaneously undergoing the cognitive dissonance of having Emperor worship replaced with democratic principles imposed by an alien power.

Over time, these multiple traumas were sublimated into a recognized artistic sensibility, characterized by an unsettling coldness or lack of sentimentality toward wartime tragedies. This *yakeato* sensibility is exemplified by Studio Ghibli's 1988 animated film *Grave of the Fireflies*, which is based on a semi-autobiographical short story by Akiyuki Nosaka about his failure to prevent his infant sister from dying of malnutrition during the chaotic period immediately after the end of the war.[2] The story is ostensibly told in the third person, but frequent appearances of phrases written in the first person betray the narrator and protagonist to be one and the same. Nosaka writes in extremely long, paratactic sentences suffused with metaphor and onomatopoeia, often ignoring conventional syntax, grammar, and punctuation in order to give a sense of the attendant panic and confusion. The effect recalls Roland Barthes's description of the way Raymond Queneau's writing is able to "contaminate all the parts of the written discourse by spoken speech, and in his works the socialization of literary language takes a simultaneous hold on all the layers of writing: the spelling, the vocabulary, and—which is more important although less spectacular—the pace."[3] This, for example, is a single sentence translated into English that is mostly loyal to the structure of the original Japanese: [4]

> From the two air raids of March 17 and May 11 he knew it was absolutely impossible with a woman and child along to put out the incendiary bombs and the shelter dug underneath their house was not to be depended on, first he had made his mother take refuge in the concrete reinforced shelter set up at the back of the fire station by the town block

association; as he began to stuff into his rucksack his father's civilian clothes from the chest of drawers with a queerily buoyant feeling the clang clang of the inspection sentries' bells filled the air with their rings, in the instant he ran out onto the porch he was enveloped by the sound of falling missiles—after the first wave passed there was an illusion because of the horror of that falling sound that a sudden stillness had descended, but the oppressive WOO-N WOO-N rumble of the B29s continued unabated—until then only once, five days before, the day of the Osaka air raid, had he from the shelter of the factory seen the formation, like a school of fish cutting through the gaps in the clouds crossing high in the sky above Osaka Bay, shapes flying toward the east, trailing clouds of exhaust so faint as to merge into nothingness, but now as he looked up that pinpoint had grown past arm's length, he could distinguish even the thick line inscribed on the underside of the fuselage of the low flying machines as they swept from the ocean toward the mountains, abruptly tilted their wings, and vanished into the west; for a second time the sound of descending bombs—as if the density of the air had suddenly thickened his body was straight-jacketed, he stood petrified—with a clattering noise the incendiary bombs, blue color, diameter only two inches, length 24 inches, rolled off the roofs, bouncing up and down the road like inchworms, spewing oil, Seita, his composure gone, for an instant dashed into the entranceway, but black smoke was already streaming slowly out from inside, going out again, but only the row of houses, the same as they had always been, not a shadow of human life, on the wall of the house before him a duster for the fires, a ladder had been left standing, anyway off to mamma's shelter; as he started off, Setsuko riding on his back sobbing convulsively, from the second floor window of the corner house black smoke was gushing out and as if by prearrangement a firebomb until then apparently smoldering in the ceiling loft simultaneously burst into flames, the splitting sound of trees crackling in the garden, fire flaming up as it ran along the eaves, a sliding door disjointed, falling, his field of vision darkened, the atmosphere was instantly sweltering, Seita as if he had been sent a staggering blow broke into a run; his previous plan had been to escape to the embankment at Ishiya River, and he ran eastward along the elevated line of the Hanshin Railway, but the area was already in a state of chaos with people dashing for shelter, people dragging large full carts, men carrying great bags of bedding, old ladies calling out for people in shrill voices, fretting with impatience he turned toward the sea, still then the sparks were flying, he was still wrapped in the cry of falling missiles, a 30 *koku* (5.4 kiloliter) sake vat filled with water broke, submerging everything in water, people trying to carry the sick off by stretcher—one block might be completely deserted while on the next street an uproar like that of spring house cleaning, people carrying out even their tatami—he went down the old national road and continued running along narrow streets; in an out-of-the-way city area—had everyone already fled?—not a man or child to be seen, the familiar sight of the black sake storage vats of Nada Gogo coming to this point in the summer the smell of salt water hangs in the air, one catches sight of from between the narrow five-foot intervals of the storage vats the sand beach shining in the summer sun and the sea deep blue rising to a surprisingly high level on the horizon, but today nothing of the kind—no prospect of a shelter in that area of the beach they had reached, just a reflexive movement of escape from the fire to the water, refugees with the same idea were huddled under the fishing boats and their pulleys for hoisting up the nets along the 150-foot wide stretch of sand.[5]

Nosaka went on to have a varied career as a writer, actor, and musician, but in whatever genre, his work was haunted by the disturbing memories of the *yakeato*.[6] Indeed, such experiences are the cause of what Sigmund Freud called traumatic neurosis, elaborated in his 1920 essay "Beyond the Pleasure Principle":

> A condition consequent upon severe mechanical shock, train crashes, and other life-threatening accidents has long since been identified and described—a condition that has come to be known as 'traumatic neurosis.' The terrible war that has only just ended gave rise to a great many such disorders.[7]

Though many of Freud's views have since been discredited, his concept of traumatic neurosis, renamed PTSD, is generally accepted in the field of psychiatry. In any case, Freud argues that the effects are profound and lifelong:

> Indeed, the term 'traumatic' has no other sense than an economic one. We apply it to an experience which within a short period of time resents the mind with an increase of stimulus too powerful to be dealt with or worked off in the normal way, and this must result in permanent disturbances of the manner in which the energy operates.[8]

Given its mandate to replace charred ruins and prevent their recurrence, architecture is the field with the most direct relationship to the effects of *yakeato*. The loss of one's family home, neighborhood, or town inspired many in that generation to become architects themselves, with the desire to not only rebuild safer and stronger structures, but to reimagine from zero what architecture and cities—and therefore society—might be. Arguably, the postwar preference for in situ concrete rather than traditional wood structures is a consequence of the *yakeato* experience. The 1960s avant-garde movement called Metabolism was morbidly fascinated by the Western technologies that led to Japan's defeat in the war, and the members originally intended to call themselves the Yakeato-ha (School of Ashes) before settling on their more optimistic name. The Metabolists made grandiose proposals for new cities projected over the scorched earth left by the bombings, or up into empty sky and across open sea. Several of the group's members have mentioned the influence of their experience of the devastation at the end of the war. Metabolist architect Kishō Kurokawa wrote:

> War helped me discover Japanese culture. As I stood amidst the ruins of Nagoya, the third largest city in Japan, there was nothing but scorched earth for as far as I could see. In contrast to the desolate surroundings, the blue of the mountain range on the horizon was dazzling to the eyes. . . . Very little was left of the Japanese cities destroyed by the air raids of World War II. Much in cities in the West is built of brick and stone, which remain as heaps of rubble after the buildings themselves have been destroyed. In Japan, on the other hand, building is mostly of wood . . . and consequently destruction usually levels Japanese cities to the ground. But even then the buildings and cities persist as vivid images in the minds and imaginations of the people. And it was in this sense that I first came into contact with several major characteristics of Japanese culture, after I had lost my home town in the war. . . .
> I belong to the fourth generation, whose point of origin is the defeat and destruction in the war. For this reason we are sometimes called the Charred Ruins School. In the hearts of all the members of this generation are the traumatic images of events that took place when we were in our formative childhood years: the sudden, tragic destruction of Hiroshima and Nagasaki by atomic bombs and the virtually total reduction of cities and buildings to ashes.[9]

Kenji Ekuan, the Metabolist industrial designer, was originally from Hiroshima, and he said in an interview:

> I was away in the navy so I wasn't there when the bomb hit, but when I stood in the ruins of the city after losing my father and sister to the bomb, there, in a world where there was nothing left at all, I felt the call

of all things man-made. The burned-out shell of a streetcar, an overturned truck, a half-melted bicycle . . . When evening came, the setting sun was just so amazingly beautiful, setting the horrific ruins aglow in its crimson light—it was as if the light of the western sun upon the atomic hellscape transformed it into a dazzling vision of paradise. The setting sun saved the relationship between the realm of things and the realm of people. That scene has continued to have a primal significance in all that I've done since. Experiences like that redirected my perception of the mutability of life from a sense of vanity and desolation to the sense that change drives new growth.[10]

Perhaps the most moving of these accounts is that of Arata Isozaki, who was not a member of Metabolism, but a friend and fellow traveler. A student of Kenzo Tange, mentor to the Metabolists, Isozaki produced a number of designs that are generally considered to be part of the Metabolist canon. The trauma that formed Isozaki's character appears frequently in his writings: the firebombing of his hometown and destruction of his family home.

> The incendiary bombs that colored the night skies over so many Japanese cities looked to me like magnificent fireworks. My memories of running for cover have somehow mingled with the thrills I felt as a child in a mirror maze or a horror show. There was certainly a feeling of terror, but somehow I wanted to stay there, running until the last possible moment. Perhaps I knew that once I had escaped the chaos there would be nothing left, nothing but a void. At dawn I saw an expanse of burnt fields. . . . When I heard the news that Hiroshima, which lay right across the bay from where I lived, had been destroyed, when I saw photographs of its ruined scenery, I still could not grasp the significance of that instantaneous flash of light. But when I saw the film of a mushroom cloud rising over Bikini Atoll, I felt ecstasy as well as terror.
> To throw myself into that explosion and be absorbed by its destruction is surely a yearning for Thanatos, but I was assailed by the feeling that I had become detached from my body, that I was floating, weightless, being sucked toward a point in the blackness of outer space.
> Boiling, swelling, dissipating. Perhaps the void would draw me in.[11]

No doubt this text comprises some over-dramatized self-mythologizing, but nonetheless, the intimations of ruin and darkness that permeate all of Isozaki's work derive from the scenes he witnessed that day. In the early 1960s Isozaki produced several visionary urban projects, titled "Cities in the Air," which introduced the idea of the "joint core": infrastructural towers placed in empty lots in an existing city, which support bridges or branches containing housing, offices, and so on. Isozaki intended these projects to be a critique-through-design of what he saw as the flaws of the Metabolist approach: its disregard of the existing city, its belief that a single architect could or should design an entire city, and its expectation of limitless growth and progress.

Dubious about his chosen profession, Isozaki was then spending much of his time socializing with a Tokyo-based art collective called the Neo-Dadaism Organizers, founded in 1960 and disbanded less than a year later. The Neo-Dadaism Organizers were united by a subversive desire to make art into an *action* as much as an *object*, so their works almost invariably ended up smashed or burned, existing in acts of simultaneous creation and destruction, with the audience often being provoked to participate in the performance or intervene in the installation. Their manifesto, formulated by founding member Ushio Shinohara, declares:

> No matter how much we dream about procreation in the year 1960, just as a single atomic bomb would easily solve our problems, even Picasso's bullfights cannot move us as much as the spray of blood from killing a stray cat. Living on the red-hot earth of the sixth decade of the twentieth century, where sincere works of art are continually crushed, the only way for us to escape the slaughter is to become the slaughterers.[12]

Fig. 3 Arata Isozaki with Masanobu Yoshimura at the Shinjuku White House, 1960.
Fig. 4 Neo-Dadaism Organizers performance at the Shinjuku White House, 1960.

Fig. 5 Arata Isozaki, “Incubation Process”.
Fig. 6 Fukushima nuclear meltdown, 2011.
Fig. 7 “Metabolism: The City of the Future” Symposium, Mori Art Museum, Tokyo, 2011.

In April 1962, Isozaki was asked to contribute to the art magazine *Bijutsu Techō* on the theme of "Contemporary Images."[13] He produced a collage that depicts one of his Cities in the Air rising above the ruins of a Greek temple, accompanied with a poem titled "Incubation Process" in which he asserts that the destiny of every city is to become a ruin. However, Isozaki was not nihilistically celebrating chaos. As implied in the title, he was suggesting that cyclical destruction is necessary for creation. Ruins are the incubator of new growth. Later that year, Isozaki published a provocative essay, or short story, titled "City Demolition Industry, Inc.," in *Shinkenchiku* magazine. It is the tale of a former hitman and poet who establishes a company that aims to destroy cities using three methods: physical destruction, functional disruption, and the encouragement of utopian planning proposals. Isozaki here condemns all urban planning as futile, and contends that a literal implementation of even the conventional plans being produced by bureaucrats would mean the death of the city.

> The aim of his company, therefore, was to destroy cities by all possible means. Tokyo, for him, was especially easy to undermine. It was like a building whose foundations had decayed, walls collapsing and water pipes getting thinner, structures barely standing, braced by numerous struts and supported by a jungle of props and buttresses, patches and stains from the leaks in the roof. Its original elegance had vanished. Imagine such a deserted house—decorated gaudily on the surface, it goes on killing people, goes on emitting a vigorous energy. A gigantic monster on the brink of extinction; a pig roasted whole; the ultimate evil of unintentional, inevitable mass massacre. . . . He said that such a city must be destroyed as soon as possible. . . . Is it really possible to carry out the physical destruction of modern cities? To answer this question, it is enough to remember Tokyo or Hiroshima of seventeen years ago.
>
> The scene there was more than ruins. It was next to nothing. Although Hiroshima at that time was sentenced to death and was expected to remain uninhabitable for the next seventy years, we have to concede that Hiroshima has come to possess a body even more substantial than it had before the war. No more Hiroshima! Resurrection like a phoenix! All right, at that time no one dared to propose the destruction of cities. Nobody will at present, either. A city with physical substance—perhaps it has never existed on earth.[14]

The following month, Isozaki was asked to contribute to an exhibition of the Metabolists and a few invited guests, under the collective name "Team Tokyo."[15] He installed a large table covered with an aerial photograph of Tokyo, beside which was a supply of colored wires, hammers and nails, with a written invitation for visitors to hammer in the nails and connect them with the wires. The aim was to produce, through the participation of random individuals, an abstract representation of the "joint core" concept. The idea of an installation as participatory performance art was inspired by the Neo-Dadaism Organizers, but the evocation of entropy and chaos was intended as a tacit criticism of the optimism and arrogance of his colleagues in the adjacent rooms.

In 2011, for the fiftieth anniversary of the founding of Metabolism, a major retrospective exhibition was held in Tokyo.[16] It included original documents as well as new models and computer animations of canonic Metabolist and related projects, notably Isozaki's controversial collage "Re-ruined Hiroshima," which shows megastructures collaged onto a photograph of the devastated city. Concurrently, Isozaki restaged his "Incubation Process" installation and performance in a small art gallery elsewhere in the city.[17] A few months before both exhibitions opened, on March 11, 2011, northeastern Japan was struck by a powerful earthquake, which caused a tsunami that wiped out entire towns, triggering a controlled shutdown at every nuclear power plant in the region. Less than an hour later, a fifteen-meter-high wave surged over the seawall at the Fukushima Daiichi Nuclear Power Plant, disabling the emergency diesel generators. Over the following days, temperatures rose out

Fig. 8 Sei'ichi Shirai, "Atomic Bomb Catastrophe Temple".

of control, causing core meltdowns in three of the six reactors. The government issued a "Declaration of a Nuclear Emergency" that has yet to be rescinded. The immediate destruction was solely a consequence of the tsunami, but the danger of radioactive contamination was the deeper fear. The only nation ever to have been attacked with nuclear weapons inadvertently allowed that same power to cause profound damage to itself and possibly to the wider world. This gave the Metabolism exhibition a new significance. At a symposium that included the surviving members of the group, there was serious discussion about whether Metabolist methods and concepts might have something to offer the post-earthquake reconstruction. Isozaki was sitting in the front row of the audience, from where he loudly mocked such suggestions.

At the same time as the disaster was unfolding, another museum in Tokyo, the Panasonic Shiodome Museum of Art, happened to be holding a retrospective exhibition on the work of Kyoto-born architect Sei'ichi Shirai, the centerpiece of which was his unbuilt design for the Temple of Atomic Catastrophes, or Genbakudō.[18] The first publication of the Genbakudō was in *Shinkenchiku* magazine in 1955, comprising a perspective drawing, floor plans, a short descriptive text by Shirai in Japanese, and an unsigned, laudatory text in English.[19] Appended to this was a longer essay on Shirai's career in Japanese, signed Tomo'o Iwata—a pseudonym used by Noboru Kawazoe, the magazine's editor and later a founding member of the Metabolists, when he was writing controversial texts. It is almost certain that Kawazoe also wrote the English text.

Though 1955 was the tenth anniversary of the bombings of Hiroshima and Nagasaki, Shirai's direct impetus for the design was the Castle Bravo thermonuclear test carried out by the United States at Bikini Atoll in March 1954. Miscalculations had resulted in an explosion more than twice the expected strength, vaporizing three islands, and rendered the neighboring atolls uninhabitable. A passing Japanese tuna-fishing boat was dusted with radioactive ash, and all twenty-three of the crew were diagnosed with radiation poisoning. The outrage was international, but in Japan it triggered a massive grassroots movement for a worldwide ban on nuclear tests. Witnessing this, Shirai felt compelled to produce the Genbakudō design, despite the lack of a client, site, or budget. He produced a set of drawings that he revised and augmented over the following year, while studying the architectural monuments of all cultures and historical periods precisely in order to avoid repeating any of them. Kawazoe describes the Genbakudō as having "its origin in the stupendous ruins of ancient civilizations around the Nile and Euphrates; while modernity is emphasized in the cantilever formed by intersection of a cylinder and a cube.[20]

MM Shirai's unrealized Genbakudō may have been an "implicit critique" of Kenzo Tange's winning Hiroshima design, but both projects share what Daniell identifies as an "aesthetic neutrality." The Hiroshima memorial's gesture of neutrality is found in a carved epigraph underneath the parabola-shaped cenotaph. Written by scholar Tadayoshi Saika, it reads in Japanese: "Let all the souls rest here in peace; for we shall not repeat the evil." The phrase has stirred debate since its unveiling in 1952. Who is the responsible "we"? Is it the Americans who dropped the bombs? Is it the aggressive Japanese empire? Or, as Saika intended, does the phrase beseech all human civilization to never use nuclear weapons again? The universalist "we" is a telling reflection of the cold war politics of the day; to assign blame to any single party would hamper the United States' plan to rehabilitate Japan as a partner in the fight against communism. The epitaph's grammatic neutrality is also an attempt to neutralize responsibility for the recent past.

How did architects engage with the question of responsibility in the postwar era? The Genbakudō was presented during the so-called "tradition debates" instigated by Noboru Kawazoe. Kawazoe invited artists and architects to locate a new origin of Japanese culture that avoided wartime themes of imperialism and militarism. In his own architectural histories, Kawazoe traced a line of continuity from his Metabolist cohorts to ancient cultures, spinning around the globe but never

Fig. 9 Sei'ichi Shirai on the cover of *Kenchiku*.

acknowledging the colonial or military architecture of the recent past. Like the epigraph, Kawazoe's universalizing gesture neutralized the question of responsibility to match the political dimensions of a new Japan-U.S. partnership. Shirai's observation that the Metabolists worked "in accordance with the system" shows that the search for an architectural "degree zero" after tragedy is nonetheless tethered to political realities.

Shirai's stated aim was an aesthetic neutrality perhaps analogous to Barthes's notion of the zero degree as "colorless writing, freed from all bondage to a pre-ordained state of language."[21] For Shirai, the ground zero of a nuclear explosion created a literal and conceptual tabula rasa, a place to begin again without the pressures of precedent or context. He later explained his intentions in a brief text:

> At first I pursued an image of deep sadness, a lone building standing on a bleak plain. It was associated with memories of brutal violence, the idea of a desolate ruin. However, as I continued to think about it, I eventually moved away from this narrative mode of thinking. I came to believe that the best thing to do was to explore the possibilities of *a priori* factors. Becoming free of biased concepts and stereotypes was a very difficult and formidable task for me at the time. It was difficult to design the eternal, collective symbol of hope rather than a metaphor defining the memory of tragedy, but I did this because I thought that the most important thing was to obtain a formal purity that had never appeared before human eyes in the past.[22]

The construction of Kenzo Tange's Hiroshima Peace Memorial Museum was also completed in 1955. Tange had attended high school in Hiroshima, and in 1946 the War Reconstruction Agency appointed a team that included Tange to undertake planning for rebuilding the city. He recorded his impressions after visiting the site:

> At first, I stood contemplating among the ghastly ruins over which there hung a pungent stench. Things like the strong will of the humans who were rising to their feet from these ruins and the gentle feeling of motherly affection that one felt could not simply be resolved by means of a plain functionalist or rationalist way of thinking. Yet I did not give up on attempting it. If anything, this experience at Hiroshima vigorously shook the naive functionalist view of architecture I had held until then.[23]

In 1949, the Hiroshima Peace Memorial City Construction Law was enacted, with the announcement of a public competition for the Hiroshima Peace Park and Peace Memorial Museum. Tange's winning design, centered on a rectilinear concrete volume raised on pilotis, was presented at CIAM 8 ("The *Heart of the City: Towards the Humanisation of Urban Life*") held in Hoddesdon, England, in 1951. Ground zero, the hypocenter of the explosion, had been Hiroshima's commercial heart, and Tange placed the museum, memorial, and plaza in axial relationships with the wider city and its existing monuments.

> The place that is called the Peace Park occupies a part of Hiroshima's ground zero. It is shaped like an elongated triangle that stretches in the north-south direction over an area of roughly 30,000 *tsubo* [approx. 99,000 square meters], and rivers flow along both of its legs. The base of the triangle abuts a tree-lined boulevard of 100 meters in width that runs across Hiroshima in the east-west direction. The construction of the Peace Park was planned on this location to memorialize the hypocenter. In my plan, I placed the cenotaph at the center of this park and positioned the Peace Halls in a linear fashion to follow the boulevard running along the base of the site.[24]

The Genbakudō might be seen as a late entry to the competition and as an implicit critique of Tange's emphasis on urban rather than architectural principles. Shirai's proposal was for an autonomous object on an anonymous site, physically and conceptually detached from its surroundings. Above a shallow pool of water, the main volume is a white box (labeled "temple") clad in ashlar masonry, cantilevered from a cylindrical tube of polished black stone that pierces the roof to create a circular skylight. The approach route begins at a large, curving pavilion (labeled "museum") set at the edge of the pool, elevated a half story above ground and thereby

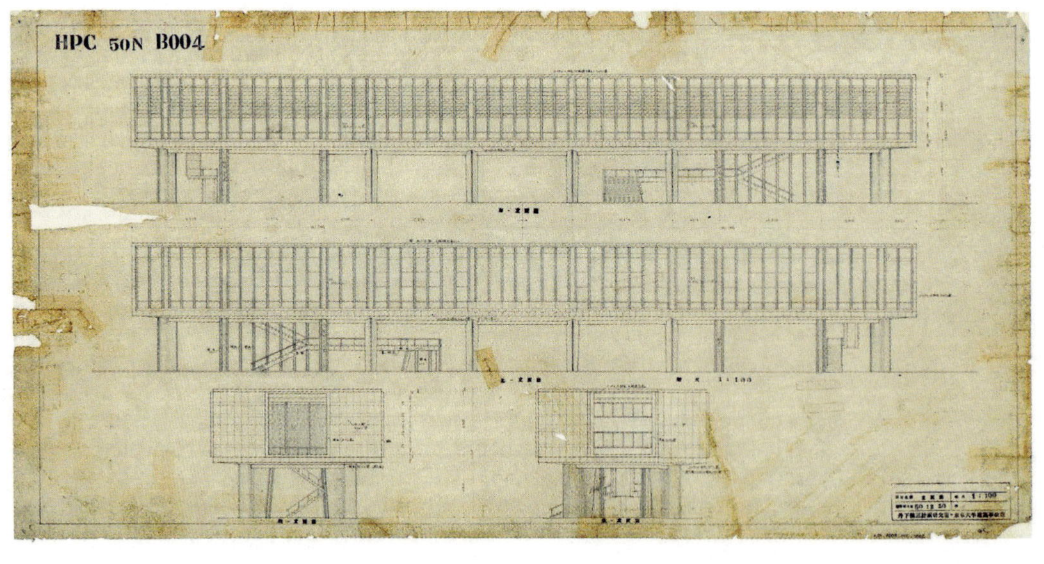

Fig. 10 Elevations of Hiroshima Peace Museum, 1955.

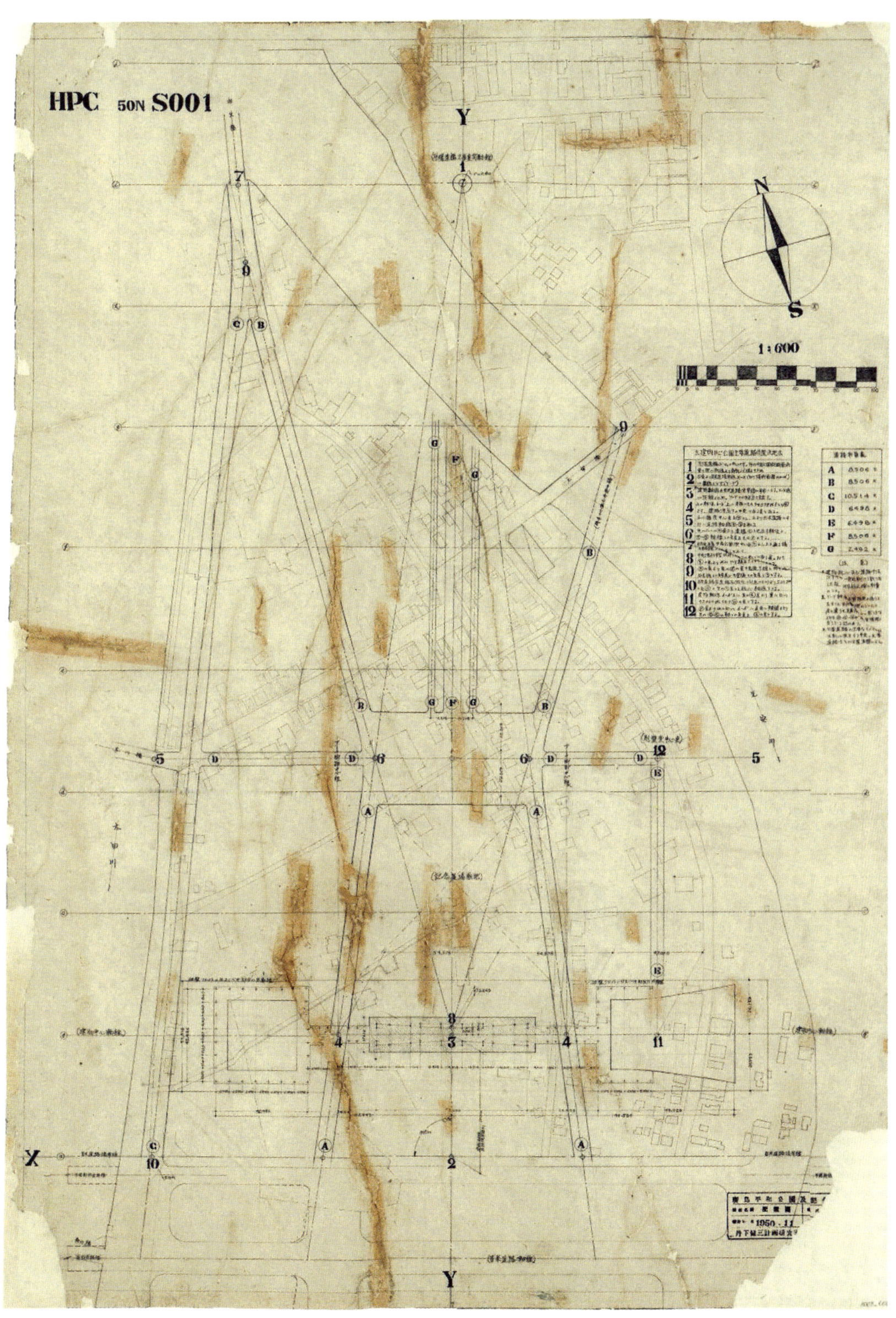

Fig. 11 Master plan of Hiroshima Peace Museum, 1955.

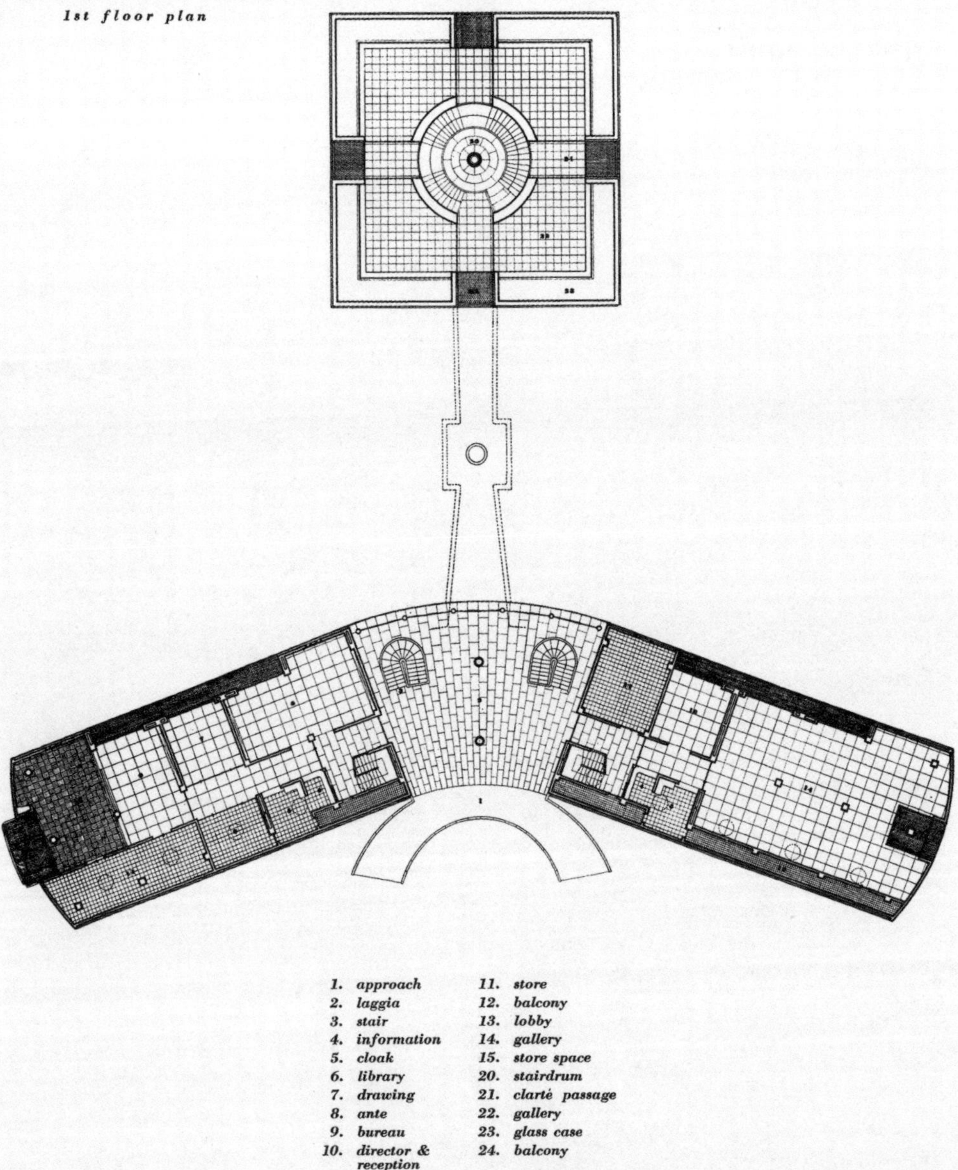

Fig. 12 Genbakudō, ground floor plan, 1955.

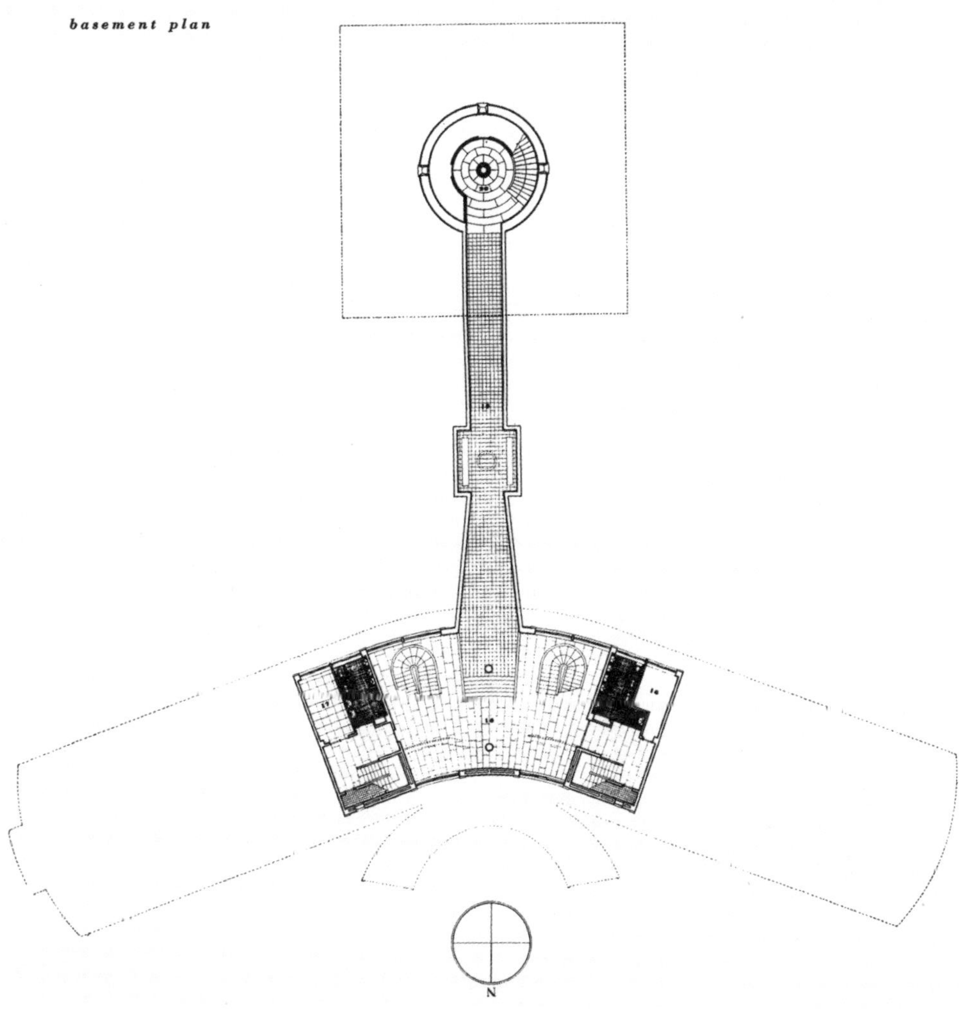

16. sub-hall
17. electric
18. service
19. sub-way
20. stairdrum

Fig. 13 Genbakudō, basement floor plan, 1955.

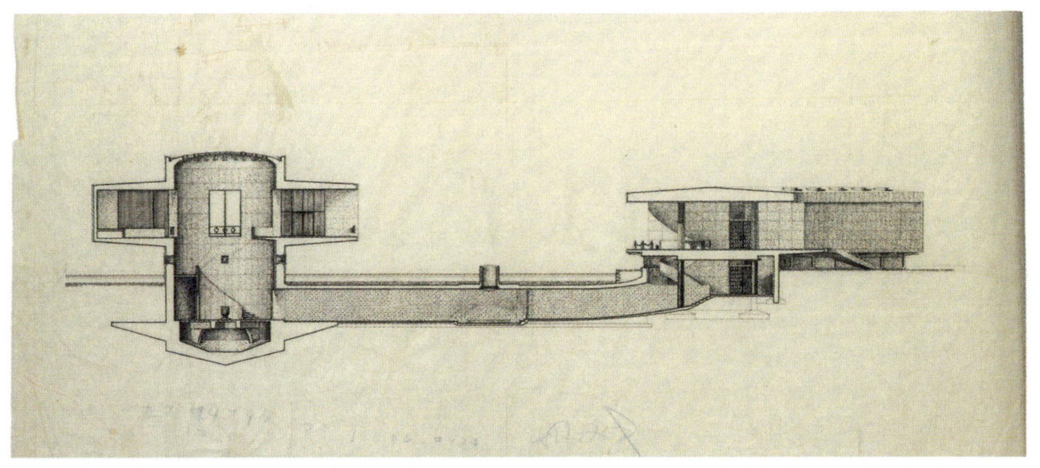

Fig. 14 Genbakudō, section, 1955.

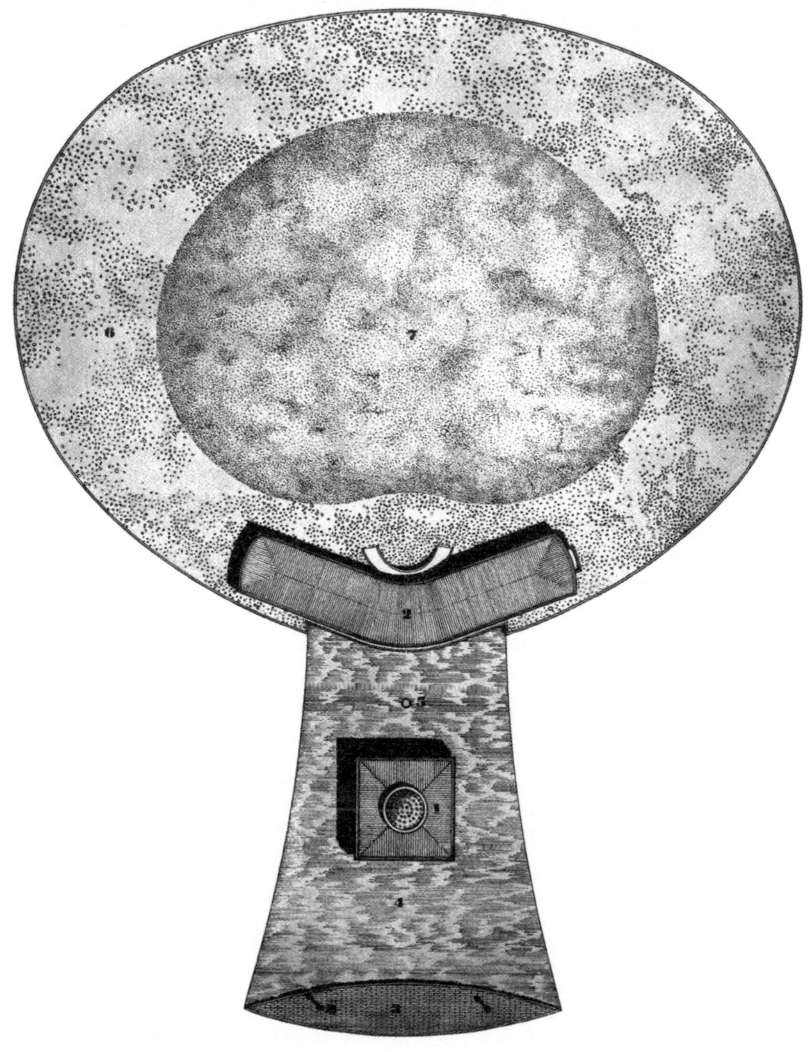

Fig. 15 Genbakudō, site plan, 1955.

blocking the view of the temple. A symmetrical pair of stairs descend to a buried passage that passes under the pool. Halfway along its length is an antechamber with a skylight projecting above the water's surface. At the far end is a spiral staircase set at the base of the black cylinder, with an unidentified urn at its center. Ascending to the temple past small windows, visitors arrive at a landing that faces back toward the entrance pavilion. The temple is symmetrical in plan and section, though what appears at first glance to be a flat roof is a shallow pyramid that is repeated on the underside of the volume. On the opposite side of the pool is a performance stage with two freestanding stone columns capped by eternal flames. Both the museum and the stage are shaped so as to follow or define the curved edge of the water. If the profile of the temple seems to suggest an abstract mushroom cloud, the shape of the site layout does so explicitly, with the pool as the stem of the mushroom and the adjacent oval-shaped plaza as its cap.

The overall plan, shown only in a small diagram, includes a second, larger oval (labeled "stadium"). The pool occupies the interstitial area, distorted to imply that the ovals are pulling away from each other, like the lobes of a living cell undergoing mitosis—a double nucleus contained within a single membrane that is beginning to cleave. Alternatively, if the overall plan is intended as a diagram of the process of nuclear fission, then the black cylinder represents the path of an emitted neutron or gamma ray, passing unimpeded through the solid mass above it. The box resembles a fortified bunker, as if it had been placed underground, then raised into the air on a hydraulic piston. Shirai precisely and painstakingly depicts its reflection (though an assistant did the actual drawing) in what he describes as a "limpid pond" of "clear water flowing so gently that the movement could not be detected by the eye,"[25] which results in the mirage of a much deeper pool with an identical volume shimmering on its floor: a levitating box made of stone is duplicated by a sunken box made of light. Shirai is known to have admired the drawings of Karl Friedrich Schinkel, who often used reflecting pools, but here the reflection is more than a scenographic device in the drawing. It also recalls the "mirror ponds" adjacent to Kyoto's Silver Pavilion and Golden Pavilion, for example, which deliberately evoke the "Western Paradise" of Pure Land Buddhism. Rather than a mushroom cloud, the temple might be a lotus flower emerging from the pond. In Buddhist iconography, the lotus symbolizes spiritual progress: roots in the mud of materialism, stem in the water of experience, and blossom in the sunshine of enlightenment.

Shirai did not give the Genbakudō an explicit religious identity, but if the temple basement is conceived as a crypt, in this case there were no corpses to be interred. The debris of Hiroshima and Nagasaki comprised a fine ash of vaporized buildings, tinctured with vaporized bodies and saturated by radioactive isotopes with half-lives measured in the millions of years. The two boxes might then represent a reactor chamber and a waste repository, the achievement of critical mass and the containment of its consequences, incubator and sarcophagus, instantaneity and eternity.

The Genbakudō was not merely polemical paper architecture. The intention to build had been there from the beginning. For *Shinkenchiku* to publish an imaginary project without any indication of where or how it might be realized was unprecedented, as was its being accompanied by a text in English. The obvious motivation was to generate enough domestic and international interest to get it financed. Kawazoe asserts in his text that Shirai developed the design as an unsolicited response to a newspaper article[26] about the artist couple Iri and Toshi Maruki, who were then working on a series of enormous paintings they called *The Hiroshima Panels*, which bore witness to their own experiences helping victims in the days after the bombing. Iri was originally from Hiroshima, and converted his family home into a makeshift hospital and morgue. In 1950, the Marukis presented the first visual representations of the effects of the bombs to be seen in Japan, a book of drawings titled *Pikadon*[27] and three large paintings that were the start of what was to become *The Hiroshima Panels*.[28] (In 1946 *Asahigraph* magazine published a photograph of the mushroom cloud over Hiroshima, but no photographs of the aftermath in Hiroshima and Nagasaki were disseminated until 1952, when the Occupation ended).[29]

The paintings were touring museums in Japan and attracting millions of visitors, so the artists were hoping to find a permanent display space, which they intended also as a memorial that could host other exhibits or performances.

Shirai had not seen the paintings before he began work on the Genbakudō—his floorplans give no clear indication as to where or how they might be hung—but associating it with *The Hiroshima Panels* was a sure way of gaining media attention and public sympathy. Before the design was published, Shirai presented it to the artists, who then assembled a group of intellectuals to evaluate it. They reacted negatively to various practical and symbolic aspects: the feasibility of Shirai's cantilevered concrete structure ("the cylinder and the beams and walls were divided into separately cast parts that were held together with hoops like those used to hold together the staves of a wooden bathtub"),[30] the cultural appropriateness of stone and symmetry, the advisability of alluding to a mushroom cloud. The artists quietly found another architect.[31]

Undaunted, Shirai self-published a twelve-page pamphlet for international fundraising, containing a revised selection of the drawings, and a new English text written by Kawazoe in which he downplays the religious aspect by referring to the project as the "Atomic Bomb Hall." The pamphlet was distributed at the first Pugwash Conference, an event instigated by the anti-nuclear manifesto written by Bertrand Russell and Albert Einstein. But these efforts were unsuccessful, and the project faded from public memory. Japanese architectural discourse in the 1960s was dominated by Metabolism. Shirai shared with the Metabolists an allegiance to Buddhism and Marxism, to the philosophical doctrine of material impermanence and the political doctrine of historical materialism, both of which find their scientific analogy in the equivalence of mass and energy, but he expressed doubts about the underlying concepts of Metabolist architecture:

> . . . to build a truly metabolic building is not to build a building that is easy to assemble and easy to disassemble. In other words, it is not a stance toward external time and society, it is to build as if one's own existence is at stake. That is, to put yourself into the metabolism of history. People like Michelangelo and Da Vinci were Metabolist in the true sense of the word. The fact that they completed their work within their own selves is, finally, the metabolism of history. I think that doing things in accordance with the era, in accordance with the system, can never be metabolic.[32]

Over the following decades Shirai pursued an increasingly personal and hermetic expression in his architecture, while further developing the compositional themes of the Genbakudō. For example, the Hansōbō Buddhist temple project (1955) appears conventional in form and construction, but the entrance hall and temple are connected by an underground passage, unprecedented in Japanese traditional religious architecture, and the Ogachi Town Hall (1957) comprises a floating cuboid volume with a central window slot, supported on a smaller, darker mass. In 1961, Shirai was commissioned to design several buildings for Shinwa Bank. The head office, located close to Nagasaki's ground zero, was designed in three phases. Phase I comprises a white, cuboid (in fact octagonal) volume supported on a black cylinder, whereas Phase II reverses the dark and light volumes, but continues the theme of levitation. Phase III is a vertically split tower, clad in rough local stone with polished granite around the entrance, incorporating oval elements that suggest an influence from Borromini or Baroque architecture. Isozaki later likened the cleaved form of the tower to both the kanji character for the Buddha and female genitalia.[33]

Shirai was still well known in the 1960s, but increasingly dismissed as an amusing eclectic and reactionary. His reputation in the Japanese architectural community was revived due to the advocacy of Isozaki, who in 1968, at the completion of Phase I of the Shinwa Bank head office, published an essay in which he explicitly rejected the common view of Shirai:

> It is wrong to assume that the blend of various styles as may be seen in the Shinwa Bank head office makes Sei'ichi Shirai an eclectic. For him,

styles are not things adopted from the outside, but are notions that flash within him at the moment he makes an instantaneous choice. It is not logical. It is the instant response of a trained body. At such moments, time surely freezes. The world that derives from this accumulation of responses is his cosmos. Consequently, this cosmos can be said to comprise the notions with which his architecture is endowed.
It is only practice that can sustain the responses of a trained body. Making architecture is, for him, the accumulation of daily practice, which is synonymous with the exhaustive excretion of defined spaces. So his nerves are always attuned to the details, diligently and comprehensively attending to the details by prioritizing the skills of the craftsmen.[34]

As a member of the Pritzker Prize committee from 1979 to 1984, Isozaki lobbied for Shirai to be nominated, which would have made him the first Japanese winner. Isozaki may have been motivated by a desire to escape personal influence and public association with the only other serious candidate from Japan, Kenzo Tange—his former teacher, employer, mentor, and father figure. Though Isozaki often asserted that he successfully convinced the jury to award Shirai the 1984 Pritzker Prize,[35] Shirai died shortly before the scheduled announcement, having fallen on a construction site in Kyoto. The 1984 Pritzker went to Richard Meier. The first Japanese winner of the Pritzker was indeed Tange, in 1987.

For many people who saw the retrospective exhibition on Shirai,[36] the Genbakudō seemed to be no longer a historical curiosity but to have gained a contemporary relevance, if not urgency. A small group of architects and historians formed a committee to raise funds for its construction, endeavoring to keep the Genbakudō in the public eye through symposiums, publications, exhibitions, and a website,[37] but they have yet to announce any committed support for its resurrection. Perhaps this is for the best. Arguably, Japanese culture has a fundamental aversion to physical monuments to tragedy and atrocity, preferring subtler methods of memorialization. The most poignant tributes to Hiroshima are the strings of origami cranes brought by visitors and left to deteriorate in the elements.

Isozaki wrote a long eulogy for Shirai, which concludes with this paragraph:

Shirai collapsed on the construction site of Unpankyo. It is said that he was building his own calligraphy hall, but he was never able to do any calligraphy there. In *Koshikyo Shojō*, the book of calligraphy he published during his lifetime, the two characters 無伴 (*muhan*, unaccompanied) are executed with special brilliance. Done early in his career, they express a sense of exaltation. However, this was a time when he was isolated in the world of architecture, so they also have a feeling of melancholy. In my opinion, they demonstrate that he had found his own style of calligraphy. At the end of his life, he used the word 雲伴 (*unpan*, accompanied by a cloud). Though he might be said to have no companions, why does a cloud suddenly appear? What did he mean by the cloud? Who was the cloud? I do not remember the source of this word, and there is no one who can explain it now. Nothing is left but a world of emptiness.[38]

Whether this "cloud" alludes to a serene cumulus formation in a blue sky or to the violent mushroom cloud over Hiroshima, Shirai's unbuilt Genbakudō remains in limbo, its expression a degree zero of architectural composition, at the nucleus of a matrix of texts, images, objects, and events that cumulatively form a conceptual ground zero in the history of modern Japan.

1 Rudolf and Margot Wittkower, *Born under Saturn: The Character and Conduct of Artists* (New York, NY: W. W. Norton & Company, 1963).

2 Akiyuki Nosaka, "A Grave of Fireflies," trans. James R. Abrams, *Japan Quarterly* XXV, no. 4 (October 1978): 445–463.

3 Roland Barthes, *Writing Degree Zero*, trans. Annette Lavers and Colin Smith (London: Jonathan Cape, 1967).

4 The translator admits to occasional compromises: "He places periods not so much to end a sentence but to conclude a train of thought, and some of his 'thoughts' run on for pages. I have tried to imitate this style of writing as much as was physically feasible, but at times could not resist inserting an extra period or changing the punctuation to make the translation more readable." See "Translator's note" in Nosaka, "A Grave of Fireflies."

5 Nosaka, "A Grave of Fireflies."

6 "When Nosaka Akiyuki received the 58th Naoki Prize in 1968 for 'A Grave of Fireflies' and 'America Hijiki,' he stated in his acceptance speech that 'everything that went into the make-up of my person today can be found in the air raids, the war ruins, and the black market.'" See "Translator's note" in Nosaka, "A Grave of Fireflies."

7 Sigmund Freud, "The Common Neurotic State," in *The Standard Edition of the Complete Psychological Works of Sigmund Freud Volume XVI (1916–1917): Introductory Lectures on Psycho-Analysis (Part III)*, ed. James Strachey (London: The Hogarth Press, 1963).

8 Sigmund Freud, "Fixation to Traumas—The Unconscious," in *The Standard Edition of the Complete Psychological Works of Sigmund Freud Volume XVI (1916–1917): Introductory Lectures on Psycho-Analysis (Part III)*, ed. James Strachey (London: The Hogarth Press, 1963).

9 Kishō Kurokawa, "The Philosophy of Metabolism," in *Metabolism in Architecture* (London: Studio Vista, 1977).

10 Kenji Ekuan interviewed in Rem Koolhaas and Hans Ulrich Obrist, *Project Japan: Metabolism Talks...* (Cologne: Taschen, 2011).

11 Arata Isozaki, "Haikyoron" [Thesis on Ruins], in *Mitate Shuhō: Nihonteki Kūkan no Dokkai* [Metaphorical Method: Readings of Japanese Space] (Tokyo: Kajima Institute Publishing, 1990). My translation.

12 Ushio Shinohara, *Zen'ei no Michi* [The Path of the Avant-Garde] (Tokyo: Bijutsu Shuppan-sha, 1968). My translation.

13 Shuzō Takiguchi, ed., *Bijutsu Techō* 14, no. 203 (April 1962), theme issue titled "Gendai no Image" [Contemporary Images]: .

14 Arata Isozaki, "Toshi Hakaigyō KK," *Shinkenchiku* 37, no. 9 (September 1962). English translation from Arata Isozaki, "City Demolition Industry, Inc.," in *Unbuilt* (Tokyo: Toto Publishing, 2001).

15 "Toshi Keikaku to Toshi Seikatsu: Anata no Toshi wa kō Naru" [Urban Planning and Urban Life: This Will Be Your City], Seibu Department Store, Tokyo (October 12–17, 1962). "Team Tokyo" comprised the four Metabolist architects Masato Ōtaka, Kishō Kurokawa, Kiyonori Kikutake, and Fumihiko Maki, with invited guests Eika Takayama, Kenzo Tange, Sachio Ōtani, and Arata Isozaki.

16 "Metabolism, The City of the Future," Mori Art Museum, Tokyo (September 17, 2011–January 15, 2012).

17 "Process," Misa Shin Gallery, Tokyo (September 9–November 12, 2011).

18 "Sirai: Anima et Persona," Panasonic Shiodome Museum of Art, Tokyo (January 8–March 27, 2011). "Shirai" is the standard transliteration of the architect's family name, though he preferred to use "Sirai" or sometimes "Schirai."

19 Sei'ichi Shirai, "Atomic Bomb Catastrophe Temple," *Shinkenchiku* 30 (April 1955): 38–43.

20 Ibid.

21 Barthes, *Writing Degree Zero*.

22 Sei'ichi Shirai, "Genbakudō ni tsuite" [On the Temple Atomic of Catastrophes], in *Shirai Sei'ichi no Kenchiku* [The Architecture of Sei'ichi Shirai] (Tokyo: Chūōkōronsha, 1974), 87. English translation taken from the exhibition

catalogue *Sirai: Anima et Persona*, ed. Akihiro Hatanaka (Kyoto: Seigensha Art Publishing, 2010).

23 Kenzo Tange, "A Plaza for Fifty Thousand People: Leading up to the Completion of the Hiroshima Peace Center," in *Tange by Tange 1949–1959* (Tokyo: Toto Publishing, 2015). Original publication, Kenzo Tange, "Goman Nin no Hiroba: Hiroshima Peace Center Kansei made," *Geijutsu Shinchō* (January 1956): 76–80.

24 Ibid.

25 Shirai, "Genbakudō ni tsuite." 26. Unsigned.

26 Unsigned, "Tōkyō ni 'Genbaku Bijutsukan': Maruki Akamatsu Ryō Gahaku ga Keikaku" [An 'Atomic Bomb Museum' in Tokyo: Planned by the Two Great Painters Muraki and Akamatsu], *Asahi Shinbun*, August 5, 1954.

27 The title is an onomatopoeia representing the "flash-bang" of an atomic bomb. Controversial, and reportedly suppressed by the Occupation authorities, the book was reissued as Iri Maruki and Toshi Maruki, *Pikadon* (Tokyo: Toho Publishing, 1982).

28 First exhibited at the Maruzen Gallery and the Mitsukoshi department store gallery, both in Tokyo, then at a venue in Hiroshima.

29 John W. Dower, *Embracing Defeat: Japan in the Wake of World War II* (New York, NY: W. W. Norton & Company, 1999).

30 Shirai, "Genbakudō ni tsuite."

31 With the exception of Panel XV, which depicts Nagasaki and is in the collection of the Nagasaki Atomic Bomb Museum, *The Hiroshima Panels* are now on permanent display at the Maruki Gallery in Saitama, which opened in 1967.

32 Isamu Kurita, Sei'ichi Shirai, and Shinpei Kusano, "Taidan: Shi to Kenchiku no Genshitsu" [Discussion: The Essential Nature of Poetry and Architecture], in *Gendai Nihon Kenchikuka Zenshū 9: Shirai Sei'ichi* [Collected Works of Contemporary Japanese Architects 9: Sei'ichi Shirai], ed. Isamu Kurita (Tokyo: San'ichi Shobō, 1970). My translation.

33 "The facade, which at first glance appears to depict female genitalia on full display, can also be justified as representing the two kanji characters for 'Buddha.' If I may make a feeble joke, in primitive times, people would pray for fertility to female figurines with spread thighs, and later generations would press their hands together in prayer and murmur, 'Hotoke-sama' [the name of the Buddha]." Arata Isozaki, "Flashback suru Shirai Sei'ichi" [Sei'ichi Shirai Flashbacks], in *Sirai: Anima et Persona* (Kyoto: Seigensha Art Publishing, 2010). My translation.

34 Arata Isozaki, "Tōketsu shita Jikan no Sanaka ni, Ragyō no Kan'nen to Mukai ai nagara Isshun no Sentaku ni Zensonzai wo Kakerukoto ni yotte Kumitaterareta, 'Sei'ichi Konomi' no Seiritsu to, Gendai Kenchiku no naka de no Mannerist teki Hassō no Imi" [The Formation of "Sei'ichi Style" as a Consequence of Confronting Naked Concepts Within Frozen Time While Gambling One's Entire Tōkyō ni 'Genbaku Bijutsukan': Maruki Akamatsu Ryō Gahaku ga Keikaku" [An 'Atomic Bomb Museum' in Tokyo: Planned by the Two Great Painters Maruki and Akamatsu] Maruzen Gallery and the Mitsukoshi department store gallery, both in Tokyo, then at a venue in Hiroshima. Being on Momentary Whims, and the Significance of Mannerist Ideas in Modern Architecture], *Shinkenchiku* (February 1968). My translation.

35 I have been unable to confirm this with the Pritzker Prize committee, as minutes were not kept.

36 Between July 2010 and August 2011, the exhibition "Sirai: Anima et Persona" toured the Kyoto University of Art and Design, the Museum of Modern Art, Gunma, the Panasonic Shiodome Museum of Art, and the Kyoto Institute of Technology Museum and Archives.

37 In particular, the exhibition "Shirai Sei'ichi no 'Genbakudō' ten: Shin na Taiwa ni mukete" ["Sei'ichi Shirai's 'Genbakudō': Toward a New Discussion"], Gallery 5610, Tokyo (June 5–30, 2018), and its associated publication, Ikuma Shirai et al., *Shirai Sei'ichi no Genbakudō: Yottsu no Taiwa* [Sei'ichi Shirai's Temple of Atomic Catastrophes: Four Conversations] (Tokyo: Shobunsha, 2018).

38 Isozaki, "Flashback suru Shirai Sei'ichi." My translation.

The Significance of the General Form: Reflections on the Degree Zero

Martin Steinmann

introduced and edited by
Irina Davidovici,
translated by
Duncan Brown

comments by
Carla Frick-Cloupet

The three short texts presented here, all previously unpublished, represent a relatively recent understanding of the degree zero in relation to architecture. Their author, the Swiss architecture critic Martin Steinmann (1942–2022), is best known for his theoretical readings of architecture in Switzerland from the 1970s to the 1990s. Trained as an architect, Steinmann became a critic and theoretician by choice. His research and writings were conceived less for academic purposes than as instruments for the articulation of design methods for practice. His forays into architectural realism and autonomy were motivated by a rejection of arbitrary gestures and the search for a rational basis for form.

The degree zero played an important part in this conceptual framework; Steinmann mentions it in relation to the work of Peter Zumthor, Herzog & de Meuron, and Diener & Diener. The architecture of the 1980s and 1990s that Steinmann was writing about espoused a reductive formal rigor that appears to have a parallel in the degree zero as a call to order against formal excess. In his essay "The Presence of Things: Comments on Recent Architecture in Northern Switzerland," published in 1994, he brings together the approaches of several German Swiss architects under a common narrative arch, in which the degree zero was the keystone. For Steinmann, "*the recherche architecturale* pursued by these architects, here representative of Northern Swiss Architecture, can be seen as a search for a *degré zéro*, at which architecture would attain a new *presence*."[1] While a frequent reference,the degree zero was nevertheless never explained, as if its definition was self-evident.

The annotated typescripts in Steinmann's archive attest that behind these fleeting statements was a detailed investigation. The three texts reproduced below were selected from a set of six typescripts in a folder entitled "Degré 0."[2] All are undated, although various clues suggest they were written in the late 1990s and early 2000s. Their conspicuous absence from Steinmann's published writings suggests they were exploratory and personal in nature—as their cursory titles suggest, mere notes, albeit very well put together, as notes go.

The translator and editor of these texts have sought to retain as much as possible their raw, unprocessed state. Stylistic editing has been kept to a minimum and only implemented in a handful of places to ease understanding. The changes made by Steinmann by hand on the typescripts, whether to add or cross out words, have been implemented. The brief references he provided in the original text have been finalized; when sources are missing altogether in Steinmann's original, they have been added and clearly marked as such. The French quotations that Steinmann incorporated have been translated into English. Finally, while the typescripts have no illustrations, Steinmann's writing suggests some possibilities, from which the editor has chosen images based on how closely they respond to those prompts.

In these private reflections, a particularly noteworthy fact is that architecture is rarely mentioned, let alone Swiss contemporary architecture. The attempt to understand the degree zero is articulated in theoretical terms, meandering through the art theory, modernist design, literature, and painting of the late nineteenth and twentieth centuries. Steinmann uses disciplinary fields to ruminate upon the generic qualities of industrial design and mass-produced objects. His starting point in exploring the degree zero is a design task: the need to specify a door handle, on the condition that it "has to be simple."

The connecting thread in Steinmann's reflections on the degree zero is the notion of *Kunstwollen* (will to art or drive to art), coined by the Austrian art historian Alois Riegl in the early 1890s to explore what motivated artists to adopt a certain formal language above others.[3] This was precisely what Steinmann sought to uncover in the act of design—namely, "the reason for form," as a set of aesthetic decisions that are nevertheless culturally predetermined.[4] Riegl understood the adherence to a given set of formal qualities, not as a question of periodization or *Zeitgeist* but as a collective drive emerging in the work of specific groups at certain times and locations. Hans Sedlmayr explains Riegl's *Kunstwollen* as "an objective will, or even specifically an objective collective will, . . . a force that is rightly conceived of by the individual as an objective power."[5]

In turn, Steinmann ponders Riegl's *Kunstwollen* to explain not those qualities that are unique to a work of architecture—or, here, of design—but rather those that are common to many. He adopts a moral stance according to which form must be justifiable beyond the intuitive or subjective gesture of its maker and dictated by a fundamental fitness to purpose. By clearly reflecting its purpose, the form of an object would express a collective creative process. Hence the forays into purism, the modern painting format developed by Le Corbusier together with Amedée Ozenfant to highlight the no-nonsense beauty of "objets-type," or standard objects. In Steinmann's understanding, the degree zero conveys the degree of form-making possessed by standard objects: that is, self-evident and objective. Thus, the philosophical category of the degree zero is enmeshed with that of "general," "banal," and "generic" artefacts. In a surprising turn at the end of the first text reproduced below, he connects the notion of the "banal," through its etymology, with notions of collective legibility and the commons. Individual creativity is repeatedly set against the tempering effects of the pragmatic collective will, the *Kunstwollen* that forms the basis for a degree zero in artistic production.

DEGREE 0, ZERO DESIGN

There has been much talk from a variety of sources in recent years about the *minimal* in architecture, ranging from minimal art to concrete art and the designs of Max Bill—that which von Moos refers to as the "minimal tradition."[6] The word *minimal* refers to forms and the relationships between forms but not to their effects. And yet the effects are great, as long as one is prepared to consider the forms themselves. This manner is determined by the intentionality that forms convey: there is nothing else that they can signal (and that intentionality includes the object to which they apply, in the sense of Riegl's "will-to-style").[7] By this I mean that an object, even if its form is one of great simplicity, or perhaps precisely because of that very simplicity, speaks not only to a certain extent of its purpose but also of the form in which that purpose is expressed. The form is itself the object of language, in a way that is independent of the thing itself; it is the object of a "will-to-form" (to adapt Riegl's terminology). This drive does not relate to the form of this thing but to form in general, to what various objects have in common through their form. It displays an attitude toward the question of form.

These thoughts were triggered by the ordinary task of having to choose door handles for a house. One thing was certain: they had to be simple. The door handle that served as starting point was known as the "Bauhaus" handle and was available in many variants. Designed by Walter Gropius in 1922, it has become, in the words of Sigfried Giedion, "a standard product in common use and almost a symbol of the vital connection between architecture and industrial production."[8] As a symbol, however, it also conveys messages beyond saying, "This is a door handle," be they messages of "standardized" machine production of the "machine age," or even of declaring, "This is a Bauhaus handle." Such meanings are not simply extracted from the form; they themselves feed back on and into it. In other words, through form, they determine what a standard form is. A form that is determined by the discourse as "purposeful" itself determines what kind of form is functional: it codifies the properties of this form, which must subsequently not only fulfill the purpose but also the code of purposeful form. But let us get back to the task in hand.

Door handles that are simple in their design, of "good form,"[9] tend to have geometric lines; the part that you hold is straight and round, while the part that goes into the lock is angled or curved and can therefore be either square-edged or rounded. The creative intention is clear enough: an elementary design requires elementary forms. These forms act, to a certain extent, as guarantors of the elementary design; their reason is less aesthetic than ethical. The elementary design is particularly evident in the Gropius door handle, in which two elementary forms, the prism and the cylinder, combine to form a kind of ABC of these forms.

Roger Diener subjected this handle to a redesign in 1981-82 (Fig. 1).[10] He stripped it back to its basic cylinder shape but also enhanced it with the option of styling it with a black (and later also a white) tube, thereby incorporating an old concept in handle design. Named after its manufacturer, the Glutz handle is an especially elegant object. Hence the first solution to the task at hand: a Glutz handle. It is not only that it is elegant, it also "says" as much: it announces that it is elegant, that it is the result of the intention to design an elegant handle (an object, which, to a certain extent, summarizes the history of the handle in a generic form).

From here, the question arises: what does a handle look like that is designed outside of a "will-to-form," if such a thing were possible?—that has, to a certain extent, designed itself? A purposeful handle that eludes the characteristics of "purposefulness," but without falling to the opposite extreme and exhibiting the characteristics of neglected purpose. The question that arises, in other words, is that of the degree zero of design. Now, in the case of the handle, I think that this degree zero does exist. It is the so-called *Waggon-Drücker*, or carriage-door handle. The name is a reference to railway design, although I cannot remember ever seeing such a handle on a carriage. One might ask where it gets its name, this form that seems to date from the 1930s and was taken up again by Max Bill during the 1950s at the Ulm School of Design, though without disturbing its self-explanatory nature, which I am now equating here with the degree zero (Fig. 2). This is what we will be going on to discuss below: the matter-of-factness of things—or to be more precise, of the form of things—which leads us to overlook them in our daily lives, to look past them, because we perceive them neither as beautiful nor as good or bad. This does not mean to say that they are not beautiful if we approach them from the perspective of the degree zero. This question is not directed at moral categories, such as modesty. It is directed at banality, or rather—since '-ity' describes a position—at the banal. And also at "the ordinary," "the everyday" (the kind of words that, when used by people such as Heinrich Tessenow, come close to being misunderstood as moral categories), or, "the general."

In their collaborative book *La peinture moderne* (Modern Painting) of 1925, Amédée Ozenfant and Charles-Édouard Jeanneret [Le Corbusier] described this characteristic as belonging to *objets-types* (object-types), which became the basis for both artists' Purist paintings (Fig. 3).[11] People use everyday objects in a direct, hands-on way, with the result that they end up being so familiar that they can scarcely be read in the painting as *sujets* [as painterly subjects in their own right]. The authors define this property as *banalité*.[12] Thus, they write, a little later:

> As one concludes, these objects have been chosen for their perfect banality, for best representing *objets-types*. . . . Moreover, these objects have the advantage of being perfectly legible and effortlessly recognizable, they avoid dispersion, the diversion of attention that would be disturbed . . . by singularities, the unknown, the unfamiliar.[13]

Let us now interrupt this revealing quote to expand on the idea of the "readability" of things. This arises from the fact that nothing, no particular feature, attracts our attention, so whatever does attract our attention is that which we do not know. To some extent, our gaze catches on it, like a hand catching a splinter sticking out from a piece of wood. This does not mean that these *objets-types* have no properties—how could they not?—but that their properties are not being individually registered in their own right, as something detached from the whole to which they contribute. It is this whole that renders them self-explanatory. Such objects also derive that self-explanatory nature from the fact that we know them so well from our own daily use, in a more or less similar form, and in forms that tend to have a universal character: "And what makes them so perfectly legible is that they've always been recreated in the most general, standard character."[14]

CFC Steinmann's interest in type-objects—such as a door handle or a piece of wood—can be linked to another chapter of this book, "Building on Conversations with Eric Lapierre," which I wrote with Lyna Bourouiba. Drawing on a series of conversations with the architect Lapierre, we addressed the notion of degree zero and the implications for his work. Lapierre calls for a new rationality in architecture, the specificity of which lies in its effort to remain as close as possible to the architectural discipline itself. Drawing on my doctoral research, we connected Lapierre's proposal to a broader trend in contemporary architecture, particularly in French and Belgian contexts, to engage with objects intrinsic to the very process of making architecture. These are objects proper to the discipline's inner functioning, which we could also call architectural type-objects. Within this trend, we observe a recurring presence of such objects: architects repurpose office tools such as Excel spreadsheets for their design potential, and buildings themselves articulate their operational systems—such as human circulation, or infrastructural elements like heating and ventilation pipes—as integral aspects of architectural expression. We concluded that "in various ways, architecture seeks to tell its own story, in terms of how it works and exists. Its contents and methods intertwine to place the discipline at the heart of architectural practice and topicality.

Does this omnipresence of the act of functioning in architecture fall within Steinmann's understanding of type-objects? If so, how might we interpret these type-objects as specific to the architectural discipline? Could the notion of degree zero, through its commitment to the essence of things, also serve as an epistemological tool that invites us to redefine the very nature of the architectural discipline?

The choice of words is not insignificant: the authors do not say "repeated" but rather "recreated." This means that if one disregards the "will-to-style," the same, elementary requirements will lead to the same forms.[15] As has been said, there are changes in this process, to a greater or lesser degree, but they lie within the range of "les caractères les plus généraux."[16] And they lead to the same forms because these are fully fit for purpose; because they are complete. (At this point, we might refer to Adolf Behne's definition of rationalism: as an approach that applies to "many cases" and therefore strives for the universal.) But the "general" in *La peinture moderne* is also situated in a French context in which the words *général*, *banal*, and even *idéal* mean much the same thing. In *Eupalinos*, Paul Valéry has Socrates say the following about tools, which are, in their own peculiar way, quite clear and understandable: "Ils se sont faits d'eux-mêmes, en quelque sorte; l'usage séculaire a trouvé nécessairement la meilleure forme, la pratique innombrable rejoint un jour l'idéal et s'y arrête." ["They have, in one sense, made themselves; centuries of use have necessarily found the best form, at some point, immeasurable amounts of practical use arrives one day at the ideal and stops there."][17] This ideal is described, however, as "la figure la plus économe et la plus sûre," that is to say, "the most economical and most dependable design." It would be useful to examine the relationship between Valéry and Le Corbusier; *Eupalinos* was published in 1922, and *La peinture moderne* in 1925, based on earlier contributions to [the magazine] *Esprit Nouveau*. (Remarkable parallels also emerge in regard to the objects that Le Corbusier later described as "objets à réaction poétique" ["objects with a poetic reaction."])[18] So far as *objets-types* are concerned, the element of commonality is emphasized in both cases; it does not come from the work of an individual, an invention, but from the work of many. Only this makes it general or generic. And it is this that makes it "banal" in the true sense of the word: *le ban* in French refers to the pastures used by the community, the common land.

DEGREE 0—NOTES (I)

Degree 0 means the banishing of form as form—as form that is presented as something special—from the creative process (removing what is "literary" from writing, that which proclaims: "this is literature," and similarly, by extension, removing the "architectonic" from the making of architecture). A passage from Robert Musil's diaries makes this clear:

> 5 September 1910. It should not say, in *Claudine*: "Somewhere a clock began to talk to itself about the time." That is lyricism. It should read: "A clock struck." ... In the first case, the author is saying, through the refinement of the simile itself: "oh, how beautiful."[19]

And yet, "a clock struck" is also an expression of "will-to-form," in that it distinguishes itself from other possible ways of saying the same thing, from richer options, and instead stands out as a sentence that restricts itself to the bare essentials. Expressing the bare essentials is also therefore form, an expression of a desire for form. And yet it is also non-form, that is to say, the simplest communication of a state of affairs. That non-form can become form by way of *difference* is an age-old story, which formalists have theorized in terms of the alienation or de-automatization of accustomed conceptions of form. The question, then, is under which conditions does this happen, and under which others does it not? What concerns us here is the question of how a banal form remains simply banal, rather than assuming the significance of banality.

According to the conventional view, minimal art is characterized by the use of banal forms and, more generally, banal objects. While artists used to tend to occupy themselves with addressing the unusual, as Barbara Rose discussed in her 1965 essay "ABC Art,"[20] they are now seeking out the banal, the ordinary, and the everyday. This seems to be a consequence of a stance being adopted among young artists that is no more suspect than the "artistic" stance. So, what do we mean when we talk about the banal in minimal art? Well, for one thing, it's the use of simple forms and structures, and for another, of industrial materials such as plywood, steel plating, Formica, fiberglass, or neon tubing. Now, while such materials may be ordinary in their original context, when transposed into the context of art, they lose their ordinariness as a self-evident quality that we tend to overlook so long as they are appearing in an industrial context. What is ordinary about boxes made of galvanized steel is thus transformed into its opposite, the extraordinary, when such boxes are seen within an art space instead of a warehouse. In such an "unaccustomed" environment, they are made visible by being alien, while in their "normal" context they are, to a certain extent, invisible. Carl Andre, who also writes poetry, once said that he would avoid using obscene or improper words in his poetry because they attracted too much attention in a society that did not yet accept such words as ordinary (as cited by Barbara Rose in her essay that was written in 1965, at a time when such words were indeed not yet part of everyday language).[21] I think that was initially also true of industrial materials, which were perceived as "improper" in the field of art. Andre thus puts his finger on a crucial point in the examination of things that are or seem banal: they are or only seem to be banal in a context in which other things confirm this characteristic (by themselves being banal). In such a context, they become invisible in terms of form and the significance of form; on the other hand, they are visible as objects for a purpose (which is what makes them significant). Does this observation lead to a definition of the banal? Such a definition would mean that in banal things, the form disappears behind the purpose that the objects serve, and completely so. The purpose has, to a certain extent, the same contours as the form, so that it covers and obscures it (Fig. 4). There is another kind of covering over to consider in the context of these observations: it consists in the fact that, to a certain extent, form fills the contours that are prescribed by convention. Insofar as convention determines the "general" form, what it corresponds to is banal; it is *itself* a general form, a form that does not attract attention because it is a standard one. Adolf Loos addressed this issue of "not standing out" in his texts on clothing: what does it mean to dress in a modern way? he asks. And then provides the answer: when you don't attract attention with your clothing.[22]

DEGREE 0—NOTES (II)

There are several lines and trains of thought running parallel to each other in this text, some of which have been on my mind for a long time, but it is only recently that I have realized how much they intertwine, and how they actually belong together, not so much, perhaps, when it comes to their *raison d'être*, but in terms of the effect they have on me. If I am to disentangle the strands, the first thing to look at is the *objets-types*, the things that have found their form and are now produced again and again with slight variations, in different locations, for reasons that are difficult to name—or may not even be valid—without anyone at the one location knowing what is going on at the other. In terms of their form, these objects have attained a degree of commonality that sets them apart, as it were, from the constant stream of the production and consumption of forms, from the rotation of form renewal and obsolescence. These things are *objets-types* because they do not owe their form to any design process that might have given the idea of the object a particular form. In a sense, they are the idea itself, or they are so close to it that it is impossible or nearly impossible to distinguish between them. And the reason why they are almost indistinguishable is because no will—in the sense of the "will-to-style"—comes into play between the idea as an end purpose and the form. These things have no style, in the sense that they have no style whatsoever, neither good nor bad—and bad is usually what we mean when we say that something has "no style." Instead of style-less, one might also say nameless or anonymous, in the sense that they cannot be associated with a designer. They owe their form to the community of all those who have produced such things without asking themselves the question of design in any sense that might be patented. They are collective designs, as in the case of the Biedermeier Chair, for example, or they have become such designs over time, like the Thonet Chair No. 14 (Fig. 5). In both cases, the question arises as to the defining characteristics that are a prerequisite for an object to become so universally recognized: for what Roland Barthes referred to for the domain of writing as the *degré zéro*.

It is characteristic of the development of language toward self-awareness that it increasingly loses its transparency—which would have been, I suppose, some time in the nineteenth century?—and words begin not only to denote things, but also to denote something else, namely their own form, their sense of "being-those-words-and-not-being-other-words." According to Barthes, however, by the time of Flaubert, at the latest, this form became the term used to describe a kind of "fabrication," like the shape of a pot. And what it signified precisely was the issue of its own fabrication. That is to say, it became something that was presented before us like some kind of show or spectacle. But this show has little to do with the things that the words describe. It is about something else, a second thing. It is also about what is actually at issue, while the things themselves provide only the material.

Valéry repeatedly described this twofold nature of words: that on the one hand they are a transparent reflection of things, and that they also exist in their own right, namely as the form behind which things disappear. "La forme coûte cher" ["form is expensive"] was what he claimed as the reason for not publishing the lectures he gave at the Collège de France. Barthes quotes this sentence and then goes on to say that there was a time when form and thought were more or less of equal value, because something was being used that already existed: "la forme n'était pas l'objet d'une propriété" ["form was not subject to ownership"]. Language was something shared, and only thoughts could be owned. "On pourrait dire que pendant tout ce temps, la forme avait une valeur d'usage" ["One might say that for all this time, form has had a practical value"].[23]

Do these ideas also apply to visual language?

The point in time when language loses its self-assured certainty coincides with the moment when bourgeois society loses its own certainty, when it emerges in consciousness as one of several hostile forms of society, when bourgeois ideology loses its universality. That's the point when different forms of writing started to flourish: "C'est alors que les écritures commencent à se multiplier" ["it's then that the writings begin to multiply"].[24] To the point of the—failed—bourgeois revolution; "c'est que l'idéologie bourgeoise a duré . . . jusqu'en 1848" ["bourgeois ideology lasted . . . up to 1848"].[25] Now, different kinds of languages and different spheres do not all necessarily develop in parallel. In architecture—in a broad sense of the word that also includes what we now tend to regard as design rather than architecture—there have been different kinds of language for expressing a thought (is it the same thought?) since the early nineteenth century. In this, Schinkel's two designs for the Werdersche Kirche [26] are undoubtedly paradigmatic. But these languages are still in the common domain, even if the way that the individual speaks them is their own. This way of speaking, however, is determined by more reasons than simply uniqueness: such as style.

"L'architecture n'a rien à voir avec les styles" ["architecture has nothing to do with styles"], writes Le Corbusier beneath the photograph of the Wilkinson silos.[27] Now, "style" can be understood in two different ways: as a set of rules that do not concern the objects themselves but rather their design, or, insofar as objects necessarily have a design, the forms-as-forms, that is to say, what Hans Schmidt called "non-essential considerations."[28] However, the term can also be understood to denote the impersonal rules that a period of time imposes, more or less consciously, on the design of its objects. These rules can be so general that the forms they determine are not perceived as something in themselves. They are rather the forms that "one" simply assigns to things. That is to say, they are the self-explanatory forms of things. This also means that one does not perceive forms as forms, as something that can be separated from the things themselves. Now we know, of course, that things do not have the particular forms that they inhabit as a matter of necessity. The necessity lies not in the design but in the perception. What is this based upon?

One answer is probably that it is based on habit. We have seen these forms so often in connection with these things that they appear as necessary forms. The *objets-types* in Le Corbusier's beautiful description are very much in this vein; furthermore, they are *objets-types* because, despite everything, there is a relationship of necessity between purpose and form: they are *objets-types* in the sense of a process of selection in which this relationship comes somewhere close to a relationship of necessity. Something strange is going on in the course of all of this: on the one hand, we no longer see the forms in these objects (we do not see them as something "in themselves,") and at the same time, we no longer see the purpose in the forms, as is the case with those bowls made of white porcelain that are used as containers for chemicals. They become pure forms. As such, however, they serve in the interest of purism, such that there is no "representationalism" to distract our attention from the relationship between forms, which is the point here. (It is not about the bottles, glasses, or whatever else can be seen in Le Corbusier's pictures, nor is it about the "âge du machinisme" that these things represent in a different context (Fig. 6).)

Valéry laments how, in our daily use of language, the form of words disappears into what it is that they mean, that is to say, that the meaning of words obscures their form. As far as everyday objects are concerned, it is possible to turn this idea into a positive; it can be seen as positive that their forms do not constantly come between us and this usage. This does not preclude us from focusing our attention on the self-evident nature of the forms of these *objets-types*, but then we change the level, from the practical use of these objects to what Max Bill referred to as their intellectual usage. (Though is it not the case that we are always operating on this level when we speak of the perception of things?)

The objects to be found in our homes, and here I am becoming normative, should leave it up to us to decide on which level we want to perceive them; they should not interfere in our lives if we don't want them to. But that's what most objects do, chairs, tables, and lamps... they all intervene with their visual noise. You can approach this question from a moral perspective, as Rudolf Schwarz did, for example, in "Neues Bauen?," his essay from 1929. There he criticizes the Neues Bauen movement for being limited to a concept of purpose that suppresses the deeper-lying needs that are associated with it:

> It (the movement) must go beyond the fiction of "aims and objectives"... and turn lovingly toward things and respond to their simple and profound demands. The movement would not need to give up any of its rigor and simplicity and yet it would have to give up everything, its very self, in order to become humble.... Humility loves the modest... things of daily life, because it is precisely the simple... things that are the deepest and the most enduring. Perhaps, if the movement is capable of undergoing a transformation, it will teach the people to love the chastity of these last things once again, just as they once knew them in their clean, poor and chaste farmhouses and workers' dwellings; perhaps life will then be filled again with things that are already something, without the need to make them into anything else, and that it will be adorned once again with the beauty of poverty. [29]

The demand for "silent" things can also be made, however, from a sensual point of view: so that the things that surround us do not impose themselves upon us.

(Hermann Czech once called for things that do not talk unless you talk to them, that only start to speak when they are called upon to do so: a beautiful, clever formulation.) This has nothing to do with modesty—one can also flaunt modesty, that is to say, turn it into a style. Instead, it has to do with a liberation from stylistic obligations, including those of "modesty." Barthes calls this kind of writing "blank," "blanche," and also "neutre," a word that not only signifies neutrality, but also suggests something akin to the suffix *-less*, i.e., depending on the context, colorless, toneless, or passionless, in short: characterless. But this absence of qualities does not mean the declaration of a position, nor any form of concealment or silence; it is a complete absence, as Barthes points out, which allows thought to retain complete responsibility for itself (it cannot therefore justify a weakness with a sense of stylistic responsibility). According to Barthes, it was in *L'étranger* by Albert Camus that this "blank writing," this writing that is completely transparent to thought, was first introduced, in a "style de l'absence qui est presque une absence idéale du style" ["a style of absence that is almost an ideal absence of style"]. [30]

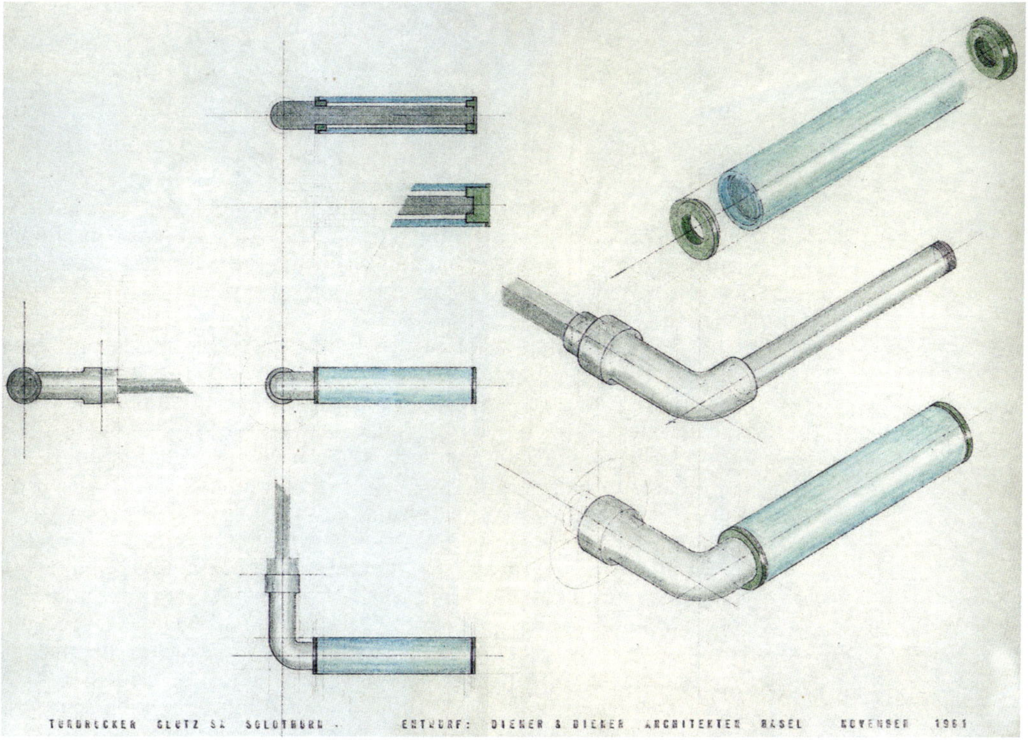

Fig. 1 Diener & Diener, drawing for the “Basel” door handle (1981) manufactured by Glutz.
Fig. 2 Door handle designed by Max Bill together with Ernst Moeckl for the Ulm School of Design (1954–55).

En fin de compte, lorsque sont techniquement résolus les multiples problèmes particuliers au purisme (et bien entendu aussi ceux de toute peinture en général), lorsque la syntaxe puriste est satisfaite, vaut le tableau ce que vaut la conception initiale de l'artiste.

L'existence de ces lois à satisfaire a fait dire que le purisme est une théorie didactique; assurément elle l'est puisqu'on peut en formuler la grammaire; et au bout, aucune grammaire n'a de valeur que si on sait l'employer.

Et certainement ne peuvent se servir de la technique puriste que ceux qui ont rompu avec les anciennes modalités de la peinture, et qui sont des êtres nouveaux, mis au point par la civilisation actuelle; la poésie que l'on veut aujourd'hui est loin des brumes où aimaient à se noyer les romantiques; Fechner, étudiant la sensibilité de l'homme, constatait que la moindre irrégularité d'un angle droit nous fait souffrir; les hommes exacts aujourd'hui repoussent l'inversion où nous avaient conduits trop d'artistes hystériques et qui affectionnaient l'équivoque des formes et des tons. En recherchant les chemins de la santé, nous nous sentons ainsi plus humains et, si nous ressentons la *beauté* comme le seul vrai bonheur, le mouvement des idées a obligé à en reformer la notion.

LA BEAUTÉ NOUVELLE

On a reproché aux théories puristes d'user de la forme scientifique; c'était la seule façon de sortir enfin des palabres des esthéticiens imprécis.

Il est curieux de constater que les écrits sur l'art admettent généralement « le beau » comme une entité précise et, cependant nul n'a jamais pu le définir; un peu de méthode dans la discussion eût permis de constater que, posé comme on le posait, le problème du beau était insoluble.

L'erreur de base était de donner comme critérium du beau l'idée de plaisir, réaction finale tout à fait personnelle et variable.

Il est, en effet, certain que la résultante des sensations et des émotions provoquées par une œuvre d'art, le *jugement* porté, varie suivant les individus; toute discussion basée sur le jugement de valeur de l'œuvre d'art était donc vicieuse; le beau était seulement ce qu'aimait le critique et ses semblables; un tableau était beau quand on en ressentait du plaisir; or, n'est-il pas connu qu'une

Fig. 3 Double spread of Amédée Ozenfant and Charles-Édouard Jeanneret [Le Corbusier], *La peinture moderne* (1925), 170–171, showing *Composition*, a painting by Amédée Ozenfant. According to Ozenfant and Le Corbusier, standard objects "of the most perfect banality" are characterised by "perfect legibility and effortless recognition" (168).

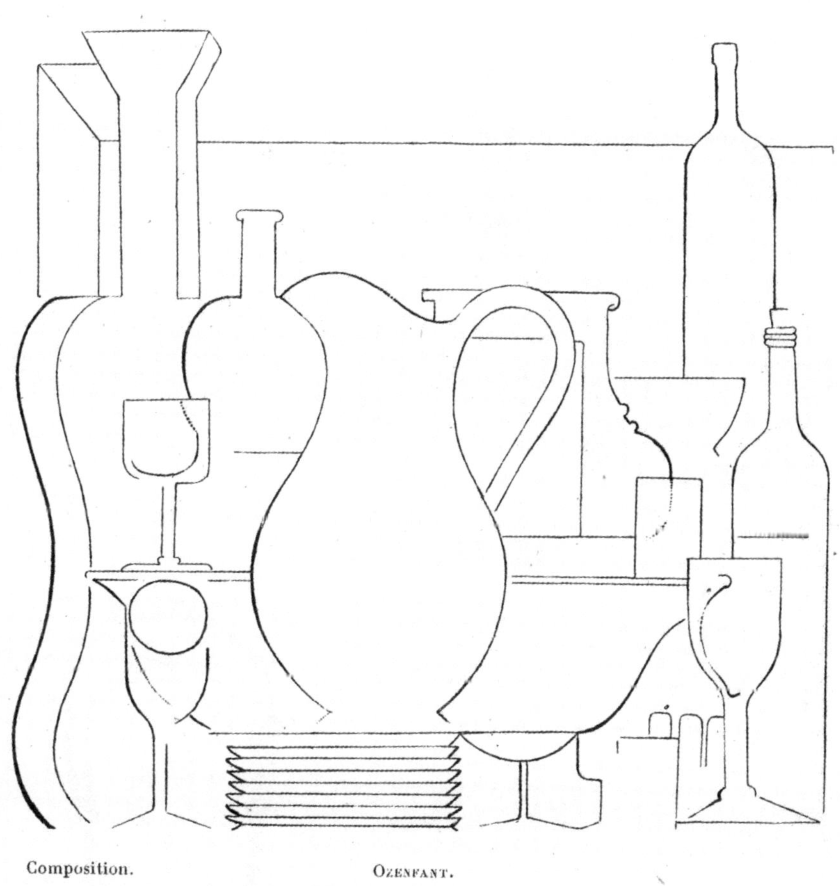

Composition. OZENFANT.

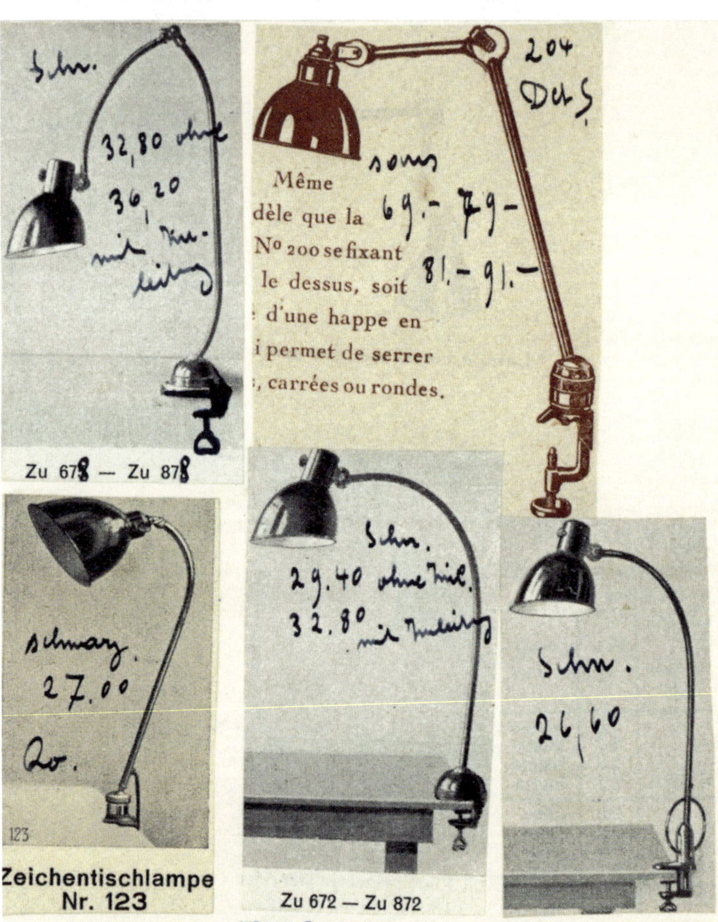

Fig. 4 "The purpose has, to a certain extent, the same contours as the form, so that it covers and obscures it." Mass-produced desklamps, manufacturers' photographs collated and annotated by Sigfried Giedion, ca. 1925–35.

Fig. 5 The Thonet Chair No. 14 (1859), or "bistro chair," designed by Michel Thonet and manufactured by Gebrüder Thonet in Vienna, known as the earliest mass-produced furniture item. Its ubiquity recalls the degree zero of design.

Fig. 6 Scenography of standard objects: Pavillon de l'Esprit Nouveau, Paris (1925).
Interior view with paintings by Fernand Léger and Charles-Édouard Jeanneret and Thonet chairs.

1 Martin Steinmann, "The Presence of Things: Comments on Recent Architecture in Northern Switzerland," *Construction-Intention-Detail: Five Projects from Five Swiss Architects* (Zurich/Munich/London: Artemis Verlags-Ag, 1994), 24 (italics in original; "*recherche architecturale*" is not italicized in the original, but since Steinmann applies them to the first use of the term, earlier on the same page, they have been added here).

2 The bequest from Martin Steinmann at the gta Archive, ETH Zurich, is currently being inventoried. The Degree 0 folder contains handwritten notes, photocopies, and six typescripts (twenty-six pages in total), of which three are reproduced below.

3 Alois Riegl, *Stilfragen: Grundlegungen zu einer Geschichte der Ornamentik* (Berlin: Georg Siemens, 1893).

4 Steinmann, "The Presence of Things," 8.

5 Hans Sedlmayr, "The Quintessence of Riegl's Thought," in *Framing Formalism* (Routledge, 2001),16. DOI: 10.4324/9781315078700-2.

6 Editor's note: See Stanislaus von Moos, "Recycling Max Bill," in Stanislaus von Moos, Karin Gimmi, and Hans Frei, *Minimal tradition: Max Bill e l'architettura "semplice" 1942–1996 = Max Bill and "Simple" Architecture 1942–1996 : XIX Triennale di Milano 1996* (Baden: Lars Müller, 1996), 41–42.

7 Editor's note: Here Steinmann is referring to Alois Riegl's *Stilfragen: Grundlegungen zu einer Geschichte der Ornamentik* (Berlin: Georg Siemens, 1893), translated into English and published as *Problems of Style: Foundations for a History of Ornament*, trans. Evelyn Kain (Princeton: Princeton University Press, 1992). As Riegl did not refer to *Stilwollen* (the drive to style), but *Kunstwollen* (the drive to art), it is possible that Steinmann conflated the title of the book, *Stilfragen*, with the notion of *Kunstwollen*. In this translation, we maintain Steinmann's formulation on the basis that his *Stilwollen* retains the meanings associated in art history with the notion of *Kunstwollen*, the drive to art.

8 Sigfried Giedion, *Walter Gropius: Mensch und Werk* (Stuttgart: Verlag Gerd Hatje, 1954), 103.

9 Editor's note: The concept of *gute Form* (good form) was first coined for the exhibition *Die gute Form* at the Swiss trade fair in Basel (1949), designed by Max Bill. Bill continued to develop the notion in his book *Form: An Overview of Mid-Twentieth-Century Trends in Design* (1952) and later summarized in the professional journal *Das Werk*. See Max Bill, *Form: Eine Bilanz über die Formentwicklung um die Mitte des XX. Jahrhunderts / A Balance Sheet of Mid-Twentieth-Century Trends in Design / Un bilan de l'évolution de la forme au milieu du XXe siècle* (Basel: Werner, 1952); Max Bill, "Die gute Form," *Werk* (Bern, Switzerland) 44, no. 4 (1957): 138–40. doi: 10.5169/seals-34150.

10 Editor's note: The "Basel" door handle designed by Diener & Diener in 1981 is manufactured by Glutz under catalogue reference number no. 569/GLU. In the manufacturer's catalogue, the door handle is named Basel, after the town where Diener & Diener's office is located.

11 Translator's note: Amédée Ozenfant and Charles-Edouard Jeanneret (Le Corbusier), *La peinture moderne* (Paris: Les Editions G. Crès, 1925). Editor's note: In the original text, Ozenfant and Jeanneret refer to the notion of "object-standard" as synonymous to "objet-type" (168). Their explanation of purism contains the following helpful quote: "Le purisme a mis en évidence la loi de la sélection méchanique. Celle-ci établit que les objets tendent vers un type qui est déterminé par l'évolution des formes entre l'idéal de plus grande utilité et celui de la satisfaction aux nécessités de la fabrication économe, qui se conforme fatalement aux lois naturelles; ce double jeu de lois a abouti à la création d'un certain nombre d'objets pour ainsi dire standardisés qui ont la vertu particulière d'être tous étroitement associés à l'homme, d'être à son échelle, d'appartenir à la même famille de formes et de se trouver par conséquent associés les uns aux autres par l'unité des lois ayant présidé à leur formation." ["Purism has demonstrated the law of mechanical selection. This establishes that objects tend towards a type determined by the evolution

of forms between the ideal of greatest usefulness on the one hand and satisfying the necessity for economical fabrication, which fatally conforms to natural laws, on the other. This double game of laws has led to the creation of a certain number of so-called standard objects, with the peculiar characteristic of being closely associated with people's bodies, their scale, belonging to the same family of forms and and therefore being related to one another through the unity of the laws that dictated their formation"] (167) (translated by Irina Davidovici).

12 Translator's note: Ibid., 168.

13 Translator's note: Ibid., 168: "Ces objets, on le constate, ont été choisis de la plus parfaite banalité, ceux qui figurent le mieux les objets-types . . . De plus ces objets ont l'avantage d'une parfaite lisibilité et reconnus sans effort, ils évitent la dispersion, la déviation de l'attention qui serait perturbée . . . par des singularités, l'inconnu, le mal connu."

14 Translator's note: Ibid., 168: "Et ce qui fait qu'ils sont d'une lisibilité parfaite, c'est qu'ils ont toujours été recrée dans les caractères les plus généraux, standards."

15 Editor's note: Hans Sedlmayr notes that Riegl's *Kunstwollen* (will to art or drive to art) is a question not of periodization or *Zeitgeist* but of a collective drive that emerges in the work of specific groups, at certain times in certain locations. At the same time, Sedlmayr writes that "it is also quite impossible to posit the 'time' or 'spirit of the age' as vehicles of the *Kunstwollen.* For if one took these vague expressions literally, all works of art of the same year, of the same era, would display the same style. Rather, the vehicle of the *Kunstwollen* is a specific group of individuals that can be of varying size. . . . Modern sociology has subsequently produced the nonatomistic theory of 'objective spirit,' and in this theoretical context there appears the concept of an 'objective collective will,' which matches perfectly the concept introduced by Riegl. . . . [W]hat is talked about here is an objective will, or even specifically of an objective collective will, and this refers to a force that is rightly conceived of by the individual as an objective power. Clearly this is precisely what Riegl means." Sedlmayr, "The Quintessence of Riegl's Thought," 16.

16 Editor's note: Ozenfant and Jeanneret, *La Peinture Moderne*, 168.

17 Editor's note: Paul Valéry, *Eupalinos ou l'architecte; précédé de L'âme et la danse*. ed. 53 (Paris: Gallimard, 1924), 187.

18 Editor's note: See for example Le Corbusier, "Les objets à réaction poétique," in Le Corbusier, *L'Atelier de la Recherche patiente* (Paris: Vincent et Freal, 1960), 209.

19 Robert Musil, *Aus den Tagebüchern* [From the Diaries] (Hamburg: Suhrkamp, 1963), 45: "irgendwo begann eine Uhr mit sich selber von der Zeit zu sprechen . . . . Das ist Lyrik. Es muss heissen: eine Uhr schlug. . . . Im ersten Fall sagt der Autor durch die Gewähltheit des Gleichnisses selbst: wie schön."

20 Barbara Rose, "ABC," in Gregory Battcock, *Minimal Art: A Critical Anthology* (Berkeley: University of California Press, 1995), 293.

21 Ibid.

22 Editor's note: "An article of clothing is modern, when it is possible to wear it in one's native cultural environment . . . and it does not attract any unwarranted attention." Adolf Loos, "Men's Fashion", ca. 1898, in *Why a Man Should Be Well-Dressed*, trans. Michael Edward Troy (Vienna: Metroverlag, 2011), 31.

23 Roland Barthes, *Le degré zéro de l'écriture* (Paris: Éditions du Seuil, 1953), 89–90.

24 Ibid., 87.

25 Ibid., 84.

26 Translator's note: The Friedrichswerder Church in Berlin.

27 Editor's note: Le Corbusier, *Vers une architecture* (Paris: Crès, 1924), 15.

28 Editor's note: In the original typescript: "sachfremde Rücksichten." Steinmann thus paraphrases the Swiss avant-garde architect Hans Schmidt, who wrote of "wesensfremden Rücksichten" (equally translatable as "non-essential considerations") in an essay accompanying the exhibition *Bauten der Technik*,

shown at the Gewerbemuseum Basel in 1929. See Hans Schmidt, "Bauten der Technik," in Hans Schmidt and Bruno Flierl, *Beiträge zur Architektur*, 1924–1964 (Basel: Pfalz, 1965), 54.

29 Translator's note: Rudolf Schwarz, "Neues Bauen?" The original article was published in *Die Schildgenossen* in 1929. Steinmann cites Rudolf Schwarz, *Wegweisung der Technik und Andere Schriften zum Neuen Bauen*, 1926–1961 (Braunschweig: Vieweg, 1979), 127.

30 Barthes, *Le degré zéro*, 109.

Building on Conversations with Éric Lapierre

Lyna Bourouiba,
Carla Frick-Cloupet

comments by
Victoire Chancel

FROM INVITATION TO CONVERSATIONS

On November 3, 2022, the architect Éric Lapierre[1] gave a one-and-a-half-hour lecture in Brussels entitled "Marvelous Architecture: Toward a Permanent Innocence,"[2] the closing talk of the two-day symposium on which this book is based. We, the authors of this chapter, invited him to discuss the possible links between his work and Roland Barthes's book *Writing Degree Zero.*[3] Among the mediatized architects of the European scene who produce a self-reflexive discourse on their work, Lapierre seemed appropriate for that keynote address for several reasons. First and foremost, we believe that Lapierre's work creates links to Roland Barthes's degree zero. The content and form of Lapierre's discourse is both efficient and erudite, both learned and accessible to a broad audience. His work questions how the responsibility of the architect-author is engaged in the architectural project both as a process and in its aesthetic manifestations. Barthes and Lapierre share a common desire: to explore the relationship between form and authorship from a social perspective; in other words, to take seriously both the responsibility of an author toward forms—whether discursive or architectural—and what those forms refer to socially and politically.

On April 22, 2024, we invited Lapierre again, this time for an interview, to pursue a dialogue of ideas. This chapter is based on these two more or less public formats of exchange.[4] It gathers and reworks our reflections that occurred before, during, and after the conference and the interview. This process enabled us to establish collective areas of thought in which everyone's preoccupations intersected and everyone could respond to each other. Therefore, this paper does not transcribe the conference talk nor the interview but rather isolates the parts that provided us with material for discussion and to relate them in a hybrid format. This approach was taken out of necessity, since it involved translating the content from different venues (invitation, conference, conversations) over discontinuous periods (between June 2022 and September 2024) into the format of this article. These acts of re-composition raised the question of transmission: what to transmit and how?

This article is both a discursive and a formal response to the need to assemble and relate a composite, individual, and collective material. It represents a retrospective and forward-looking account of Lapierre's thoughts as we understood them and as they resonated with our own questions.[5] It is based on conversations we had with each other, as well as with the authors and friends, that helped us to think,[6] in the vein of Erasmus when he wrote *The Adages*[7] or Barthes's references in *A Lover Discourse: Fragments*.[8] We use these *conversations*—"these concrete interactions viewed from the angle of the arguments exchanged"[9]—as a collaborative tool for evolving an improvised knowledge able to redistribute the roles previously assigned to each person.[10] Following Cécile Canut's words, we consider that "it is within speech and through discourses that meaning is constantly negotiated."[11] Finally, in this chapter, we try to mirror the collaborative and improvised nature of speech in the language we use when writing.[12] As will become evident, form and style are important when questioning, as Lapierre does, a degree zero in contemporary architecture.

A "NEW RATIONALITY," AS CLOSE AS POSSIBLE TO ARCHITECTURE

As a social art, architecture is exposed to everyone, and everyone is subjected to it. For Lapierre, this specific place in the social world makes rationality necessary for architecture to be public. A building may express extravagant and sophisticated forms, identifiable as an author's signature. But Lapierre wonders if it contributes to a shared and possibly cumulative culture or, on the contrary, if it reinforces the myth of the architect-author and solitary artist. Nevertheless, Lapierre does not aim for fully objective architectural processes. He sees the architect's suspension of subjectivity as an impossible and undesirable goal and seeks instead to celebrate subjectivity by making it collective.

Indeed, Lapierre defends the need for not only rationality but a "new rationality" in architecture. If Lapierre can consider this rationality as "new," it is because he

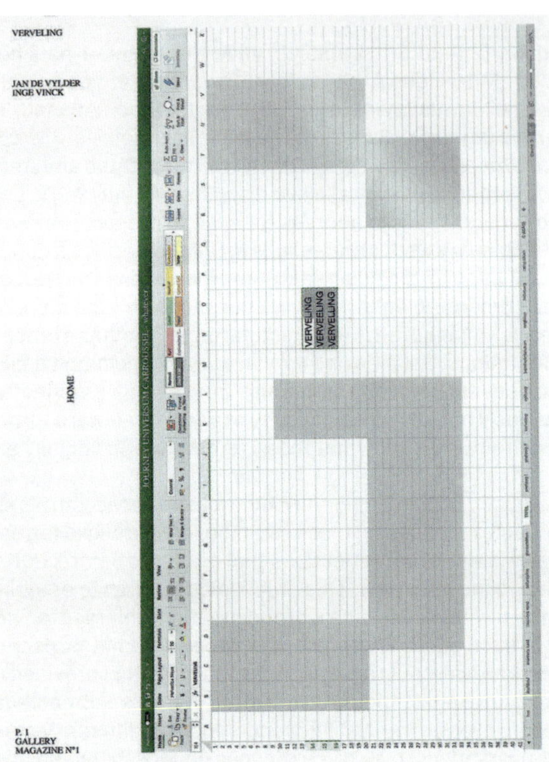

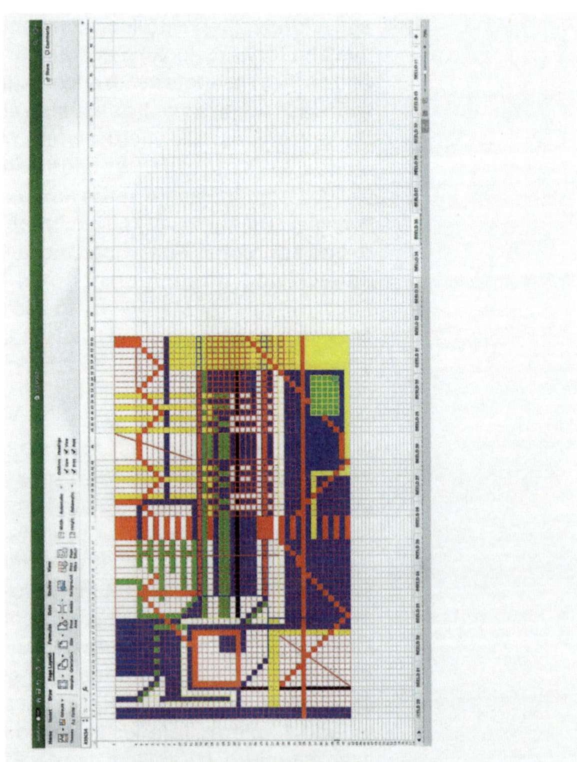

Fig. 1 Inge Vinck and Jan De Vylder's Excel spreadsheets become graphic prints.

first identifies the limits of another rational mode, Cartesianism, the incompleteness of which he points out in relation to a specific architectural rationality that needs to be elaborated. This rationality, he says,

> is good at finding solutions, things with a single answer that can be measured. But what is beautiful, pleasant, and practical cannot be quantified. However, we will all agree on architecture when it is there, which means that there is a form of rationality in architecture, something that can be shared. [13]

This "new rationality" also differs from earlier rational regimes that can be retraced in the history of architecture. Lapierre gives the examples of functionalism, which places function at the heart of architecture's operating principles, and constructive rationalism, which focuses on the role of structure as a vector of architectural and spatial expression. Such theories have in common the goal of making intelligible the intellectual priorities that must be implemented to achieve them.

However, with "new rationality," Lapierre tries to formulate a rationality specific to architecture and elaborated under new conditions. He wants to understand "how architecture works."[14] He invites us to consider a rationality that would also include non-measurable dimensions (the beautiful, the pleasant, the practical), since architecture emerges from the non-hierarchical interplay between measurable (hitherto easily rationalized) and non-measurable elements. We interpret Lapierre's "new rationality" as a paradox of trying to objectify what, a priori, cannot be objectified. Above all, we analyze it as a desire to theorize a concept that would be as close as possible to a definition of architecture itself, in all its complexity and wholeness.

The need to get as close as possible to the essence of architecture seems more than ever to be at the heart of the contemporary architectural discourse in which we evolve, so much so that this notion of functioning shapes practices and projects and the ways in which architects talk about them.[15] Design tools that are usually invisible, because internal to the practice, are increasingly highlighted and used for their creative potential over and beyond the pragmatic aspect of their necessity. The specific visibility that Ghent architects Inge Vinck and Jan De Vylder give to their Excel spreadsheets, which they present in a stand-alone book[16] or transform into graphic print, is a clear illustration of this (Fig. 1). Beyond the means, the human organization that surrounds the project—in other words, the various forms of collaboration and alliances that are forged in both the design and the construction phases—also tends to be embodied within the buildings themselves.[17] The English collective Assemble, for example, draws a parallel between its collaborative approach and how its projects are assembled, bringing together the cooperation mechanisms with the construction systems. Finally, the buildings themselves seem inclined to share their operating methods. They are becoming increasingly transparent in terms of their function—of both human and non-human activity, whether articulating the circulation of human traffic or the pipes for heating and ventilation. In the *Moteur action forme*[18] exhibition, the Parisian office of Bruther emphasized the technical devices of its buildings to show how architectural comfort is made possible (Fig. 2). In various ways, architecture seeks to tell its own story, in terms of how it works and exists. Its contents and methods intertwine to place the discipline at the heart of architectural practice and topicality. The production of Experience, Lapierre's office, is also part of this contemporary momentum. It attempts to reduce the gap between a project's representational elements and a project as a constructed object. Sections, plans, and models almost seem to ask to be built the way they end up within a project. In describing the Point du Jour art center in Cherbourg (2008), Lapierre says he wanted to get as close as possible to the model produced during the design phase of the project (Fig. 3). For the logistics platform at Toulouse Fondeyre (2021), he aimed to build what the section represented (Fig. 4).

The desire to attain accuracy by getting as close as possible to the foundations of a discipline also appeals to us because it strongly resonates with Barthes's degree zero in the field of literature. Barthes aimed for a form of rationality in literary writing that places a common culture at the center of literature's priorities. This practice would be as close as possible to the act of writing itself, the act that turns to its primary tools—language and words—and that holds formalism responsible for the erasure of the collective in favor of a mythical bourgeois culture.[19] In his lecture, Lapierre cited the writer Céline to draw a parallel between Barthes's degree zero and his own desire to reduce the gap between what the Point du Jour model represented and what the building effectively represents:

> Céline has not taken the popular language as something picturesque, seen from a distance. It's the raw material of the book itself and you are completely existentially involved in it. What does it mean? It means that it's a work about trying to be as close as possible to the thing itself.[20]

Here, Barthes's reflections on the degree zero and those of Lapierre on "new rationality" seem to converge in a similar commitment.

VC One might find something peculiar in Lapierre's view of culture, upon which architecture relies. Lapierre argues that architectural forms must be rooted in a shared and cumulative culture. Yet he also maintains that architecture is received with a certain immediacy, reflecting this common basis—for, as he puts it, "we'll all agree on architecture when it's there."

However, culture could be understood differently: as a continuous process of construction, always situated, and in constant evolution over time. From this standpoint, the idea of an immediate and universally shared recognition becomes difficult to uphold.

The connection between Lapierre's thinking and Barthes's *Writing Degree Zero* reveals what I see as a paradoxical view of culture. Culture is depicted as so fundamental that it appears almost absolute—outside of history. Beyond its cumulative process of variations, there would exist a stable and permanent common foundation, making it fundamentally recognizable. From this perspective, culture closely resembles what could be seen as its conceptual opposite: essence.

Although the reasons for such a paradigm shift in architecture today are challenging to identify, we do not seek to answer them unequivocally. Instead, we formulate hypotheses. The attempt by contemporary architects to get as close as possible to architectural tools, means, and modes of collaboration within the form and processes of an architectural project could reflect a profound crisis in the discipline: the original distinction between the design and the building phase is being compromised, a crisis in which those in the discipline are trying to redefine that discipline, using its own means of expression to better grasp its issues and reasons.[21] While form is less a key topic than it might have been twenty years ago, overtaken as it is by more vital considerations such as resources or the very necessity of continuing to build, it remains no less substantial. What may have changed lies in the ways by which architects think of how the form specifically articulates a practice: indissociable from a *manner* of being an author and relative to a *mode* of practicing and discussing it.[22] It might lead us to another hypothesis. The social issue Barthes saw in the degree zero when inviting writers to consider the political relationship between authorship and literary form seems symptomatic of a crisis of modernity that has profoundly shaken the myth of the solitary genius and a bourgeois culture. How architects desire to redefine their practice—by being as close as possible to how the discipline functions and looking for other relationships between authorship and form—resonates with Barthes's proposal. What we identify in architecture today could also find its *raison d'être* in the effects of the critics of modernity that still operate in the cultural field, outside of the logic of the architectural discipline itself.

THE "MARVELOUS ELEMENT" AS A METHOD

For Lapierre, any good architecture is not just a matter of (newly) rational thinking. It must also be capable of provoking surprise.[23] Lapierre considers the notion of surprise as an unconditional feature of architecture. He pursues it in his projects and seeks to identify it in the work of his contemporaries and predecessors. Surprise, however, cannot result from purely gratuitous intentions. It must also correspond to the rational conceptual framework put in place by the architectural project. Lapierre called this a quest for the "marvelous element."

For Lapierre, the "marvelous element" is a factor that could explain any good building—any building capable of provoking surprise—and sums up the main intention of architectural projects. If surprise meets rationality as a first complexity, it then faces a second complication of design involving the designer's cultural background. By becoming architects, we lose a kind of innocence by appropriating a learned architectural culture. Lapierre asks himself, "How to create surprise in a project when we have lost our architectural innocence?"[24] But, he adds, to "produce good architecture the surprise must also be permanent."[25] Lapierre also draws on the ideas of others to work with this notion. The architect Auguste Perret, for example, stated that surprise should be mistrusted because, "by definition, it is not permanent."[26] Lapierre argues instead that with this idea of "the marvelous," we would be able to identify buildings that are a permanent surprise, where architecture exists and "where boredom never happens."[27] For him, that things appear as new every time, and therefore manage to surprise us constantly, would be the hallmark of any durable architecture. He then continues this "call to friends"[28] by looking to the poet Louis Aragon, who defines the marvelous as the contradiction that appears in the real. Lapierre shares this idea as an unambiguous one; in his view, "it is by definition architecture."[29]

Although presented by Lapierre as an ideal to be found, the "marvelous element" also serves as a guide for analyzing architectural projects. At the time of the conference, the projects studied were those carried out with Experience. For example, in the Point du Jour in Cherbourg, the "marvelous element" was its materiality. The Paxalumin cladding, usually used for waterproof roofs, covers the entire building, making it particularly significant. For Lapierre, this use of an unusual material sums up the architectural ambition of the project and its surprising character (Fig. 5). In the Toulouse logistics platform, which is a purely utilitarian building, the surprise appears through the project's technical elements such as the ventilation systems. The "marvelous element" is created from what is apparently useless: the commonly secondary or even anecdotal elements of a building are here considered as important as the structure. In the house for a collector in the Pyrénées (2012), the ontological nature of the sixteen-square plan allows us to take the full and surprising measure of the project—the building's "marvelous element" (Fig. 6). Lapierre's concept, finally, appears to us as a means of identifying and justifying the expression of the author's subjectivity in the architectural project, where the "new rationality" seems to act as a method of allegiance to the common culture.

However, we felt that introducing those projects this way contradicts Lapierre's desire to get as close as possible to the essence and entirety of architecture. For us, the "marvelous element" as a method segments the understanding of the projects in all their complexities and prevents a faithful and complete reading of them. By establishing categories such as "materiality," "the apparently uselessness," or "the ontology of the plan," the "marvelous element" appears to generate reductions. In *Complexity and Contradiction in Architecture*,[30] the architect and theorist Robert Venturi proposes other modes of analysis that we consider more nuanced. Admittedly, many of his tools—like Lapierre's "marvelous element"—are used according to the constraints or scales of the projects (materiality, context, structure, etc.). However, Venturi is interested in the very contradictions of these logics, so he invents modes of linguistic analysis that avoid partial understanding of projects. The most striking example seems to be the phenomenon of the "both-and," by which elements are defined as "both this" and "both that." This element of language necessarily leads the author to use examples.[31] In this way, the meaning of the "both-and" cannot be purely theoretical, essentialized, or extracted from situated projects. As a result, the projects analyzed by Venturi are not classified according to their constraints but rather to common postures whose establishment this element of language allows.[32]

When we discussed this Venturian method with Lapierre, he said that a complex reality can be recomposed after an act of division. For him, the "marvelous element" enables us to understand a building from various angles, all of which work together to approach it in its entirety. For Lapierre, segmenting is not incompatible with a desire for totality, especially regarding the complexity of defining architecture. He also advances the argument of transmission of architecture: the "marvelous element" also could be an architectural theory handbook for first-year architecture students in which everyone could add its chapter. The "marvelous element" thus appears to us more as an invitation to approach and manipulate theory than a tool for analyzing architecture. In so doing, the question shifts from methods to the discursive modes through which ideas are transmitted.

STYLE GATHERS FORM AND VALUE

Together with Lapierre, we discussed the idea that the current architectural crisis and the debates on the notion of authorship should not lead to a categorical retreat of the notions of architectural artwork and author. We believe architects should assume these constitutive notions of the discipline to reform them. Then, and within a broad spectrum of possible responses, we can still ask: How can one be an author without being a demiurge? To avoid any ambiguity, we do not argue in favor of maintaining the myth of the solitary genius and their associated authority—quite the opposite. But neither do we believe in erasing the notion of artwork and author from the architectural discipline. In our view, the architectural and theoretical production of Lapierre and his office tries to make a stand within this thorny and topical debate. He attempts to propose conceptual benchmarks (such as "new rationality" and "marvelous element") and to bring them into the contemporary architectural debate.

To emphasize the value he attaches to his commitment to the architectural form, Lapierre employs the notion of *style*. For him, any architecture induces individual writing (a style) based on the author's interests. Nevertheless, this subjectivity must speak to everyone.[33] Form and style synthesize the collective culture and the individualistic passions without opposing them. For Lapierre, designing equates to "carving a foreign language into a common language."[34] The form is also essential in this foreign but collective language. Once again relying on literature and language, Lapierre says that even visually, the writer Céline's use of French "doesn't look like French!"[35] Therefore, to engage within the form, architects must reach a sufficient level of rationality, evidence, and common language. At the same time, as authors, they must bring their singularities. Through style, the notion of architectural artwork thus emerges. Nevertheless, while Lapierre defends style, he carefully distinguishes it from productions characterized by overly mannered, exuberant, and arbitrary forms, which distort the notion by reducing it to a purely aesthetic architectural language.

In *Styles: Critique de nos formes de vie*, the historian of literature and essayist Marielle Macé also looks at the notion of style (Fig. 7).[36] She considers that this concept has been emptied of the plurality of its meaning by two main phenomena. The structuralist approach of the social sciences (such as that of Pierre Bourdieu) brought the concept closer to a social and structural meaning, while liberalism has monopolized the notion by making identity, appearance, and people's social status consumable. In contrast to these two acts of essentialization and confiscation, Macé seeks to restore the political nature of style by emphasizing how values are hidden behind forms. Indeed, both Lapierre and Macé share an interest in style and a desire to defend it against contemporary criticisms—whether productivist or functionalist—that accuse stylists of being apolitical aesthetes. Just as Macé does with forms-of-life, Lapierre says that architectural style always carries commitments and that denying it is also a political statement. Both strive to defend style against a utilitarian reduction, advocating that culture not be sacrificed "in times of crisis."[37] In their respective fields of thought, style is not a mere aesthetic whim but something meaningful. Thus, we invite Lapierre to fictitiously continue the conversation we have begun together, this time alongside Macé, to discuss the requalification of this notion within the architectural discipline. Could architects, too, restore a contemporary depth to style, distancing it from its partnership with neo-liberal architecture from which it suffers and reconstructing it on the side of common culture and authorial commitment? How can we reopen the notion of architectural style, which has been reduced to a formalist issue, to its political dimension?

For Macé, style is a manner, a way, a regime, a conduct, or even a gesture that reveals stances taken in the world. Style questions the meaning we attach to our actions and how we perform them. In conceiving it as such, Macé invites us to consider the values behind our forms, the ability of forms to embody values about what they mean in a political commitment. In this article, we approach style as "a knot between form and value."[38] By reformulating and extrapolating the thoughts of others, we construct a conversation from various formats of exchange. We experiment with a balance between subjectivity, otherness, and shared knowledge and, in doing so, question the forms of a collective range, since "the questions posed by scholars do not arise from a solitary exercise of the faculty of thinking: they are born from interactions with others. With the dead, sometime... But more often, with the living."[39]

Fig. 7 Cover of *Styles: Critique de nos formes de vie* (Paris: Gallimard, 2014).

Fig. 2 *Moteur action forme* exhibition by Bruther, Carlotta Darò, and Laurent Stalder, in 2021-22 at Arc-En-Rêve, Bordeaux.

Fig. 3 (a, b) Building the Point du Jour art center in Cherbourg as its model, 2008.

Fig. 4 Building the postal logistics platform as its section, 2021.

Fig. 5 (a, b) The paxaluminium as the marvelous element of the art center, 2008.

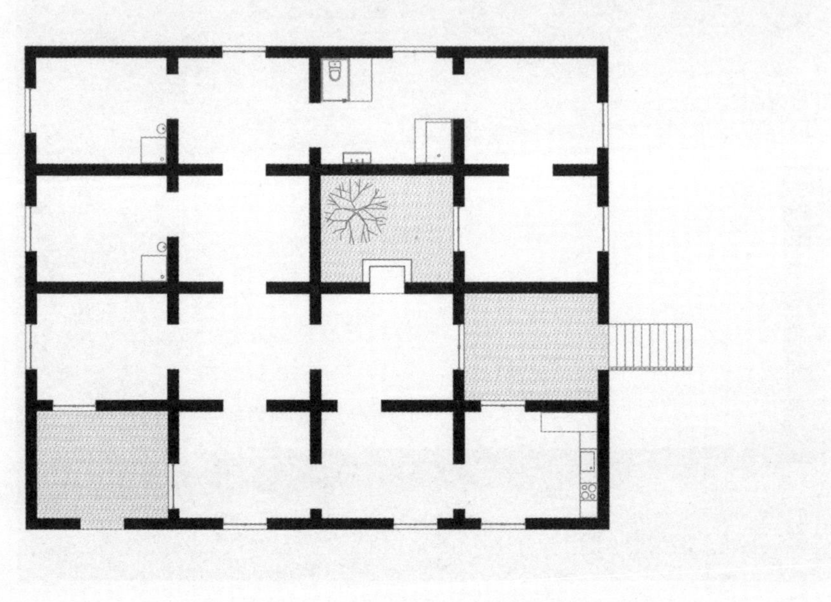

Fig. 6 (a, b) The plan as the marvelous element of the house, 2012.

1 Éric Lapierre runs a practice called Experience. It was given this name in 2023 to bring together Éric Lapierre, Tristan Chadney, and Laurent Esmilaire. Before Experience was formed, Éric Lapierre's practice, founded in 1999, operated under the name Éric Lapierre EXPERIENCE.

2 The conference was open to the public and has been filmed. While the video is unavailable online, anyone who wants to access it can request it from the symposium organizers, the editors of this book.

3 Roland Barthes, *Le degré zéro de l'écriture* (Paris: Seuil, 1953).

4 Éric Lapierre, interview with Lyna Bourouiba and Carla Frick-Cloupet, Brussels, April 22, 2024; Éric Lapierre, "Marvelous Architecture: Toward a Permanent Innocence," recording of paper for the symposium "The Zero Degree of Architectural Writing: Theorizing, Drawing, and Debating the 'Third Term,'" November 2–3, 2022.

5 While we aim to reproduce Lapierre's thoughts as faithfully as possible, we cannot guarantee precise accuracy, since they have been filtered through our interpretations.

6 We particularly thank Victoire Chancel, Eric Lapierre, and Wouter Van Acker for their precious feedback during the writing of this article.

7 Érasme, *Les Adages* (Paris: Éditions Les belles lettres, 2019).

8 Roland Barthes, *A Lover's Discourse: Fragments* (New York: Hill and Wang, 2010), originally published in French as *Fragment d'un discours amoureux* (Paris: Seuil, 1977).

9 The French historian and sociologist Christian Topalov is also interested in conversations to study how ideas circulated between scholars and to develop a social history of knowledge. Christian Topalov, *Histoires d'enquêtes: Londres, Paris, Chicago (1880–1930)* (Paris: Classiques Garnier, 2015, 30). All translations are ours unless otherwise noted.

10 Will Holder is interested in the act of publishing and in conversation as a "model and tool for a mutual and improvised set of publishing conditions," as described by the Dutch Art Institute and others institutions (https://dutchartinstitute.eu/page/5265/will-holder). He is a typographer, an artist, and a writer, and edits books with artists and musicians. With the co-operatively run, non-profit contemporary art venue castillo/corrales, he published a collection of texts jointly, called *The Social Life of the Book* (Paris: Paraguay Press, 2011–2015).

11 Cécile Canut, *Langue* (Paris: Anamosa, 2021), 24.

12 Speech and language correspond to the distinction Canut makes between "parole" and "langue" in the French language. She describes how the institutionalization of language has imposed ways of expressing, while speech allows greater freedom of enunciation and invention in language.

13 Lapierre, interview, 00:58.

14 Ibid., 00:34:40.

15 Our practices are based in Brussels. The architectural discourses we are referring to are mostly from Northern Europe.

16 Jan De Vylder and Inge Vinck, *Verveling*, special issue for *Gallery Magazine*, no. 1, 2020, 62 (Sint-Amandsberg: Art Paper Edition, 2020), 62.

17 For a more detailed examination of the correlations between authorship and aesthetic achievement in collective architectural practices, see Bureau FL5.2, "(In)visible authors," *OASE*, no. 113 (2023): 56–65.

18 Bruther, Carlotta Darò, and Laurent Stalder, *Moteur action forme*, exhibition, 2021–2022, Arc-En-Rêve, Bordeaux.

19 In her PhD dissertation, Lyna Bourouiba studies the translation of Barthes's degree zero in architectural history, theory, and criticism. While Barthes's book is typically analyzed as a formalist approach to writing, she proposes a socio-political reading of Barthes's book through the lens of social class conflict.

20 Lapierre, interview, 1:17:10

21 In her PhD dissertation, defended in 2024, Carla Frick-Cloupet studies the architectural practices of Experience, Advvt, OFFICE kgdvs and Bruther.

The notion of functioning that we point out above, as well as this hypothesis, comes from this Phd research, entitled *Architecture Langagière: analyse performative d'une posture architecturale émergente.*

22 The terms *manner* and *mode* refer to Marielle Macé and her book *Styles: Critique de nos formes de vie* (Paris: Gallimard, 2014). The link between practice and form will become obvious at the end of the chapter.

23 Lapierre, "Marvelous Architecture," 00:41:07.

24 Lapierre, interview, 01:02:24.

25 Lapierre, "Marvelous Architecture," 00:42:22.

26 Ibid., 00:41:44.

27 Ibid., 00:42:41.

28 Bruno Latour, *La science en action* (Paris: La Découverte, 1989) 47–68, cited by Topalov in *Histoires d'enquêtes*, 32–33.

29 Lapierre, "Marvelous Architecture," 00:45:38.

30 Robert Venturi, *Complexity and Contradiction in Architecture* (New York: The Museum of Modern Art, 1966).

31 For example, here Venturi is referring to church plans to explain the "both-and" phenomenon: "The basilica, which has mono-directional space, and the central-type church, which has omnidirectional space, represent alternating traditions in Western church plans. But another tradition has accommodated churches which are both-and, in answer to spatial, structural, programmatic, and symbolic needs. The Mannerist elliptical plan of the sixteenth century is both central directional. Its culmination is Bernini's Sant' Andrea al Quirinale, whose main directional axis contradictorily spans the short axis." Ibid., 32.

32 In Carla Frick-Cloupet's PhD dissertation, Venturi's book *Complexity and Contradiction in Architecture* inspired her to propose analytical tools that use language in a performative way so that architecture can be analyzed without essentializing the project's constraints one by one.

33 Lapierre, interview, 01:24:00.

34 Ibid., 01:17:00.

35 Ibid., 01:17:39.

36 Marielle Macé, *Styles: Critique de nos formes de vie.*

37 Lapierre, interview, 01:33:46.

38 On February 7 and 8, 2024, Lyna Bourouiba, Anne-Laure Iger, and Alice Paris organized a seminar at the Faculty of Architecture, La Cambre Horta of the ULB, on the work of Marielle Macé. The goal was to explore collectively, in the presence of Macé, what it means to write. The phrase "style is a knot between form and value" comes from their unpublished notes analyzing Macé's book *Styles*.

39 Topalov, *Histoires d'enquêtes*, 31.

The Right to Architecture

Geert Bekaert

translated and introduced by
Christophe Van Gerrewey

comments by
Pierre Chabard

STICHTING
POST-
DOKTORAAL
ONDERWIJS
IN HET
BOUWEN

SYLLABUS VAN DE LEERGANG

LESSEN IN ARCHITEKTUUR.2

Gehouden op 8 + 9 oktober 1980

TECHNISCHE HOGESCHOOL DELFT

Fig. 1 Cover of *Lessen in architektuur 2*, ed. Joost Meuwissen, Technische Hogeschool Delft, 1980.

INTRODUCTION TO THE TRANSLATION

The discourse that architecture facilitates and provokes is produced by architects, clients, academics, students, users, and inhabitants, but also by critics. Geert Bekaert (1928–2016) was one such critic. From the early 1950s until the beginning of the twenty-first century, he wrote, mainly in Dutch, about architecture in Belgium and the Netherlands, but also about more historical and theoretical evolutions. As one of the "generalists" of the postwar generation of architectural writers in the Western world, he addressed all kinds of topics and phenomena related to architecture at large, combining history, theory, and criticism.[1]

In 1974, Bekaert became the first professor of history and theory of architecture at the Technical University of Eindhoven. In that capacity, he was invited to participate in a lecture series, called Lessons in Architecture, at the Technical University of Delft, organized by Joost Meuwissen. The first session took place in 1979; the second, in which Bekaert participated, on October 8 and 9, 1980. His text, which is translated here, called "Het recht op architectuur" ("The Right to Architecture"), was published in the reader of the series, but also, a few months later, in the journal *wonen-TA/BK* (which would later become *Archis* and, more recently, *Volume*) (Fig. 1).[2] Two decades later, part of it was included in the Dutch anthology *Dat is architectuur* from 2001, a collection of key theoretical texts from the twentieth century.[3]

At the beginning of "The Right to Architecture," Bekaert immediately addresses the impossibility of architectural criticism—of talking about architecture to an audience of architects. The problem is, he says, that he was annoyed by current architecture—and by current Dutch architecture in particular. His criticism is based on the observation that architects set goals that they cannot achieve. In doing so, he argues, they deny the specificity of their discipline, as well as its historical continuity. Attempts to make architecture more social or to use architecture to immediately improve and change society are not only pretentious, they are also part of the history of modern architecture itself. Architects who, at that moment in the late 1970s, claim to be able to fight all kinds of social injustices in a novel way or to allow buildings to communicate smoothly with as many people as possible cherish some of the same illusions as their predecessors from previous centuries. Moreover, they also forget what architecture can really be capable of.

On the one hand, Bekaert's analysis—and he admits as much—is pessimistic, much like the perspectives of Manfredo Tafuri and other postwar theoreticians who fundamentally doubted the social and semiotic potential of architecture. On the other hand, Bekaert refuses to condemn architecture to a kind of zero degree and its accompanying isolation, uselessness, and silence. Or rather: in his view, the zero degree of architecture forms the basis of the social contribution it can make.

Of course, this is a paradoxical position. Bekaert's definition and defense of architecture's autonomy does not lead to an endorsement of formalistic experiments that turn architecture into an otherworldly, experimental, and absurd activity. It is by guaranteeing the confrontation with architecture—by respecting the right of every society to architecture—that buildings and architectural projects can become part of that society and at the same time continue to differ from it.

Although this plea is clearly inspired by the structuralism in Dutch architecture at the time, it can also be regarded as a call to continue to fight for the fundamental and critical otherness of architecture, compared to what is dominant and omnipresent in a culture and a society, at some point in history. Although he mentions not a single building in his lecture, Bekaert does refer to the competition for the Dutch Parliament Extension, de Tweede Kamer, in The Hague in 1978, as an example of "the threat of integration" of architecture by making it harmless, dull, and obedient. That competition caused quite a stir, mainly because the project by OMA and Rem Koolhaas that won the first prize of the first competition was pushed aside so that another, second competition could be organized. Bekaert praises many different forms of architecture in his critical writings, but in the project by OMA for the extension of the House of Representatives, he encountered some of the architectural and intellectual "intelligence" that he was looking for in his plea for the right to architecture (Fig. 2-3).[4]

It is possible to argue that, by doing so, he also heralded the era of star architecture—of strange, surprising, singular but soon also spectacular and sculptural buildings that attract attention with their often-outrageous alterity. And yet it is also true that this lecture from 1980 contains a warning precisely against that kind of practice: once the exception has become the norm, it is the task of architects to look for other exceptions that once again escape those conventions and customs.

PC ORPHEUS AND PROCRUSTES. ESCAPES FROM THE POTEMKIN VILLAGE

Sharp and nuanced, pessimistic and fiery, Geert Bekaert's text deals with the possibility of a language or even poetry in architecture, this practice "condemned to constantly speak without saying anything." If a building may hope to attain a form of poetry, it is, paradoxically, on the condition that the architect renounces any poetic pretense or intention and immerses himself entirely in the concrete and rational reality of his profession, "to continually renew its 'truth' in concrete works." Following Bekaert, the architect resembles the figure of Orpheus summoned up by Roland Barthes in *Writing Degree Zero* to illustrate the cruel dilemma of writing: "Suspended between forms either disused or as yet unknown, the writer's language is not so much a fund to be drawn on as an extreme limit; it is the geometrical *locus* of all that he could not say without, like Orpheus looking back, losing the stable meaning of his enterprise and his essential gesture as a social being."[5]

But the sobriety which Bekaert urges architects to adopt seems to refer less to Barthes's *Writing Degree Zero*—which he does not cite—than to recent controversial events in the architectural microcosm. He gave his "Lesson in architecture" at TU Delft in October 1980; a few weeks earlier, during a summer trip to northern Italy with Jeanne and Charles Vandenhove, Lieve and Geert Bekaert visited the Strada Novissima at the first Venice Architecture Biennale. The respective photographic archives of the critic[6] and of the architect bear witness to their interest in OMA's polemical contribution, aptly entitled "La nostra nuova sobrietà" and deliberately opposed to the prevailing "cruel Procrustean arsenal"[7] of postmodernism that was a "celebration of architecture" as well as "a progressive dismantling of its ambitions."[8] While Vandenhove photographed every single sheet of the two projects presented (Dutch Parliament Extension, 1978, and Koepel Prison, Arnhem, 1979), Bekaert focused on the strange translucent veil that closed OMA's alcove, promising an architecture that is at once silent and efficient, ambiguous and erotic, conscious of its own power.

THE RIGHT TO ARCHITECTURE

Let us try to keep a cool head, to not let words run wild, because if they smell architecture or architects, however odorless they may be, they easily become savage and can no longer be controlled. This means that talking about architecture to an audience of architects is a perilous, if not impossible, undertaking. . . . Spontaneously, I no longer embark on this adventure, although I remain convinced that it is necessary and legitimate to get annoyed.

That annoyance, at least that's what I think, does not come from a more than average degree of narrow-mindedness, unwillingness or frustration, nor from an excessive idealism or late romanticism. It is not connected with some preconceived universal architectural truth and even less with a glorification of the past in which everything was so good.

This annoyance originates in the unimaginable insignificance of the work of architects, which presents itself with enormous pretensions as unique, original, personal, innovative, social and who knows what else, and which fails to live up to this pretension in any way; it is evidence of a gross disregard for one's own means and of ignoring one's own discipline in its historical continuity.

. . .

Architecture is considered to be everything that presents itself as such. That is more or less the entire built environment. What the building has to say or not to say is central. So I am not talking about the distance that exists between what is said or written about a building and the building itself. I know that the distinction is subtle and the objection is obvious that a building does not exist outside the story that is told about it; that a building, like everything else, exists only in language and can only be recognized as such.

But even if we accept that, which I am not inclined to do immediately, it is not an objection, because then my arguments against architecture must be described as an annoying, stupid, mind-numbing and mendacious use—not even abuse—of language. In and with language nothing happens, or if you like, a great deal. In multiple, almost inexhaustible, combinations, the same well-known figures always return automatically, as it were, under new names. The signs that are presented as new are perfectly interchangeable, a unique confirmation of Baudrillard's analysis of symbolic exchange and death.

. . .

The starting point is therefore the triviality, the general and internal triviality of the current architcotural concept. Triviality should not be confused with unimportance. Even something trivial can be very important.

By internal we mean that no external criteria are applied to the concept, but that the criteria that the concept itself provides are accepted as a standard of assessment in the first instance and to the extent possible. In other words: We play along with the role of the architect.

By general we mean that we see no reason to make a distinction in the architectural production of the moment. . . . A text entirely in capitals or entirely in lowercase remains the same text, even if it disrupts our reading habits in both presentations. What is at stake here is the text. With this I do not want to make a statement, as I said, about whether or not architecture is text, or whether or not we can analyze architecture as a language. For the time being I regard these as academic questions of contention and start from a much simpler, everyday experience, that a building, every building, presents itself, explicitly or implicitly, as a rationally considered intervention in the course of events. The rationale, that is, the concept, must be revealed, as far as possible. A building is made at a specific moment and therefore not by chance, no matter how accidental it may seem. Apart from the intentions of the maker, it cannot escape meaning... The meaning of a building, I want to make it explicit, applies not only to the architecture of the architect, but also to the most anonymous "vernacular," even to the purest repetition of pre-given models; it applies to what is called expressive and what is called banal architecture, to what is calculated for effect or happens intuitively, to what wants to be a conscious contribution to history or to what does not give a damn about history, to what wants to be socially responsible or what wipes the floor with society.

Whether a building aims to be a formal expression or a personal one, it doesn't matter much at this point, compared to this one still undefined and probably never completely explicable fact: that it concerns a trace of intelligence, presupposes an activity of thinking, whether thinking is done with the hands or with the mind. And whether that intelligence aims to communicate or not—it probably doesn't aim to do so in the first place—it presupposes in any case the principle of communicability. In other words, it does not have to be understood in order to be understandable, it does not have to have a message in order to be comprehended.

...

What does architecture have to tell us, and first of all what does architecture tell us about itself? How does it present itself? What role does it assign itself? Architecture is apparently embarrassed about itself... It can no longer give itself a clear reason for existence. It grasps at random for reasons to legitimize itself. It does not want to appear as a useless, superfluous luxury. . . . But architecture—and this is not a negligible fact—is slow to learn and still does not seem to be ready for plans of suicide, although the necessary techniques and methods were and are being developed with exaggerated zeal. There are even specialized institutes. In its insignificance, architecture continues to exist. But the reason for all of this is apparently not at all clear to architecture.

Where, for example, are those buildings that are openly called architecture; in which architecture demonstrates its own legitimacy, its self-sufficiency, its autonomy, independent of function or program, without a guilty conscience about its elitist character, aware that architecture finds its responsibility, when it asks for responsibility, in itself, in its form, a form that builds its own logic with its own resources, a form that is real, even without people in or around it, a form that is useless, that is dangerous, and irreducible to anything else?
Are there formalist buildings in that noble and full sense of the word?

However, we neither witness the opposite: hopeless, nonconformist, provocative, hallucinatory, extravagant architecture, buildings that resist the code to which they are subject, taking the liberty of doing everything exactly different from what has been done for centuries, with or without humor, making architecture creak so intensely that it emerges even more strikingly when injured. There are also no attempts at anarchist architecture, pastiche architecture, at metaphorical or figurative architecture, that make façades like a face, cafes like a beer barrel, eateries like a hot dog or a Greek temple.

...

For this kind of extreme excess, let us assume, there is indeed no place here. In architecture, things should be viewed somewhat soberly. But then my question is, where is that sober architecture? Architecture that has no need for embellishment, but clearly, lucidly, and precisely puts together a program, making use of the most suitable techniques, without prejudice, without ulterior motives of beauty, belonging together, fitting in with the environment and other of those aesthetic clichés; like how a farmer used to build, but hasn't done for a long time, since he too has been placed under the realm of architecture.

...

But why think in opposites? Why play formal architecture off against functional architecture? Can't architecture be everything at once? A harmonious dosage of these opposites that don't have to be opposites, a universal reconciliation or a transcendence? That would of course be wonderful if it were true, or if it were possible. But it isn't. It's not even conceivable! Such universal buildings, which every designer dreams of at some point—or perhaps always—are simply unthinkable; they undermine their own hypothesis.

...

If architecture is apparently no longer concerned with itself, if it no longer possesses or wants to possess any singularity as a discipline, then what is it concerned with? We can, it seems to me, sum it up in one word: the social. Since the mid-eighteenth century, architecture has been searching for its role as a social activity, it has been focused on building a civil, well-ordered, problem-free society, in which everyone has their place and above all in which everyone is satisfied with that place once and for all, the city as an architectural earthly paradise, the materialization of the ideal Platonic state, from which, according to Plato's own prescription, all possible troublemakers—to be clear: the poets and the artists, the useless, the idlers, all who cannot cope with that ideality or with any ideality—are banished in advance, whereby in other words the social is emptied of all possible content, except that of a satisfied, happy, and vegetative submission. And the emptying of the social is accompanied by the emptying of architecture. The hole of the social is filled with architecture, that is to say, with nothing. One empty sign charges itself on the other, and both, together, can stand for any arbitrary content without any problem.

An example! One of the most recent signs under which the social of architecture appears is the city—no longer the utopian, the dreamed city, but the real, historical city, or rather the idea of the real historical city. . . . The city is everything and more; it is in any case the frame of reference for architecture and the raison d'être of the architect who must save the city and thereby also saves themself. In the city the social becomes concrete. Here the architect finds the subservient, integrated role that they were looking for. The architect only has to put on paper, so to speak, what the city prescribes to them, repair the torn fabric as invisibly as possible. The city has replaced the garden district, the primitive village, the kasbah.

But what a city! The city of the social, the cozy, idyllic, old-fashioned picture. Not the city as political reality, not the city of Machiavelli, not the city of the romantics, not the city of Flaubert, Zola or Baudelaire, not the city of Joyce or Döblin, but also not the city of Haussmann, not the city of the social revolution, not that of mass culture, not the dynamic city of the futurists, not that of psychoanalysis, not the metropolis, the city of Rem Koolhaas, not the invisible, the imaginary city, and so on, nothing, truly nothing of what was ever connected with the concept of the city is found in the social city of the architect. The city at most stands for the neighborhood (and then, which neighborhood?) and that is where it ends: the pedestrian and the residential area, the paradise of narrowness and boredom.

. . .

With these few examples of meaningless, blunt and perfectly interchangeable terms . . . we have already said something about the attitude towards history. After its rejection by modernism—where it served merely as a reference against which to be benchmarked—it is now being triumphantly welcomed back and its arsenal of images is drawn upon with childlike amazement. . . . There is hardly any time left to build architecture. And the worst thing is that if a new trend is not immediately recognized and given a name, it no longer exists, because it is completely focused on the immediacy of consumption, the immediacy of the packaging industry. Loos spoke disparagingly of the architect as a fashion designer, as a draftsman, a bad draftsman at that.

. . .

I am not going to give a history of the dissatisfaction with architecture here—although it is an attractive subject—but it is good to also place our architectural annoyance in historical perspective. I will address the French theoretical tradition, not only because it is the best known, but also because it has had by far the most influence, also in the Netherlands. Already in the juicy writings of Philibert De L'Orme, a friend of Rabelais from the middle of the sixteenth century, when there was hardly any talk of architecture, criticism of the architect resounds in every chapter of his book, the bad architect, that is. . . . In the middle of the eighteenth century—I am taking long strides—Marc-Antoine Laugier no longer has that delightful obviousness of the craftsman, which he is not, and he is well aware of it. He wants to regain that certainty and discovers it in the vision of the primitive hut that becomes for him the frame of reference of the architectural concept. . . . Much has happened in the two centuries that separate Laugier from De L'Orme. Laugier no longer sets the good architect against the bad. He anticipates Loos by subjecting architecture as a discipline to a general critique and he calls on architects to reflect on their profession and to ground it in the same way as the other arts, so that it, like theatre, can be judged and enjoyed by every intelligent citizen with taste. The two go together.

...

The concept of architecture undergoes a clear shift here. It is emptied, completely demystified and transparent, scientificated, but at the same time, in one and the same movement, subordinated to a higher reason, that of the social. Architecture becomes a manipulable policy instrument and as such loses its autonomy. It is given a task and placed at the service of others. Lessons in architecture are lessons in civic virtue, that is to say: they must give the civic ideal its cultural legitimacy by beautifying the city, no longer the ideal city, but the real everyday city. And this beautification can only be based on a good organization that removes all disruptive elements from the hygienic city: illness, death, poverty, crime, even labor no longer have any right to exist in the purified city, nor does history. Architecture cannot eliminate all these ills, but it can make them invisible, among other things by banishing them from the city.

...

I began our brief historical excursion with Loos. It was he who, with rare lucidity, denounced the universalist and moralistic social idealism of modern architecture from the very beginning, with Henry van de Velde, in fierce terms and irrefutable arguments. He elevated the antagonism between the social and art, which architecture sought to ignore, to the level of dogma.

...

This modernism with its universal aspirations became the focus of the architectural discussion in the 1950s, also expressed in the Netherlands, a country that appears to have to rely on clearly defined movements and ideas and wants to know at any given moment where it stands exactly in the evolution of international trends. Dutch building has indeed been one of the most convincing expressions of modernism, from Rietveld's Schröder House to Oud's Kiefhoek.

At one point this modernism and all its consequences are rejected in a way as equally radical as the way in which it was espoused. The last CIAM congress didn't take place in Otterlo by coincidence. One would start over, for the umpteenth time. But rejecting modernism is like refusing to acknowledge that the French Revolution took place. And what often happens with such abrupt reversals: the best of modernism is thrown away and the weakest aspects are adopted. Where modernism had sought an objective basis for making architecture, as a condition for a social life liberated from architecture and the environment, the reaction starts to subjectivize architecture again and simply links it to its experiential value in a blunt, deterministic way. The residue of subjectivism, the weak point of modernism, is brought out and exalted. The objective nature of architecture as a guarantee for the subjectivity of the user is replaced by the subjectivity of the designer. The medium of architecture is, as it were, bypassed, so that the designer can identify directly with the user and give their "social" dimension some content.

Is it the tragedy or comedy of modern architecture to be able to appear only in fleeting metamorphoses? Is it condemned to constantly speak without saying anything? ... Is it more, to use Laugier's term, than a mechanical art? Does it have what I would like to call an independent poetic function, which sets it apart from all considerations of utility and grants it an irreducible autonomy?

...

The simplest conclusion is of course to answer no immediately, and to deny any autonomous poetic or imaginary power to today's architecture, as Baudrillard does, for example. ... Architecture is then condemned, as in Laugier's system, to reproduce the system itself. It has no power over the system itself. ... On this point, Tafuri shares Baudrillard's opinion. According to him, the only way to practice architecture is that of the formalists and rationalists who cultivate architecture as an autonomous, visual discipline, but their work cannot be assigned any social significance. The poetic function has come to an end with the death of the avant-garde.

A way out of this impasse is not easy to substantiate. After all, Baudrillard and Tafuri appear to be right. Baudrillard does acknowledge an attack on the system, but not from within, not from institutions embedded into the system. . . . Like Tafuri, he introduces here a historical determinism that he himself does not accept. The mass media are powerless to change their status.

I am inclined, partly on the basis of arguments by Tafuri and Baudrillard, to turn that proposition around and to assume (with Derrida and Enzensberger) that if anything is to change in the system, it will have to happen from within. That architecture will have to be fought with architecture. One can declare architecture dead and occupy oneself with other things, but that will not prevent architecture from living on and from becoming ever more strongly what we have already described, being increasingly left to quacks and taking on more and more oppressive forms every day, because architecture is not innocent. If there is a way out, if the pretension of architecture is legitimate, we must start from Tafuri's dilemma and turn to those who consciously commit to architecture as an autonomous discipline, not to ask them what "architecture" is to them, because that question is explicitly irrelevant, but to see what they do when they engage with architecture.

. . . When formalists are occupied with architecture, they are occupied with nothing else, not with the social, the functional, the semiotic, the moral, which does not necessarily mean that they are not social, functional, charged with meaning or moral. It is the essence of their activity that it contains no reference other than that to itself and it is this activity, this fight with a reality that constitutes itself only in this fight, that matters. The building, as a provisional and ever-renewable result of this activity, is its own responsibility, possesses its own internal logic. It solves no problem, except the one it sets itself. Completely useless, completely superfluous, it possesses no message outside its own existence. It is what it is, outside of any form of communication. *La rose, c'est la rose, c'est la rose*. But the building is what it is, not like a flower but as a rational construction in a concrete historical context. And it is here that the formalists in general drop out.

They reclaim the right to architecture . . . but they content themselves with a theoretical right within the space of the system, the space that Baudrillard and Tafuri have described. They restore the poetic status of architecture as a historical fact and also, and rightly, place therein its only social relevance, but the historical material is so restricted in advance that it quickly becomes impoverished. They do not ask humans or society whether they need architecture or what they want to do with it, but assert, with great certainty, but without any external persuasiveness, that humans are potentially architectural beings, inhabiting the earth poetically, and that the history of architecture can only be understood as a poetic event. However, they remain stuck in a bourgeois conception of that poetry... One then quickly thinks of something exceptional, a separate world, an artificial paradise, a utopia, something, as Loos thought, that had nothing to do with the everyday world and the everyday man; something that one can think of when all the other work has been done. Poetry, like death, is inevitable, but one should not think about it. No matter how often our bourgeois culture has tried to push poetry out of the everyday, it has never completely succeeded. Despite all scientific efforts to grasp reality, it is poetry and not science, insofar as we can set them against each other, that is a true factor of reality. It is in poetry that we live. It is poetry that, in whatever form, creates the mental images from and through which our reality arises. Poetry does not project another world. It makes our everyday, historical reality.

That this possibility is given to poets or writers might still be accepted. The poet needs at most paper and pen to write. And not even that. What he needs is language, and that is at everyone's disposal. But an architect? He literally drowns in a materiality over which he has no control, from guidelines and regulations to the rules of construction production, from program offices to aesthetic review committees, from clients to residents, from consultation committees to drafting firms, not to mention the financing or the endless analyses about the marginality of the professional situation as a wage earner. I do not want to detract from that. But all that is his language, his historical material, the only thing with which a poem, the building, must be made. And that this is no illusion is proven daily, even if it is per absurdum, by the viscous poetry, the doggerel, the flattery in the occasional verses of a socially integrated architecture.

There is no choice. No architecture can be made outside that concrete reality, and that architecture is by definition a poetic sign, just as airport novels are poetic signs. . . . The battle of poetry, of architecture, must be fought on two fronts, if one so wishes. First and foremost, against the disregard of architecture by architecture itself, against its self-denial, which is nothing but a betrayal. But that "deconstruction" of the institutionalized architectural concept can only be conducted in a positive, constructive, assertive way, by continually introducing new formal concepts, which are not as easily reducible as the current concepts of today, even though the threat of integration remains ever present, as, to give just one example, is evident from the results of the competition for the Tweede Kamer. You can see how concrete and topical what I am saying here is.

These offensive concepts are not ready-made, readily graspable syntheses, not universal visions of humanity or society, nor repressed ideals or frustrated utopias. A truly poetic concept breaks them down, punctures them. It cannot do much with general ideas, because it is precisely so extremely concrete, so directly involved with its material and its materiality.

. . .

The result is always unexpected, even for the creator. It cannot be predicted. Creators have no control over their product and they are therefore unreliable. This does not mean that they are irresponsible. On the contrary, they are the ones who fully assume responsibility for the product (and society), because they focus only on the work and nothing else, refusing to be confined in certain expectations in advance. Each time, the creator must begin the work anew, from scratch. If architecture has a reason for being, it is to continually renew its "truth" in concrete works.

Why should architecture no longer be capable of this? Does a poet have an easier time with language? Whoever concludes that the poetic function of architecture is impossible does not do so because they are realists, but precisely because they are not realistic enough, because they seek to escape reality too easily, too evasively, because they prefer to hide behind universal ideals rather than plunge into the only reality, that of the unknown. He is not concerned with spectacular results, on the contrary, nor with brilliant exceptions, original discoveries, talent or skill, or what other excuses I know of, it is not about what architecture is or could be, about artificial paradises, about the improvement of the human race. . . , but about tearing open the veil . . . of meanings behind which it is hidden in what is called architecture, mercilessly ripping open the discourse in which it is concealed and shamelessly admitting its (sublime) uselessness, and in this way not giving up but realizing the pretensions for which we have called it out, if only to save appearances and keep the game going in a more intelligent way than is currently the case.

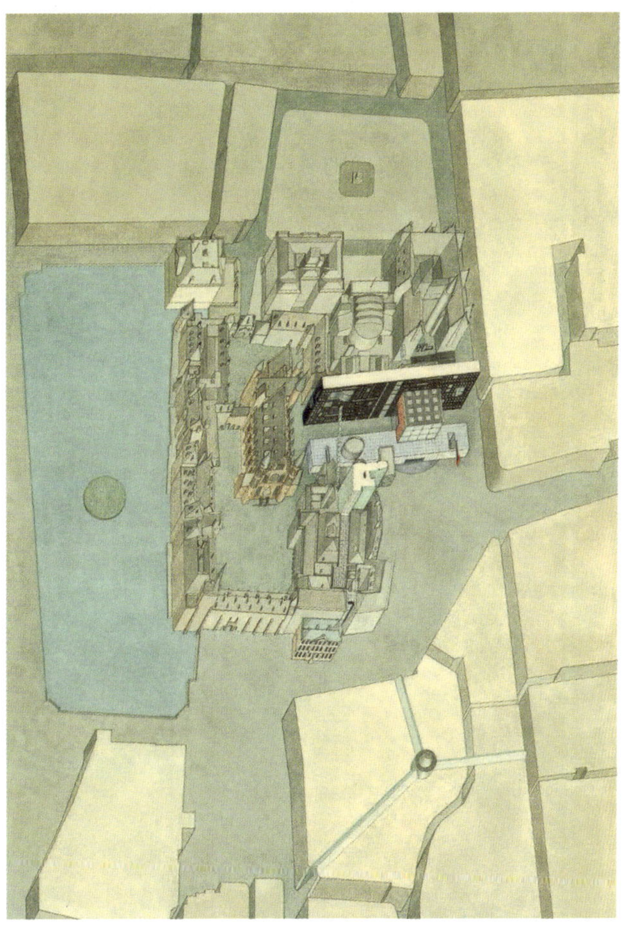

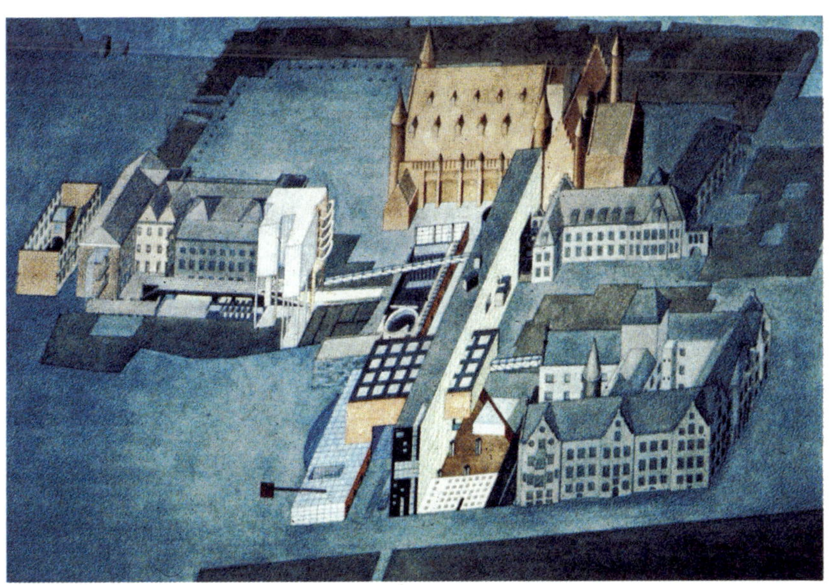

Fig. 2 Axonometric drawing by Zoe Zenghelis of the Tweede Kamer, or the Dutch Parliament Extension, by OMA/Rem Koolhaas, 1978.
Fig. 3 Watercolor painting by Madelon of the Tweede Kamer, or the Dutch Parliament Extension, by OMA/Rem Koolhaas, 1978.

1 For an overview of his writings, see Christophe Van Gerrewey, "The Right to Architecture: Geert Bekaert (1928–2016), a Critic from Belgium," *Journal of Architecture*, no. 4 (2020): 444–471.

2 Geert Bekaert, "Het recht op architectuur," in *Lessen in Architectuur* 2, October 8–9, 1980, ed. Joost Meuwissen (Delft: THDelft, 1980), 33–52. Republished in *wonen-TA/BK*, no. 4 (1981): 9–17 and in the third volume of Bekaert's collected writings: Geert Bekaert, *Hierlangs*, 1971–1980 (Ghent: WZW, 2007), 396–414. This translation is based on the final, WZW version from 2007. For reasons of brevity or clarity, in the case of very specific references, some passages have been elided.

3 *Dat is architectuur: Sleutelteksten uit de twintigste eeuw*, ed. Hilde Heynen, André Loeckx, Lieven De Cauter, and Karina Van Herck (Rotterdam: 010Publishers, 2001), 541–545. An anthology of English translations of Bekaert's writing was published in 2011, but without "Het recht op architectuur": Geert Bekaert, *Rooted in the Real: Writings on Architecture* (Ghent: WZW, 2011).

4 See also Christophe Van Gerrewey, "Hope Has Returned: The Glorious Reception of OMA/Rem Koolhaas in the Dutch-Speaking World," *Architectural Theory Review*, no. 3 (2013): 356–371.

5 Roland Barthes, *Writing Zero Degree* (New York: Hill & Wang, 1968 [1953]), 10.

6 I warmly thank Christophe Van Gerrewey for having shared Bekaert's pictures of this visit.

7 Rem Koolhaas and Elia Zenghelis, "La nostra nuova sobrietà", in *La Prensenza del Passato* (Venice: La Biennale di Venezia, 1980), 214.

8 Rem Koolhaas, "Less is More", in *S, M, L, XL* (New York: The Monacelli Press, 1995), 47.

Degree Zero Revisited. A Look Back on Swiss Architecture at the Turn of the Twenty-first Century

Irina Davidovici

comments by
Thomas Daniell

PROLOGUE 2024

Some 20 years have passed since I first explored the notion of degree zero in relation to the Swiss architecture of the late 1980s and 1990s, in the essay reproduced below.[1] At the time, by "Swiss architecture" I meant a cultural construct, whose international circulation, albeit undisputed, could only be qualified through numerous provisos. The notion referred specifically to the German-speaking parts of Switzerland, and was further fragmented by the necessity to acknowledge distinctions between architecture in the Graubünden, in Basel, Zurich, and so forth. The tenuous consensus of what was meant by "Swiss architecture" in the early 2000s was nevertheless justified by the international currency of the label—however indiscriminate its application. From the outside, "Swiss architecture" denoted above all the buildings of end-of-the-century Swiss masters—Herzog & de Meuron, Burkhalter Sumi, Peter Zumthor, Diener & Diener, Gigon/Guyer, Meili Peter, and Peter Märkli are among the best known—whose tendencies towards volumetric simplicity, raw materiality, and a certain monumental stillness has justified their association with the degree zero of architectural expression.

The essay reproduced below was written in 2007–08 and first published in 2012.[2] Its original aim was to contextualize an already established connection between this situated understanding of Swiss architecture and the theoretical "degree zero". The impulse to investigate it further ultimately focused on clarifying possible connections between Swiss architecture and art-historical minimalism. To that end, the argument focused on the direct interaction between viewer or observer and self-referential artwork or building. The Swiss architecture of the late 1980s and 1990s had previously, on account of its volumetric simplicity and elaborate surfaces, generated mainly object-based analyses, focused on the craft of construction and conceptual rigor. With this essay, I sought to explore the cultural associations and meanings attached to "the reduced form"—a claim that would seem only to confirm the pervasiveness of formal analysis. In hindsight, I would reiterate that the interest in the formal reductivity was itself motivated by a belief in its place-specific, cultural significance.

TD Like many national architectural styles—Japanese, Spanish, Dutch, and so forth—a precise definition of contemporary Swiss architecture may be difficult, but we know it when we see it.

The irony of minimalism in architecture is the maximization of work on the part of the architect and builder. Eliminating minor elements (skirtings, dadoes, cornices, flashings, eaves, power outlets, light switches) for esthetic reasons often requires just as much effort and expense as concealing them with elaborate ornamentation. The Swiss climate obviously demands gabled roofs and projecting eaves, not the pure volumes of minimalist architecture. In inverse proportion to their visual simplicity, immaculately smooth surfaces and invisible connections entail far more work and risk than conventional methods, both in initial creation and later maintenance. One must do more to "say" less.

Of course, the intention is not less effort in conception and construction, but rather to confront people with the raw, physical presence of the building, or more precisely, the building materials, notably monolithic concrete. These abstract, subdued volumes may occasional use patterned and tessellated envelopes, but only to reinforce the absence of conventional architectural elements.

The paradox of such formal reduction and gestural inhibition, supposedly predicated on a return to direct, bracketed phenomenological experience—to "reality"—is that the results so often seem surreal, otherworldly: heavy monoliths become shimmering phantoms in their painstaking denial of convention.

Indeed, one could identify two types of minimalism: the former a sleek, neutral precision achieved with great care and at great expense, exemplified by the Swiss tradition of subdued rationality and refinement; the latter a cheap, ad hoc improvisation that arises from exigency rather than choice, exemplified by the slums of the developing world. Both exemplify a degree zero of architecture, but a degree zero attained from diametrically opposed directions.

Revisiting this argument from today's perspective offers a different basis for discussing the degree zero of architecture. In the early 1990s, the prominent Swiss architecture critic Martin Steinmann had already identified and theorized Swiss architecture's "search for a degree zero, at which architecture would attain a new presence".[3] Fifteen years later, I was taking his emphasis on "presence" for granted, although, today, I am more intrigued about the "new". This is partly because, a couple of architectural generations later, the notion of "Swiss architecture" as circulated in the early 2000s has lost many of its initial connotations. It no longer denotes a small core of widely recognized architects-auteurs, most of them born around 1950. Nor is it possible to connect the more recent work produced in German-speaking Switzerland to the tenets of formal reduction, withdrawal from gesture, and emphasis on material presence. The primacy of concepts in driving formal decisions has lost much of its appeal, not least because the adherence to autonomous concepts seems to distance the built architecture from its social responsibilities. Even the deeper cultural index that justified the architecture's qualification as "Swiss" has lost some of its immediacy. Under the understandable pressures of sustainability and climate change, the basic motivation for new buildings in themselves is increasingly critically scrutinized. The suspicion towards form-determining concepts has been overtaken by a wider suspicion—not merely towards form-making, but towards the very act of construction. Out with the new (construction), in with the (refurbished) old.

The new professional agendas notwithstanding, the younger generations have often embraced other historical references than their teachers and mentors. The current architecture of the internationally significant figures of the 1980s and 1990s—Herzog & de Meuron, Peter Zumthor, Diener & Diener and others—is no longer clearly distinguished from the stream of new buildings covered in architecture publications, and many students no longer follow their next project with bated breath. Young architects now tend to gravitate towards the ecological urban activism of a yet older generation of architects, active since the 1950s, who were themselves marginalized in the 1980s and 1990s discourse. At the same time, the postmodernism that had been rejected as alien to Swiss culture has meanwhile been rediscovered as a valued precedent and a welcome outlet for a previously missing "irony". The moderate Swiss high-tech, earlier snubbed as architects sought more "authentic" forms of expression (pure geometries, natural materials), is today finding a new audience, attracted by the futility of its technological utopian visions as much as the conservation challenges it poses.

In this new situation, Barthes's theoretical provisions regarding the possibility of a degree zero have not only been long confirmed, but, also, overtaken by events. Over the last three decades, Swiss architecture has undergone profound transformations. By the early 2000s, the focus on the minimal form had already led to the rut earlier predicated by Barthes's theorization. Namely, the abstract interpretations of reality attempted by the architects newly active in the 1980s and 1990s had, ten years later, entrenched themselves in the mainstream. Swiss architecture followed the predictions that Barthes had made with regards to literature: the new simplicity of the 1990s had already by the late 2000s become a formal cliché. The design methods tentatively sketched out in the 1980s and crystallized in the early 1990s became the main tools received by students during their architecture training—a default mode from which they now, naturally enough, seek to break away.

Twenty years ago, I posited the degree zero of Swiss architecture in terms of a search for authenticity. By the third decade of this century, however, we find the very concept of authenticity as a strangely anachronistic, possibly suspicious construct, hardly relevant in practice. Younger architects are faced with a more elemental questioning of the very basis of their profession: the capacity to build. This redefined degree zero questions the modus operandi of late Western neoliberalism, and seeks—idealistically, paradoxically, frenziedly—a different set of societal values. The discussion has veered sharply away from aesthetics and towards the political aspects of architecture. Today, the degree zero is no longer about the ordinary, the object-type, the performatively simple volume that Steinmann had so powerfully theorized as the *forme forte*.[4] It has taken another meaning, more blunt and more immediate: a zero-sum game, aimed at a form of survival.

DEGREE ZERO

The formal strength and material focus of Swiss projects invite, primarily, an object-based analysis. A first glance registers simple volumes wrapped in active surfaces—prisms whose skin is textured, patterned, three-dimensional, expressing tectonic or ornamental urges. Rather than explain this treatment of forms and materials as a topic in itself, this essay is about the second glance. It hopes to introduce some of the meanings and messages implied, rather than expressed, in the accomplished artefacts. Its theme is the reduced form.

The manifest preference for stark primary volumes suggests an avoidance of obvious formal gestures, although many architects clearly delight in incident to imprint specificity on the general *parti pris*. Almost anything could provide a basis for meaningful irregularities: not only the as-found pattern of natural materials and their weathering but also the geometric peculiarities imposed by site constraints, regulations, or structural efficiency. Whatever the cause, any formal transgressions are carefully justified within the overall conceptual discipline, even where concepts are mostly a cover for authorial licence. Thus it is not gestures that were avoided at all costs but gestures that were deemed arbitrary, intellectually unaccounted for.

In the absence of justifications for visual incident, the default mode of this architecture remains formal neutrality: the pure prism, the blank canvas, the degree zero of formal determinism. This explains why, in the early years of international exposure, this production was widely associated with a minimalist sensibility. Swiss critic Martin Steinmann, the foremost scholar of this production, presented this connection in experiential, phenomenological terms. As in minimal art, the focus of this architecture was on the object and the experience it engendered in the viewer. This connection to minimalism was rooted in the aesthetic domain. At the same time, however, Steinmann associated the Swiss works with the pop subversion of market imagery, and the appropriation of everyday consumerist motifs in design.[5] He thus established a clear dialectic at work, between an almost solemn retreat into the form and materiality of the object on one side and the opening towards everyday images on the other. Each of these tendencies establishes its own distinct truth: the reassurance of concrete substance, respectively the domain of the familiar and the ubiquitous; as it were, reality itself.

This dialectic suggests that the withdrawal from gesture witnessed in Swiss architecture had wider implications. Understandably, practitioners were cautious about associations between their work and minimalism, acknowledging the tendency toward formal reduction, though never merely as the result of aesthetic choice. Rather, their preference for recessive formalism was explained as a cultural predisposition, an attitude with respect to the world, in which some identified an ethical ambition.

Martin Steinmann described this production as the "search for a *degré zéro*, at which architecture would attain a new presence".[6] There is an obvious relation between the "degree zero" metaphor and this reductive sense of form, poised between abstraction and familiarity. Steinmann was not alone in finding a literary qualification for this tendency. The degree zero formulation has been, occasionally, used interchangeably with "empty sign", as in Peter Zumthor's ambition for buildings that "reach beyond signs and symbols", that are "open, empty".[7] These enticements worked on the strength of association, as if the implied meaning was to be grasped through allusion rather than definition.

The structuralist roots of the "degree zero" formulation indicate its literary origins. Roland Barthes coined the term in 1953 to denote "a sort of basic speech, equally far from living languages and from literary language proper".[8] This primary, reticent mode of expression was to anchor the text in absolute and permanent values, as the "social or mythical characters of a language are abolished in favor of a neutral and inert state of form".[9] A minimum of incident would provide a clearing in the ever-growing profusion of ideas, materials, and objects put forth by the market economy, which Walter Benjamin famously described as a perpetual addition of cultural debris.

The direct communication established through degree zero writing avoided the vagaries of subjective aesthetics. Through it the literary work would uncover an elusive essence, and be able to claim ethical status:

> If the writing is really neutral, and if language . . . reaches the state of a pure equation, which is no more tangible than an algebra when it confronts the innermost part of man, then Literature is vanquished, the problematics of mankind is uncovered and presented without elaboration, the writer becomes irretrievably honest.[10]

The degree zero of art is therefore an art that seeks authenticity. Transposed to architecture, this pertains to the capacity to express through reduced means a fundamental dimension of human existence. Nevertheless, Barthes was aware that this potential is limited by the constant re-presentation of fundamental issues in history. In particular, the bourgeois consumption culture renders the degree zero only momentarily effective, without duration. The artwork's fate in the market culture suggests this gesture of freedom will inevitably return to the *status quo* which it first resisted:

> Mechanical habits are developed in the very place where freedom existed, a network of set forms hem in more and more the pristine freshness of discourse. . . . The writer, taking his place as a 'classic', becomes the slavish imitator of his original creation, society demotes his writing to a mere manner, and returns him a prisoner to his own formal myths.[11]

Thus the pursuit of the degree zero is utopian. The authenticity that it purports is unattainable; the wider conditions for communication are undermined by the established social order.

> Writing. . . is a blind alley, and it is because society itself is a blind alley. . . . The search for a non-style or an oral style, for a zero level or a spoken level of writing is, all things considered, the anticipation of a homogeneous social state . . . there can be no universal language outside a concrete, and no longer a mystical or merely nominal, universality of society.[12]

In other writings, Barthes's parallel between writing and society expanded to commentaries regarding culture as a whole. The *Mythologies* essays (1957) presented culture as a self-renewing package of artistic emancipatory attempts and commercial constructs, offered as self-evident and natural values. This makes more explicit the debt to Ferdinand de Saussure's structuralist linguistics, indicating a belief in culture's readability as a system of signs.[13] Structuralist thinking performs, at a wider level, the oscillation between form and meaning manifested in architecture in the ambivalence of type, and with the same limitations.

The structuralist notion of language as a structure for the transmission of messages does not grasp its role in enabling understanding and communication. Similarly, the existing belief in the deep structures of culture is inhibited by the idea that culture can be understood scientifically, according to epistemological criteria of certainty. The question raised by Barthes's degree zero is therefore whether one can find a human language that is not embedded in its culture, or, in an architectural equivalent, an architecture conceived in abstraction from its circumstances.

The degree zero of architecture, understood as a distilled medium of primary forms devoid of compositional manipulations, is likewise a purely conceptual proposition. Seeking authenticity as an end in itself is a corollary of instrumental thinking; it places architecture on a conceptual level, where the unselfconsciousness of "authentic" objects is itself unavailable.

At face value, the constant and inevitable assimilation of autonomous avant-gardes into the bourgeois cultural value system also applies to the reductive trend of late twentieth-century Swiss architecture. Indeed, the cohesion within this particular phenomenon can only be identified during a brief period from around 1985 to 1995. Thereafter, as the celebrated Swiss *auteurs* turned in different directions in search of personalized modes of expression, the possibility of a common degree zero became ever more elusive.

The implementation of the degree zero thematic places the Swiss works philosophically under the province of structuralism.[14] Indeed, the debt to structuralist thinking could be traced back to the popularity of Barthes among ETH students during the 1970s, and to the semiology courses that Steinmann ran with Bruno Reichlin at gta at that time. This teaching was itself informed by Rossi's (and, indirectly, Manfredo Tafuri's) attempts to apply Saussurian structural linguistics to architecture. While Barthes's literary model has proven uncannily stimulating for Swiss architectural production, it has determined for it the same limitations. Structuralism itself saw the commercial manifestations of market culture as hidden dimensions of culture, declaring economical mechanisms as eternal arbiters of human existence. Architecture's outward dependence on these mechanisms makes its position more difficult.

BETWEEN CULTURE AS OBJECT AND CULTURE AS SIGN

The closer descendent of Barthes's degree zero in the visual domain is 1960s minimal art. In its effort to engage with reality, minimalism was a compelling, if paradoxical, proposition. Its products embodied a philosophical resistance to the crisis of modernism, as manifested through abstract expressionism. Minimal art proposed to counteract this crisis through the production of objects freed from any reference except to themselves.

To avoid any compositional or anthropomorphic associations, the artists shunned conventional artistic means (figuration, the canvas as window), mediatory devices (pedestals, frames, narrative titles) and materials (bronze, marble, watercolor). Minimal art's materials were taken from contexts other than the gallery. Often "aggressively" industrial, they were formed into inert, solitary objects, manifesting a bid to approach what Clement Greenberg had deemed "non-art".[15] These objects stated their difference from the realm of representational aesthetics through their directness, declaring themselves as *objects* precisely in opposition to artworks.

Early on, Greenberg had remarked that minimalism's claim to objecthood was fatally undermined by its reliance on a conceptual framework.[16] Nevertheless, his analysis was itself restricted to objects and their theoretical armature. The focus on corporeal interactions between viewer and object, as stated by Michael Fried in an apparent attack on Greenberg's critique, continued to overlook the deeper context for phenomena, suggesting that deeper meanings are located solely in this relationship.[17] These poles of minimalist critique are indeed closer then they may seem. The debates converge in the assumption that meaning can reside in the art object and the gallery.

Marshall Berman has identified two contradictory modernist attitudes in 1960s culture: the "withdrawn" and the "affirmative".[18] Barthes and Greenberg illustrate the former strand, whereby as a form of societal commentary art turns inwards, to its own terms of expression. As Greenberg wrote, "each art had to determine, through the operations peculiar to itself, the effects peculiar and exclusive to itself. By doing this [it] would narrow its area of competence, but [...] make its possession of this area all the more secure".[19] One notes here a parallel with Cartesian epistemology—perhaps useful for certain conclusions in the sciences but ill-suited to the domains of art and architecture. This positivism sought to determine the content of each discipline as an autonomous medium. Barthes returned literature to language, Greenberg restored painting to the flat canvas, just as Aldo Rossi refocused architecture on type.

The notion of architectural autonomy can be interpreted as a characteristic of "withdrawn" modernism, seeking the return to the essentials of the medium (form, type, material) as a common basis for intelligibility. Nevertheless, this retracing of boundaries has only served to undermine the fragile continuity of a fragmenting culture, replacing potential richness with a field of thoughtful yet solitary gestures:

> An art without personal feelings and social relationships is bound to

> seem arid and lifeless after a little while. The freedom it confers is the freedom of a beautifully formed, perfectly sealed tomb. [20]

In contrast, "affirmative" modernism found potential and beauty in the everyday, seeking to blur the boundaries between art and other domains of activity.[21] This set in motion the enthusiasm for a supposed 'popular culture' that can be identified both in pop art and architectural postmodernism.

One recognizes in the formal strategies of 1980s Swiss architecture a debt to both of these modernist variants, together with the attempt to filter out their shortcomings. The existing references to minimal and pop art reinforce this dependency.[22] The early works, responding to a complex context through multifaceted, heterogeneous designs, seem more concerned with the representational content of communicative "images".[23] In the later stages, from the late 1980s onwards, the production tends towards unified objects, whose materiality and tectonic expression strove to the totality implied in Gestalt theory.[24]

One recognizes in some autonomous objects of Swiss architecture the framework of form and material, and the emancipation from context, characteristic of minimalism. Donald Judd's interest in "objectivity" led to the production of three-dimensional, unitary forms with an "obdurate" material identity.[25] The focus of his art was on the object as an assembly of directly expressed characteristics. "The thing as a whole, its quality as a whole, is what is interesting. The main things are alone and are more intense, clear and powerful."[26]

Herzog & de Meuron's works circa 1990, equating architecture with what they called "the autonomous reality of a painting or a sculpture", reflect to some degree Judd's stipulations.[27] An important characteristic of the Swiss degree zero discourse was the conflation of meaning with a basic geometry. In 1988, Herzog & de Meuron stated their position as "a search for perception and meaning, a search of something hidden, something that is integral to nature... A search that must fail at the moment I believe I have found my geometry".[28] A set of forms is constantly assimilated to the currents of capitalism, thereby projecting the creator further on his or her search for self-definition.

The oft-made connection between art-historical minimalism and the species of Swiss architecture also deemed minimalist during the 1990s stands for more than a formal comparison. Indeed, Greenberg's critique of minimalism as "too much a feat of ideation, and not enough anything else" can also be seen to apply.[29] In particular, the "Swiss box" motif is symptomatic of the tension between aesthetic ambitions and the acts of everyday inhabitation, familiarity, wear and tear, and clutter.

German Swiss architects' relationship to art in general and to minimalism in particular is ambiguous: on one hand they resist the charge of literal adoption and the vexed question of architecture in relation to art, on the other they invoke it as a means to escape the burden of reality through self-imposed objectivity and conceptual coherence. Ultimately, Swiss architecture's claims of integrity stem from its orientation not towards art but towards the common Issues raised in relation to the city and Western urban society. It is this horizon of commonality that warrants access, as Meili has implied, to the constant values of human existence:

> We seek a kind of "authenticity of usage"... we are no longer interested in the optimisation of the modes of usage in buildings but in the process of sedimentation of meanings into forms, such as results through the incessant repetition of everyday use.... An architecture that could embody more general significations ... could be realized through a focus of design on the problem of form, provided that our proposals would achieve a more comprehensive understanding of "use" than their scorned modernist predecessors ... Thus our incursions in the world of the ordinary and the everyday constitute a search for collective meanings.[30]

This quest for a direct and intelligible architecture frames what Meili calls "authenticity", as the dilemma between pure form and the impositions of lived life.

This differs from the meaning Kenneth Frampton has ascribed to "authenticity" as an inherent value of the architectural object.[31]

The gravitas of empty, resonant spaces, the fascination with simple but tactile volumes has provided ample ground for essentialist readings, both inside and outside the Swiss camp. Yet Meili's proposal is more ambitious than an aesthetic of authenticity, readable directly from the surrounding culture. Equally significant is the intuition that this commonality resides not solely in form but also in a better understanding of how architecture is being used. To once again paraphrase Barthes, architecture should be seen as an unwritten pact between architect and society. The belief that form could encompass, in and by itself, cultural patterns, transposes to architecture Greenberg's attempt to redefine an art form in crisis. It reiterates the boundaries, and the fundaments, of its medium.

Fig. 1 Peter Zumthor, Kunsthaus Bregenz, Bregenz, 1990–97, model.
Fig. 2 Valerio Olgiati, School, Paspels, Graubünden, 1996–98, interior.

Fig. 3, 4 Peter Märkli, La Congiunta, Giornico, Ticino, 1989–91, interior.

Fig. 5 Herzog & de Meuron, Stone House, Tavole, project 1982, realisation 1985–88. Detail of external wall and pergola.

Fig. 6 Gigon/Guyer, Kirchner Museum, Davos, Graubünden, 1989–92.

1 These early explorations were part of my doctoral work: Irina Davidovici, "Between Typology and Typicality: German-Swiss Architecture 1980-2000" (PhD diss., University of Cambridge, 2003 to 2008).

2 This is a re-edited and expanded version of the essay "Degree Zero" published in Irina Davidovici, *Forms of Practice. German-Swiss Architecture 1980-2000* (Zurich: gta Verlag, 2018, second revised edition): 285-292.

3 Martin Steinmann, "The Presence of Things. Comments On Recent Architecture In Northern Switzerland," in *Construction Intention Detail: Five Projects from Five Swiss Architects* (Zurich, Munich, London: Artemis, 1994): 8-25, here 24.

4 The notion was originally coined in Martin Steinmann, "La forme forte- En deça des signes", *Faces. Journal d'architectures*, no. 19 (Spring 1991): 4-13.

5 Martin Steinmann, "The Presence of Things. Comments On Recent Architecture In Northern Switzerland", in *Construction Intention Detail* (Zurich: Artemis, 1994): 8-25.

6 Steinmann, "The Presence of Things," 24.

7 Peter Zumthor, "A Way of Looking at Things" (1988), in *Thinking Architecture* (Basel: Birkhäuser, 2006): 17.

8 Roland Barthes, *Writing Degree Zero* (1953), trans. Annette Lavers and Colin Smith (London: Jonathan Cape, 1984): 64.

9 Ibid.

10 Ibid., 65.

11 Ibid.

12 Ibid., 72.

13 See Graham Allen, *Roland Barthes*, ed. Robert Eaglestone (London: Routledge, 2003): 39-41; Jonathan Culler, "Structuralism," London: Routledge, http://www.rep.routledge.com/article/N055SECT2.

14 For a clear illustration of this debt see Martin Steinmann, "The Most General Form. On the Development of Diener and Diener's Work," in *Diener & Diener. Projects 1978-1990*, ed. Ulrike Jehle-Schulte Strathaus and Martin Steinmann (New York: Rizzoli, 1991): 25-31, here 25.

15 Clement Greenberg, "Recentness of Sculpture" (1967), in *Minimal Art. A Critical Anthology*, ed. Gregory Battcock (New York: E.P Dutton, 1968): 180-186.

16 Ibid., 183.

17 Michael Fried placed Minimalism under the rubric of theatricality. See Michael Fried, "Art and Objecthood" (1967), in *Minimal Art. A critical anthology*, ed. Gregory Battcock (New York: E.P. Dutton, 1968): 116-147.

18 Marshall Berman, *All That Is Solid Melts Into Air: The Experience of Modernity* (London: Verso, 1983): 29-30.

19 Clement Greenberg, "Modernist Painting" (1961), in *Art In Theory 1900-1990*, ed. Charles Harrison and Paul Wood (Oxford, Cambridge MA: Blackwell, 1992): 755.

20 Berman, *All That Is Solid Melts Into Air*, 30.

21 Ibid., 31.

22 For example see Jacques Herzog and Theodora Vischer, "Conversation, May 1988," in *Herzog & de Meuron 1978-1988*, ed. Gerhard Mack (Basel: Birkhäuser, 1997): 213-15.

23 This is the case for example with Herzog & de Meuron's Blue House (Oberwil, 1978-79) and Photographic Studio Frei (Weil-am-Rhein, 1981-82), or Diener & Diener's Hammerstrasse I (Basel, 1978-81) and Burgfelderplatz building (Basel, 1982-85).

24 Virtually all the case studies presented earlier illustrate this development, including the Stone House, which in this respect, too, was ahead of its time.

25 Donald Judd quoted in Fried, "Art and Objecthood" (1967), 143. Also see Donald Judd, "Specific Objects" (1965), in *Art In Theory 1900-1990*, ed. Charles Harrison and Paul Wood (Oxford, Cambridge MA: Blackwell, 1992): 809- 813.

26 Judd, "Specific Objects" (1965), 813.

27 Jacques Herzog & Pierre de Meuron, "The Hidden Geometry of Nature" (1988), in *Herzog & de Meuron*, ed. Wilfried Wang (Zurich, Munich, London: Artemis, 1992): 144.

28 Ibid., 142.

29 Greenberg, "Recentness of Sculpture" (1967), 183.

30 Marcel Meili, "Ein paar Bauten, viele Pläne," in *Architektur in der Deutschen Schweiz*, ed. Peter Disch (Lugano: ADV Advertising Company, 1991): 22–27, here 22. Translation by author.

31 Kenneth Frampton, "Minimal Moralia: Reflections On Recent Swiss German Production" (1996), in *Labour, Work and Architecture. Collected Essays in Architecture and Design* (London: Phaidon Press, 2002): 324–331.

Notes on Architecture, Barthes's Zero Degree, and AI Imaging

Sunil Manghani

comments by
Adil Mansure

Following an invitation to speak at the symposium "The Zero Degree of Architectural Writing",[1] and listening to what *else* was said at the event, I present here a reading of Roland Barthes's literary term "zero degree", which is pertinent to a visual practice discourse. I cannot claim to settle on an answer to a specific 'question' (e.g. regarding the degree zero vis-à-vis architecture), nor would I think that this is necessarily appropriate. Rather, I hope the reader will allow me to 'thicken the picture'; to take an idea for a walk. In weaving together various parallels between degree zero and architecture, or more broadly *spatiality*, I evoke notions of acoustics and computation. In turn, this leads to a contemporary subject matter, the (mathematical) 'space' of AI generated imagery.

Barthes is best known for his work on the nature of language, myth, and semiotics. However, he has little to say on architecture per se, though some of his writings indirectly touch upon the subject. Most obvious is Barthes's famous essay on the Eiffel Tower.[2] In a laconic remark, he suggests how the only place in Paris where the structure is not visible is when you are standing on it, looking out. As such, the Eiffel Tower serves as a kind of focal point; a signifier, embodying various myths and narratives about modernity. In *The Semiotic Challenge*, he has a short essay on semiology and urbanism, which builds upon his theory of the production of signs (referring to the city as poem), and which can be applied to architectural studies, analyzing buildings and urban spaces as systems of signs. There are also crossovers with his technical study of the 'fashion system'.[3] Architecture, much like fashion, can be said to be comprised of a specific language, through which societies express values, desires, and identities. Finally, in his late lecture courses, notably *How to Live Together*, Barthes draws attention to questions of habitat and forms of life.[4] Thus, while Barthes did not provide an explicit critique or exploration of architecture, his semiotic and cultural theories have inevitably enabled valuable means for understanding how architectural forms carry and produce meaning in society.

Yet what can *really* be said regarding his literary term "zero degree" vis-à-vis architecture? As a critical concept pertaining to the production of literature, Barthes only explicitly references the term in his first book, *Writing Degree Zero*.[5] Nonetheless, at the end of his life, in his second to last lecture course, on the Neutral, he underlines his life-long concern, equating what he called "the Neutral" to the degree zero, "insofar as its referent inside me is a stubborn affect (in fact, ever since *Writing Degree Zero*)".[6] In its simplest sense zero degree specifies "a 'neutral' aesthetic situated in response to and outside of the dominant order";[7] furthermore, as elaborated elsewhere, it is pertinent to expand from the 'work' (whether a literary, artistic, architectural or musical work, etc.) and its specific context in order to consider "the *capacity* of response as constrained by medium and site of engagement: the frames of seeing."[8] But, there is another compelling quality of the zero degree: the mathematical. "There is always the conundrum as to the whether or not zero is part of the number system, or as that which must stand outside it. . . . Zero also, of course, constitutes an intellectual shift . . . that results in the basic 0/1 binary division for computer code."[9]

For Barthes, the appeal to degree zero aims to situate someway between form and content, whereby we understand something is not 'formed' as such, but through which is revealed the possible grounds of meaning. In this sense the degree zero is not straightforwardly the site of the 'new' (it is *not* the preserve of the avant-garde), nor is it a 'thing' as much as a position—a sightline—from which it is possible to see the conditions of meaning (and on occasion to thwart them). The degree zero might best be considered the *possibility* of becoming. It suggests an ability to see all the calculations of the 'data' *before* coalescing as an entity, as a representation. As soon as the zero degree is 'uttered'—brought into an available, discursive form—it is folded back into the already existing patterns of representation.

AM Through the degree zero, Manghani compellingly invites us to think about the "possibility of becoming" in the context of the mathematical operations and spaces that yield machine-generated imagery. The following are further questions that this article productively raises, as it focuses our gaze into the endless pit of the procedures of information technology. If, in social spheres, the degree zero harkens to a shared space of meanings, symbols, and associations—which are recognizable in common words, gestures, and actions and recognizable in patterns but not reducible to them—then what might the machine equivalents be? If intelligence, natural or artificial, can be thought of as giving weight not to efficiency or reproducibility—which no doubt machines excel in—but to the ability to draw from common realms of experience, how then might we assess the permutations, combinations, and reconfigurations of information bits as they yield imagery? What composes data itself as vectors move 0s and 1s around in arithmetic space that tile into suitable right adjacencies and contiguities to congeal into representations? What also need reconsideration are perhaps the very histories of art that read visual space algorithmically or arithmetically, the inverse of which of course yields the logic of machine learning and machine-produced imagery. If we look into what these histories overshadow, what shared social cultures underneath might come to the fore? We might not be able to "utter" them but we do sense them. This perhaps is the precise affordance of the degree zero, its staying power in the "possibility of becoming," and, crucially, its agential role therein.

In architectural terms, we might relate the idea of a 'possibility of becoming' (and of seeing the conditions of meaning) to the history of avant-garde designs, which often enough are equal part iconic and imaginary (a form of in between, a *structuring*, rather than structure). Think, for example, of Etienne-Louis Boullée's Cenotaph for Newton (1784) (Fig. 1), Vladimir Tatlin's Tower (1919), Frank Lloyd Wright's Automobile Objective and Planetarium (1925), Louis Kahn's City Tower (1955), Kiyonori Kikutake's Marine City (1958), Buckminster Fuller's Manhattan Dome (1960), Kenzo Tange's 1960 Master Plan for Tokyo, Jean Nouvel's Endless Tower (1989), Israel López Balan's Church Without God (2015), and Wai Think Tank's Palace of Failed Optimism (2021). These projected structures have impacted upon architectural discourse in the very absence of their realization, and as such *continue* to persist, morph and interweave. As Susan Buck-Morss notes, "Much of avant-garde 'architecture' consisted of maquettes and drawings rather than blueprints and buildings." They are readily more 'textual' than most realized architectures. "Perhaps not the object but its critical interpretation is avant-garde," she adds.[10] The *aesthetic experience* of unrealized work hovers 'somewhere,' accessible as a possibility, yet remains intangible. As a zero degree they remain always in circulation.

Underpinning the degree zero is what Barthes later calls the "enormous Text": a 'space' or store of *potential* meanings; wherein the zero degree can be understood as a form (or *operation*) of a virtual, preparatory space[11]—here my reference to 'space' is purposefully mathematical, suggestive of the vector space techniques of generative artificial intelligence, which arguably provide *direct* access to the degree zero. Notably, the emergence of image diffusion models trace through the massive archive of images (including architectural images and language) to denoise meaning before rendering never previously seen imagery and designs.[12] At the time of writing, for example, in prompting ChatGPT to "draw an architectural design: Cenotaph For Newton," the response is an immediate reference to the "famous architectural drawing" of Boullée, yet with the offer to create "an original architectural design" inspired by the architect. The resulting design is described as featuring "a massive sphere within a circular base, crafted in a contemporary style with glass and steel, and includes lighting effects to simulate a starry sky" (Fig. 2).

Fig. 1 Etienne-Louis Boullée, Cenotaph for Newton, 1784.

Fig. 2 *After* Etienne-Louis Boullée's *Cenotaph for Newton*, image rendered by OpenAI ChatGPT by the author.

AN ACOUSTICS OF THE TEXT

In the essay "Diderot, Brecht, Eisenstein,"[13] Barthes reminds us representation is not merely a matter of imitation or mimesis. It is the line of sight, the lines of inscription and projection. It is the very instrument of thought. Wherever there is a subject (including building-as-subject) directing the gaze towards a horizon, Barthes explains, there is a projection from "the base of a triangle of which his eye (or his mind) would be the apex" (*sic*). Representation is always made up of a double logic of "the sovereignty of ... projection and the unity of the subject doing the projecting."[14] In making these remarks, Barthes focuses on the "dioptric arts" (theatre, painting, cinema and literature), but touches upon an underlying interest or lament for music, or what we might refer to as Barthes's lament for *an acoustics of the Text.*[15]

I make this reference to an acoustics as a proxy for the architectural—as a way of evoking a syntax or a mathematics of three-dimensional signifying space. Barthes actually asks us to imagine an affinity between mathematics and acoustics; an affinity that he suggests is more taxing to discern, since it has been set in opposition to and is overridden by the "link connecting geometry and theater ... that line which intersects the optic beam."[16] Barthes presents music as the "counter-proof" to the representationalism of the dioptric arts. As such, music operates as a metaphor or a key to Barthes's evocation of the Text, which in his widely referenced article "From Work to Text" he describes as a "social space," as a network space of meanings and an "archive" of possibilities of speech.[17] Music captures his interest in *langue* and *parole*, structure and event, or to remain with musical terms, harmonic structure and vibration. Meaning can only come of "speech" (movement), yet that speech must have a holding form. The zero degree is like a tuning fork: identifying structures of meaning prior to any specific, motivated articulation. The zero degree as a 'space' (an acoustics) of meaning *through* which all degrees of representation must frequent.

THEORETICAL VISION, BEYOND LANGUAGE

Barthes makes clear his indebtedness to Julia Kristeva's account of semiotics, which gave him "personally and principally the new concepts of *paragrammatism* and *intertextuality*."[18] Even in *Writing Degree Zero*,[19] originally published in French in 1953, Barthes provides an early, if less sustained account that later resonates with Kristeva's *Revolution in Poetic Language*.[20] Barthes opens with a reference to a journalist writing in *Le Père Duchesene* (a radical newspaper of the French Revolution) (Fig. 3). The journalist Jacques Hébert, he notes, would always begin his articles with a series of obscenities. "These improprieties had no real meaning," Barthes explains, "but they had significance." They embodied a revolutionary situation through "a mode of writing whose function is no longer only communication or expression, but the imposition of something beyond language, which is both History and the stand we take in it."[21]

To give a more contemporary example, we might think of how the singer Rihanna delivers the lines of her song "Work" (2016). The repetition of certain words (work, dirt, learn, tired) perform a critique of the repetitiveness of work, which is further pronounced by her slurring of the words ("When you a gon' nah nah nah nah nah nah"), bending them into something indeterminate. In terms of a 'spatial' reading, the words have a malleability or dimensionality, allowing a refiguring with "work" melding to "nah nah ...". This is no revolution of course, but it makes for an imposition, or at least resilience. Here, we can recognize something *beyond* language, a certain responsibility to *form*, which Barthes calls "writing" ("*écriture*"); a movement of both (or in-between) form and content that equates with an acoustics: we might imagine being *inside the formation* of letters in a word as they push and pull into shape; or inside a picture or mode of seeing. Hence we move beyond language per se (beyond human units of meaning) towards a zero degree

Fig. 3 Masthead from Jacques Hébert's *Le Père Duchesene* (No. VI of 15 frimaire year 2 [5 December 1793]), with the motif 'Je suis le véritable pere Duchesne, foutre!' [I'm the real father Duchesne, fuck!].

technique for rendering new, fluent, meaningful forms.

To elaborate on an 'acoustics' (or spatial mathematics), consider the later work of Victor Burgin, in which he produces CGI-based digital projections. Responding to a commission for the Istanbul Biennale, Burgin was inspired by a partially disappeared coffee house by the Bosphorus, which he could only render *virtually* for what became *A Place to Read* (2010) (Fig. 4). Crucially, Burgin is no longer engaging in photography or video but rather compiling and *projecting* environments.[22] As with all 'projects,' these later works are speculative. At the same time, they are tethered to history and politics, especially of space.[23] Zero degree seeing relates to Burgin's work through the impossible perspective that CGI environments allow; algorithmically constructed, revolving in a panoramic virtual space from an incorporeal position. Burgin writes:

> Composition is the corollary of framing, but the panoramic scanning of a still image produces a frame that is 'acompositional' (much as one speaks of the 'atonal' in music) [...] This is an incorporeal form of vision, the view of a disembodied eye turning upon a mathematical point of zero dimensions. [...] This is a theoretical vision.[24]

We can begin to understand a *visual* degree zero, or a 'theoretical vision,' as a means to see in multiple directions, simultaneously; a *capacity* to predict, prepare, project. This is to go beyond the 'new objectivity' of the camera (which still required the subjective human operator). Degree zero seeing is not merely to take pictures mechanically. It evokes a 'theoretical' *structuring* of units of meaning, to in-form spaces of signification; to handle, to situate between structure and event, form and content.

Fig. 4 *A Place to Read*, Victor Burgin, digital projection, 2010.

THE ENORMOUS TEXT

Reference has already been made to Barthes's term of the "Text", understood beyond simply the textural, the literary. In the lengthy essay "Réquichot and His Body,"[25] Barthes extends the Text to the visual practice of painting. He concludes with the suggestion that "[t]o recognize Réquichot's signature... is to possess an additional sign in the chaos of the enormous Text which is written without interruptions, without origin, and without end."[26] The description reveals Barthes's continued search for the Text that has no beginning or ending. Again Barthes appeals to a sense of *both* structure and event, with painting being a "Text" without interruptions—the movement of paint operates seemingly without grammar or syntax. At the time when Barthes was writing, the "enormous Text" suggests endlessly resounding collisions of meaning. Today, we might well evoke this notion as a way of understanding recent computer vision techniques and generative AI image diffusion models, which draw effortlessly upon an enormous corpus of big data, thus 'reading' the image via 'units of meaning' (or tokenization) very different in scale and significance to human vision, and equating to levels of syntax beyond our own comprehension.

THE WORLD AS DATA

Keeping in mind the new order of information, I return now to the philosophical concerns of degree zero. As noted, in "The World as Object," written in the same period in which he was working on the first drafts of *Writing Degree Zero*, Barthes presents Saenredam as offering a *modern* aesthetic. Saenredam is only mentioned briefly, yet he operates as a key pivot for the overall account. He is the antithesis of an antithesis: "... a paradox," writes Barthes, "he articulates by antithesis the nature of classical Dutch painting, which has washed away religion only to replace it with man and his empire of things." Barthes' description is almost flippant, reminiscent of Bataille writing on Manet.[27] His references to how "Saenredam painted neither faces nor objects, but chiefly vacant church interiors, reduced to the beige and innocuous unction of butterscotch ice cream" or how his "sugary, stubborn surfaces" rejected "the Italian overpopulation of statues" could be lines from *Mythologies*.[28] Yet, like Bataille, Barthes is not colluding with myth in order to unseat it, rather he is on the side of these paintings, which he sees as a confrontation.[29]

The double negation of Saenredam has to be understood against the dominant view of 17th-century Dutch painting more generally. The realism of Dutch painting has frequently been taken to undermine the works as 'art' (a precursor to the debates over photography as a mechanical, 'artless' art). The writer Henry James, for example, remarked upon the difficulty of knowing what is an original (i.e. a real landscape) and what is the copy. In *The Art of Describing*, different to the dominant perspectival account, Svetlana Alper sets out a thorough analysis of how we gain an "optical" account of the image from looking at 17th-century Dutch painting, different to the then dominant perspectival account.[30] In brief, there are two modes of picturing the world. "[O]n the one hand the picture considered as an object in the world, a framed window to which we bring our eyes," as in the Italian tradition. It is a mode epitomized by the work of the Italian Renaissance polymath Leon Battista Alberti (Fig. 5, top). On the other hand (as with the Dutch tradition), the picture takes "the place of the eye with the frame and our location thus left undefined." [31] Vermeer's *View of Delft* is a good example, whereby it is remarked that the scene of Delft "is hardly grasped, or taken in—it is just there for the looking.... The Dutch artist... adds actual viewing experience to the artificial perspective system of the Italians. In this wide vista, which presumes an aggregate of views made possible by a mobile eye, the retinal or optical has been added on to the

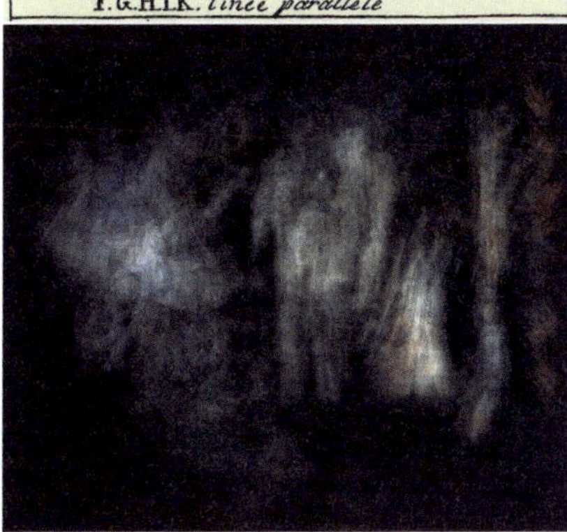

Fig. 5 On top, figure from *Della pittura* showing the vanishing point, 1450, by Leon Battista Alberti. Bottom *MJ Unstable RTI*, 2016.

Fig. 6 *The Art of Painting* and detail of *The Art of Painting*, by Johannes Vermeer, oil on canvas, c.1666–68.
Fig. 7 *Interior of St Bavo's Church in Haarlem*, by Pieter Jansz Saenredam, oil on panel, 93.7 cm x 55.2 cm, 1636.

perspectival."[32] Put simply, we move from a rendering of visual space according to a fixed gaze (a vanishing point, as demonstrated by Alberti) to a 'worldly' vista, without frame or boundary (here the gaze must *roam*, analogous to point of view computer games).

Johannes Kepler, the German mathematician and astronomer, takes us a step further, unpacking the relationship between scientific observation and the aesthetics of Dutch painting. As Alpers argues, Kepler turns our attention away from "seeing the world" to insisting the human eye only has access to its representation, as a picture on the retina. Taking this on board, Alpers writes:

> We might then consider Vermeer's *View of Delft* not as a copy done after a camera obscura or as a photograph (both of which claims have been made in the past), but as a display of this notion of artifice. A claim is made on us that this picture is at the meeting-place of the world seen and the world pictured. That border line between nature and artifice that Kepler defined mathematically, the *Dutch made a matter of paint*.[33]

Echoing Burgin's "theoretical vision," Kepler effectively "deanthropomorphizes vision," with the world picturing itself upon a passive eye (like a screen), and with Dutch painting capturing this 'zero degree' vision. Underlying this reading is a notion of painting *light* itself, not objects or forms. It is pre-emptive of the contemporary computational photographic method known as Reflectance Transformation Imaging (RTI), a forensic method that can reveal surface information otherwise undisclosed through direct empirical examination.

RTI generates information from a series of photographs using a stationary camera, with the light source projected from multiple but known directions (typically using a small black reflective ball as a fixed control measure). Lighting information is mathematically synthesized to create a model of an object's surface. Sculptor Ian Dawson usefully defamiliarizes these images. By inverting the process, using a static light but affixing the light control to the camera and moving it around the object, he has recorded a dynamic form of RTI (Fig. 5, bottom). No single 'image' does justice to what Dawson reveals (they are best seen as film-like sequences), but as we watch the succession of pictures, tracking the movement of the imaging technique, we begin to discern the *tracing* of imaging itself, as if observing an ethereal world of a myriad of viewpoints. We are inside the enormous Text, coursing dynamically through all its data points: a live space of degree zero, an unlabeled, untrammeled acoustics.

MORE THAN THE EYE CAN SEE

While Dutch painting is full of color, it shares something with so-called colorless, neutral writing. Like an unadorned 'style,' in which authors such as Camus reject the adjective, the Dutch painter presents only what is before them. As Laurence Gowing writes: "Vermeer seems almost not to care, or not even to know, what it is that he is painting. What do men call this wedge of light? A nose? A finger? What do we know of its shape? To Vermeer none of this matters, the conceptual world of names and knowledge is forgotten, nothing concerns him but what is visible, the tone, the wedge of light."[34] Focus, for example, on just a small detail in Vermeer's *The Art of Painting* (Fig. 6). Looking just at the hand of the painter, "[O]ur experience is vertiginous," Alpers writes, "because of the way the hand is assembled out of tone and light without declaring its identity as a hand."[35] Here, again, can be *heard* connections with how AI and computer vision 'sees'. It does not look, it *locates*, via pixels, data, clusters of pixels, and patterns, not things or defined objects or outlines.

Here, we can return to Saenredam, whose deceptively seamless church interiors offer 'more than the eye can see.' Today, we might read these images as akin to the orthographic composites of 3D gaming environments—scenes that keep building and rebuilding as you move about within the scene: the space is frameless, boundless. *Interior of the St. Laurens Church at Alkmaar* (1661), for example, presents multiple views: "The eye passes low through two doors and through free space to the left, and is stopped by a high, lean slice of space behind the pillar at the right.

...The small figures at the right are markers ... of the horizon line."[36] The organ case is high up, forcing us to physically lift our gaze. In other examples, figures within the picture space take up the artist's viewpoint, making their object of sight into our own. In *Interior of the Church of St. Bavo in Haarlem* (1636) (Fig. 7), for example, the eye point runs from the bottom of the pillar to the right foreground.

> It is from here that the view could be seen across the nave into the complex of space beyond and also up into the vault with the painted shutters of its great organ. One could see this, that is, if one adjusted one's gaze. Once again the surface traversed by the eyes is the field of vision that the panel lays out for us. The definitive gaze of the human eye is then fortified with the figure of a man.[37]

Saenredam's innovation is to use the upward gaze of this figure to establish the view of the organ; he is "literally a captive of that view."[38] He deploys a geometric, orthographic drafting technique, known as distance point construction. It refers to a method of rendering objects onto a flat surface without designating the viewer and picture plane, without the Albertian frame. In this technique, the 'eye point' is placed multiply, so that *theoretically* it would be possible to move around the objects depicted. These points are "functions of the world seen" rather than specific, external points of view. "The many eyes and many things viewed that make up such surfaces," Alpers suggests, "produce a syncopated effect. There is no way that we can stand back and take in a homogeneous space."[39] Again, these echoey Church spaces might be compared to spatial coordinates of CGI environments. Saenredam offers an "acoustics" of space; a space that is—or seems—in the process of calculating and recalculating its viewing dynamics, giving a "syncopated effect" (to repeat Alpers's musical reference).

Barthes's equating of Dutch painting and the gaze turns the picture itself into a question about picturing and our being looked at. Arguably the more famous example of such a phenomenon is Velasquez's *Las Meninas*. The scale of the work and its manner of looking out at those who stand before it never fails to raise questions about spaces and frames of representation (Fig. 8). It prompts Michel Foucault to emphasize the painting's push and pull of our being seen in/by *Las Meninas*: "[I]n the midst of this dispersion which it is *simultaneously grouping together and spreading out before us*, indicated compellingly from every side, is an essential void."[40]

Fig. 8 After Velasquez's *Las Meninas*, image extended via OpenAI DALL-E 2 by the author.

Foucault's writing on *Las Meninas* forms the opening to *The Order of Things,* in which he charts the emergence of "man" as an object of knowledge—one which famously, of course, can be erased "like a face drawn in sand at the edge of the sea."[41] Here, Foucault alludes to how the very structures of knowledge (based upon the compartmentalizing of modern science) create the discourse of the human "subject," a productive force that simultaneously places subjectivity under domination. In contemporary terms, we have become data out of our own quest for knowledge. We have invented the archive of knowledge that must then be continually traversed, and which over the *longue durée* has enabled recent developments in Big Data and probabilistic AI.[42] If we think of the diachronic and synchronic axes of signification, they are perpendicular. Upon the diachronic we unfold temporally (eventfully) the meanings we exchange, but always we are choosing (at right angles) from the vast store of the synchronic—all the available data of possible meanings. The point of intersection, just prior to an utterance, is the degree zero: the moment in which we could say something else; we could formulate differently. Today, with AI, we can now massively scale this process to a point where we may no longer even draw that face in the sand to begin with. AI leads us to a radical objectivity—wherein the degree zero (as the situating of signification) is both full and empty at the same time.

AT THE RIGHT ANGLES...

Erasure and the "order of things" leads to a final observation. As a political aesthetic, we need to remind ourselves that the inside/outside of the picture frame (or rather its unbounded nature) nonetheless intersects (at right angles) with our 'real' world (i.e. lived experience). It is at this *incidence* when we read images, formulate sentences, and of course build buildings; when we demarcate through architecture. As such, actually existing architecture never can be at the zero degree, but, nevertheless, like the Eiffel Tower, can be the vantage point from which we extend the possibilities of the gaze. For Foucault, this is the "contract" that *Las Meninas* never fails to invoke: "[I]n this precise but neutral place, the observer and the observed take part in a ceaseless exchange. No gaze is stable, or rather, in the neutral furrow of the gaze piercing at a right angle through the canvas, subject and object, the spectator and the model, reverse their roles to infinity."[43]

Consider, for example, the NASA 'photograph' of the earth *made* in 2012; "made" as in *assembled* from many satellite images. From the orbit of satellites it is not possible to see the full view of the earth, hence the need to stitch partial views together. The original "Blue Marble" photograph of the Earth taken by Jack Schmitt in 1972 from the vantage point of the Apollo 17 mission is the only genuine photograph available (which, as Nicholas Mirzoeff remarks, had a profound effect on the way we came to see the 'world').[44] No one, since 1972, has ever witnessed this full view. These multiple viewpoints act as a metaphor for how we traverse the 'right angles,' the intersections of meaning (and the making of meaning). What links the various historical threads in this chapter is an 'eye' that is picturing/coding itself; embedded in the configuring and reconfiguring of space. This is the vision of a simulation, a virtual 'world,' which must be constantly made (or frequented, as one must traverse the spaces of Saenredam), operating upon the principle of the unbounded frame. Like the virtual space of the computer game, the zero degree is always ahead of (and before) our every move; a calculation just out of sight and yet equally what makes all seeing possible.

1 "The Zero Degree of Architectural Writing", Brussels Faculty of Architecture, La Cambre Horta, November 2–3, 2022. https://zerodegreesymposium.wordpress.com.

2 Roland Barthes, *The Eiffel Tower and Other Mythologies*, trans. Richard Howard (Berkeley: University of California Press, 1997).

3 Roland Barthes, "Semiology and Urbanism," in *The Semiotic Challenge*, trans. Richard Howard (Berkeley: University of California Press, 1994), 191–201; Roland Barthes, *The Fashion System*, trans. Matthew Ward and Richard Howard (Berkeley: University of California Press, 1990).

4 Roland Barthes, *How to Live Together: Novelistic Simulations of Some Everyday Spaces*, trans. Kate Briggs (New York: Columbia University Press, 2013).

5 Roland Barthes, *Writing Degree Zero*, trans. Annette Lavers and Colin Smith (New York: Hill and Wang, 1968).

6 Roland Barthes, *The Neutral: Lecture Course at the Collège de France* (1977-1978), trans. By Rosalind E. Krauss and Denis Hollier (New York: Columbia University Press, 2005), 8.

7 Ryan Bishop and Sunil Manghani (eds.), *Seeing Degree Zero: Barthes/ Burgin and Political Aesthetics* (Edinburgh: Edinburgh University Press, 2019), 3.

8 Ibid.

9 Ibid., 8.

10 Susan Buck-Morss, *Dreamworld and Catastrophe: The Passing of Mass Utopia in East and West* (Cambridge: MA., MIT Press, 2000), 63.

11 Sunil Manghani, "Preparatory Space: Roland Barthes and Large Language Models", *Barthes Studies* 10 (November 2024).

12 Jane Birkin and Sunil Manghani, "From Dürer's Rhinoceros to AI Image Diffusion Models," *HOLOTIPUS Rivista di Zoologia Sistematica e Tassonomia* 5, no. 1 (2024).

13 Roland Barthes, "Diderot, Brecht, Eisenstein," in *The Responsibility of Forms: Critical Essays on Music, Art, and Representation*, trans. Richard Howard (New York: Hill and Wang, 1985), 89–97.

14 Ibid., 90.

15 Sunil Manghani, "Neutral Seeing: Saenredam, Barthes, Burgin," in *Seeing Degree Zero: Barthes/Burgin and Political Aesthetics*, eds. Ryan Bishop and Sunil Manghani (Edinburgh: Edinburgh University Press, 2019), 109–135.

16 Ibid., 89.

17 Roland Barthes, "From Work to Text," in *The Rustle of Language*, trans. Richard Howard (Berkeley: University of California Press, 1989), 56–64.

18 Roland Barthes, *The Semiotic Challenge*, trans. by Richard Howard (Berkeley: University of California Press, 1994), 6.

19 Barthes, *Writing Degree Zero*.

20 Julia Kristeva, *Revolution in Poetic Language*, trans. by Margaret Waller (New York: Columbia University Press, 1984).

21 Barthes, *Writing Degree Zero*, 1.

22 Ryan Bishop and Sunil Manghani (eds.), *Barthes/Burgin: Notes Towards an Exhibition* (Edinburgh: Edinburg University Press, 2016); Bishop and Manghani, *Seeing Degree Zero*.

23 Victor Burgin, *The Remembered Film* (London: Reaktion Books, 2004); and Victor Burgin, "Beginning", *Barthes Studies*, Vol. 10.

24 Victor Burgin, *Components of a Practice* (Milan: Skira, 2008), 92.

25 Roland Barthes, "Réquichot and His Body", in *The Responsibility of Forms: Critical Essays on Music, Art, and Representation*, trans. by Richard Howard (New-York: Hill and Wang, 1985), 207–236.

26 Ibid., 236.

27 Georges Bataille, *Manet* (London: Macmillan/Editions d'Art Albert Skira, 1983).

28 Roland Barthes, *Mythologies*, trans. by Annette Laverse and Siân Reynolds (New-York: Vintage Books, 2009).

29 Sunil Manghani, "Barthes/Bataille: The Writing of Neutral Economy", *Theory, Culture & Society* 35, no. 4 (2018): 193–215.

30 Svetlana Alpers, *The Art of Describing: Dutch Art in Seventeenth Century* (London: Penguin Books, 1989).

31 Ibid., 43, 45.

32 Ibid., 27.

33 Ibid., 35, emphasis added.

34 Laurence Gowing, *Vermeer.* (London: Faber and Faber, 1952), 19.

35 Alpers, *The Art of Describing*, 37.

36 Ibid., 64.

37 Ibid.

38 Ibid.

39 Ibid., 58.

40 Foucault, *The Order of Things*, 17, emphasis added.

41 Ibid., 422.

42 Birkin and Manghani, "From Dürer's Rhinoceros to AI Image Diffusion Models".

43 Ibid., 5.

44 Nicholas Mirzoeff, *How to See the World* (New York: Basic Books, 2016), 1–9.

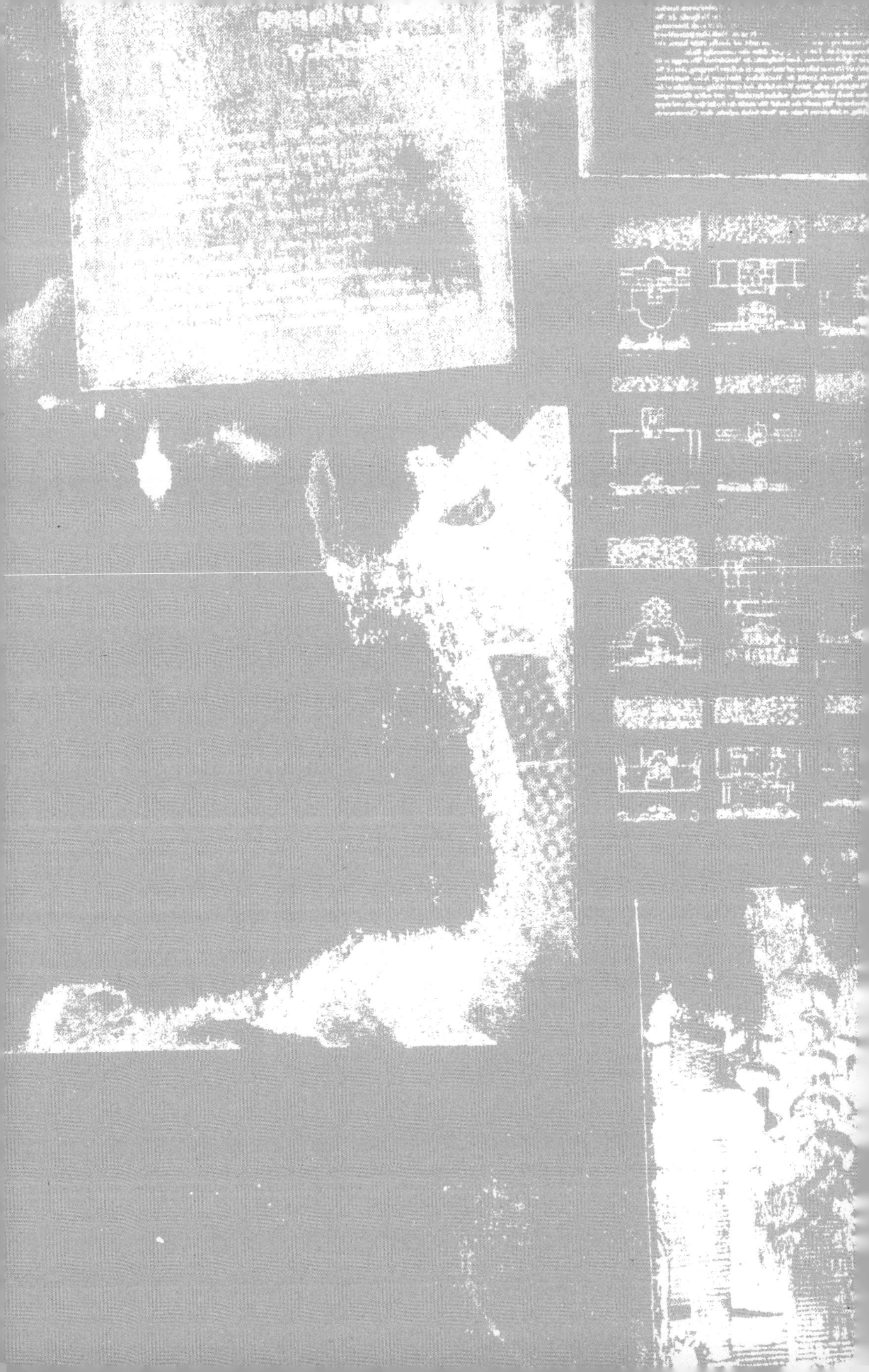

II

Ways for Knowledge to Be a Research Object

155
BORROMINI '67
Andrew Leach
comments by
Gilles Malzac,
Giulia Tellier

171
AT THE MARGINS: CHOMSKY, PALLADIO, AND THE COMPUTER
Pablo Miranda Carranza
comments by
B. Beril Kapusuz-Balcı

187
GAUGING TSCHUMI'S POINT ZERO: WEAVING AND WRITING AN ARCHITECTURAL TEXT WITH DERRIDA, BARTHES, AND BATAILLE
Ole W. Fischer
comments by
Pablo Miranda Carranza

215
EXPRESSIONIST ZEROING. ANACHRONISM IN BRUNO ZEVI'S PARADIGMATIC COUNTER-HISTORIES
Wouter Van Acker
comments by
Irina Davidovici

237
ZERO DEGREE, CAPITALISM, AND ARCHITECTURE: MANFREDO TAFURI, BRUNO ZEVI, AND THE TRANSLATION OF A LITERARY CONCEPT INTO ARCHITECTURE
Gilles Malzac,
Giulia Tellier
comments by
Andrew Leach

II Ways for Knowledge to Be a Research Object

Borromini ’67

Andrew Leach

comments by
Gilles Malzac,
Giulia Tellier

On the morning of Thursday 28 September 1967, at the Accademia nazionale di San Luca in Rome, Nikolaus Pevsner (1902–83) launched a ten-day programme of lectures, roundtables, museum visits, and guided tours of archives and buildings around the city.[1] All of this activity concerned the work of Francesco Borromini (1599–1667), the commemoration of whose suicide three centuries earlier offered an assembly of scholars from across Europe and the US an occasion for analysis and reflection. It also presented a setting in which competing historiographical stances were brought together around a common figure. How should one write and speak about the architect? About the architect's work? Or about the forces acting upon each—from the internal workings of the artist's mind to the economy in which his buildings were produced?[2] The program described in these pages (a *celebrazione*) included a series of discrete lecture and screening events, exhibitions, and a conference, drawing Borromini in as many directions that the discipline of the history of architecture then allowed. In one sense, then, it embodied in the study and representation of this architect the extent to which the methods and frames used by the discipline's institutions legitimately treated figures, works and themes. In another sense, the event describes the limitations and latencies of the same field, such that scholars of subsequent decades might be tempted to read consistency in difference and methodological conflict.

The conference was part of a months-long program launched in Rome that May 1967 with a lecture by Rudolf Wittkower (1901–71) and marked by exhibitions of both a speculative and documentary bent; films, lecture programs, discussions, and thousands of pages dedicated to new books and articles all addressed, one way or another, the architecture, life and entanglements of the architect Francesco Borromini. Where this event might on another occasion—earlier, but also later—have had a more inert character, the 1967 commemoration of the baroque master occurred in a moment of historiological change, when the architectural historian's tools and tasks were up for grabs, when the questions introduced by the generation that had professionalized architectural history in the post-war era were being taken up and reorientated by their children.[3] It also occurred in a moment in which such a wide-ranging commemoration of a figure like Borromini could naturally form part of the Roman cultural calendar and command an audience that would not, for instance, be matched by the events staged to mark the quatercentenary of his birth at the century's end.[4]

Among the voices addressing Borromini in 1967, that of Bruno Zevi (1918–2000), in particular, promoted an idea of history bound to the present by a superhistorical, common spatio-plastic architectural language. Zevi demonstrated how his own search for the irreducible of architecture over time and geography inflected what we might now read as a highly idiosyncratic form of architectural history.[5] In his later writing, as the present volume attests, he would recast this search in terms borrowed from Roland Barthes and his study of language—the degree zero. Consistent across any changes to Zevi's terminology, however, is the instinct that the past and present have a common denominator that the architectural historian can isolate and convey. This commonality, allowing historical works to be read in a modernist key, or showing the "degree zero" binding 17th and 20th-century works as one architectural field, was essential, too, for the extraction of lessons from the past, for the present.

GM, GT We should remember that, for Marx, all the analytical categories of political economy —labor, commodity, value, technique—exist only in the specific mediations and social relations of capitalist modernity. Architecture, which is itself determined by a specific social division of labor, techniques, and ideologies, is a historically specific institution, interdependent with the differentiated spatialization of capital over time. We suggest that readers meditate on the necessity of considering architecture and its defining categories as suprahistorical or transhistorical.

What is the nature of this transhistoricity?

Is it a question of building "analogical bridges" between periods (putting Borromini directly in contact with the modern world, or replacing plasticity with spatiality as a critical theme in

Michelangelo's work), using form to close the temporal gap between past and present, at the risk of canceling out historical differences, ruptures, and socio-political contexts? Or, is it a question of reopening the possibility of an alternative to capitalist modernity, triggering the explosive charge of the past in the present, as Massimiliano Tomba suggests in his book *Marx's Temporalities* (2013), and following a certain "warm stream" of Marxism? According to Tomba, there is a qualitative difference between "actualizing" and "presentifying" the past.

Here again we would like to suggest a reflection on the way "transhistoricizing" can lead to an acritical distancing that would result in the essentializing of the categories of architecture. It is then much easier, in a heretical gesture, to think of their reform, their contestation, and to ignore their active participation in the logics of capital's mutation and reproduction. And thus the need to overcome these logics.

While applied to the figure of Borromini in 1967, this stance was entirely consistent with Zevi's treatment of Michelangelo (1475–1564) just three years earlier.[6] Placed, however, within the multivalent treatment of Borromini that a gathering like that at the Accademia di San Luca made inevitable, the events of 1967 throw Zevi's approach into relief—and his insistence upon it sits briefly at a table surrounded by competing stances on history's materials, purpose, procedures, traditions, and promise.

To appreciate the demands on this event as a "third space", consider the people involved and the individual or institutional stakes they brought to the proceedings in Rome. The honorary committee, for instance, included everyone from Prime Minister Aldo Moro (1916–78) and Rome Mayor Amerigo Petrucci (1922–83) on down, including the directors of museums in Italy, Austria, the United Kingdom and Sweden, who had leant materials for the various exhibitions staged in the program, and several key academic directors of the major Italian art history institutes. Three notable scholars of Borromini and the Roman *Settecento* stand out among those named: Eberhard Hempel (1886–1967), whose monograph on Borromini appeared in 1924; Hans Sedlmayr (1896–1984), author of the 1930 *Die Architektur Borrominis*, written in the structure-analysis mode of the later Wiener Schule; and Rudolf Wittkower, who had decisively shaped the historiographical landscape for an architectural baroque of which Borromini was exemplary.[7] Hempel died a fortnight before the conference began. Wittkower did not live to see the conference acts published. The latter's own contribution offered a psycho-historical profile of the architect that informs more effectively than any other source the idea of Borromini as a melancholic genius—and hence of a particularity against which Zevi railed.[8] Both stand for the historiographical status quo: the image of Borromini as a historical figure, which would be variously tested and reinforced by the discussion.

Working alongside the convenors Giovanni Muzio (1893–1982), a Milanese alumnus of Novecento Italiano, and the architect Guglielmo De Angelis d'Ossat (1907–92), a large consultative committee included Giulio Carlo Argan (1909–92), Roberto Longhi (1890–1970) and Bruno Zevi. A smaller group took on the executive roles of the overall event, and this included Lidia Bianchi (1912–98), then Director of the Gabinetto Nazionale delle Stampe, who had co-curated a monographic show on Pietro da Cortona in 1956; Carlo Ceschi (1904–73), an architect and historian who would soon thereafter write an important book on restoration; and Carlo Pietrangeli (1912–95), an art historian who, as Director of the Vatican Museums, is best known for overseeing the restoration of the frescos of the Capella Sistina.[9] Group members better known to present-day readers were Paolo Portoghesi (1931–2023) (Fig. 1) and Luigi Moretti (1907–73): Portoghesi, whose *Roma Barocca* first appeared in 1966 alongside his volumes *Borromini nella cultura Europa* (1964) and *Borromini:*

Fig. 1 Paolo Portoghesi in *Francesco Borromini: Bissone 1599–Roma 1667*, still, dir. Steefano Roncoroni, 1967 (Radiotelevisione Svizzera), rsi.ch.

Architettura come linguaggio (1966); [10] and Moretti, an architect whose debt to Borromini and attention to his work is widely acknowledged, not least by Moretti himself.[11]

These names add up to something like a directory of the establishment, circa 1967, and its successors both appointed and self-appointed. In particular, Portoghesi, Moretti and Zevi had each asserted—and long thereafter continued to assert—their investment in the Borrominian legacy as an origin, of sorts, for a Modernism conceived first and foremost as spatial. Who was Borromini, in fact, and in history? Who was he to this establishment? And who was he to those who would supplant it? Particularly for a figure like Zevi, the question was also who Borromini was to the present.

For a ten-day program, the number of speakers—and hence topics—was mercifully short. Day one, 28 September, began with Pevsner's lecture on Borromini's legacies in British architecture, which was followed by the opening of an exhibition of Borromini's own drawings—one of several, including another at the Palazzo dei Filippini. The program favored a small number of morning events followed by evening events including both formal talks and receptions and informal gatherings. To establish a clear figure, papers presented by a young Marcello Fagiolo (b. 1941) (Fig. 2), the restoration architect Paolo Marconi (1933–2013), and the architect and historian Furio Fasolo (1915–87) tracked Borromini's career during pontificates spanning from Paul V (1605–21) to Alexander VIII (1655–67).[12]

By the end of day two the subject's scope was established, linking art and circumstance in a sequential, phased development clearly bound to the shifting possibilities open to Borromini through the papal families he served. The day had begun with a screening of the new documentary film *Il linguaggio di Francesco Borromini* (Fig. 3), directed by Stefano Roncoroni (b. 1940) and narrated by Paolo Portoghesi, through which the primary strain of the reception of baroque spatiality and fluidity was clarified through the medium of a modernist cinematography. The day ended with a visit to the Archivio dello Stato at the Palazzo della Sapienza, home to significant documents concerning Borromini's life and works (in the shadow of his Sant'Ivo), where an exhibition named *Ragguagli Borrominiani* had been staged for the occasion.[13] The extent, foundations, and possibilities of Borromini-as-subject were thereby settled as a foundation on which scholars could tussle over questions of method, interpretation, and significance.

Consider the themes explored in the sessions that followed. Fagiolo spoke once more, on Borromini's critical fortunes and introducing the question of historiographical determinacy. Next came Cesare Brandi (1906–88)—who, beyond having written the famous *Teoria del restauro*, taught a monographic course on Borromini at Palermo.[14] Brandi spoke on the "codes" and "structures" in Borromini's work—taking up a linguistic analogy that Eugenio Battisti (1924–89) would amplify in turn in his own contribution (quite lengthy in its published form), and which Brandi himself would further explore in his 1970 *La prima architettura barocca*.[15] Battisti addressed the role of symbol and allegory in Borromini's work and the sources available to him as an erudite architect.[16] Battisti's subject occupied a complex historical setting, neither autonomous nor subordinate to his moment. Architecture shared weak borders with painting, letters, symbolism, economy, building technology, and science. It is difficult to say whether ideas flowed from one person to another as Borromini's critical legacies continued to be explored in the aftermath of the event, or whether they went from the lecture hall into later works. We can, however, regard this event as an inflective device, at the very least—with the methodological possibilities laid bare, all future choices among those gathered in Rome were informed choices.

In his lecture on Borromini's "structural series," Moretti pursued on more spatial terms the theme that Brandi had earlier addressed. To Moretti, Borromini's codes and structures (as Brandi had it) were less concerned with how architecture-works as language, for him, than with how his work exposed a common language of architecture, rooted in space. This extended Moretti's project in the journal *Spazio*

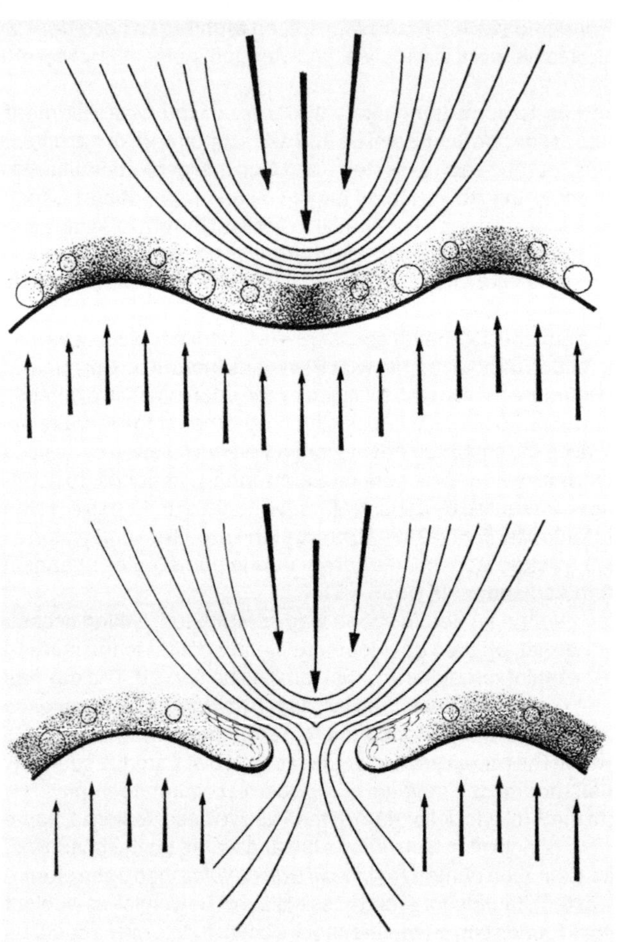

Fig. 4 Luigi Moretti: “Patterns of the ideal tensions of the interior space that, with its super natural, spiritual, force of expansion, pushes, curves, transcends the human, pagan, wall structure that is set to enclose it, limit it, almost repel it. From these contrasting tensions arise those hallucinatory Borrominian gravitational fields that distort, bend, with a metaphysical force, the elements of his architecture.” Drawing by Luigi Moretti.

(1950–53) and exercised against other architects as alert as Borromini to this irreducible language. Moretti's work insisted that diagrammatic analysis of form, space, and structure acted to close the temporal gap between past and present (Fig. 4). He showed how reading works of architecture with the mentality of an architect—looking for spatial relationships, structural logics, the anticipation of experience through form and sequencing—could make historical cases available to the present through a process of geometrical and strategic abstraction, rendering historical work atemporal.

Extending the theme Pevsner had introduced at the outset, a series of papers on Borromini's uptake at a distance located the architect's importance outside Rome: Wladimir I. Piliawskij (Vladimir Ivanovič Piljavskij, 1910–84) spoke on the Russian reception of the baroque style (Fig. 5); Germain Bazin on the Eastern European and Latin American reception of Borromini and the baroque (three contestable historico-politico-geographical categories meeting around the one architect); Werner Hager on the "resonances" and "amplifications" of the Roman baroque to be found in Central Europe and Scandinavia; and Christian Norberg-Schulz (1926–2000) on Borromini's legacy in Santini (Fig. 6), Dietzenhofer (Fig. 7), and their Bohemian compatriots.[17]

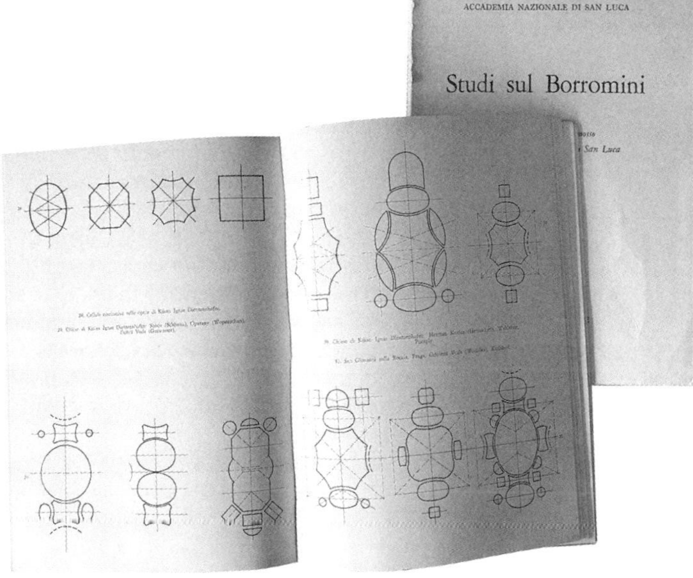

The presentation of these papers was spread across the program and offered a cross section of reflections on the mobility, influence, and communication of this architect's work and its lessons beyond any direct influence we might claim for him. In the program itself, Pilyavski was immediately followed by Giulio Carlo Argan, who addressed the commonly celebrated "rivalry" between Borromini and Bernini, the two disciples of Maderno, read through a discourse on technique and *mimesis*—a variation of Argan's most famous paper on the baroque and rhetoric concerning the artist's agency in view of institutional and political forces, returning to the question of invention.[18] Another paper concerned with relationships was presented by the American art historian Howard Hibbard, who considered Borromini's powerful relationship with Maderno—what does one take up from one's teacher? How does one generation surpass that which precedes it?[19] At the center of this third space, we were reminded, is a figure, a persona, an individual life.

Sunday afternoon was given to leisure before the delegates faced another week's worth of papers and visits. Monday welcomed the first of three roundtables in which scholars directly engaged one another in debate (and to which we will shortly return),[20] before attending the next two presentations of papers, in the Palazzo della Sapienza: in Sant'Ivo, Riccardo Pacini, Superintendent of Roman Monuments,

Fig. 7 Christian Norberg-Schulz, planimetric diagrams of the churches of Kilian Ignaz Dietzenhifer, vol. 1, page spread.

spoke on the later adaptation and restoration of Borromini's work, major and minor (Fig. 8); in the Biblioteca Alessandrina, Marcello Del Piazzo addressed the architect's documents (Fig. 9) – Del Piazzo being among Borromini's most astute and systematic collocators.[21] His work on the Alexandrine collection was published the following year as *Ragguagli borrominiani* (roughly, "Reuniting Borromini's Works"). In forecasting this (day five) contribution, Zevi could not help himself from suggesting that Pacini's talk was at the Guggenheim, drawing Wright and Borromini into direct conversation on the basis of form and space – demonstrating Zevi's enduring habit of turning to Wright (and Borromini and Michelangelo) to exemplify both the figure of these architect and their work:

> The analogies between Borromini and Wright are stupefying: consider their spatial inventions, their studies into compressed and dilated cavities, their monitoring and qualification of light, their use of triangles, hexagons, and coils, their treatment of the shell as a diaphragm between interior and exterior and, most importantly, a common design methodology that extends from simple initial schemes to ever more complex conceptions, and a system of recesses that can unite as well as juxtapose in order to concentrate energy only to disperse it over the city and landscape.[22]

On the program's sixth day, everyone headed to an exhibition of drawings at the Biblioteca Apostolica Vaticana and at the Palazzo Carpegna, home of the Accademia di San Luca (under whose auspices the exhibition was presented). This was principally curated by Portoghesi, who also had a hand in most of the exhibitions associated with the entire commemorative program.[23]

The three aforementioned roundtables variously explored the themes of Borromini's design methods; his legacies in Italy; and his relationship with "tradition" – the last staffed by Emilio Garroni, Portoghesi (appearing once again), and Manfredo Tafuri under the chairship of d'Angelis d'Ossat. The roundtables gravitated to the import of knowing the work of such a historical figure as Borromini in the present, and each roundtable reshaped the figure of Borromini. The "lessons of history" were posed in these discussions as more complicated matters involving the interrelationships of historical research, projective motivations, exemplification, and anachronism – not to mention preservation and restoration as ongoing matters for Italian architects.

Over the course of 1967, Borromini piled up, each impression and the reconstructed world from which it was drawn rounding out the figure and denying him clarity as a historical subject. There were biographical sketches and interpretations, close analyses of the documents for signs of invention, interpretations of those same documents alongside readings of his buildings and case studies of their preservation or restoration. Borromini's relationships with his patrons, contemporaries, mentors, and disciplines, and his influence throughout Italy and Europe: all of these were held under the magnifying glass. In many respects this is what we should expect from such a complex commemorative program, and to this extent it was not especially noteworthy. These perspectives, however, pulled together the breadth of preoccupations in architecture's historiography at that moment, on a single institutional plane, demanding the exchange of ideas and forms of provisional reconciliation: preoccupations concerning method, formation and propriety of subject, geographical differences and institutional agendas, audience and its role in determining the import of the historian's work. As Zevi noted in his concluding address "L'attualità di Borromini" (The Contemporaneity of Borromini), the conference was a virtual tug of war, in which formal analysis, symbolism and iconography, psychology, politics and rhetoric, technical questions of construction and materials, institutional procedures, artistic insight, philology and personal politics were quietly but firmly employed to describe Borromini but also the history of architecture, in the round. As Zevi himself observed:

> In the blazing and melancholy setting of baroque theatricality, Borromini personified the task of a systematic and desperate contestation that, with regards

to the seventeenth century cultural frame, assumes the value of a heresy. Hence, on ethical grounds, his pregnant actuality: the entire history of modern architecture is made of contestations and heresies—battles against an ever resurgent academic classicism, and against that more subtle and insidious classicism seeking to crystallize the linguistic conquests of the last century, to render them static, to close off their problems. That Borromini constitutes a font of inspiration for contemporary architects more inclined to research appears natural and, now, almost self-evident.[24]

This quotation is a perfect example for the point of view we expressed in our first comment, concerning the neutralization of history.

The multivalent historicism this final impression allows presents a model for speaking and writing about the status quo of contemporary architectural culture. Especially from Zevi's perspective, around Borromini's font of inspiration can be gathered those who understand tradition and a normalized idea of history but who have no faith in it. As he declared: "After the time of Wright and Le Corbusier, we act in a difficult context, but a context that is undoubtedly rather less oppressing and paralyzing. We have the right and the duty to go forward with a joyous perspective that is revealed by the revolutionary heritage of modern architecture."[25]

The use of the adjective "revolutionary" to describe the legacy of modern architecture raises a number of questions and doubts. Pier Vittorio Aureli addresses this issue in his article "Do You Remember Counterrevolution? The Politics of Filippo Brunelleschi's Syntactic Architecture".[26]

To summarize, Aureli argues that a formal revolution may, from a political and social perspective, be counterrevolutionary. The real questions, then, when assessing whether something is revolutionary or not, could be: does it alter social relations in an emancipatory way? Does it break, reverse, or destabilize the social, economic, and political order? Moreover, we must keep in mind that counterrevolution also shapes "new mentalities, cultural habits, tastes, customs, and modes of production."[27]

There is a risk in reading too much into an event designed to attend to established and emerging scholarship and scholars, to pragmatic and intellectual matters in Borromini's life, work, and legacy and the issues to which they give rise, and to new calls for a platform serving an international scholarly community.

Herein, though, is evidence of a setting in which the figure of Borromini becomes a methodological cipher (Fig. 10). For one thing, the agencies of Zevi and Moretti insured that Borromini as a figure was placed into a super-historical relationship with the architects of the Modern movement on the basis of his reduction to essential architectural qualities: modest budgets became a determination to create form and space unencumbered by ornament or other forms of artifice; structural and geometrical complexities gave rise to unified spatial compositions—but also a model both for the architect and for the cultural critic. One could, indeed, had to be something of a heretic, since the alternative was the reinstatement of orthodoxy. At the same time, the event invited in all the complexity that allowed Borromini to be seen in the round, as well as the pure language of architecture sought out by Zevi to be complicated by institutional histories, circumstances of patronage, practices of collection, archiving, cataloguing and accessing the drawings, restoration, and his legacies as an operative figure in the history of art of the preceding century; at once a hero of the Wölfflinian baroque and an exemplar of all that had gone wrong in the classical tradition. Borromini was, in 1967, all of these things and none of them.

Fig. 2 Borromini: Facade of the Oratorio dei Filippini.
Fig. 3 *Il linguaggio di Francesco Borromini 1599–1667*, still, dir. Steefano Roncoroni, 1967 (Radiotelevisione Svizzera), rsi.ch.

Fig. 5 Church of the Transfiguration, Kihzi Island, Lake Onega.

Fig. 6 Jan Santini Aichel, Chapel of Lomec, interior.
Fig. 8 The vault of the Chiesa dei Re Magi of the Propaganda Fide, showing the restoration works of 1955.

Fig. 9 Drawing for a moulding by Borromini, Albertina, Vienna.
Fig. 10 Lieven Cruyl, view of the Quattro fontane looking toward Santa Maria Maggiore, ca. 1667, Cleveland Museum of Art.

1 *Celebrazione Borrominiane: Manifestazione in onore di Francesco Borromini* (program of events), Accademia San Luca (Rome, 1967), box 62, folder 07/20 1967, Fondazione Bruno Zevi, Rome. While often redundant, the inclusion in this essay of the dates for each figure begins to show generational relationships and differences over the course of the event.

2 The full proceedings of the formal *anno borrominiano* were published as *Studi sul Borromini. Atti del Convego promosso dall'Accademia Nazionale di San Luca*, ed. Guglielmo De Angeles d'Ossat, 2 vols (Rome: De Luca Editore, 1972) (hereafter *SB*).

3 Indexical of this generational change is the argument offered in Manfredo Tafuri, *Teorie e storia dell'architettura* (Rome: Laterza, 1968) – arguably the founding document of the so-called Venice School of architectural history. The Borromini conference followed by mere weeks an event further north, at Vicenza's Centro Internazionale di Studi di Architettura "Andrea Palladio", in which disciplinary luminaries and hopefuls had likewise met to resolve the study of mannerism in architecture. Many of the same figures introduced in the present essay were already present, and the discussion anticipated that the Rome meeting participants would benefit from the gains of the Vicenza meeting. Rodolfo Pallucchini in "Cronaca del IX Corso internazionale di storia dell'architettura", *Bollettino del Centro Internazionale di Studi di Architettura "Andrea Palladio"* 9 (1967), 449. On this earlier meeting, see Andrew Leach, "At Midnight they Returned to the City", *gta Papers* 10 (2025), forthcoming.

4 Most authoritatively captured in Richard Bösel and Christoph L. Frommel, eds., *Borromini e l'universo barocco*, 2 vols (Milan: Electa, 1999). Zevi's preparations for the event are documented in box 14; box 19, folder 06.02/56 1999; and box 65, folder 07/51 1999, Fondazione Bruno Zevi.

5 This is explored in, among other sources, Roberto Dulio, "From Michelangelo to Borromini: Bruno Zevi and Operative Criticism", in *The Baroque in Architectural Culture, 1880–1980*, ed. Andrew Leach, John Macarthur and Maarten Delbeke (Farmham: Ashgate, 2015), 185–93.

6 These are best captured in Bruno Zevi and Paolo Portoghesi, eds, *Michelangiolo architetto* (Turin: Einaudi, 1964). An index of the kind of cultural programming the quatercentenary of Michelangelo allowed, and on which the anno borromiano was modelled three years later, is offered by the commentary on this figure at the end of the didactic opening scene of *The Agony and the Ecstasy* (dir. Carol Reed, 1965), in which Charleton Heston (who plays the artist in the film) comments on the gathering of the world's Michelangelo scholars in Rome on the occasion of this anniversary year.

7 Eberhard Hempel, *Francesco Borromini* (Vienna: A. Schroll, 1924); Hans Sedlmayr, *Die Architektur Borrominis* (Berlin 1930) – quoting also from Anthony Blunt, *Borromini* (London: Thames and Hudson, 1979), 224. Rudolf Wittkower, *Art and Architecture in Italy 1600–1750* (London: Pelican, 1958); and *Studies in the Italian Baroque*, ed. Margot Wittkower (London: Thames and Hudson, 1975).

8 Wittkower's death may have precipitated the reshuffle in the table of contents from the conference program as delivered, provoking Blunt's erroneous observation that Wittkower, rather than Pevsner, delivered the first address (Borromini, 225). To delve deeper into the melancholic construction of genius in Wittkower's work, see Rudolf Wittkower and Margot Wittkower, *Born Under Saturn: The Character and Conduct of Artists* (New York: WW Horton and Co., 1969). In later editions, Margaret Wittkower is named first.

9 Mario Salmi, ed., *Mostro di Pietro da Cortona* (exh. cat.) (Rome: De Luca Editore, 1956), with an essay by Lidia Bianchi on the drawings; Carlo Ceschi, *Teorie e storia del restauro* (Rome: Bulzoni, 1970).

10 Paolo Portoghesi, *Roma Barocca* (Rome: Bestetti e Tumminelli, 1966); *Borromini nella cultura Europa* (Rome: Officina Edizioni, 1964); *Borromini: Architettura come linguaggio* (Milan: Electa, 1967). On Portoghesi (who died shortly before this present essay was revised for publication), see Silvia Micheli and Léa-Catherine

Szacka, *Paolo Portoghesi: Architecture Between History, Politics and Media* (London: Bloomsbury, 2024).

11 Most recently in Bruno Reichlin and Letizia Tedeschi, eds, *Luigi Moretti. Razionalismo e trasgressività tra barocco al informale* (Milan: Electa, 2010); cataloguing the exhibition curated by Maristella Casciato and Anna Viati Navone, *Luigi Moretti. Dal razionalismo al informale*, MAXXI, November 2010, Rome. Moretti's own contribution to the conference program ("Le serie di strutture generalizzate di Borromini", *SB*, 1: 197-228) was included in English and Dutch translation in "Barock"/"Baroque", ed. Maarten Delbeke, Tom Vandeputte, Christoph Grade, David de Bruijn, Job Floris, and Ruben Molendijk, Oase 86 (2011): 56-60.

12 These were first published as, respectively, Nikolaus Pevsner, "Borromini e l'Inghilterra", *SB*, 1: 381- 408; Marcello Fagiolo, "L'attività di Borromini da Paolo V a Urbano VIII", *SB*, 57-89; Paolo Marconi, "Le fabbriche pamphiliane di Borromini", *SB*, 91-127; Furio Fasolo, "L'ultimo decennio dell'attività del Borromini", *SB*, 129-153. In his review of the English edition *The Rome of Borromini: Architecture as Language*, trans. Barbara Luigi La Penta (New York: Braziliier, 1968), Henry A. Millon provides a helpful guide to the production of this year. Beyond the academic program introduced above, he writes, "[T]here were exhibitions of Borromini's drawings at the Vatican, the Accademia di San Luca, documents and drawings at the Archivio di Stato, and photographic essays in some of Borromini's buildings. The major scholarly work to appear was the first volume of Heinrich Thelen's monumental and painstakingly prepared catalogue of all known Borromini drawings (*Francesco Borromini, die handzeichnungen*, I [Graz, 1967]). Thelen also prepared the catalogue for the Borromini drawings and documents in the Vatican (*Francesco Borromini. Disegni e documenti Vaticani* [Vatican City, 1967]). Portoghesi wrote the catalogue for the drawings exhibited at the Accademia di San Luca (*Disegni di Francesco Borromini* [Rome, 1967]). The documentary exhibition held in the Archivio di Stato was accompanied by a full catalogue (M. del Piazzo, ed., *Ragguagli Borrominiani. Mostra documentaria* [Rome, 1968])." These, he notes, were accompanied by an extensive library of books and articles. He notes in conclusion: "Any endeavor, however tedious, that reveals facets of Borromini's intent and achievement is patently rewarding. Coping with the fertile and subtle mind of a contemporary architect/critic/historian may provide yet other compensations." Henry A. Millon, review of *The Rome of Borromini, Journal of the Society of Architectural Historians* 31, no. 3 (October 1972), 244, 245.

13 Stefano Roncoroni (dir.) and Paolo Portoghesi (narr.), *Il linguaggio di Francesco Borromini* (1967).

14 Cesare Brandi, *Teoria del restauro* (Rome: Ed. di storia e letteratura, 1963). Documentation of Brandi's course at Palermo is held at the Fondazione Bruno Zevi.

15 Mario Fagiolo, "I temi della poetica borrominiana nella storia della critica", *SB*, 1: 157-72; Cesare Brandi, "Codici e strutture nel Borromini", *SB*, 1: 173-95; Eugenio Battisti, "Il simbolsimo in Borromini", *SB*, 1: 229-303; noting, too, Cesare Brandi, *La prima architettura barocca. P. da Cortona, Borromini, Bernini* (Bari: Laterza, 1970).

16 It will be notable for some readers that Battisti's paper offers a sustained response to Leo Steinberg's (1920-2011) dissertation on San Carlo alle Quattro Fontane, written 1958-59. In its published form, it was widely read and highly popular but largely dismissed by specialists. While Steinberg had no formal role in the program, his project was remarkably similar to Zevi's: to make Borromini's work accessible in the present. Leo Steinberg, "San Carlo alle quattro Fontane: A Study in Multiple Form and Architectural Symbolism", 2 vols (PhD diss, Columbia University, 1960). Michael Hill has more recently located Battisti's response to Steinberg as one of the more serious responses to a study (at that moment still an unpublished dissertation) that would define geometrical analyses of the San Carlino plan in the latter decades of the 20th century. See Michael Hill, "Steinberg's Complexity", in *The Baroque in Architectural Culture*, ed. Leach, Macarthur and Delbeke (Aldershot: Ashgate, 2015), 217.

17 Wladimir I. Piliawskij, "Lo stilo barocco nell'architettura russa", *SB*, 1: 409-18; Germain Bazin, "Borromini et le borrominisme en Europe occidentale et an Amérique latine", *SB*, 1: 419-30; Werner Hager, "Risonanze e amplificazione borrominiane nei paesi dell'Europa centrale e scandinavi", *SB*, 1: 431-52; Christian Norburg-Schulz, "Borromini e il Barocco boemo", *SB*, 1: 453-96.

18 Giulio Carlo Argan, "Borromini e Bernini", *SB*, 1: 305-13, In this, Argan returned to themes he had previously explored in *Borromini* (Milan: Mondadori, 1952) and *The Europe of the Capitals, 1600-1700* (Milan: Skira, 1964).

19 Howard Hibbard, "Borromini e Maderno", *SB*, 1: 497-506.

20 All documented in *SB*, 2: 5-113.

21 Riccarco Pacini, "Alterazione dei monumenti borrominiani e prospettive ri destauro", *SB*, 1: 315-72; Marcello Del Piazzo, "Documenti borrominiani", *SB*, 373-79.

22 Bruno Zevi, "Attualità di Borromini", *SB*, 1: 510. This phrasing is borrowed from Dulio and a passage translated by myself and Maarten Delbeke in Dulio, "From Michelangelo to Borromini", 190.

23 On the exhibition programme, see n. 12 above.

24 Zevi, "Attualità di Borromini", 509-10; trans. in Dulio, "From Michelangelo to Borromini", 189.

25 Zevi in "Riposta di B. Zevi a P. Portoghesi", *SB*, 1: 526, trans. in Dulio, "From Michelangelo to Borromini", 191.

26 Pier Vittorio Aureli, "Do You Remember Counterrevolution? The Politics of Filippo Brunelleschi's Syntactic Architecture", *AA Files*, no. 71, Winter 2015: 148), drawing on Paolo Virno's ideas: Virno, Paolo, "Do You Remember Counterrevolution?," in *Radical Thought in Italy: A Potential Politics*, eds. Paolo Virno and Michael Hardt (Minneapolis: University of Minnesota Press, 1996), 241-259.

27 Pier Vittorio Aureli, "Do You Remember Counterrevolution?," 148.

At the Margins: Chomsky, Palladio, and the Computer

Pablo Miranda Carranza

comments by
B. Beril Kapusuz-Balcı

Fig. 1 A frame from the video of the lecture at MIT, "Virtual Palladio," October 24, 2000. Seated, Howard Burns; standing at the back, Stanford Anderson; speaking, Kurt Forster, talking to Peter Eisenman and William Mitchel, seated in the first row.

PALLADIO'S TOILS

On october 24, 2000, Stanford Anderson organized a symposium, "Virtual Palladio: Two Views," at the Department of Architecture at MIT. The event pitched two different readings of Palladian architecture against each other: one represented by his old friend Peter Eisenman[1] and the other by his colleague and then dean of architecture at MIT, William Mitchell. Anderson came up with the idea after reading about a presentation by Peter Eisenman at The Cooper Union, in which he showed work that he would publish fifteen years later in the book *Palladio Virtuel*.[2] Since Mitchell had made his preoccupation with Palladio one of the core themes of the Design and Computation Group that he created at MIT, Anderson conceived of a small symposium in which a conceptual reading of Palladio would confront a technical one. In this architectural showdown, Eisenman and Mitchell would each enlist to their cause a Palladian scholar: to Mitchell's side, Howard Burns, with whom he had previously collaborated, and to Eisenman's, Kurt Forster, one of the co-editors at the journal *Oppositions* (Fig. 1).

In the existing video of his lecture, Forster concisely details the reasons behind the modern interest in Palladio. According to him, Palladio's role as the indicator of a paradigm shift during the High Renaissance would be virtually unthinkable without *The Four Books*. The second book in particular functions as the first *oeuvre complète* in architecture: it presents, for the first time, the theory proposed by an architect as coincident with their own work. Forster explains how Palladio coordinates the plans, elevations, and sections to present idealized versions of his own work, linking them at the same time to classical examples from antiquity. This graphical systematization of his own projects and buildings set the stage for its future interpretations. It implies, particularly for modern readers, the presence of an underlying system or principle. During the twentieth century, Rudolf Wittkower, Colin Rowe, and their followers,[3] conforming to the method of formalist criticism, took up the readily abstracted plans of *The Four Books* and further bracketed their graphical configurations from the social and economic conditions that had given rise to them (Fig. 2–3).[4]

BBKB Could this kind of abstraction explain why Palladio remains an intellectual touchstone across different eras, serving as a flexible model rather than a historically situated figure?

Forster points out how Palladio had already relegated any information external to the drawings to the explanatory text that accompanied each villa in *The Four Books*, from accounts of the client's wishes to the topography of the site, among other details of what today we would call the program. The exclusion of any technical, material, or programmatic information from this systematic graphical representation of architecture also set the conditions for the subsequent interpretations of Palladio. For the English-speaking readership of the seventeenth and eighteenth centuries, the plans in *The Four Books* encoded into abstract patterns a new type of country house, patterns that had the intellectual appeal of their universality, and suggested their practical applicability as templates for new buildings. Also inscribed in their abstractions was the new type of subject that identified with the new villa type: a new gentry class, from Palladio's original Venetian clientele to British squires and American plantation owners, who, while tied to the economic exploitation of land, had humanistic pretentions and city tastes.[5]

The separation between architectural form and its causes in *The Four Books* anticipate later modernist habits of abstraction. In his comparison of Palladian plans and Le Corbusier's villas, Colin Rowe substantiates the same separation by prefacing his essay with Christopher Wren's distinction between *natural* and *customary* beauty: the first geometrical and universal, the second related to use.[6] Searching for this *natural* beauty of geometrical and universal principles, Rowe, following Wittkower, abstracts Palladio's plans beyond their graphical reductions in *The Four Books*. By focusing exclusively on the master houses and disregarding the wings with their barns or *barchesse*, Rowe and Wittkower fully dislocate their geometries from program and site. The syntaxes of these central volumes became thus the artistic and symbolic expression of a humanist culture manifested through proportions, ratios, and symmetries, rather than indexes of the political, social, and technical conditions behind them. Palladio's systematization of design could equally have been seen as a response to the rising demand for a new type of farming state, after the reorientation of the Venetian Republic's economy toward the intensive agricultural exploitation of its Terraferma domains. But these would have been *customary* explanations of Palladio's systematicness, contrary both to the methodological estrangement at the basis of formalism and to the formulation of architecture's disciplinary autonomy at the hands of Rowe and others.

In these mid-twentieth century interpretations, the plans in *The Four Books* came to signify the historical origin of architecture as a discipline of architectural form. During the 1960s these disciplinary definitions became conflated with the linguistic theories underpinning the rise of structuralism, leading, once more, to the rehashing of recurrent analogies between architecture and language.[7] Prominent among the concepts underpinning this analogy is Barthes's idea of a degree zero of writing, "in which the social or mythical characters of a language are abolished in favor of a neutral and inert state of form."[8] Nowhere is this more apparent than in *Oppositions*, the journal begun by Eisenman and for which Forster was an editor and both Anderson and Rowe were contributors.[9] The very title of the journal is a deliberate play on its alternative reading as "zero positions," a nod to Barthes.[10] From 1971 to 1984, the period when *Oppositions* was published, the term *degree zero* was often used to refer to the sought-after neutrality of a pure architectural language,[11] or instead to address its alienation from any social or political referent, most prominently by Manfredo Tafuri.[12]

While also having Rowe and Wittkower as its sources, Mitchell's formalism follows scientific and technical inclinations in contrast to the continental thought that informs *Oppositions*. Its influence was admittedly marginal, but not insignificant: through his teaching at the Harvard GSD, as dean of architecture at MIT, and through his many publications,[13] Mitchell's views on architecture were important in shaping its future digitalization.[14] But Mitchell's and Eisenman's analyses of Palladio share more than their object of study; both make use of the generative linguistic theories of Noam Chomsky to propose two contrasting views on architecture: one that preserves the figure of the architect as an author and another that substitutes it by a combinatorial mechanism. The remainder of this text will examine these two distinct and perhaps even antagonistic interpretations of architecture as language, both of which take Palladio's villas as their paradigmatic objects.

PETER EISENMAN AND THE SEMIOTICS OF THE VILLA

A characteristic of formalism is the search for the intrinsic constituents of any artistic form, from what is literary in literature to what makes a painting a painting.[15] Correspondingly, the diagrams traced by Wittkower, Rowe, and their followers over Palladio's plans came to define what was inherently architectural in them.[16] Eisenman reiterates this search for the intrinsically architectural in his own presentation at the MIT symposium,[17] which begins with a memory from his trips to Italy to study Palladio: "In a very hot summer day in 1961," Eisenman recalled, "I was placed in front of a villa by Colin Rowe, who delighted in doing this to people, ... and he said 'you sit there until you can tell me something you see.'"[18] What Rowe wanted Eisenman to see, he explains, was not the visible attributes of the villa but its *virtual* aspects, as Eisenman describes them during the symposium.[19] This *virtual* form had been Eisenman's preoccupation during the previous thirty years, one that in his doctoral thesis he calls *generic* as opposed to *specific*, and which a few years later he reformulates under the respective Chomskian concepts of *deep structure* as opposed to *surface structure*.[20]

Chomsky first proposes the distinction between *deep* and *surface* structure in *Aspects of the Theory of Syntax* of 1965, as part of his concept of *generative gram-*

mars.[21] In this work, Chomsky 'tries to explain the generation of phrase structures in language, a process that he describes as the application of a *grammar*, a set of rules defined in terms of formal logic. A phrase in English such as "the man hit the ball," Chomsky explains, results from a process of substituting symbols according to a set of rules: an initial symbol "Sentence" is substituted by the symbols "NP" and "VP"; these in turn are substituted according to the rules in the grammar, until the final sentence is generated (Fig. 4).

The particular application of rules like the one above make up a sentence's logical form, which Chomsky describes as its *deep structure*. In comparison, its *surface structure* is the result of the eventual application of further transformations, such as turning a sentence into its passive or interrogative form, and of its phonological interpretation. The deep structure of a sentence defines its sense at a more elemental level than the specific meaning of its words.[22]

In his application of these concepts to architecture, Eisenman explains how the specific aspects of the surface structure of buildings are plain to anyone, while those he consecutively defines throughout his career, first as their *deep structure*, then as *generic*, and finally as *virtual*, are only accessible to architects as the composers of architecture. The virtual aspect is something that is "not there," something beyond the physical presence of buildings, but which at the same time cannot be fully separated from it. This elusive architectural signifier is the product of a constant but ultimately impossible process of estrangement of architecture from its conditions.[23] The conceptual architecture that Eisenman had proposed, thirty years prior to the symposium, using Chomsky had evolved by that time into what he calls "a critical practice," one that had originated with Palladio, he argues.[24]

Palladio's architecture then, he explains, should not be read as variations of an *ideal* diagram, as in Wittkower and Rowe,[25] but as the realizations of *virtual* schemata: the longitudinal organization of Palladio's palaces and villas are the actualizations of a syntax consisting of an ABCBA sequence of spaces, and its lateral one of an ABA arrangement. This basic code is realized into overlapping, merging, or disappearing spaces in Palladio's different projects (Fig. 5). In Eisenman's consecutive interpretations, this *virtual condition* is the furtive signifier of architecture; deciphering and embedding it into buildings defines the disciplinary domain of architecture. This pure architectural sign is always threatened by the presence of a context exterior to it, its motivation, in the guise of its program, function, and physical and material limitations. In Eisenman's view, Palladio stands for the historical origin of this dilemma at the heart of architecture as an autonomous discipline. Palladio's architectural syntax, purged of any "'accidents' or secondary meanings," is nothing else than a "degree 'zero'" of architectural language, according to Tafuri's criticism of Eisenman.[26]

PALLADIO, THE ROBOT

Mitchell's interpretation of Palladio presented at the symposium was grounded, like Eiseman's early theorizations, in the use of Chomskian linguistics; but rather than metaphorically, Mitchell deploys Chomksy's generative grammars as the technical means to produce and explain architecture. While Eisenman posits competence in architecture as a form of literacy, the ability to read and write architectural form,[27] Chomsky instead defines linguistic competence as the double capacity to produce new sentences and to reject others as ungrammatical, a competence given in terms that are anything but humanistic. In Chomsky's formulation a language is understood as all possible sequences of symbols—for example, all possible sequences of morphemes in English—that are grammatical. A grammar is in turn conceived in terms of a finite set of rules for substituting symbols. The understanding of linguistic competence as something reducible to a mechanical procedure—rather than an inalienable human prerogative—is underscored by one of Chomksy's principal theses, known subsequently as the Chomsky hierarchy: it proposes a correlation between grammatical categories and various automata classes capable of either generating or recognizing grammatical sequences of symbols (Fig. 6).

(7) 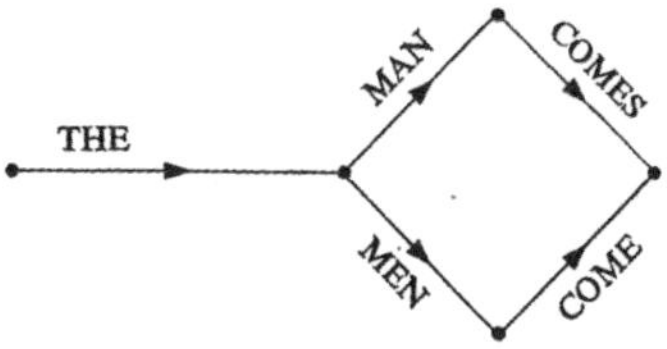 THE MAN COMES MEN COME

(8) 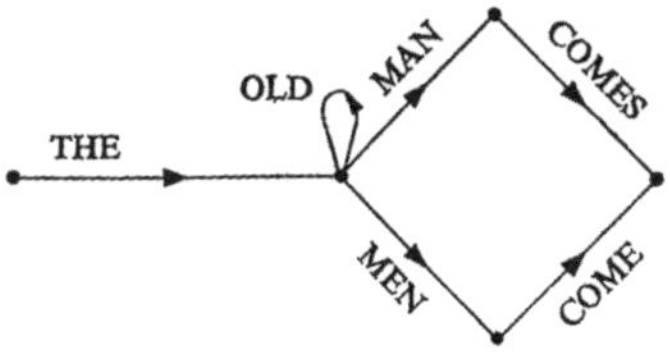 THE OLD MAN COMES MEN COME

These equivalences between linguistic competence and machines made Chomsky's generative grammars especially useful to the theorization of computer languages and the technologies of programming,[28] and became the rationale behind Mitchell's understanding of Palladio.

Mitchell began working on the ideas he presented at the symposium in the 1970s. While at the Martin Centre for Architectural and Urban studies at the University of Cambridge, he began a collaboration with George Stiny, then at the Open University's Centre for Configurational Studies at Milton Keynes (Stiny later became a professor of design and computation at MIT). In "The Palladian Grammar" and "Counting Palladian Plans," published in consecutive issues of *Environment and Planning B* in 1978,[29] Mitchell and Stiny present the application of a Chomsky-inspired mathematical formalism to Palladio's architecture. Rather than sentences in a language, these "Shape Grammars" (Fig. 7) would generate the plans of the villas from the second of Palladio's Four Books, as well as many others that "look Palladian."[30]

Mitchell and Stiny's shape grammar can be seen as a sort of technical double of Eisenman's project for a conceptual architecture: in 1971 Eisenman had compared the architecture of Palladio with the conceptual art of Sol LeWitt in "Notes on Conceptual Architecture" and found in both the presence of an underlying syntax that he identified with Chomsky's *deep structure*.[31]

Eisenman's figure-figure urbanism challenges the traditional figure-ground paradigm; yet, from a satellite perspective, Palladio's villas appear as figures imposed upon the Venetian landscape, with their expansive gardens forming an artificial ground. This recalls Eisenman's treatment of the ground as a critical medium, as discussed in his *Architectural Review* interview.[32] If Eisenman's conceptual architecture aligns with LeWitt's systemic abstraction, could Palladio's villas —understood as formal interventions within the landscape—be seen as an early architectural counterpart to conceptual art's engagement with structured systems and territorial delineations?

Palladio's early training as a sculptor brings to mind the idea of artistic formalism at a territorial scale, where his villas act as systematic sculptural forms shaping the landscape through controlled variation. This reminds me of Rosalind Krauss's concept of "sculpture in the expanded field," in which objects extend beyond their immediate site into a broader spatial logic. Rather than isolated compositions, Palladio's villas appear as a network of spatial iterations—a structured yet evolving approach to land intervention that, like Eisenman's figure-figure urbanism, unsettles conventional figure-ground relationships.

The same year, Stiny, together with computer scientist James Gips, described for the first time "shape grammars" as a mathematical formalism to generate paintings and sculptures in the geometrical abstract style typical of the previous decade (Fig. 8), of which LeWitt's work was a main example.[33] Thus shape grammars can be seen as a technical translation of precisely the same conceptual art at the heart of Eisenman's theorizations at the time. This technical double was part of a project intended to establish architectural disciplinarity as a science of form. It began at the Department of Architecture at the University of Cambridge during the 1960s, inspired by Wittkower's and Rowe's influence in British architecture at that time, and more directly by Rowe's teaching at the department—it was at Cambridge where Eisenman had met Rowe, shortly before the Palladian tour recounted in his presentation. The goal at Cambridge was to fulfill the modernist synthesis of science and art, following constructivist calls for a scientific theory of the calculation of form.[34] Responding to how the new

Fig. 6 A grammar represented as a finite State Automaton, the simplest type of automata in the Chomsky hierarchy. Starting from the point to the left (the initial state of the automaton), the arrows show possible sequences of state transitions, eatch transition adding a word to the sentence in the correctly syntactic order.

mathematics of the computer were affecting fields like geography or archeology, the work begun at Cambridge proposed a new scientific theory of architecture based on the transcription of formalism into the new algebras of set theory and graph theory.[35] The Martin Centre at the University of Cambridge, where Mitchell was based when he wrote "The Palladian Grammar" paper, was the continuation of the Centre for Land Use and Built Form Studies, or LUBFS, the institution that came to embody these approaches. The Centre for Configurational Studies at Milton Keynes, where Stiny was at the time, was its offshoot.[36]

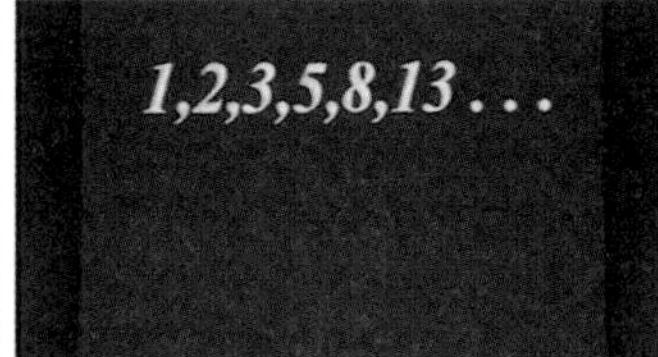

This was the background to the Palladian shape grammars that Mitchell showed during his talk at MIT. The problem for Mitchell was not so much that of discovering some essential architectural quality in Palladio's villas, but that of inferring a logic for their production. Mitchell explains this in his presentation, resorting to what he describes as a "parlor trick." He shows a slide (Fig. 9) with a numerical sequence: 1, 2, 3 ... , which could initially be assumed to be a sequence of natural numbers, followed by 4, 5, 6, 7... . But he explains how 1, 2, 3 ... could also be part of a Fibonacci series, in which each element in the series is the sum of the two previous ones. Then the next elements in the series would instead be 5, 8, and 13.[37]

According to Mitchell, shape grammars make it possible to apply the same type of inference to architectural form and to deduce the rules that would generate new cases (plans, elevations, details, furniture, buildings) from a "corpus" of architectural examples (Fig. 10). The choice of the word *corpus* is indicative of Mitchell's theoretical enterprise. Chomsky uses it to explain how grammars of a language were identical to a theory of it: if in physics or chemistry a theory can explain previous observations and predict future ones, the rules inferred from a corpus of utterances could generate existing ones as well as new utterances conceivably belonging to it.[38] But Chomsky never claims that grammars, as theories or hypotheses, describe anything other than linguistic competence, a capacity to produce utterances in a language. He does not argue that these grammars were models of thought.[39] Similarly, the "Palladian grammars" do not answer, as Wittkower tried to do, the question of "what was in Palladio's mind" when he experimented with the same elements.[40] In the application of this grammatical model to the villas of Palladio, shape grammars represent a scientific theory for the calculation of their forms, one that could explain the existing corpus and generate villas beyond it.[41]

As part of an effort toward a science of architectural form, shape grammars had all the trappings of mathematical rigor and of a commitment to the universal algebras that Jacques Derrida had identified with the project begun by Gottfried Leibniz of a *Characteristica universalis*, of an "originary and preor meta-phonetic writing that... Leads to nothing less than an '"overtaking"' of speech by the machine."[42] But despite all appearances of rigor, the commitment to shape prevented the translation of shape grammars into pure mechanical writing. The obstacles were both technical and discursive. Technical, because the equivalences between Chomsky's grammars and machines hinged on the possibility to carry them out as computations, a possibility that Chomsky had outlined rigorously,[43] and which was not the case for shape grammars in general.[44] Discursive obstacles were the reason for the unwillingness to abandon shape. Modernism had made of shape the central object of knowledge of architecture and design. Understood under the premises of Gestalt psychology, shape—the flattened and abstracted version of form—had been

Fig. 9 William Mitchell's slides from his presentation at the "Virtual Palladio" symposium October 24, 2000. The slides illustrate the process of induction.

postulated as part of an experience untranslatable to discourse, and by extension to any algebraic writing.[45]

THE DIALECTICS OF ARCHITECTURAL LANGUAGE

What led to these strange confluences of Palladio and Chomsky, one pointing toward a *conceptual* and critical architecture, the other to a science of architectural form? Was this perhaps just a conceptual reprise of the modernist conflict between systematic and individual expression, between a mechanical and a humanist rationality, one demanded by modern forms of production, the other necessary to architecture's status as an artistic discipline? In "From Structure to Subject: The Formation of an Architectural Language," Mario Gandelsonas outlines the history of what he defines as the "*vanishing subject* of post-humanism."[46] In his view, Palladio and Jean-Nicolas-Louis Durand represent two distinct expressions of the articulation between linguistic structure and speaker, between system and subject. In Palladio, the syntactic variations of the villas are an index of *invenzione*,

The Italian word *invenzione* carries meanings that enrich Gandelsonas's distinction between Palladio and Durand. In one sense, *invenzione* refers to ideation and the realization of an original solution, reflecting Palladio's role as a creative subject who operates within a structured system yet introduces variation and innovation. Another meaning suggests imaginative fabrication, aligning with the interpretive, even fictional nature of architectural composition—an element of imagination and manipulation.

of him as a creative subject. In Durand, on the other hand, the autonomy of the architectural object reaches its logical conclusion, flattened "to a pure combinatory system" where "the *subject* is *reduced to zero*" and creativity is reduced to a structural property of the system organized as a language. Eisenman, Gandelsonas argues, avoids falling "into the static and entirely autonomous *zero degree* of a Durand" precisely through his use of Chomsky to conceptualize architecture as language.[47] Gandelsonas interprets Chomsky's generative grammars from a humanist standpoint, always implying a creative subject. Mitchell instead uses them, in his interpretations of Palladio, to reduce creativity—at least in theory—to computation, a mechanical process that could very well claim the same *degree zero* Gandelsonas assigns to Durand's systematizations.

In light of the fundamental tension in architectural theory—between authorship and systematicity, as illustrated by the contrast between Palladio and Durand, between architecture as an expressive act and architecture as a self-generating linguistic structure, the paper's examination of zero-degree in architecture provides an alternative questioning regarding authorship: does the quest for an autonomous architectural syntax diminish the architect's agency, or does it redistribute authorship within a broader framework? This provokes further reflection on the shifting function of the architect in contemporary design methodologies and practices.

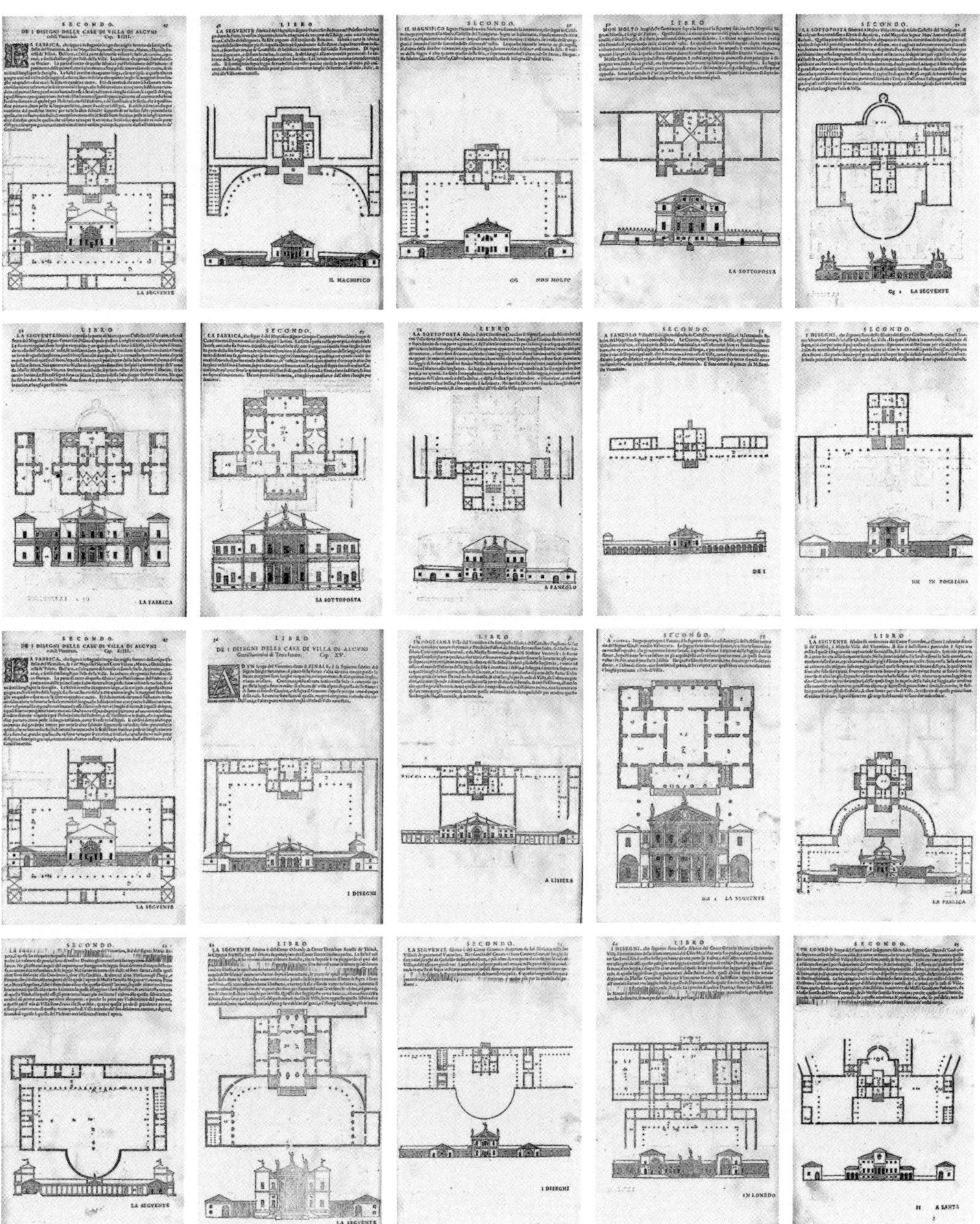

Fig. 2 Villas from the Second Book by Andrea Palladio, *I quattro libri dell'architettura*, 1581, 47–65.

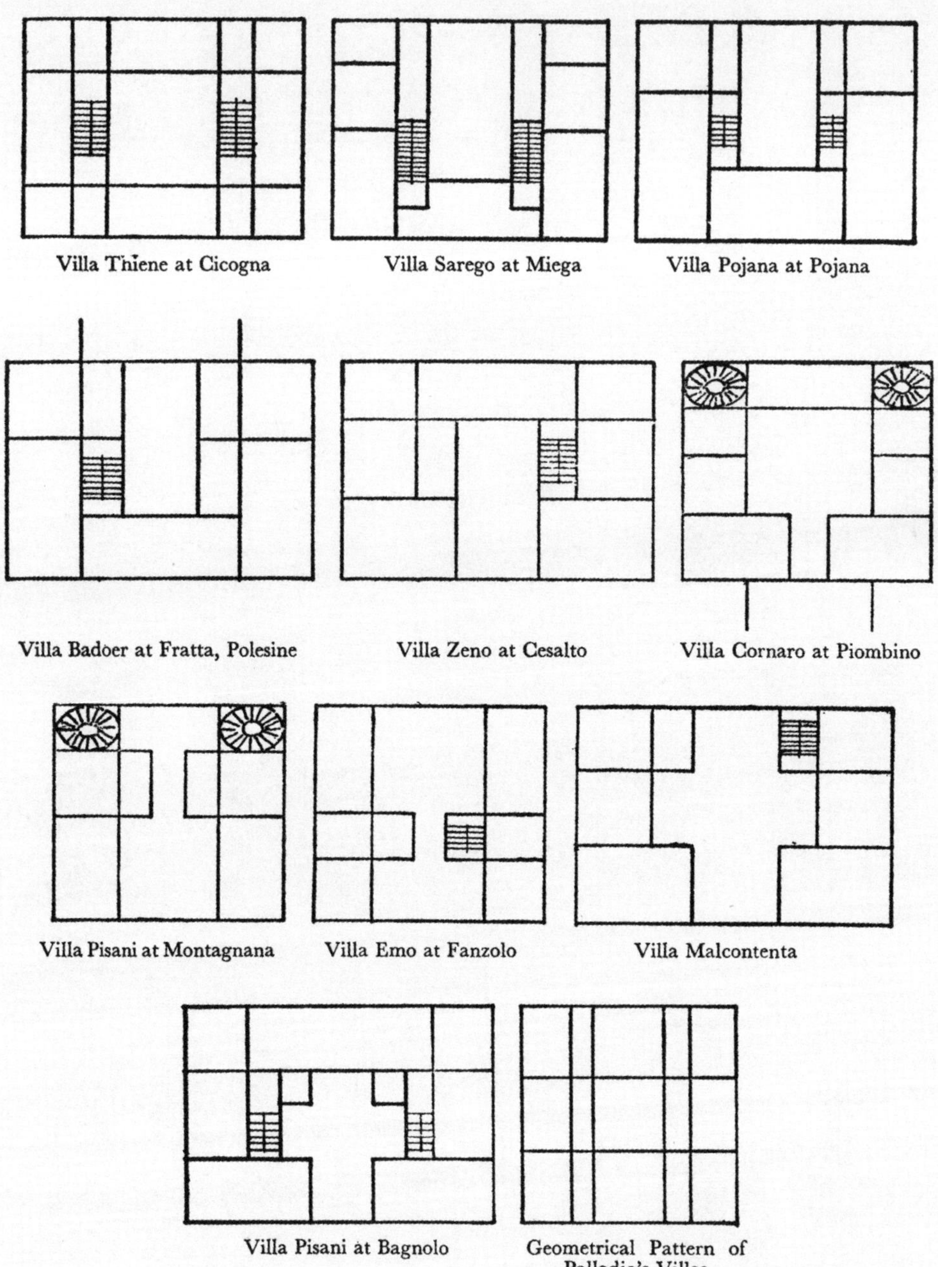

Fig. 3 The original eleven villas (ten plus the idealized one) from Rudolf Wittkower's "Principles of Palladio's Architecture," *Journal of the Warburg and Courtauld Institutes* 7 (1944): 110.

(13) (i) *Sentence* → *NP* + *VP*
(ii) *NP* → *T* + *N*
(iii) *VP* → *Verb* + *NP*
(iv) *T* → *the*
(v) *N* → *man*, *ball*, etc.
(vi) *Verb* → *hit*, *took*, etc.

(14) *Sentence*
NP + *VP* (i)
T + *N* + *VP* (ii)
T + *N* + *Verb* + *NP* (iii)
the + *N* + *Verb* + *NP* (iv)
the + *man* + *Verb* + *NP* (v)
the + *man* + *hit* + *NP* (vi)
the + *man* + *hit* + *T* + *N* (ii)
the + *man* + *hit* + *the* + *N* (iv)
the + *man* + *hit* + *the* + *ball* (v)

(15)

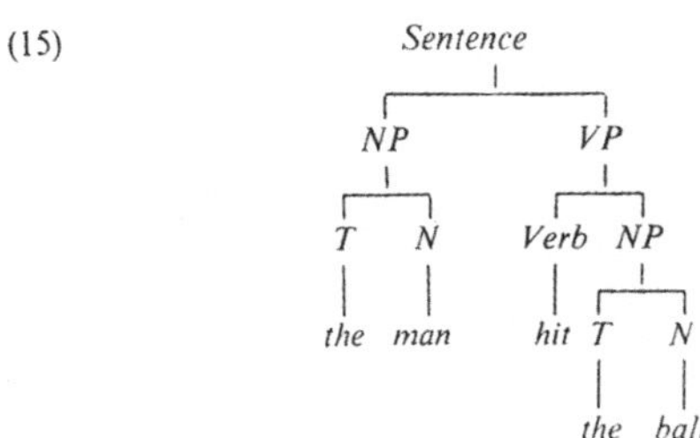

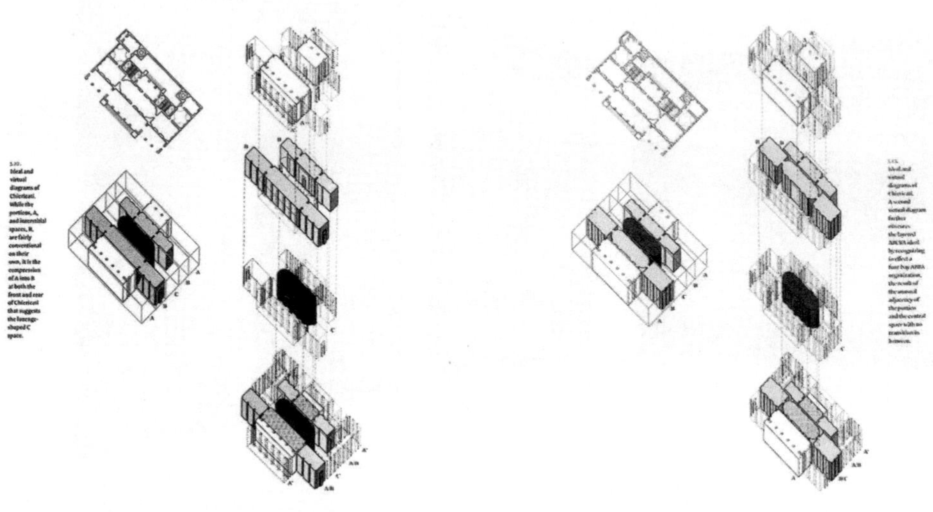

Fig. 4 Grammar and derivation tree, from Noam Chomsky, *Syntactic Structures*, Janua Linguarum, no. 4. (The Hague: Mouton, 1957), 26–27.
Fig. 5 Analysis of the Palazzo Chiericati, from Peter Eisenman, Palladio Virtuel, (New Haven: Yale University Press, 2015), 86–87.

Fig. 8 Example of an application of shape grammars to generate paintings.

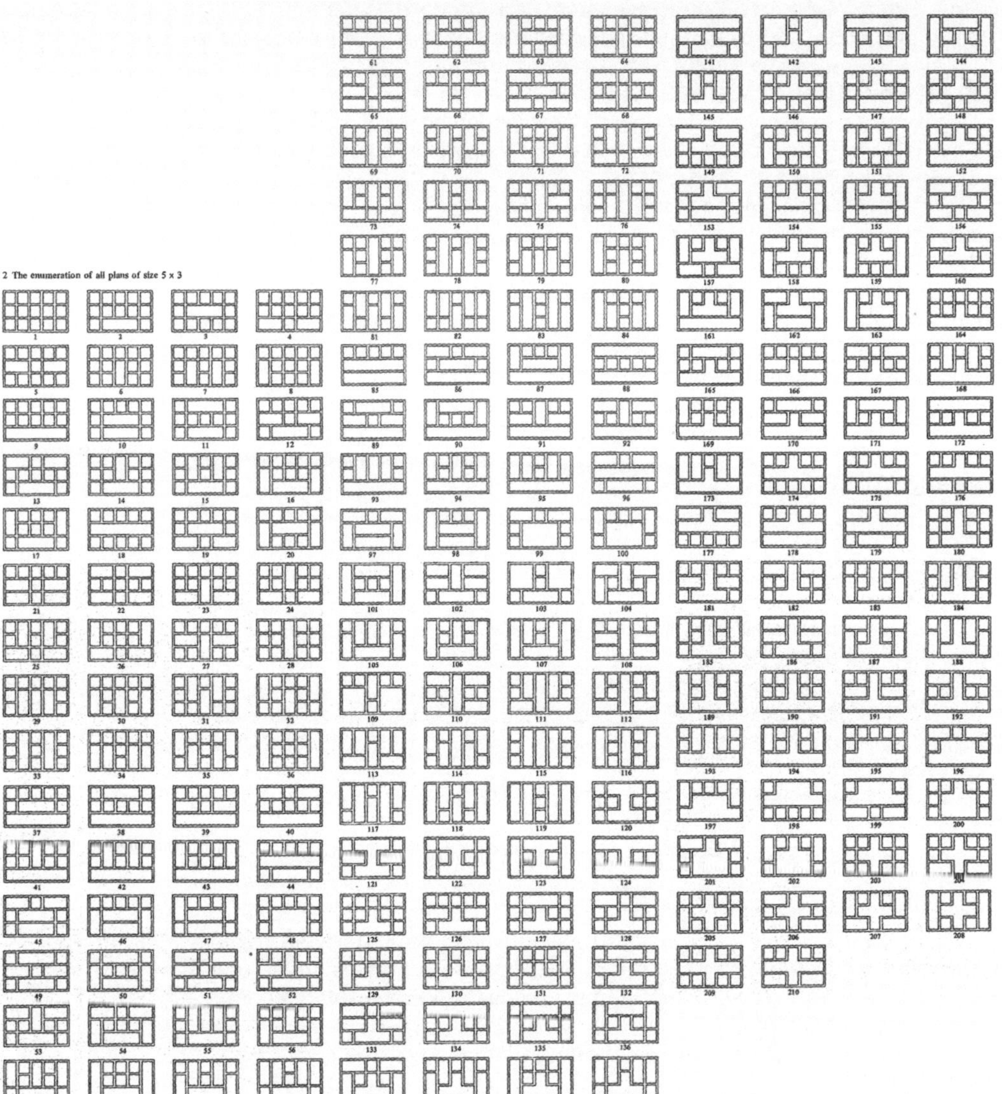

Fig. 10 The 210 possible Palladian plans in a 5 × 3 grid, presented in George Stiny and William Mitchell, “Counting Palladian Plans,” *Environment and Planning B: Planning and Design* 5, no. 2 (1978): 193–198.

1 Kurt W. Forster, Peter Eisenman, and Stanford Anderson, "Virtual Palladio: Two Views," MIT Department of Architecture Lectures Series, October 24, 2000, video recordings held at Massachusetts Institute of Technology, Department of Architecture records, AC-0260. Anderson was a close friend and colleague of Peter Eisenman, a relationship that began when Anderson was a doctoral student at Columbia, and both were members of The Conference of Architects for the Study of the Environment (CASE) in the 1960s.

2 Peter Eisenman and Matt Roman, *Palladio Virtuel* (New Haven: Yale University Press, 2015). The original presentation was part of the Gwathmey lectures at The Cooper Union.

3 Colin Rowe, "The Mathematics of the Ideal Villa: Palladio and Le Corbusier Compared," *Architectural Review* 101 (1947): 101–4; Rudolf Wittkower, *Architectural Principles in the Age of Humanism*, Studies of the Warburg Institute, 19 (London: The Warburg institute, University of London, 1949); Rudolf Wittkower, "Principles of Palladio's Architecture," *Journal of the Warburg and Courtauld Institutes* 7 (1944): 102–22; Giulio Carlo Argan, "The Importance of Sanmicheli in the Formation of Palladio," in *Renaissance Art*, ed. Creighton E. Gilbert (New York: Harper and Rowe, 1973), 173–79.

4 Fredric Jameson, *The Prison-House of Language: A Critical Account of Structuralism and Russian Formalism* (Princeton: Princeton University Press, 1972). In this book, Jameson describes the motives for this ahistorical "bracketing" typical of formalism.

5 James S. Ackerman, *Palladio, The Architect and Society* (Harmondsworth: Penguin, 1966), 78.

6 Rowe, "The Mathematics of the Ideal Villa."

7 Georgia Clarke and Paul Crossley, eds., *Architecture and Language: Constructing Identity in European Architecture, c. 1000–c. 1650* (Cambridge: University Press, 2000).

8 Roland Barthes, *Writing Degree Zero, and Elements of Semiology*, Beacon Paperback, 350 (Boston: Beacon Press, 1970), 77.

9 Beatriz Colomina, Peter Eisenman, and Urtzi Grau, "Interview with Peter Eisenman, Oppositions Editor 1973–1982," in *Clip, Stamp, Fold: The Radical Architecture of Little Magazines, 196X to 197X* (Barcelona: ACTAR Publishers, 2010), 261–64.

10 Joan Ockman, "Resurrecting the Avant-Garde: The History and Program of Oppositions," in *Architectureproduction*, Revisions—Papers on Architectural Theory and Criticism 2 (New York: Princeton Architectural Press, 1988), 181–99.

11 Kenneth Frampton, "Industrialization and the Crises in Architecture," *Oppositions*, no. 1 (September 1973): 70; Kenneth Frampton, "On Max Bill: A Review of the Albright-Knox Exhibition Catalog," *Oppositions*, no. 4 (October 1974): 157; Kurt W. Forster, "Readings of the Dom-ino," *Oppositions*, nos. 15–16 (1979): 89. These are just a few examples of the frequent use of the term in *Oppositions*.

12 Manfredo Tafuri, "L'architecture dans le Boudoir: The Language of Criticism and the Criticism of Language," *Oppositions*, no. 3 (May 1974): 38; Manfredo Tafuri, "The Dialectics of the Avant-garde: Piranesi and Eisenstein," *Oppositions*, no. 11 (1977): 79.

13 William J. Mitchell, *City of Bits: Space, Place, and the Infobahn* (Cambridge: The MIT Press, 1996). This is perhaps his best known book, of a long list that includes books about digitalization, CAD, and the use of digital technology in design education.

14 Greg Lynn, "New Variations on the Rowe Complex," *ANY: Architecture New York*, nos. 7–8 (1994): 38–43. Greg Lynn used Mitchell's Palladian studies, for example, to argue for his own type of computer-generated formalism.

15 Jameson, *The Prison-House of Language: A Critical Account of Structuralism and Russian Formalism*, 83; Greenberg, Clement. "Modernist Painting." In *Art and Literature: An International Review*, no. 4 (Spring 1965): 193–201.

16 Tafuri, "L'architecture dans le Boudoir"; Manfredo Tafuri, *Architecture and Utopia: Design and Capitalist Development* (Cambridge: MIT Press, 1976), 150–69.

17 Eisenman and Roman, *Palladio Virtuel*; Peter Eisenman, "Digital Scrambler: From Index to Codex," *Perspecta* 35 (2004): 40–53; Peter Eisenman, *The Formal Basis of Modern Architecture* (Baden: L. Müller, 2006), 378–81. Many of the ideas and events described in his presentation appeared in texts published in the following years.

18 Eisenman in Forster, Eisenman, and Anderson, "Virtual Palladio"; Eisenman and Roman, *Palladio Virtuel*. Eisenman also recalled this episode in the introduction to the publication fifteen years later.

19 Rosalind E. Krauss, "Death of a Hermeneutic Phantom: Materialization of the Sign in the Work of Peter Eisenman," *A + U: Architecture and Urbanism*, no. 112 (January 1980): 189–219. In this text, Krauss develops her view on the relation between the *virtual*, Rowe, formalism, and Eisenman's linguistic interest.

20 Peter Eisenman, "Towards an Understanding of Form in Architecture," *Architectural Design* 33, no. 10 (1963): 457–58; Peter Eisenman, "Notes on Conceptual Architecture," *Casabella*, nos. 359–360 (1971): 49–56.

21 Noam Chomsky, *Aspects of the Theory of Syntax*, Massachusetts Institute of Technology Research Laboratory of Electronics Special Technical Report, no. 11 (Cambridge: The MIT Press, 1965); Noam Chomsky, *Syntactic Structures*, Janua Linguarum, no. 4. (The Hague: Mouton, 1957).

22 Chomsky, *Aspects of the Theory of Syntax*, 16.

23 Tafuri, *Architecture and Utopia*, 152; Victor Shklovsky and Marion Reis, "Art as Technique: Russian Formalist Criticism: Four Essays," Trans. Lee T. Lemon and Marion J. Reis (Lincoln and London: University of Nebraska Press, 1965). Strangement, or *ostranenie*, was a basic technique of formalism, as described by Victor Shklovsky in 1917, and was used by Tafuri in his critique of formalism and semiotics in architecture.

24 Eisenman in Forster, Eisenman, and Anderson, "Virtual Palladio."

25 Wittkower, "Principles of Palladio's Architecture."

26 Manfredo Tafuri, "Peter Eisenman: The Meditations of Icarus," in *House of Cards* (New York: Oxford University Press, 1987), 170.

27 Peter Eisenman, "The End of the Classical: The End of the Beginning, the End of the End," *Perspecta* 21 (1984): 155–73.

28 Noam Chomsky, "On Certain Formal Properties of Grammars," *Information and Control* 2, no. 2 (1959): 137–67; Noam Chomsky, "Three Models for the Description of Language," *IRE Transactions on Information Theory* 2, no. 3 (1956): 113–24; John E. Hopcroft and Jeffrey D. Ullman, *Introduction to Automata Theory, Languages, and Computation*, Addison-Wesley Series in Computer Science (Reading, MA: Addison-Wesley, 1979).

29 Mitchell and Stiny were acquainted from their time at UCLA. Stiny was based at the Centre for Configurational Studies, headed by Lionel March, while writing "The Palladian Grammar." Previously, March had led the Land Use and Built Form Studies (LUBFS) group, the predecessor to the Martin Centre, where Mitchell was then based. Additionally, March was the founding editor of *Environment and Planning B*, the journal where the two papers were published.

30 George Stiny and William J. Mitchell, "The Palladian Grammar," *Environment and Planning B: Planning and Design* 5, no. 1 (1978): 5–18; George Stiny and William J. Mitchell, "Counting Palladian Plans," *Environment and Planning B: Planning and Design 5*, no. 2 (1978): 189–98.

31 Eisenman, "Notes on Conceptual Architecture"; Sol LeWitt, "Paragraphs on Conceptual Art," *Artforum* 5, no. 10 (1967): 79–83; Casey Reas, "{Software} Structures: A Text About Software and Art," (https: //artport.whitney.org/commissions/softwarestructures/text.html, 2004). References to Sol LeWitt's statement that "the idea becomes a machine that makes the art" continue to appear in algorithmic and generative art.

32 Iman Ansari, "Interview: Peter Eisenman," *The Architectural Review*, 2013, https: //www.architecturalreview.com/essays/interview-peter-eisenman.

33 George Stiny and James Gips, "Shape Grammars and the Generative

Specification of Painting and Sculpture," in *IFIP Congress* (1971): 1460–65.

34 Lionel March, *The Architecture of Form*, Cambridge Urban and Architectural Studies 4 (Cambridge: Cambridge University Press, 1976), vii; Altino João Magalhães Rocha, "Architecture Theory, 1960–1980: Emergence of a Computational Perspective" (PhD thesis, Massachusetts Institute of Technology, 2004).

35 Philip Steadman, "Research in Architecture and Urban Studies at Cambridge in the 1960s and 1970s: What Really Happened," *The Journal of Architecture* 21, no. 2 (2016): 291–306; Lionel March, "Modern Movement to Vitruvius: Themes of Education and Research," *RIBA Journal* (March 1972): 101–9.

36 Mary Louise Lobsinger, "Two Cambridges: Models, Methods, Systems, and Expertise," in *A Second Modernism: MIT, Architecture, and the "Techno-Social" Moment*, ed. Arindam Dutta (Cambridge: The MIT Press, 2013), 651–85.

37 Eisenman in Forster, Eisenman, and Anderson, "Virtual Palladio."

38 Chomsky, *Syntactic Structures*, 49; Chomsky, *Aspects of the Theory of Syntax*, 24.

39 Chomsky, *Aspects of the Theory of Syntax*, 140.

40 Wittkower, *Architectural Principles in the Age of Humanism*; Wittkower, "Principles of Palladio's Architecture."

41 George Stiny and William J. Mitchell, "The Palladian Grammar," *Environment and Planning B: Planning and Design* 5, no. 1 (1978): 5–18.

42 Jacques Derrida, *Of Grammatology*, 1st American (Baltimore: Johns Hopkins University Press, 1976), 85.

43 Chomsky, "On Certain Formal Properties of Grammars."

44 George Stiny, "Shape," *Environment and Planning B: Planning and Design* 26, no. 1 (February 1999): 7–14. Stiny emphasizes how a defining characteristic of shape grammars is their irreducibility to computation and their dependence on human perception and interpretation.

45 Rudolf Arnheim, *Art and Visual Perception: A Psychology of the Creative Eye* (Berkeley: University of California Press, 1954).

46 Mario Gandelsonas, "i," *Oppositions*, no. 17 (1979): 7–29; Mario Gandelsonas, "From Structure to Subject: The Formation of an Architectural Language," in *House X* (New York: Rizzoli, 1982), 7–31 (italics in the original). "From Structure to Subject," which first appeared in *Oppositions* in 1979, formed the introduction to Eisenman's *House X* in 1982.

47 Gandelsonas, "From Structure to Subject," 1979, 19.

Gauging Tschumi's Point Zero: Weaving and Writing an Architectural Text with Derrida, Barthes, and Bataille

Ole W. Fischer

comments by
Pablo Miranda

In 1985 the French philosopher Jacques Derrida contributed an essay to the folio volume *La case vide: La Villette 1985*, edited by the New York-based Franco-Swiss architect Bernard Tschumi during his tenure at the Architectural Association School of Architecture (AA) in London in 1985–86.[1] In this invited piece, Derrida acknowledged Tschumi's winning design for the Parc de La Villette competition in Paris of 1982-83, whose reworking, planning, and execution continued until 1987. Tschumi's ventures into architectural teaching, writing, and design in the 1970s and 1980s were influenced by Derrida, Roland Barthes, Georges Bataille, and Michel Foucault, and others—writers whose work would soon be labeled "French theory." His Parc de La Villette design was a fruitful conclusion of this philosophically informed practice developed over the previous decade. Derrida's response, as a philosopher, in turn reflected back on architecture, both as human artifact and as philosophical metaphor, which would undergo a process of deconstruction/reconstruction in Tschumi's design.

Interested in phenomena of translation and reception, this essay traces, first, the writing of Tschumi on teaching and architecture, and second, his design process, both of which appropriate concepts from the reading and writing practices of Barthes, Bataille, and Derrida, in order to discuss the reflection of Derrida back onto Tschumi's design. What becomes apparent is a loop of an architect's use of literature and philosophy to weave a philosophically informed design practice that in turn becomes the subject of a philosophical reading of this type of architectural texture/writing/work. Significantly, in his analysis of Tschumi's design for the Parc de la Villette, Derrida employs the term "degree zero" to move beyond a pure description of the multiple linguistic processes that are written, performed, and signed by Tschumi in his undoing of the architectural text. He emphasizes the affirmative and productive aspects of Tschumi's open design work.

The course of this essay will not stop at a close reading of a text on an architectural work informed by texts of the same author, among others. It asks critical questions about the success of this self-referential and inter-textual archi-writing and speaking: in retrospect, the Parc de la Villette seems less to "anticipate the architecture to come" that Derrida hoped for[2] and more to draw a conclusion, an endpoint, for a specific form of architectural writing of the 1980s—the "degree zero" that the work of Tschumi exemplifies. What opportunities and pitfalls does Tschumi's sort of philosophically informed architectural practice entail, and what are the lessons to be learned for architectural thinking today?

AVANT-PROPOS: THREE POINTS ON POINT ZERO

The three questions raised by the Brussels conference on Roland Barthes, the "Degree Zero," and the "Third Term" in architecture—"① translating and theorizing 'zero degree', ② drawing and spatializing 'zero degree,' ③ and debating the 'Third Term' in the 'Third Space'"[3]—are all pertinent for an analysis of Tschumi's development in the 1970s leading to the Parc de la Villette. This article addresses these questions with three hypotheses, so that one can take the temperature of the following preliminary points:

① A translation of Barthes's "degree zero writing" into the discipline of architecture (specifically, through Tschumi and Derrida) undermines a purely dialectical structuralist reading of society, space, and architecture in favor of a "third term," situated between high and low, literature and pop, and in this case in particular, linked to the nondialectical, the antirational, and the non-partisan. Tschumi's translation into architecture refers to his critique of both the tradition of modern architecture *and* of popular postmodernism *à la* Charles Jencks, Robert Venturi, Hans Hollein, and others, in order to open architecture up for concepts like play, pleasure, eroticism, taboo and performance.

② Tschumi uses multiple methods of drawing and spatializing "degree zero" in his designs of the time, especially the Parc de la Villette, such as notation, score, matrix, storyboard, film (stills),

PM I find very interesting the idea of seeing a "degree zero of writing" in the notations, scores, matrices, storyboards, film stills, and other material outside the tradition of drawings, diagrams, and text. I wonder if it is the inclusion of these materials that reveals traditional architectural design and discursive techniques also as forms of writing, and enables Derrida's interpretation of Tschumi's work as spacing—a characteristic that he had ascribed to linear writing in *Of Grammatology*.[4]

and theoretical writing (weaving). Both Tschumi and Derrida, his critic, emphasize the proliferation of media, genres, and representations, of rules of high and low, of accepted and transient behavior (such as transgression, eroticism, rot). Furthermore, Tschumi was interested in jump cut montage, or "the structure of the narrative and that of the architectural space."[5]

③ The "third places" that Tschumi employs, performs, and stages are multiple: the places where he explored adaptation and transposition of literature, literary theory, philosophy, and linguistics into architecture. These "places" are the teaching formats at the AA London and the locations where theory is produced, at conferences and in journals (such as *L'Architecture d'aujourd'hui, Studio International, Oppositions, Architectural Design AD*, and *Artforum*) as well as in exhibitions, catalogs, and fictional projects (such as *The Manhattan Transcripts*). Another locus of this disciplinary translation is within design itself, with Tschumi's competition entry for Parc de la Villette informed by the philosophers and writers commonly associated with "French theory." In turn, this locus of the design undergoes a re-reading in Derrida's writing on Tschumi on the occasion of the exhibition at the AA in London and the resulting folio *La case vide* of 1986. Finally, Derrida's text is a place where multiple lives and re-readings are gathered through acts of translation: composed in French, it is published in Tschumi's folio alongside its acknowledged English translation, immediately followed by a German edition, which, in another turn, as will be discussed later, remains closer to Barthes than the French original and its English counterpart.

STARTING FROM ZERO: BARTHES, ZERO DEGREE WRITING, THIRD TERM, PLEASURE

Before one can grasp Tschumi's interpretation of the concept of "degree zero" and the endless mirrors of references between literature, linguistics, philosophy, and architecture, it is necessary to frame this term in both its original and its contemporary context. As introduced by Roland Barthes in *Le degré zéro de l'écriture* (1953), it is borrowed from physics (the absolute zero of the Kelvin scale,

In physics the absolute zero describes also a theoretical and virtual condition, a limit, and not necessarily a state within a corresponding actual reality.

where all particles stop moving), meteorology (the freezing point of the Celsius scale), and mathematics (the point of origin). In the contemporary context, Barthes's concept has been summarized by Ryan Bishop and Sunil Manghani: "Degree zero represents a neutral aesthetic situated in response to, and outside of, the dominant cultural order."[6] Barthes refers to the impossibility of the writer to label oneself as belonging to the field of "literature"—to which one can add "art" or "architecture"[7]—since modern writing. Gustave Flaubert and Stéphane Mallarmé developed a literary form different from the transparent language of the earlier Classical and Romantic Western canon. According to Barthes, this modern writing would aim at the destruction of language and literature itself, leaving behind a "corpse."[8] The result is a form of writing characterized by neutrality, absence, negativity, and cold, white colorlessness (Fig. 1-2).[9] Barthes distinguishes three dimensions of literary writing: first, "language" as transparent during the classical period (the ancien régime); second, "style" as a biological and biographical "given," hence also beyond the reach of the author; and third, writing (*écriture*) that he defines as "formal reality independent of language and style," a "third dimension of Form" that "binds the writer to his society."[10] In the context of the post-war French literary debate, Barthes targets Jean-Paul Sartre, a writer, existentialist philosopher, and anti-bourgeois public intellectual, by debunking a mode of writing that is both political and intellectual as "para-literature" that would "lead only to complicity and impotence."[11] Without entering deeper into the literary debates around Marxism of postwar France at the time, Barthes questions the conflation of the political orientation of the author with the literary quality of a text and re-introduces the category of form into literary criticism. As examples of the neutral mode of writing he describes, Barthes refers to the texts of Albert Camus and Alain Robbe-Grillet as well as the post-novel tradition of French literature, which he distinguishes as a "late form,"[12] alienated, problematic, and self-annihilating, although only as one of the multiple modes of modern writing.

In the same text, Barthes employs the term "degree zero" with a more linguistic inclination when he describes how a "neutral state" of a word reaches a "generic form" freed from specifications.[13] He compares "degree zero" to an "amodal form" of language, that is, beyond the intention of the speaker or author, something that is likely, desirable, or permissible. Similarly, Barthes uses the linguistic concept of modality to illustrate his use of the term "neutral" writing, or "degree zero" writing, as an "indicative mood," between the subjunctive and the imperative, and compares it to the non-emotional matter-of-fact writing of journalism, which is an "instrumental" mode of language that could attain the quality of "pure equations" in algebra (Fig. 3-4).[14]

Finally, Barthes relates the term "degree zero" to the performative side of linguistics, to speech acts unlike the written text,[15] especially to a form of "basic speech, equally far from living languages and from literary language proper."[16] Barthes goes on to elaborate the topic in his *Éléments de sémiologie* (1964),[17] where he implies that he borrowed the term "degree zero" from phonology, a branch of linguistics that studies the use of spoken language (sounds, dialects, signs), to refer to the "unmarked" or "significant absent" sign and its use in speech, logic, ethnology, and rhetoric.[18] To conclude this short excursus into terminology, Barthes's change of focus from written literature to (neutral) matter-of-factness to unmarked speech acts seems relevant in this discussion, since Tschumi aims for an immediate form of architectural writing, a writing of the moment, maintenant, similar to performative language.

comme spectacle et imposée). Mallarmé, enfin, a couronné cette construction de la Littérature-Objet, par l'acte ultime de toutes les objectivations, le meurtre : on sait que tout l'effort de Mallarmé a porté sur une destruction du langage, dont la Littérature ne serait en quelque sorte que le cadavre.

Partie d'un néant où la pensée semblait s'enlever heureusement sur le décor des mots, l'écriture a ainsi traversé tous les états d'une solidification progressive : d'abord objet d'un regard, puis d'un faire, et enfin d'un meurtre, elle atteint aujourd'hui un dernier avatar, l'absence : dans ces écritures neutres, appelées ici « le degré zéro de l'écriture », on peut facilement discerner le mouvement même d'une négation, et l'impuissance à l'accomplir dans une durée, comme si la Littérature, tendant depuis un siècle à transmuer sa surface dans une forme sans hérédité, ne trouvait plus de pureté que dans l'absence de tout signe, proposant enfin l'accomplissement de ce rêve orphéen : un écrivain sans Littérature. L'écriture blanche, celle de Camus, celle de Blanchot ou de Cayrol

Fig. 1 Roland Barthes, *Le degré zéro de l'écriture* (Paris: Seuil, 1953), 12–13.

par exemple, ou l'écriture parlée de Queneau, c'est le dernier épisode d'une Passion de l'écriture, qui suit pas à pas le déchirement de la conscience bourgeoise.

Ce qu'on veut ici, c'est esquisser cette liaison ; c'est affirmer l'existence d'une réalité formelle indépendante de la langue et du style ; c'est essayer de montrer que cette troisième dimension de la Forme attache elle aussi, non sans un tragique supplémentaire, l'écrivain à sa société ; c'est enfin faire sentir qu'il n'y a pas de Littérature sans une Morale du langage. Les limites matérielles de cet essai (dont quelques pages ont paru dans Combat *en 1947 et en 1950) indiquent assez qu'il ne s'agit que d'une Introduction à ce que pourrait être une Histoire de l'Ecriture.*

This is important: literary form may henceforth elicit those existential feelings lying at the heart of any object: a sense of strangeness or familiarity, disgust or indulgence, utility or murder. For a century now, every mode of writing has thus been an exercise in reconciliation with, or aversion from, that objectified Form inevitably met by the writer on his way, and which he must scrutinize, challenge and accept with all its consequences, since he cannot ever destroy it without destroying himself as a writer. Form hovers before his gaze like an object; whatever he does, it is a scandal: if it stands resplendent, it appears outmoded; if it is a law unto itself, it is asocial; in so far as it is particular in relation to time or mankind, it cannot but mean solitude.

The whole nineteenth century witnessed the progress of this dramatic phenomenon of concretion. In Chateaubriand it is still only a trace, a light pressure of linguistic euphoria, a kind of narcissism in which the manner of writing is scarcely separable from its instrumental function and merely mirrors itself. Flaubert – to take only the typical stages of this process – finally established Literature as an object, through promoting literary labour to the status of a value; form became the end-product of craftsmanship, like a piece of pottery or a jewel (one must understand that craftsmanship was here made manifest, that is, it was for the first time imposed on the reader as a spectacle). Mallarmé's work, finally, was the

Fig. 2 Roland Barthes, *Writing Degree Zero* (Boston: Beacon Press, 1970), 4–5.

crowning achievement of this creation of Literature as Object, and this by the ultimate of all objectifying acts: murder. For we know that the whole effort of Mallarmé was exerted towards the destruction of language, with Literature reduced, so to speak, to being its carcass.

From an initial non-existence in which thought, by a happy miracle, seemed to stand out against the backcloth of words, writing thus passed through all the stages of a progressive solidification; it was first the object of a gaze, then of creative action, finally of murder, and has reached in our time a last metamorphosis, absence: in those neutral modes of writing, called here 'the zero degree of writing', we can easily discern a negative momentum, and an inability to maintain it within time's flow, as if Literature, having tended for a hundred years now to transmute its surface into a form with no antecedents, could no longer find purity anywhere but in the absence of all signs, finally proposing the realization of this Orphean dream: a writer without Literature. Colourless writing like Camus's, Blanchot's or Cayrol's, for example, or conversational writing like Queneau's, represents the last episode of a Passion of writing, which recounts stage by stage the disintegration of bourgeois consciousness.

What we hope to do here is to sketch this connection; to affirm the existence of a formal reality independent of language and style; to try to show

(On sait tout ce que cette hypothèse d'un Mallarmé meurtrier du langage doit à Maurice Blanchot). Ce langage mallarméen, c'est Orphée qui ne peut sauver ce qu'il aime qu'en y renonçant, et qui se retourne tout de même un peu ; c'est la Littérature amenée aux portes de la Terre promise, c'est-à-dire aux portes d'un monde sans Littérature, dont ce serait pourtant aux écrivains à porter témoignage.

Dans ce même effort de dégagement du langage littéraire, voici une autre solution : créer une écriture blanche, libérée de toute servitude à un ordre marqué du langage. Une comparaison empruntée à la linguistique rendra peut-être assez bien compte de ce fait nouveau : on sait que certains linguistes établissent entre les deux termes d'une polarité (singulier-pluriel, prétérit-présent), l'existence d'un troisième terme, terme neutre ou terme-zéro ; ainsi entre les modes subjonctif et

Fig. 3 Roland Barthes, *Le degré zéro de l'écriture* (Paris: Seuil, 1953), 108-109.

impératif, l'indicatif leur apparaît comme une forme amodale. Toutes proportions gardées, l'écriture au degré zéro est au fond une écriture indicative, ou si l'on veut amodale ; il serait juste de dire que c'est une écriture de journaliste, si précisément le journalisme ne développait en général des formes optatives ou impératives (c'est-à-dire pathétiques). La nouvelle écriture neutre se place au milieu de ces cris et de ces jugements, sans participer à aucun d'eux ; elle est faite précisément de leur absence ; mais cette absence est totale, elle n'implique aucun refuge, aucun secret ; on ne peut donc dire que c'est une écriture impassible ; c'est plutôt une écriture innocente. Il s'agit de dépasser ici la Littérature en se confiant à une sorte de langue basique, également éloignée des langages vivants et du langage littéraire proprement dit. Cette parole transparente, inaugurée par *l'Étranger* de Camus, accomplit un style de l'absence qui est presque une absence idéale du style ; l'écriture se réduit alors à une sorte de mode négatif dans lequel les caractères sociaux ou mythiques d'un langage s'abolissent au profit d'un état neutre et inerte de la forme ; la pensée garde ainsi toute sa responsabilité, sans se recouvrir d'un engagement accessoire de la forme dans une Histoire qui ne lui appartient pas. Si l'écriture de Flaubert contient une Loi, si celle de Mallarmé postule un silence, si d'autres, celles de Proust, de Céline, de Queneau, de Prévert, chacune à sa manière, se fondent sur l'existence d'une nature sociale, si toutes ces écritures impliquent une opacité de la forme, supposent une problématique du langage et de la société, établissant la parole comme un objet qui doit être traité par un artisan, un magicien ou un scripteur, mais non par un intellectuel, l'écriture neutre retrouve réellement la condition première de l'art classique : l'instrumentalité. Mais cette fois, l'instrument formel n'est plus au service d'une idéologie triomphante ; il est le mode d'une situation nouvelle de l'écrivain, il est la façon d'exister d'un silence ; il perd volontairement tout recours à l'élégance ou à l'ornementation, car

Fig. 3 Roland Barthes, *Le degré zéro de l'écriture* (Paris: Seuil, 1953), 110-111.

ces deux dimensions introduiraient à nouveau dans l'écriture, le Temps, c'est-à-dire une puissance dérivante, porteuse d'Histoire. Si l'écriture est vraiment neutre, si le langage, au lieu d'être un acte encombrant et indomptable, parvient à l'état d'une équation pure, n'ayant pas plus d'épaisseur qu'une algèbre en face du creux de l'homme, alors la Littérature est vaincue, la problématique humaine est découverte et livrée sans couleur, l'écrivain est sans retour un honnête homme. Malheureusement rien n'est plus infidèle qu'une écriture blanche ; les automatismes s'élaborent à l'endroit même où se trouvait d'abord une liberté, un réseau de formes durcies serrent de plus en plus la fraîcheur première du discours, une écriture renaît à la place d'un langage indéfini. L'écrivain, accédant au classique, devient l'épigone de sa création primitive, la société fait de son écriture une manière et le renvoie prisonnier de ses propres mythes formels.

III

word between two layers and sets it off less as a fragment of a cryptogram than as a light, a void, a murder, a freedom. (We know all that this hypothesis of Mallarmé as a murderer of language owes to Maurice Blanchot.) This language of Mallarmé's is like Orpheus who can save what he loves only by renouncing it, and who, just the same, cannot resist glancing round a little; it is Literature brought to the gates of the Promised Land: a world without Literature, but one to which writers would nevertheless have to bear witness.

In this same attempt towards disengaging literary language, here is another solution: to create a colourless writing, freed from all bondage to a pre-ordained state of language. A simile borrowed from linguistics will perhaps give a fairly accurate idea of this new phenomenon; we know that some linguists establish between the two terms of a polar opposition (such as singular-plural, preterite-present) the existence of a third term, called a neutral term or zero element: thus between the subjunctive and the imperative moods, the indicative is according to them an amodal form. Proportionately speaking, writing at the zero degree is basically in the indicative mood, or if you like, amodal; it would be accurate to say that it is a journalist's writing, if it were not precisely the case

Fig. 4 Roland Barthes, *Writing Degree Zero* (Boston: Beacon Press, 1970), 76-77.

that journalism develops, in general, optative or imperative (that is, emotive) forms. The new neutral writing takes its place in the midst of all those ejaculations and judgments, without becoming involved in any of them; it consists precisely in their absence. But this absence is complete, it implies no refuge, no secret; one cannot therefore say that it is an impassive mode of writing; rather, that it is innocent. The aim here is to go beyond Literature by entrusting one's fate to a sort of basic speech, equally far from living languages and from literary language proper. This transparent form of speech, initiated by Camus's *Outsider*, achieves a style of absence which is almost an ideal absence of style; writing is then reduced to a sort of negative mood in which the social or mythical characters of a language are abolished in favour of a neutral and inert state of form; thus thought remains wholly responsible, without being overlaid by a secondary commitment of form to a History not its own. If Flaubert's writing enshrines a Law, if that of Mallarmé postulates a silence, and if others, those of Proust, Céline, Queneau, Prévert, each in its own way, is founded on the existence of a social nature, if all these modes of writing imply an opacity of form and presuppose a problematic of language and society, thus establishing speech as an object which must receive treatment at the hands of a craftsman, a magician or a scriptor, but not by an intellectual, then neutral writing in fact rediscovers the primary condition of classical art: instrumentality. But this time, form as an instrument is no longer at the service of a triumphant ideology; it is the mode of a new situation of the writer, the way a certain silence has of existing; it deliberately forgoes any elegance or ornament, for these two dimensions would reintroduce Time into writing, and this is a derivative power which sustains History. If the writing is really neutral, and if language, instead of being a cumbersome and recalcitrant act, reaches the state of a pure equation, which is no more tangible than an algebra when it confronts the innermost part of man, then Literature is vanquished, the problematics of mankind is uncovered and presented without elaboration, the writer becomes irretrievably honest. Unfortunately, nothing is more fickle than a colourless writing; mechanical habits are developed in the very place where freedom existed, a network of set forms hem in more and more the pristine freshness of discourse, a mode of writing appears afresh in lieu of an indefinite language. The writer, taking his place as a 'classic', becomes the slavish imitator of his original creation, society demotes his writing to a mere manner, and returns him a prisoner to his own formal myths.

Fig. 4 Roland Barthes, *Writing Degree Zero* (Boston: Beacon Press, 1970), 78.

INTERTEXTUALITY: TSCHUMI ON BARTHES, BATAILLE, AND DERRIDA

Tschumi enters the stage when he was teaching at the AA in London in 1970, just before the almost bankrupt school reinvented itself under its longtime chairman, Alvin Boyarsky. Before coming to the AA, Tschumi had studied at the ETH Zurich and worked for Georges Candilis in Paris, where he participated in the events of May 1968. In the aftermath of revolt and a general strike, he searched for the revolutionary potential of architecture and the do-it-yourself city.[19] While in the beginning Tschumi advocated, as revolutionary practices, "counter design," the tactic activism of "exemplary actions" inspired by the Situationists, and urban squatting,[20] by the mid-1970s he had repositioned himself with a series of theoretical essays against both the tradition of the modern movement and postmodern notions of typology, history, image, sign, and syntactics. At the same time, in his teaching at the AA, he moved away from urban politics to injecting literature as a "program" for his architectural studio. At a time when modern architecture, with its credo of "form follows function," was under scrutiny, Tschumi did not dismiss this relation altogether, but he undermined it by interpreting pieces of literature—such as *Don Juan* and *Finnegans Wake*—as prompts for spaces and events.[21] For these, Tschumi's AA unit explored alternative modes of representation by which to draw movement, narratives, and temporal actions, such as photo stills from *film noir*, notational systems from choreography, montages and jump cuts from the revolutionary film theory of Sergei Eisenstein, and so on, which overlapped with fictive or real places, such as Hyde Park in London. Texts were key to Tschumi's teaching of architecture at the time, since he shifted the focus from how an author tells a narrative or generates meaning to the manipulation of the means to do so—words and language. Architecture was to learn from literature and literary criticism.

And this is where Roland Barthes comes in: the notion of degree zero in literature echoes in Tschumi's own reflection on the state of politically engaged architecture. After the perceived failure of 1968, architecture seemed caught between a complicit status quo of the discipline as providing design services for the dominant societal forces and the impotence to revolutionize society with design. Tschumi had to acknowledge that capitalism proved able to incorporate even subversion, criticism, and revolutionary practices and turn them into sophisticated products of culture. Similarly, in *Teorie e storia dell'architettura*, the historian and critic Manfredo Tafuri, with references to Roland Barthes and Walter Benjamin, questioned the "operative practice" of modern architecture to change society with planning and the notion of engaged "operative criticism" of modern historians like Nikolaus Pevsner, Sigfried Giedion, Giulio Carlo Argan, and Bruno Zevi, who would instrumentalize the past for poetic and political goals.[22]

In 1975, Tschumi wrote "Questions of Space: The Pyramid and the Labyrinth," published in *Studio International*, where he explores a "double paradox of architecture."[23] He identifies, on the one hand, a split within modern avant-garde architecture between its utopian claims versus its limited, if not negative, impact on social reality. On the other hand, for contemporary architecture, he attests a split in the perception of space: it could either be sensually experienced or rationally understood, either practiced or represented—though not at the same time.[24] Tschumi interprets this split between "ideal" and "real" space, using Henri Lefebvre's concept of a "product of social praxis,"[25] as an ideological construct: this "paradox of architecture" is in itself political. The inability to question and experience space simultaneously pushes architecture toward an "expression of a lack, of a shortcoming, or something incomplete."[26] As a result, Tschumi concludes, architecture has to choose between acknowledging its social determination or retreating into artistic autonomy—both of which, however, remain within capitalist structures and status quo conservatism. Tschumi warns that architecture runs the danger of being driven into silence, even self-annihilation, referring to Tafuri's sharp analysis of (neo)avant-garde design approaches following the modern movement in "L'architecture dans le Boudoir" of 1974.[27] Tafuri criticizes the futility of the formalist design experimentation of autonomous architecture and the impossibility of escaping from the vicious circle of a linguistically informed architecture.

Tafuri's association of this futility of formalism with a "degree zero" of architectural language emptied of "all dreams of social function and any utopian residues" (in "L'architecture dans le Boudoir") was also the basis of his critique of Peter Eisenman's work in his contribution to *House of Cards*, published in 1987. I think it can be useful to bring to the fore this contrast between Tschumi and Eisenman (another important figure in this articulation of a practice around theory).[28]

Instead, Tschumi proposes its radical uselessness as way out of the conudrum.[29] Or, as Tschumi suggests, in the essay "Architecture and Transgression" of 1976, perhaps there is "another way around this paradox," another way "to refute the silence the paradox seems to imply, even if this alternative proves intolerable."[30]

Tschumi borrowed from Bataille the eponymous metaphors of the "pyramid"—which stands for concept, representation, discourse, dematerialization, absence, the abstract, autonomous, and the ideal—and the "labyrinth," which represents life, subjectivity, sensuality, experience, immediacy, materiality, presence, and the real. Or rather, he took them from Denis Hollier's 1974 essay on Bataille in another act of translation.[31] According to Hollier's interpretation, Bataille pictured the "Pyramid of Reason" as a millennia-old attempt by Western philosophy to overcome nature, human drives, and human emotion. The pyramid is imagined to be erected upon the inescapable "labyrinth" of subjective senses, bodily functions, and irrationality.[32] Bataille did not simply pose pyramid against labyrinth dialectically as "alternatives," since one would imply the other. Rather, he used these metaphors to attack the "philosophical edifices" of Immanuel Kant and Georg Wilhelm Friedrich Hegel, the architectonics of Western idealism,[33] and their reliance on structure, concepts, and words.[34] Against their transcendentalism and what he calls their "mathematical frock coats" ("redingotes mathématiques"), Bataille proposes "interior experience" ("l'expérience intérieure") as bodily, imaginative, and subjective meditation, even as "drunken" and "mystical" ecstasy. Yet while Bataille directed his criticism against Western philosophy, Tschumi translates these concepts to architecture when he asserts that every form of representation, such as "words, plans, or pictures," would already be "outside architecture," "extraterritorial," a "world of death."[35] "Real life" would only be found in subjectivity, sensuality, and spatial experience. Hence against the threat of dematerialization through conceptual architecture, structuralist linguistics, or semiotics, Tschumi suggests an immediate experience bridging between sensuality and reason.[36] To him, the "paradox of architecture" and the silence it entails could be overcome with spatial praxis and subjectivity ("interior experience"). He employs Bataille's example of "eroticism" to ignite a temporary flash between reason and pleasure, a conceptualization of the act and the sensual engagement with the Other.[37] Applied to architecture, eroticism would provide for both system and excess,[38] a singular event where real and ideal space are able to meet momentarily.

With this transfer from literature and philosophy to architecture, Tschumi perverts his reference text of Bataille, which is known to characterize architecture in terms of a prison, an institution, and the representation of the "mathematical frock coats" of form, rationalism, and geometry.[39] While Bataille distrusts architecture as a discipline, he favors "l'informe" of dust, spit, or spider.[40] Yet the coupling of "pleasure" and "excess" in Tschumi's argument is not only informed by Bataille but also by Barthes and his *Le plaisir du texte* from 1973.[41] In this personal and meandering essay, Barthes distinguishes between a text that creates "plaisir" (in the sense of Sigmund Freud) and confirms the reader's subjectivity, and a reading experience that provides "jouissance" (translated as bliss, but can also be understood as orgasm), which challenges the reader's expectations, fragmenting their subjectivity and transgressing the codes of literature and society. His prime example for the latter is the erotic novels of Bataille: "Neither culture nor its destruction is erotic; it is the seam between them, the fault, the flaw, which becomes so.... [W]hat pleasure wants is the site of a loss."[42] Tschumi develops this train of thought in more detail in his essay "The Pleasure of Architecture," published in *Architectural Design* in 1977,[43] the third text of the mid-1970s that directly references Barthes. Yet where Barthes contemplates the resistance of literature to semiology as an infinite chain of metaphors, which would constitute its erotic component, Tschumi is quick to replace literature for architecture as the desired body for the reader/observer, and to frame it as an assemblage of fragments—in a text that was a fragmentary montage in itself.

In 1976, Tschumi published "Architecture and Transgression" in *Oppositions*,[44] an article that is built again around transfers from literature to architecture. The article echoes Bataille's négation when Tschumi claims that architecture would only survive when it negates society's expectation of form and use.[45] He exemplifies this with a retrospective description of a student field trip in 1965 to the shattered ruin of the Villa Savoye in Poissy by Le Corbusier, which he found surprisingly "erotic." Tschumi learned lessons from Bataille on rules and taboo, eroticism and rot, the moments when life meets death, when modernist reason collides with subjective experience of space—at least momentarily—and where architecture demonstrates its essential non-necessity. Tschumi also echoes Barthes's reflections on both the subjective and universal character of the pleasure ("jouissance") of the text.[46] For Barthes, the reader's experiences are highly subjective and particular, yet considered universal—or at least shared—human attitudes.[47]

Finally, in the series of articles "Architecture and Limits I, II, III," published in *Artforum* in 1980 and 1981,[48] Tschumi discusses the discipline not as "knowledge of form," but as "a form of knowledge" ("episteme"),

The recurrent concern of architects from the second half of the twentieth century:
to describe architecture as knowledge, and its domain (rather than as a practice or a profession).
I take up some parallel discussions on architecture as a science or a (humanist) discipline
of form in my own contribution to this volume.

and establishes the small-scale projects ("folies") as an architecture of/at the limit that will later populate his Parc de la Villette design.

By the mid-1970s, in the aftermath of the 1968 revolt, as Louis Martin argues, Tschumi shifted his interests away from an engagement with Marxist and structuralist urban theories, such as those of Henri Lefebvre and Guy Debord, toward the literary theories of Barthes, Foucault, Derrida, and others of the Tel Quel group.[49] Barthes's notion of the endless metaphorical dimension of urban semiology and the continued exploration of this motive in literature, as discussed in *Le plaisir du texte*, informed Tschumi's "Pleasure of Architecture." Similarly, he discovered the writings of Bataille through those of Hollier and Barthes. From literature to architecture, Tschumi directly adapted, applied, and translated oppositions such as pyramid/labyrinth, eroticism/rot, sex/death, and taboo/transgression. His discovery of Bataille led Tschumi to appreciate the ruin and the folly of the English landscape garden as non-functional and non-semiotic architecture. This path opened references to Foucault's discussion of social norms and "folie," or madness,[50] as well as discussions about the limits of the discipline.

INFINITE DEFERRAL, OR DERRIDA ON TSCHUMI: *POINT(S) DE FOLIE—NULLPUNKT DER VERRÜCKTHEIT*

This intertextual process of translation and transposition of literature, philosophy, and linguistics into architecture came full circle in 1986, when Derrida elaborated on Tschumi's winning design of 1982-83 for the Parc de la Villette. The text, whose French title is "Point de folie—Maintenant l'architecture," was written on the occasion of the exhibition on the project that same year at the Architectural Association London (under its chairman Alvin Boyarsky), and published in Tschumi's book, whose title, *La case vide*, literally means "the empty box," a reference to the quantity of zero. While Tschumi had originally in mind a contribution by Jean-François Lyotard, whom he also hoped to involve in the design of the Parc de La Villette, but who declined, he began a dialogue with Derrida rather by accident—or serendipity. The "box" contains Tschumi's introduction, folio prints of drawings and diagrams for the Parc, a text by Anthony Vidler, a conversation with Boyarsky, as well as Derrida's text, both the French original and the English translation by Kate Linker for this bi-lingual publication. A German translation of Derrida's essay by Michael Wetzel appeared in *Wege aus der Moderne* in 1988, edited by Wolfgang Welsch.

Derrida's text is fragmentary and meandering, poetic and playfully engaging, with its infinite chain of metaphors and references. Written by a philosopher on a philosophically informed architectural design that took cues from that very same author, the text is prized today as a key example of "deconstructivist architecture."[51] However, is such a thing possible? Should one not discuss "deconstruction" as an analytical reading strategy for complex textual corpora—and hence using the verb "deconstructing"—rather than as a style in architecture, especially since its questions are directed against subject, form, hierarchy, structure, and institution? Derrida's text is beyond comprehension, since its point to point structure echoes Tschumi's design for the La Villette—open ended and meant to remain open, side-stepping any attempt of hermeneutic finality. Nevertheless, without claiming to summarize or analyze it fully, I would like to provide a few "points" for this argument on architectural writing.

Derrida introduces the notion of "spatial writing" ("écriture de l'espace")[52] in Point 3 together with the notion of the event ("évènement") which he characterizes not only as an architecture that makes room for the event, but an architecture *of* the event. He emphasizes the now ("maintenant") of the speech act, or rather, a form of writing as immediate as speech. This dimension of the event would enter directly the architectural apparatus ("dispositif"), and hence dislocate architecture from its metaphysical social function as ground, foundation, and inhabitation for the *socius*.

In Point 9, Derrida explicitly employs the term "degree zero"—and hence references Barthes—when he describes the "architectural writing" of Tschumi, although in form of a rejection: Derrida claims that Tschumi's dislocation and destabilization of "architecture" as a discipline and of "the architectonic" in Western thought could be seen not as—or not only as—destructive and negative, but rather affirmative, constructive, and operative (for lack of a better word for "oeuvre"), or as one would say today, "projective":

> "*Maintenant* we will take the measure of the *folies*, of what others would call the immeasurable *hybris* of Bernard Tschumi and of what it offers to our thought. These *folies* destabilise meaning, the meaning of meaning, the signifying ensemble of this powerful architectonics. They put in question, dislocate, destabilise or deconstruct the edifice of this configuration. It will be said that they are 'madness' in this. For in a *polemos* which is without aggression, without the destructive drive that would still betray a reactive affect within the hierarchy, they do battle with the very meaning of architectural meaning, as it has been bequeathed to us and as we still inhabit it. We should not avoid the issue: if this configuration presides over what in the West is called architecture, do these *folies* not raze it to the ground? Do they not lead back to the desert of **anarchitecture, a zero degree of architectural writing** where

this writing would lose itself, henceforth without finality, aesthetic aura, fundamentals, hierarchical principles or symbolic signification, in short, in a prose made of abstract, neutral, inhuman, useless, uninhabitable and meaningless volumes?
Precisely not. The *folies* affirm, and engage their affirmation beyond this ultimately annihilating, secretly nihilistic repetition of metaphysical architecture."[53]

Here, Derrida describes an architecture of "degree zero" not only as a state of cold, neutral, generic, or minimalist presence

I cannot but wonder what must have gone through Derrida's mind at this point, when he was simultaneously engaged in a collaboration with Peter Eisenman for a garden in Tschumi's La Villette, and while it was never built, it became the book *Chora L Works*.[54] I read many of his comments as references to Eisenman's own "degree zero" of architecture.

(with neither historical "rhetoric" nor "style" in the sense of postmodernism à la Jencks), but rather as "anarchitecture." The term combines anarchy and architecture, it negates architecture through the *alpha privative*, and finally it refers to the group of artists around Laurie Anderson and Gordon Matta Clark in New York City in the early 1970s.[55] On another level, Derrida repeatedly references Martin Heidegger's phenomenological *Bauen, Wohnen, Denken* of 1951 and playfully undermines his naturalization of the built environment as/for human inhabitation and the building as thing gathering the metaphysical fourfold.[56] Unlike the inhuman and uninhabitable, the *folies*—and therefore metonymically the design of the entire Parc de la Villette—would propose another architecture of the event. Derrida develops this form of architectural writing/weaving of the event in relation to performative speech, to a promise, and to a social contract—as something that is non-permanent, transient, and transgressive, and connecting high and low, concept and space, rationality and sensuality, even if only momentarily, as Tschumi claimed in his theoretical essays. Derrida echoes in the same Point 9 the architect's critique of autonomous architecture as formalism (and re-semantization), whereas he gives Tschumi's *folies* the benefit of supposedly "crossing" architectural writing with what is "most singular" in other texts (photographic, cinematographic, choreographic) through narrative montage (again with reference to the film theory of Sergei Eisenstein and to Tschumi's translation into *Manhattan Transcripts*). As Derrida goes on to suggest, this "crossing" leads to an interwoven, intertextual "transarchitecture."

When one reads the French, English, and German texts in parallel, there is a significant mistranslation of "point de folie" in the German version as "Nullpunkt der Verrücktheit." This phrase seems much closer to the German translation of Barthes's *Le degré zéro de l'écriture* as *Am Nullpunkt der Literatur* (1982). Hence the German interpretation of Derrida's text on Tschumi suggests a reference to Barthes's degree zero, much more than the French original title and its official English translation, where "point de folie" remains without translation. And the German version shows two more counts of Barthes's term "Nullpunkt" in Derrida's text: in Point 13, with regard to the paradoxical character of the *folies* that dislocate and assemble or gather,[57] as well as in Point 15 with regard to the "double bind" of each point/*folie* to both repeat within the external grid *and* be differentiated within the internal organization of the cube (Fig. 5).[58]

However, since both the French original ("point de folie rassemble ce qu'il vient juste disperser") and its English translation ("the point of folie [French: point de folie = no folie] gathers together what it just has dispersed") do not directly refer to Barthes, this innuendo must have been added by the German interpreter,

tikalität, weder der Natur noch der Kultur, weder der Form noch des Grundes, noch des Zwecks. Der Architekt schrieb mit Steinen, das war es, was er an Lithographien in ein Raumbuch [volume] einrückte – und Tschumi spricht von ihnen als *Folianten*. Ein Raster entsteht [se trame] bei dieser Paginierung [foliotage], dessen Stratagem – aber auch Würfelwurf – mich an einen Verdacht des Littré erinnert: Was den zweiten Wortsinn von *folie* angeht, den von Häusern, die den Namen ihres Unterzeichners tragen, „desjenigen, der sie hat bauen lassen, oder des Ortes, in dem sie gelegen sind", wagt der Littré folgendes im Namen der Etymologie: „Man sieht dort für gewöhnlich das Wort *folie*. Aber das wird zweifelhaft, wenn man in den Texten des Mittelalters findet: *foleia quae erat ante domum* und *domum foleyae* und *folia Johannis Morelli*. Der Verdacht wird erweckt, daß dort eine Abwandlung des Wortes *feuillie* [belaubt] oder *feuillée* [Laubwerk] vorliegt." Das Wort *folie* hat nicht einmal mehr den Gemeinsinn, es verliert selbst noch die versichernde Einheit seines Sinns. Die Verrücktheiten [folies] von Tschumi spielen zweifellos auch mit dieser „Abwandlung" und überdrucken, gegen den Gemeinsinn, mit diesem anderen Sinn, diesem Sinn des anderen, der anderen Sprache, die Verrücktheit dieser Asemantik.

12. Als ich das Werk Bernard Tschumis entdeckte, habe ich eine leichtfertige Hypothese abwenden müssen: daß der Rekurs auf die Sprache der Dekonstruktion, auf das, was sich in ihm kodieren konnte, auf ihre am meisten insistierenden Worte und Motive, auf bestimmte Strategien von ihr, nur eine *analoge* Übertragung, ja sogar eine *Applikation* der Architektur sei. In allen Fällen gerade das Unmögliche! Denn der Logik dieser Hypothese zufolge, die nicht lange Widerstand leistete, hätte man sich fragen müssen: Was könnte wohl eine dekonstruktive Architektur sein? Ist das, was die dekonstruktiven Strategien zu destabilisieren beginnen oder aufhören, nicht gerade das strukturale Prinzip der Architektur (System, Architektonik, Struktur, Fundierung, Konstruktion etc.)? Diese letzte Frage hat mich dagegen zu einer anderen Wendung der Interpretation geführt: Diejenige, zu der uns die *Manhattan Transcripts* oder die *Folies* von La Villette verpflichten, ist der *obligatorische Weg* einer Dekonstruktion in einer seiner intensivsten, affirmativsten und notwendigsten *Bewerkstelligungen*. Nicht *die* Dekonstruktion *selbst*, es gibt niemals dergleichen, sondern dasjenige, was den Anstoß über die semantische Analyse, die Kritik dieses Diskurses oder der Ideologien, der Begriffe oder der Texte, im traditionellen Sinne des Ausdrucks, hinausträgt. Die Dekonstruktionen wären schwach, wenn sie negativ wären, wenn sie nicht konstruieren würden, vor allem aber wenn sie sich nicht zunächst mit den Institutionen darin messen würden, was sie an Solidität *anstelle ihres größten Widerstandes* haben: den politischen Strukturen, den ökonomischen Entscheidungshebeln, den materiellen und phantasmatischen Dispositiven der Verkoppelung zwischen Staat, bürgerlicher Gesellschaft, Kapital, Bürokratie, kulturellen Kräften und der Lehre der Architek-

Fig. 5 Jacques Derrida, "Am Nullpunkt der Verrücktheit – Jetzt die Architektur," in Wolfgang Welsch, ed., *Wege aus der Moderne. Schlüsseltexte der Postmoderne-Diskussion* (Weinheim: VCH, 1988), 227.

tur – diesem so sensiblen Relais –, aber auch zwischen den Künsten, von den schönen Künsten zu den Kriegskünsten, der Wissenschaft und der Technologie, der alten und der neuen. Es gibt so viele Kräfte, die in einer Operation von der Spannweite der Architektur voranstürzen, erhärten oder zementieren, vor allem wenn diese Operation den Körper einer Metropole näherbringt und mit dem Staat verhandelt. Das ist hier der Fall.

13. Man erklärt nicht den Krieg. Zwischen Feindseligkeiten und Verhandlung entsteht das Raster [se trame] einer anderen Strategie. In seinem allerstriktesten, wenn nicht buchstäblichsten Sinn verstanden, führt das Raster [trame] der Verrücktheiten ein singuläres Dispositiv in den Raum der Transaktion ein. Der eigentliche Sinn von „Raster" wird nicht versammelt. Er durchquert. Ein Raster einschießen heißt durchqueren, durch Ritzen hindurchdringen. Es ist die Erfahrung einer Permeabilität. Und die Durchquerung erfolgt nicht durch ein schon gegebenes Gewebe, sie webt, sie erfindet die Gewebestruktur eines Textes, wie man im Englischen sagt von etwas „fabric". Fabrique, so sei am Rande vermerkt, das ist der französische Name – mit einem ganz anderen Sinn –, den einige Entschlossene an die Stelle des beunruhigenden Titels *folies* zu setzen vorgeschlagen hatten.

Der webende Architekt. Er erstellt ein Raster, und er verflicht die Fäden der Kette, seine Schrift stellt ein Netz auf. Immer noch ein Raster, Raster in mehreren Sinnen und jenseits des Sinns. Ein Netz-Stratagem, folglich ein singuläres Dispositiv. Welches?

Eine aufgelöste Serie von „Punkten", von roten Punkten, bildet das Raster, in dem sie eine Vielheit von Matrizes oder Erzeugungszellen verräumlicht, deren Transformationen sich nie in einem Kontinuum zufriedenstellen, stabilisieren, installieren, identifizieren lassen. Als selbst teilbare punktieren diese Zellen auch die Bruch-, Diskontinuitäts- und Disjunktionsmomente. Aber gleichzeitig, oder vielmehr durch eine Serie von Unzeiten [contretemps], von rhythmisierten Anachronien oder aphoristischen Abschweifungen, versammelt der Nullpunkt der Verrücktheit das, was er just gerade zerstreut hat, versammelt er es *als* Zerstreuung. Er versammelt es in einer Vielheit von *roten* Punkten. Ähnlichkeit [ressemblance] und Versammlung [rassemblement] laufen nicht auf dieselbe Farbe hinaus, aber die *chromographische* Erinnerung spielt dabei eine notwendige Rolle.

Was ist folglich ein Punkt, *dieser* Nullpunkt der Verrücktheit? Wie stoppt er die Verrücktheit? Denn er hebt sie auf und stoppt sie in dieser Bewegung, aber *als* Verrücktheit. Haltepunkt [arrêt] der Verrücktheit: überhaupt keine Verrücktheit, keine Verrücktheit mehr, keine Verrücktheit. Auf einen Schlag entscheidet er darüber, aber durch welches Dekret, welchen Entscheid – und welche Gerechtigkeit des Aphorismus? Was macht das Recht? Wer macht das Recht? Es teilt *und* stoppt die Teilung, es *hält* diesen Punkt der Verrücktheit *aufrecht*, diese Chromosomen-

Michael Wetzel.[59] Hence, if one considers the additional "reference" to Barthes as accidental—or rather, as a translational error made by matching "point" with "Nullpunkt"—the historic aspect of this discussion must be regarded as unstable, if not questionable. Nevertheless, the translations appear to exemplify Derrida's idea that there is no conclusive end to reading and final interpretation, but rather a continued unstable process of new (and sometimes unintended) meanings and possible readings. And in the same course of thought, is this mistranslation truthful in any way to Derrida's own playful interpretation of Tschumi's project of *La Villette*, in which infinite metaphors and references are latent and multiple meanings come to the fore as if the process of reading remains unfinished, held open, and set aside?

CODA: AFTER (FRENCH) THEORY?

What (if anything) is to be learned from this translational process—linguistics to philosophy to architectural theory to design and back to theoretic interpretation by a philosopher? From an architecturally informed philosopher writing about a philosophically informed architect? (Mis)translations from French to English and French to German and back? Should one unmask them as "language games," as Tafuri has it with regard to linguistically informed architecture of the early postmodern moment?[60] Or should one playfully enjoy the excess of thinking, meaning, interpretations, and their paradoxical relation and succumb to the pleasure (or *jouissance*) of the interwoven text, which takes architecture to its limit condition necessary for it to overcome itself, as Tschumi would probably argue with Barthes? How does one today—in a time when many people search for simple answers to complex problems, in architecture as in other areas, and when architectural criticism is reduced to promotion through social media and public relations—look back toward a poetics of nonunderstanding (or misunderstanding) characterized by maintaining paradoxical terms in tension (from Nietzsche through Bataille to Barthes to Derrida)—even if only momentarily? In retrospect, the design for the Parc de la Villette did deliver less on its promise of an "architecture to come,"[61] but it can be interpreted historically as an end point of a specific form of postmodern academic culture, where a cult of "difficult" concepts, often half-understood and metaphorically applied in design, formed the academic capital for those who claimed it. Derrida attempted to deconstruct an Architecture (with capital A) that celebrated the humanist scholar as imagined by Leon Battista Alberti—and that has haunted the discipline since the Italian Renaissance—by criticizing its conservative social function (permanence), its servile nature (function), and its imagined second nature (inhabitation), and decried it as the "last fortress of metaphysics."[62] Instead, he offered a pledge for a different way of making architecture and another persona of the architect.[63] Despite these well-meant intentions, it seems that Derrida contributed to one of its most spectacular and late reiterations: form follows French theory.

1 Jacques Derrida, "Point de folie—Maintenant l'architecture," in Bernard Tschumi, *La case vide: La Villette 1985* (London: AA, 1986), 4–19.

2 Ibid., 19.

3 Lyna Bourouiba and Wouter Van Acker, eds., *Degree Zero*, from the call for papers: "The Zero Degree of Architectural Writing. Theorizing, Drawing, and Debating the 'Third Term,'", https://zerodegreesymposium.wordpress.com/.

4 Jacques Derrida, *Of Grammatology*, trans. Gayatri Chakravorty Spivak (Baltimore: Johns Hopkins University Press, 1976).

5 Bourouiba and Van Acker, eds., *Degree Zero*, 3.

6 Ryan Bishop and Sunil Manghani, eds., *Seeing Degree Zero: Barthes/Burgin and Political Aesthetics* (Edinburgh: Edinburgh University Press, 2019).

7 Roland Barthes, *Le degré zéro de l'écriture* (Paris: Seuil, 1953); Roland Barthes, *Writing Degree Zero*, trans. Anette Lavers and Colin Smith (Boston: Beacon Press, 1970), 1.

8 Barthes, *Writing Degree Zero*, 5.

9 Ibid., 5; in French: Barthes, *Le degré zéro de l'écriture*, 12–13. "Degré zero de l'écriture" is translated into German as "Schreibweise im Nullzustand," in Roland Barthes, *Am Nullpunkt der Literatur* (Frankfurt am Main: Suhrkamp, 1982), 11.

10 Barthes, *Writing Degree Zero*, 5–6.

11 Ibid., 28.

12 Ibid., 67: "Neutral writing is a late phenomenon to be invented only much later than Realism by authors like Camus, less under the impulse of an aesthetics of escape than in search of a mode of writing which might at last achieve innocence." "Neutral writing" is translated into German as "die neutrale Schreibweise," in Barthes, *Am Nullpunkt der Literatur*, 78.

13 Barthes, *Writing Degree Zero*, 48: "It [the word] therefore achieves a state which is possible only in the dictionary or in poetry—places where the noun can live without its article—and is reduced to a sort of zero degree, pregnant with all past and future specifications. The word here has a generic form; it is a category." "Generic form" is translated into German as "eine Art Nullzustand," in Barthes, *Am Nullpunkt der Literatur*, 58.

14 Barthes, *Writing Degree Zero*, 76–78; in French: Barthes, *Le degré zéro de l'écriture*, 108–111.

15 Barthes, *Writing Degree Zero*, 87: "Writing therefore is a blind alley, and it is because society itself is a blind alley. The writers of today feel this; for them, the search for a non-style or an oral style, for a zero level or a spoken level of writing is, all things considered, the anticipation of a homogeneous social state; most of them understand that there can be no universal language outside a concrete, and no longer a mystical or merely nominal, universality of society."

16 Ibid., 78.

17 Roland Barthes, "Éléments de sémiologie," in "Recherches sémiologiques," special issue, *Communications*, no. 4 (1964): 91–135; Roland Barthes, *Elements of Semiology*, trans. Annette Lavers and Colin Smith (New York: Hill and Wang, 1968).

18 Barthes, *Elements of Semiology*, 77–78: "The second problem arising in connection with privative opposition is that of the unmarked term. It is called the *zero degree* of the opposition. The zero degree is therefore not a total absence (this is a common mistake), *it is a significant absence*. We have here a pure differential state; the zero degree testifies to the power held by any system of signs, of creating meaning 'out of nothing': 'the language can be content with an opposition of something and nothing.' The concept of the zero degree, which sprang from phonology, lends itself to a great many applications: in semantics, in which *zero signs* are known ('a "zero sign" is spoken of in cases where the absence of any explicit signifier functions by itself as a signifier'); in logic ('A is in the zero state, that is to say that A does not actually exist, but under certain conditions it can be made to appear'); in ethnology, where Levi-Strauss could compare the notion of mana to it ('... the proper function of the zero phoneme is to be opposed to the absence of the phoneme

... Similarly, it could be said ... that the function of notions of the "mana" type is to be opposed to the absence of signification without involving in itself any particular signification'); finally, in rhetoric, where, carried on to the connotative plane, the absence of rhetorical signifiers constitutes in its turn a stylistic signifier."

19 Bernard Tschumi and Fernando Montes, "Do-It-YourselfCity," *L'architecture d'aujourd'hui*, 148 (February- March 1970): 98-105; cf. Louis Martin, "Transpositions: On the Intellectual Origins of Tschumi's Architectural Theory," *Assemblage*, no. 11 (April 1990): 22-35.

20 Bernard Tschumi, "The Environmental Trigger," in *A Continuing Experiment: Learning and Teaching at the Architectural Association*, ed. James Gowan (London: Architectural Association, Diploma School, 1975); cf. Bernard Tschumi's "Introduction" in his book *Architecture and Disjunction* (Cambridge, Mass: MIT Press, 1994), 2-23, here: 10.

21 Bernard Tschumi, "Le jardin de Don Juan ou la ville masquée," *L'architecture d'aujourd'hui* 187 (October- November 1976): 82-83; Tschumi, *Architecture and Disjunction*, 17; cf. Claire Jamieson and Rebecca Roberts Hughes, "Two Modes of a Literary Architecture: Bernard Tschumi and Nigel Coates," *Architectural Research Quarterly* 19, no. 2 (2015): 110-122.

22 Manfredo Tafuri, *Teorie e storia dell'architettura* (Bari: Laterza, 1968); in English: "Operative Criticism," chapter 4 in Manfredo Tafuri, *Theories and History of Architecture* (London: Granada, 1980), 141-170; see also Barthes's sarcasm against the "well-behaved writing of revolutionaries" of realism, naturalism and the socialist realism of his times, in Barthes, *Writing Degree Zero*, 73.

23 Bernard Tschumi, "Questions of Space: The Pyramid and the Labyrinth (or the Architectural Paradox)," in *Studio International* 190 (September-October 1975): 137-142.

24 Ibid., 137.

25 Bernard Tschumi, "Architecture and Transgression," in *Oppositions* 7 (Winter 1976): 58; cf. Bernard Tschumi, "Review of Henri Lefebvre's 'Le droit a la ville,'" *Architectural Design* 42, no. 9 (September 1972): 581-582.

26 Tschumi, "Architecture and Transgression," 58; note how the wording echoes Barthes's description of contemporary literature in *Writing Degree Zero*.

27 Tschumi, "Questions of Space," 139, reference to Manfredo Tafuri, "L'architecture dans le Boudoir: The Language of Criticism and the Criticism of Language," *Oppositions* 3 (May 1974): 38-62.

28 Peter Eisenman. *Houses of Cards* (New York: Oxford University Press, 1987).

29 Tschumi, "Questions of Space," 142.

30 Tschumi, "Architecture and Transgression," 58.

31 Tschumi, "Questions of Space," 140, here a reference to Denis Hollier, *La Prise de la Concorde: Essais sur Georges Bataille* (Paris: Gallimard 1974).

32 Ibid., 140.

33 George Bataille quoted in Denis Hollier, *Against Architecture: The Writings of Georges Bataille* (Cambridge, MA: MIT Press, 1989), 57, original French: George Bataille, *La Prise de la Concorde: Essais sur Georges Bataille* (Paris: Gallimard 1974).

34 Hollier, *Against Architecture*, 72: Hollier confirms that for Bataille the labyrinth is also language; since words are only relational, they render individual experiences as something mediated, not immediate.

35 Tschumi, "Architecture and Transgression," 57.

36 Tschumi, "Questions of Space," 142.

37 Georges Bataille, *L'Érotisme* (Paris: Éditions de Minuit, 1957); Georges Bataille, *Erotism: Death and Sensuality*, trans. Mary Dalwood (San Francisco: City Lights Books, 1986); cf. Renata Hejduk, "Death Becomes Her: Transgression, Decay, and eROTicism in Bernard Tschumi's Early Writings and Projects," *The Journal of Architecture* 12, no. 4 (2007): 393-404.

38 Tschumi, "Questions of Space," 142; Tschumi, "Architecture and Transgression," 59: "Sensuality is as different from eroticism as a simple spatial

perception is different from architecture. 'Eroticism is not the excess of pleasure, but the pleasure of excess': ... the 'pleasure of excess' requires consciousness as well as voluptuousness. Just as eroticism means double pleasure that involves both mental constructs and sensuality."

39 Martin, "Transpositions," 28.

40 Georges Bataille, "Informe" ("Formless"), *Documents* 7 (December 1929): 382; cf. Yve-Alain Bois and Rosalind Krauss, *L'informe: Mode d'emploi* (Paris: Centre Georges Pompidou, 1996); in English: Georges Bataille, *Formless: A User's Guide* (New York: Zone Books, 1997).

41 Roland Barthes, *Le plaisir du texte* (Paris: Édition de Seuil, 1973); in English: Roland Barthes, *The Pleasure of the Text* (New York: Hill and Wang, 1975).

42 Barthes, *The Pleasure of the Text*, 7; Barthes continues to differentiate on p. 14: "The text of pleasure [plaisir]: the text that contents, fills, grants euphoria; the text that comes from culture and does not break with it, is linked to a *comfortable* practice of reading. The text of bliss [*jouissance*]: the text that imposes a state of loss, the text that discomforts (perhaps to the point of a certain boredom), unsettles the reader's historical, cultural, psychological assumptions, the consistency of his tastes, values, memories, brings to a crisis his relation with language."

43 Bernard Tschumi, "The Pleasure of Architecture," *Architectural Design (AD)* 47, no. 3 (March 1977): 214–218.

44 Bernard Tschumi, "Architecture and Transgression," *Oppositions* 7 (Winter 1976): 55–63.

45 Ibid., 61; see also "Advertisement for Architecture" that accompanies this essay on p. 56.

46 Ibid., 59; Barthes, *The Pleasure of the Text*, 62.

47 Tschumi, "Architecture and Transgression," 60.

48 Bernard Tschumi, "Architecture and Limits," *Artforum* 19, no. 4 (December 1980): 36; Bernard Tschumi, "Architecture and Limits II," *Artforum* 19, no. 7 (March 1981): 45; Bernard Tschumi, "Architecture and Limits III," *Artforum* 20, no. 1 (September 1981): 40.

49 Martin, "Transpositions," 22–35; see also Hejduk, "Death Becomes Her," 393–404.

50 Michel Foucault, *Folie et déraison: Histoire de la folie à l'âge Classique* (Paris: Librairie Plon, 1961); in English: Michel Foucault, *Madness and Civilization: A History of Insanity in the Age of Reason* (New York: Random House, 1965).

51 Philip Johnson and Mark Wigley, eds., *Deconstructivist Architecture* (New York City: The Museum of Modern Art, 1988); on the problem of the curated term "deconstructivism" and the misleading labeling of a heterogenous group of then emerging academic architects under a constructed philosophical umbrella term, see Joan Ockman, "Talking with Bernard Tschumi," *Log*, nos. 13–14 (Fall 2008): 166; for a critical assessment, see, for example, the introduction by C. Greig Crysler, Stephen Cairns, and Hilde Heynen, "Introduction—1: Architectural Theory in an Expanded Field: Revisiting Parc de la Villette," in their edited volume *The Sage Handbook of Architectural Theory* (London: Sage, 2012), 1–4.

52 Derrida, "Point de folie," 4.

53 Ibid., 11 (emphasis in bold by the author; italics in original); cf. in French: "un degré zéro de l'écriture architecturale," 10; in German: "Nullpunkt der zur Architektur gehörenden Schrift," Jacques Derrida, "Am Nullpunkt der Verrücktheit - Jetzt die Architektur," in Wolfgang Welsch, ed., *Wege aus der Moderne: Schlüsseltexte der Postmoderne-Diskussion* (Weinheim: VCH, 1988; Berlin: Akademie Verlag, 1994), 221. Citations refer to the Akademie Verlag edition.

54 Jacques Derrida, Peter Eisenman, Jeffrey Kipnis, and Thomas Leeser, *Chora L Works* (New York: Monacelli, 1996).

55 Cf. the database of the Spatial Agency website: https: //www.spatialagency.net/database/the.anarchitecture.group (last accessed April 10, 2024).

56 Derrida, "Point de folie," 9; cf. in French: 8; cf. Martin Heidegger, "Bauen, Wohnen, Denken," lecture held at the 2nd Darmstädter Gespräch 1951, published

in Otto Bartning, ed., *Mensch und Raum: Das Darmstädter Gespräch 1951* (Darmstadt: Neuen Darmstädter Verlagsanstalt, 1952); in English: Martin Heidegger, "Building Dwelling Thinking," in Martin Heidegger, *Poetry, Language, Thought*, trans. Albert Hofstadter (New York: Harper & Row, 1975), 145–161.

57 Derrida "Am Nullpunkt der Verrücktheit," 227.

58 Ibid., 229; cf. Derrida, "Point de folie," 16 and 17: "Die Vielheit öffnet nicht jeden Punkt *von außen her.* Um zu verstehen, inwiefern sie zu ihm auch von innen her kommt, muß man das *double bind* analysieren, dessen Nullpunkt der Verrückheit den Knoten zuschnürt, ohne das zu vergessen, was ein *double bind* mit der Spaltung [schize] und der Verrücktheit verbinden kann" (emphasis in original).

59 Derrida, "Point de folie," 14 and 15.

60 Tafuri, "L'architecture dans le Boudoir," 53.

61 Derrida, "Point de folie," 18 and 19.

62 Ibid., 9.

63 Ibid., 19.

Expressionist Zeroing. Anachronism in Bruno Zevi's Paradigmatic Counter-Histories

Wouter Van Acker

comments by
Irina Davidovici

In the second half of the twentieth century, Bruno Zevi's long-standing preoccupation with expressionist architecture occupied an increasingly untimely position in architectural criticism. While his fascination with expressionist architecture began early in his career, it was only in the 1970s that Zevi adopted the idea of "degree zero" as a trope through which he demonstrated the recurrence of an expressionist lineage within architectural history.[1] "Expressionist zeroing," he said, had developed in the work of architects like Erich Mendelsohn and Antoni Gaudí in the first decades of the twentieth century in parallel with rationalism, and was followed by a plethora of expressionist revivals in the "postrationalist organic era."[2]

ID Without having read Zevi's build-up to it, this pairing sounds to me like a contradiction. I tend to associate the degree zero with muted, neutral reactions, with the deliberate retreat from expressing anything. Therefore, I see expression as having an inherent added value, and expressionism as having an inherent stylistic quotient. A personal expression, even when meant as a guttural, unarticulated expression of one's id, is still an expression of a personal style, even if this is unfettered, unfiltered, or anti-canonical.

The spatial concept of expressionism had a direct operative relevance too: expressionism could be mobilized as a keystone by which to revisit the past and envision the future. From this counter-historical perspective, Zevi treated various cases as evidence of a continuity of an expressionist mindset from pre-history to modernism and beyond. To examine the persistence of his advocacy for expressionist architecture, and why Zevi equated Roland Barthes's idea of the "degree zero" with the expressionist conception of architectural space, we will make some time jumps to several of his conference papers and articles.

REBIRTH IN THE YEAR ZERO

At the conference he convened in Modena in 1997, three years before his death, Zevi gathered colleagues, architects, and students one last time to celebrate the essence of his thought and pass the torch to them. Nearly eighty years old when he opened the conference with his talk on "Landscape and the Zero Degree of Architectural Language," Zevi proudly declared that architecture had won a long battle, finally realizing Frank Lloyd Wright's 1924 vision, as expressed by Mendelsohn, for an architecture "without prescriptive models, movement in three and four dimensions . . . a joie de vivre expressed by space."[3] After the degree zero eras of caves, Roman catacombs, and the High Middle Ages, a modern era of degree zero of architectural writing had dawned.

The idea of a zero degree in architecture refers to the will to be free from conventions, norms, and the canon, an attitude which, in Zevi's interpretation, lay at the heart of modernism, and which was incorporated in prehistorical architecture and reincarnated in more recent developments. Among these more contemporary instantiations, he hailed the triumph of deconstructivism over postmodernism, and exemplified this victory with Daniel Libeskind's Jewish Museum and Frank Gehry's Vitra Museum. For Zevi, this triumph marked the rebirth of an expressionist lineage stretching from Gaudí to Reima Pietilä and from the Jørn Utzon to Bruce Goff. In the publication of this Modena lecture, Zevi gathered a pinboard of examples to illustrate this argument.

Among the other lectures in Modena, Dennis Sharp and Peter Blundell Jones most clearly backed Zevi's heroic view of the recurrency and longevity of expressionism. The friendship between these men went back some time. Zevi and Sharp were long-time allies in the International Committee of Architectural Critics, or CICA, founded in 1978, over which Zevi presided. Sharp was one of its co-directors.[4] Blundell Jones became a member of CICA in 1987, after Zevi had awarded him the CICA prize "best periodical of the last three years" for his "Organic" Issue of *The*

Architectural Review.[5] Their lectures in Modena thus extended and represented a similar conception of modernist space that found much sympathy within CICA.

The plea for expressionism's continued relevance played out in Sharp's lecture at Modena, "Linking Expressionism, Urban Planning and Landscape Design," through an exploration of the work of Arthur Korn, who had worked at Erich Mendelsohn's office and had been Sharp's tutor at the Architectural Association. Sharp's lecture referred to the renewed interest in landscape, organic forms, and the ecological debate, treating "Nature" as "the book of books."[6] Blundell Jones, for his part, dealt with the work of Hugo Häring. He cautioned the conference attendees against any unwitting replication of organicist models, providing examples, such as the work of Häring, drawn from what Reyner Banham called the "silent zone"—a group of projects outside the mainstream canon of modern architecture.[7] In their lectures, both Sharp and Blundell Jones paid tribute to Zevi's foresight in *Toward an Organic Architecture* (1945), where he championed the architecture of Frank Lloyd Wright and expressionism at a time when Corbusian revivalism colored the postwar architectural landscape.

The Modena message was also promulgated by Zevi in the press, where he professed that the "expressionism of American deconstructivism" had illuminated the path toward the architecture and city of "the year zero."[8] Swept along by a sense of millenarianism, the year 2000 was prophesized as a pivotal moment—a point in time around which architectural regression and progression would swirl, a point of reference for what would soon become the past or else serve as a launchpad for architecture to project itself into the future.

Because it occurred so late in Zevi's career, the Modena conference provides a fitting entry point for unpacking his strained efforts to synchronize his understanding of expressionism with prevailing trends. But to come to grips with Zevi's expressionist conception of architectural space, and the meaning of the phrase "expressionist zeroing," we need to move back in time to conference papers he wrote earlier.

REORIENTING MODERNISM'S HISTORY

Since the beginning of his career, Zevi had insisted on the necessity of a "cultural revision" of the place given to expressionism in the modernist legacy. In his 1949 lecture at the CIAM Congress in Bergamo, he had forcefully challenged the historical outlook presented in the programmatic book by Siegfried Giedion, *Space, Time and Architecture*, of 1941—a work to which CIAM, as Zevi reminded its members, was institutionally bound.[9] While acknowledging Giedion's influence on his own thinking—Giedion as secretary-general of CIAM was present in the audience—Zevi asserted that in *Toward an Organic Architecture*, all he "did was translate" Giedion's book, but "with one modification: I transposed the chapter on F. Ll. Wright so that it followed the one on Le Corbusier."[10] In Giedion's biological outlook on the modern movement—organized, according to Zevi, in three stages, infancy, maturity, and decadence—Le Corbusier's Villa Savoye and the Bauhaus were placed at the apex of perfection. This orientation revealed critical omissions in the lineup of precedents of the modern movement, Zevi said, in particular Giedion's dismissal of expressionism as a "transitory phenomenon and not a constituent element of modern architecture." For example, he said, Giedion did not mention Erich Mendelsohn "once" in the book's 601 pages.[11] This neglect, Zevi argued, extended to CIAM itself, which inadequately represented the New Empiricism movement and overlooked the young postwar generation of architects who adhered to the Wright school and revered the work of Alvar Aalto.[12]

The historiographic revision that Zevi continued to call for was carried out in the '60s and '70s with the publication of such books as Ulrich Conrads and Hans Sperlich's *Fantastic Architecture* (1960), Sharp's *Modern Architecture and Expressionism* (1966), Franco Borsi and Giovanni König's *Architecture of Expressionism* (1967), and Wolfgang Pehnt's *Expressionist Architecture* (1973).[13] In his own writings, Zevi did not shy away from referencing his own publications as essential to this list, such as his publication of the drawings and sketches of such masters of Italian neo-expressionism as Giovanni Michelucci, and more importantly his publication of the sketches of Erich Mendelsohn. Through his friendship with Mendelsohn's wife, Luise Mendelsohn, Zevi collected and republished Mendelsohn's sketches, first in the journal *L'architettura* in 1963 and then in *Erich Mendelsohn: Opera Completa of 1970*, which formed a valuable reference work for many Mendelsohn scholars.[14] All these publications strengthened a body of literature which corrected expressionism's place in and against the established canon.

The revisions to architectural historiography, particularly to expressionism, continued in several symposia, covering expressionism's early death as an avant-garde movement, its oblivion, and its resurrection under the banner of neo-expressionism in that same period. During the 1962 symposium "Architecture 1918–1928: From the *Novembergruppe* to the CIAM (Functionalism and Expressionism)," organized by the Avery Architectural Library and Columbia University, the issue surfaced in different lectures.[15] Its speakers were divided on the question of whether there was a revival of 1920s expressionism in the 1950s; George Collins and Henry-Russell Hitchcock weighed in on opposite sides, Collins finding resemblances while Hitchcock did not believe in a resurrection nor in the fact that expressionism had ever been dead. A similar division arose at the 1964 conference on expressionism at the Palazzo Vecchio in Florence.[16] Oswald Mathias Ungers thought expressionism belonged to World War I and quickly disappeared after the war. John Summerson attacked the very foundation of the term, saying that expressionism was an artistic label that could well be eliminated in favour of a specific analysis of the masterworks of that period. Zevi, on the other hand, defended expressionism as a continuous force rebelling against the academy.

RE-EVALUATING THE TEMPORALITY OF AN UNTIMELY AVANT-GARDE

The 1980 symposium "Architectural Expressionism: A Re-evaluation" at the AA School, organized by Sharp, carried the momentum and brought together a significant group of historians, including Collins, Wolfgang Pehnt, Julius Posener, Tim Benton, and Paul Oliver.[17] Their task was to address the unresolved question of expressionism's temporality and to re-evaluate expressionism as both a historical phenomenon and a present-day interpretation. At the symposium, Zevi contributed a talk on Mendelsohn and expressionism, in which he connected Einstein's scientific concept of space-time to a morpho- and anti-static understanding of matter as energy. This topic aligned with the international competition "Spazio-tempo einsteiniano e processo architettonico," which the Faculty of Architecture at the University of Rome had organized the previous year. The competition sought new expressions of Einstein's theories of relativity and the spatial field as recorded by "the Rationalist, Expressionist and Futurist movements."[18] The jury, presided over by Zevi during his last year as professor at the University of Rome, awarded the first prize in the architect category equally to Pietilä and Luigi Pellegrin (Fig.1).[19]

Using these different revisions in his talk in London in 1980, Zevi provoked the audience through an approach that he would later call "counter-history," or *controstoria*.[20] Just as Michelangelo's drawings or Utzon's Opera House could be mobilized to clarify Mendelsohn's work, so could expressionism function as a pivot when re-reading the major works of the past and projecting such a reading back to the future. This counter-history allows for an anachronistic reading of recurrent manifestations of expressionism, from the Roman catacombs to Louis Kahn. The purpose of this "critical-operative" method, in Zevi's words, is "involving, updating, and reproposing the past as an irreplaceable moment to understand the contemporary period, in seeing it not passively, as a given to be subjected, but as a choice to be accepted or rejected, recovering it in a modern key or condemning it."[21]

By contrast, at the same symposium, the German architectural historian Rosemarie Haag Bletter presented a critical assessment of the historiographic revision of the preceding decades.[22] If Giedion had done an injustice in his coverage of expressionism, describing the Einstein Tower as "flaccid as jellyfish," then in the

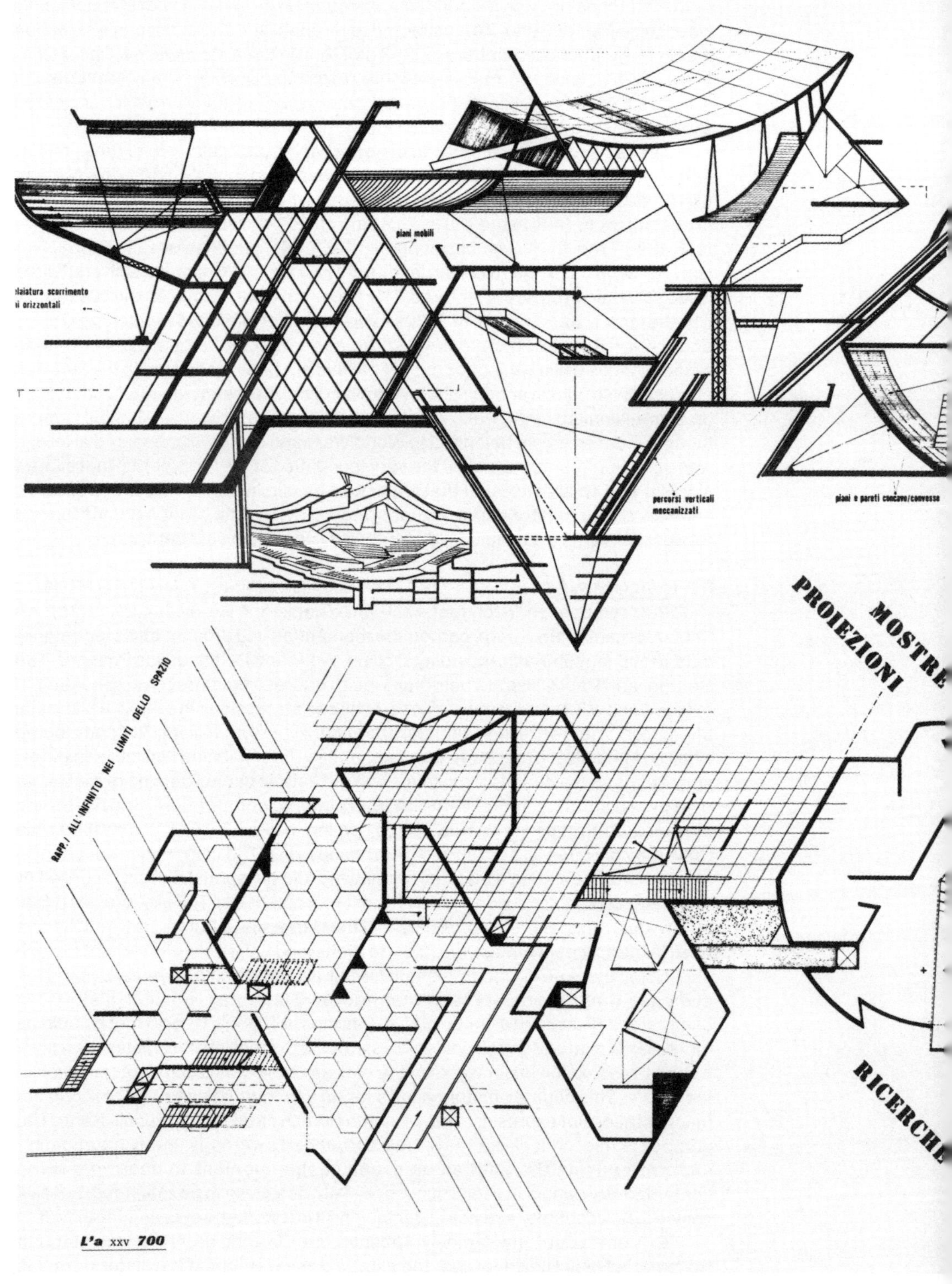

Fig. 1 The international competition *Spazio-tempo einsteiniano e processo architettonica*, Faculty of Architecture, University of Rome, 1979. Project by Rocco Roberto Bray, 2nd place in the students' section.

Rocco Roberto Bray

Alfred Whitehead ha sottolineato il merito della teoria di Einstein nell'aver compreso la visione organica del mondo. « Non è possibile l'esistenza locale isolata di una particella: l'ambiente entra nella natura di ogni cosa ». È evidente la coerente corrispondenza dell'architettura wrightiana alla relatività. Nella maggior parte delle realizzazioni e progetti di Wright nessun'opera è a sé. Le esperienze espressioniste percorrono talvolta un unico binario della ricerca architettonica; il maestro americano azzera sempre... in lui, le verità delle equazioni di Einstein sono visibili e verificabili nei fatti.
Non conosciamo, né nella storia dell'architettura moderna né nell'attuale presente, altre vie d'uscita per esprimere i concetti einsteiniani. Qualsiasi esperienza progettuale che, sia nei contenuti che nelle scelte architettoniche, di linguaggio, si muova da tale assunto ci sembra stimolante. Su tale linea appare indispensabile sperimentare, vedere, dimostrare attraverso gli strumenti del nostro specifico.
Realizzata nel tempo, la struttura progettata è mutevole, si adegua a differenti situazioni funzionali e spaziali, intrinseche e di intorno. Le possibilità di sviluppo sono multiple. La maglia di partenza non è condizionante: talvolta propone solo l'assetto compositivo. Presenza di un telaio reticolare - romboidale solo su parte di essa, per lo scorrimento (orizzontale e verticale) dei piani orizzontali. La struttura si innerva sui percorsi, verticali e orizzontali, meccanizzati e non.
Fruizione di spazi piani, obliqui, concavi e convessi. Essi individuano le attività, implicano rapporti plurimi, anche nel comportamento. Testimoniano la dinamicità delle relazioni: coinvolgono la luce, integrata nell'architettura come elemento di primaria partecipazione.

Anche il progetto che conclude questa rassegna è giunto senza relazione. Rinviamo in parte a quanto vale per il gruppo Maltese (pag. 685), e in parte alla lettura di Sergio Musmeci (pag. 708).

recent revisions by Pehnt, as she wrote in a revised version of the paper, "the jellyfish has grown into a nasty octopus that is threatening to gobble up all European movements in its path."[23] She demonstrated the conceptual continuity in the utopian thought of Bruno Taut before World War I, when he worked on urban planning projects at the firm of Theodor Fischer in Stuttgart, and Taut's work as designer of housing estates in Berlin and as a city planner in Magdeburg. From this segment of Taut's work, Haag Bletter could insist on the existence of close links, rather than allowing a divide, between new objectivism and expressionism. A more *contextual* approach, she concluded, shows expressionism's intent to reassert "human sensibility and social congregation as prime form givers" and its resistance to modern alienation, which is why it remained relevant and continued to be pursued in the architecture of Le Corbusier and Louis Kahn in the '50s and '60s.[24]

These debates about the missed locus of expressionism in the continuity between modernism and the contemporary moment resonate with more recent assessments of the untimeliness of expressionism and, more broadly, of the historical avant-garde.[25] For the philosopher Friedrich Nietzsche, untimeliness is the precondition of art's direction to be out of step with the times in order to act on its time, and therefore for a time to come.[26] The perception of expressionism as outdated, or critically distant from the present, endows it with the troubling force of resisting any claim of actuality—a point of contention that divided both camps of the debate outlined above.

From the contextualist historical perspective, the angst-ridden traumatic visions of modernity, the utopian yearnings of salvation, and the pathos-filled gestures in expressionist art were indissociably linked to the closed period of World War I and its aftermath.

I find it difficult to contest the reading of Summerson et al., namely the need for historical contextualization. As human beings in time we—whether as history writers or artists—are inevitably circumscribed by the times we live in. Historical undercurrents carry even the most independent members of the avant-garde; the very need to recreate, to issue appeals to order, is historically conditioned. In the case of Expressionism, it seems irrefutable that at its core is an expression of the times: of personal trauma, of radical reorderings of society and culture, of the convulsions between a disappearing worldview and the emergence of another.

In addition, repeated suspicions about alliances with totalitarianisms make it difficult for expressionism to be reconsidered having any actuality, unless as a space of thought that unsettles a contemporary sense of normality. From the architectural and operative camp, on the other hand, expressionism is not a style but an avant-garde attitude, an experimental architectural poetics of motion and empathic emotion that is antithetical to the rationalist domino-structure and geometry of the box, a spatial mindset that can be re-discovered and updated in the present without regard to differences in historical context.[27]

An avant-garde attitude among many others that are possible? Rejecting established wisdom can occur in many ways, and being outside of the canon is not necessarily being ahead of it.

Detached from the pathos of madness and the loss of historical expressionism, its primacy as form is taken up as a rebellious language, the relevance of which was rewrapped to stay in tune with the late modern and postmodern times.

A RETURN TO ZERO, OUTSIDE THE CRISES OF HISTORY

Beginning in 1973, Zevi regularly invokes Barthes's term "degree zero" when repositioning expressionism's counter-historical temporality against and outside of postmodernity. In *The Modern Language of Architecture*, a degree zero is associated primarily with the avant-garde's logic of the new, of a return to zero, a rejection of architecture's institutionalized linguistic and codified system of communication. This line of reasoning extended his much criticized heroic narrative and overtly patriarchal rhetoric, by which he claimed that many architects preferred to "remain dependent children under the authority" of the father figures who died in the 1950s and '60s—"Wright, Le Corbusier, Gropius, Mies van der Rohe, Mendelsohn, and a few years later, Louis Kahn"—and that the "orphan architects, without a father to turn to, head back to the maternal womb of the academy."[28]

Not unlike Kahn's concept of "Volume Zero," Zevi's degree zero exists not only outside but also before history. It is appropriated as a new origin outside of writing, in "a prehistory that has continued to exist."[29] Captivated by the tomes of English history, Kahn, in a 1972 speech at Aspen, lingered on how, in "harking back" through the first chapters of the first volume of such a national history compendium, he intuited a hypothetical "Volume Zero," and finds for himself a beginning in the archaic and the prehistoric.[30]

This reminds me of a specific genealogy of isolated figureheads in Swiss architecture: Rudolf Olgiati and Peter Märkli, the former a mentor to the latter. Olgiati's self-imposed exile from the modernism mainstream manifested itself through the appeal to archaic forms and an essentialist withdrawal from (his own) time, resulting in an architecture of thick columns without capitals, walls of white mass, an architecture of sharp shadows and bright light. Märkli's other intellectual figurehead was the sculptor Hans Josephsohn, another artist who created his work in deliberate, though not lofty, isolation from the contemporary discourse, an isolation that took decades to achieve and that ended up, only shortly before his death, being incorporated into the mainstream art market. Märkli's own architecture stands out in its time in a similar manner and reflects his preoccupation with archaic, "early periods," and prehistories in Western art.

Such a *Volume Zero* might include the pyramids at Giza, the castle of Carcasonne, or the Piazza della Cisterna in San Gimignano, but only to project an imagined time.[31] Similar to this circumventing maneuver, Zevi generalized an accumulation of "'out-of-time' aggregates"—the Neolithic village of Balla in northern Rhodesia, the Matamata village in southern Tunesia, the "primitive village" of the Dogon in Mali—in short, "everything that art historians have thus far disdainfully banned from their books," to set the stage for a now architect who "descends to the 'zero degree' of his culture."[32]

If degree zero is a way to subscribe to the linguistic turn in architecture and the insight that language "speaks us,"[33] or speaks before we learn to speak, it also marks a turning point in Zevi's thinking. In his 1983 lecture "Architecture versus Historic Criticism" for the RIBA in London, he stated that from "1948 to 1973, I believed that history could provide a consistent and scientific methodology to design. In other words, I believed in modern Mannerism.[34]" But "after 25 years teaching history as a methodology for design," he found that "Mannerism was not enough." He explained elsewhere that "Mannerists work from results, from finished products, and neglect the process that developed the products."[35] "White" writing in architecture is by contrast "a continuous process, a game that always destroys its own rules all the time and has to be reinvented every day." It takes to heart the idea that "the cathedrals were white"—white because they were new. It is this "intrinsic power of regeneration, of dying and resurrecting" that a postmodernist such as Jencks, Zevi posited, does not understand—Jencks who had declared modernism dead since 1972, and to Zevi's great annoyance claimed Utzon's Opera House and the Ronchamp chapel as precursors of postmodernism.

Fig. 2 Mario Deluigi, *La visione informale dell'ultima opera, Santa Maria degli Angeli*, created for the 1964 exhibition on Michelangelo, curated by Paolo Portoghesi and Bruno Zevi.

BARTHES'S AND ZEVI'S PARADIGM

In referring to Barthes, Zevi presented the idea of degree zero as a strategy to bypass binary oppositions, in his case as a way to overcome the impasse between modernism and postmodernism. This dialectic was essential to Barthes's definition of the idea that he developed in 1978 in the course on "the Neutral" for the Collège de France. Barthes defined the Neutral as "the idea of a structural creation that would defeat, annul, or contradict the implacable binarism of the paradigm by means of a third term, the *tertium*."[36] The Neutral is "everything that eludes the paradigm," and the paradigm is "the opposition of two virtual terms from which, in speaking, I actualize one to produce meaning."[37] The Neutral is neither A nor B but the invention of a complex or degree zero of A and B. It transcends the paradigm that is an opposition of two meanings.[38]

The singular expressive nature of Zevi's interpretation of the degree zero, however, contradicts various aspects of Barthes's definition. At the 1981 meeting of CICA at the UIA World Congress in Warsaw, Zevi cobbled together a highly personal disciplinary understanding of Barthes's *Writing Degree Zero* of 1953.[39] Grounded as he was among scholarly companions at the meeting, Zevi drew extensively and selectively from Barthes to define a "degree zero of architectural writing."[40] One passage from *Writing Degree Zero* that Zevi quotes at length deals with the historical necessity of a "search of a non-style, or an oral style, for a zero degree or spoken degree of writing" that can be found in the "possible area of a new humanism."[41] This humanism, Barthes writes, has "finally integrated History in the image of man," reinvestigated the civilized world as true Nature, a Nature that speaks and that develops living languages from which the writer is excluded. After Barthes, who concluded that *L'Étranger* by Albert Camus is the book that inaugurated "a style of absence that is almost an ideal absence of style," Zevi declared the degree zero the unattainable ideal for architecture as it searches for a way out of the paralyzing struggle between the oppositions of the Greek and the Gothic, the classic and the organic, the classicist legacy and the modernist one.[43] In reaction to the regression of postmodernism to Beaux-Arts academism, postmodern bizarre facadism, or pseudo-vernacular regionalism, it was necessary to reconquer the values of the modern movement that, in his view, obsessively returned to zero, as such sidestepping the traditional cycle of crises followed by weak compromises.

Zevi illustrated his argument in the 1981 lecture in Warsaw with some of the paintings that Barthes had made that were inspired directly by the haiku and his travels to Japan and had been shown with others in Rome immediately after his death.[44] These paintings struck Zevi as a clear attempt to "translate the 'zero degree' of literary writing in figurative writing." Zevi aligned Barthes's paintings with an expression of bodily movement in space that he found in American abstract expressionism, such as in the work of Jackson Pollock or in the Italian postwar art movement known as spatialism, exemplified by the work of Mario Deluigi (Fig. 2). Zevi's formalistic reduction of Barthes's idea contrasts with Barthes's adherence to an ethical minimalism that neutralized the object-subject relationship through a harmonizing between a maximum of internal but a minimum of external intensity.

But above all, the set of exemplary architecture that Zevi promotes in his lecture to illustrate an architecture of degree zero—the Roman catacombs, Santa Sofia, Le Corbusier's Ronchamp, Mendelsohn, deconstructivism—does not transcend a paradigm in the way Barthes understood a paradigm, as an opposition of two terms, or, in Zevi's transposition, the opposition of modernism and postmodernism. Instead, Zevi affirmatively sides with modern architecture, or at least a specific lineage of modernism. As he explains in *How to See Architecture* (1948), there are two big spatial movements in modern architecture. The first is functionalism; it has Le Corbusier as its protagonist, and the functionalist conception of space crystalizes in the Villa Savoye. The second is the organic movement as defended by Wright.[45] The organic conception of space has Fallingwater as its masterpiece. Zevi consistently championed this second movement and defended a vision of organic space that is rich in movement and reflects the movements of the users who dwell in that space.

As Zevi acknowledges, the architectural space conception he adhered to is more broadly rooted in the German aesthetic theory of empathy (*Einfühlung*) of the late nineteenth and early twentieth century.[46] This empathic way of seeing architecture actively is lucidly explained by August Schmarsow, in his description of architecture as "the intuited form of three-dimensional space" that arises psychologically through "the experiences of our sense of sight."[47] Through bodily movement viewers project themselves into space using their visual and tactile faculties. The viewer and the building thus enter into a subject-object union. Architecture coerces the viewer to play an active part in the unfolding of the play of light and movement, of motion and emotion. This empathic understanding of architectural space underpinned much of the thinking of expressionist architecture.[48] When Zevi uses the phrase "expressionist zeroing," it pertains to this aesthetic vision of space essential to expressionism: architecture can only be understood by moving through space, by projecting our bodies into space through movement.[49]

It is this embodied and spatial form of vision, which is not static but spatial, that Zevi detects in architecture of various ages and ties together in what we could call an expressionist paradigm—with "paradigm" understood here as philosopher Giorgio Agamben defines it: a logic of exemplarity. A paradigm, according to Agamben, is a tool that enables us to rethink by means of examples foundational concepts (such as modernist space, in this context). For Agamben, the single example through which the paradigm operates both belongs to the set of examples it represents and stands apart from it. Through a form of analogical exemplarity that runs from one example to another, the paradigm for Agamben exhibits its own knowability.[50] Agamben's definition of the paradigm captures well the logic of exemplarity that ties together Zevi's temporal chain of architectural examples.

The paradigmatic example of Zevi's chain of particulars, which in Agamben's words could be said to be "excluded by means of its very inclusion," could be argued to be the cave or natural grotto. The cave, a classic trope of expressionism, reintegrates architecture and nature, roof and wall, synchrony and diachrony.[51] Paradigmatic in the hypothetical supposition of the principle of the "unfinished," the cave stands for an architecture of growth and change, an "architecture without architects" that belongs to pre-history. The cave is a form associated with a past that lies outside of history, before the invention of writing, but which can easily be projected in a futuristic space-time of science fiction. Historical time is naturalized and mythologized. The cave is the paradigmatic example of expressionism and thus, by extension, of Zevi's lineage of exemplars of his dynamic space conception (Fig. 3).

The cave/grotto is also a definitive motif of *Cinquecento* Mannerism, representing the tension between *natura naturans* and *natura naturata*, the former expressing the active, generative principles of nature and the latter its passive, created results. The cave is indeed a recurring motif in art history, not only having gained its own moniker in "grotesque", but emerging again in the geological metaphors of surrealism.

If the cave is the paradigmatic example in Zevi's family of exemplary architecture, some buildings could be pointed out to nearly perfectly exemplify this cave-figure. Mendelsohn's Einstein Tower comes close to incarnating this exemplarity. Walls and ceilings merge to form one continuous, enveloping form.

Again, the negation of structural logics and the merging of actual and represented surfaces are motifs of art-historical Mannerism in architecture, as expounded in John Shearman's masterly *Mannerism* (1967).

An architecture of interior spaces, the exterior of the Einstein Tower turns the figure of the cave inside out. Other candidates in Zevi's architectural list are Le Corbusier's chapel at Ronchamp, Utzon's Sydney Opera House, and Scharoun's Berlin Philarmonic, which all align with the experience of an architecture that moves us as we move through the architectural space (Fig. 4). In the end, these projects and many others all add to a thread of exemplars interchangeable throughout time.

A final demonstration of how Zevi applied this logic of analogical exemplarity was evident in his response to the 1998 exhibition on German expressionism at the Palazzo Grassi in Venice. Here, a 6-meter-high scaled replica of Mendelsohn's Einstein Tower was displayed in the atrium (Fig.5).[52] Zevi criticized the curators for limiting the exhibition to the first wave of expressionism, from before 1924. In his view, they overlooked the second wave, which included the chapel at Ronchamp, which he considered the "neo-expressionist masterpiece,"[53] and the third wave of deconstructivist expressionism, which emerged in the work of Jean Renaudie, Zvi Hecker, Günther Behnisch, Libeskind, and Gehry.

At the end of reading this piece, my understanding of Zevi's understanding of Expressionism has shifted towards a more general understanding of Mannerism as a recurring motif in history (including, but not restricted to, *Cinquecento* art and architecture). It is possible to identify Mannerist motifs not only in the architecture of the *Cinquecento*, but also that of the late twentieth-century architecture, from Robert Venturi to OMA and Herzog & de Meuron. Some of these formal motifs, the grotesque included, have resurfaced recurrently in ways that echo Zevi's "zeroing". These recurrences can however be forever historically contextualized. Mannerism was understood as a manifestation of eras of great uncertainty, at the fault lines of established worldviews: in the sixteenth century the Reformation and its brutal Counter-Reformation; in the early 20th century World War I, and in the late 20th century the so-called "end of history" (which has proven anything but).

But in Zevi's temporal logic, these waves also extend backwards in time, to pre-history and the age of caves. Recurrence is the temporal mode of Zevi's exemplarity, not continuity or some Barthian dialectic. Expressionist zeroing is above all an act of anachronism. It circumvents the order of time through the recurrence of counter-historical moments and rebirths of spatial experiences of a higher type.

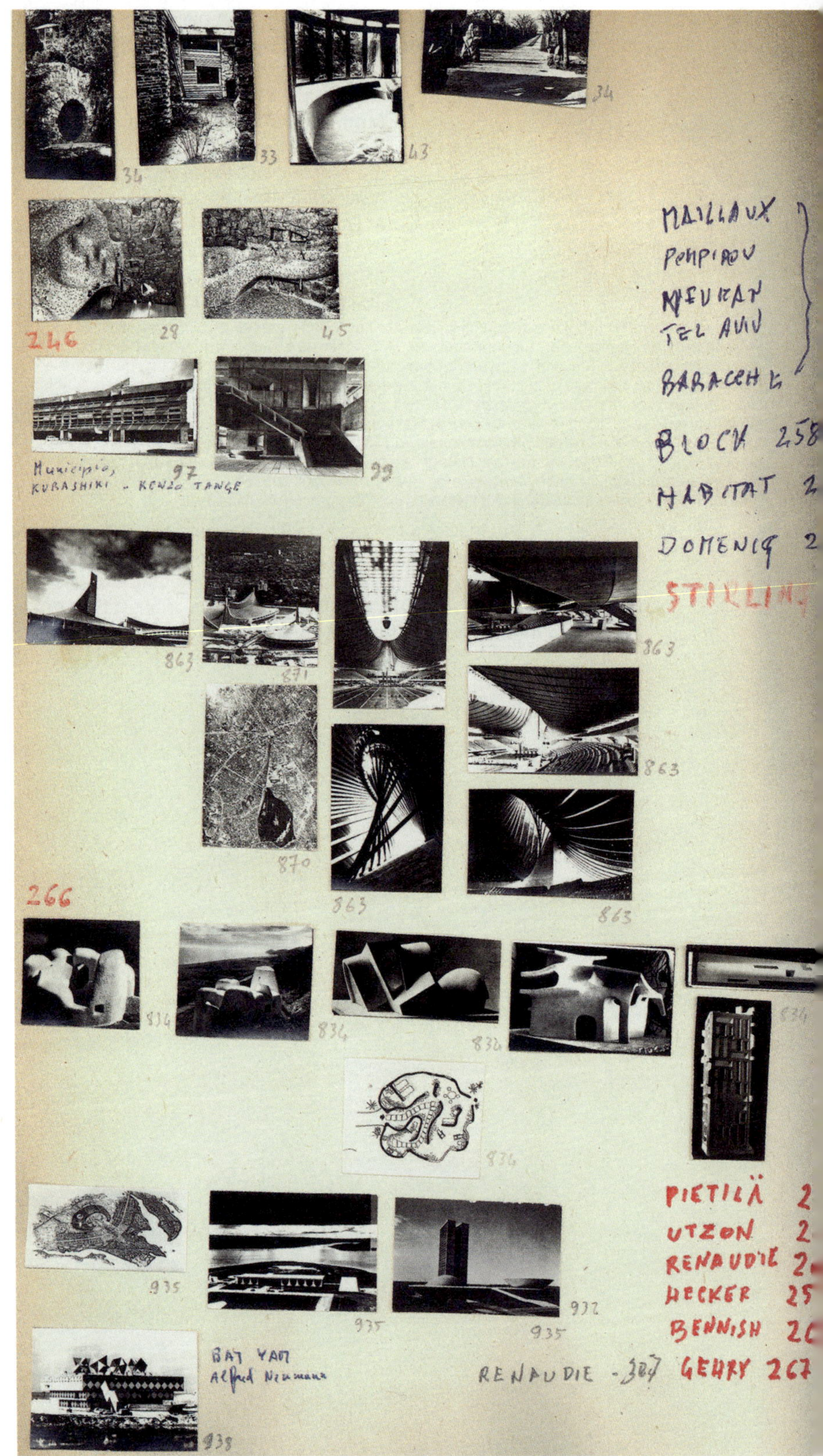

Fig. 3 Last page of Bruno Zevi's scrapbook.

Fig. 4 Hans Scharoun, Berlin Philarmonic, Berlin, 1963. Photographs from Bruno Zevi's scrapbook.

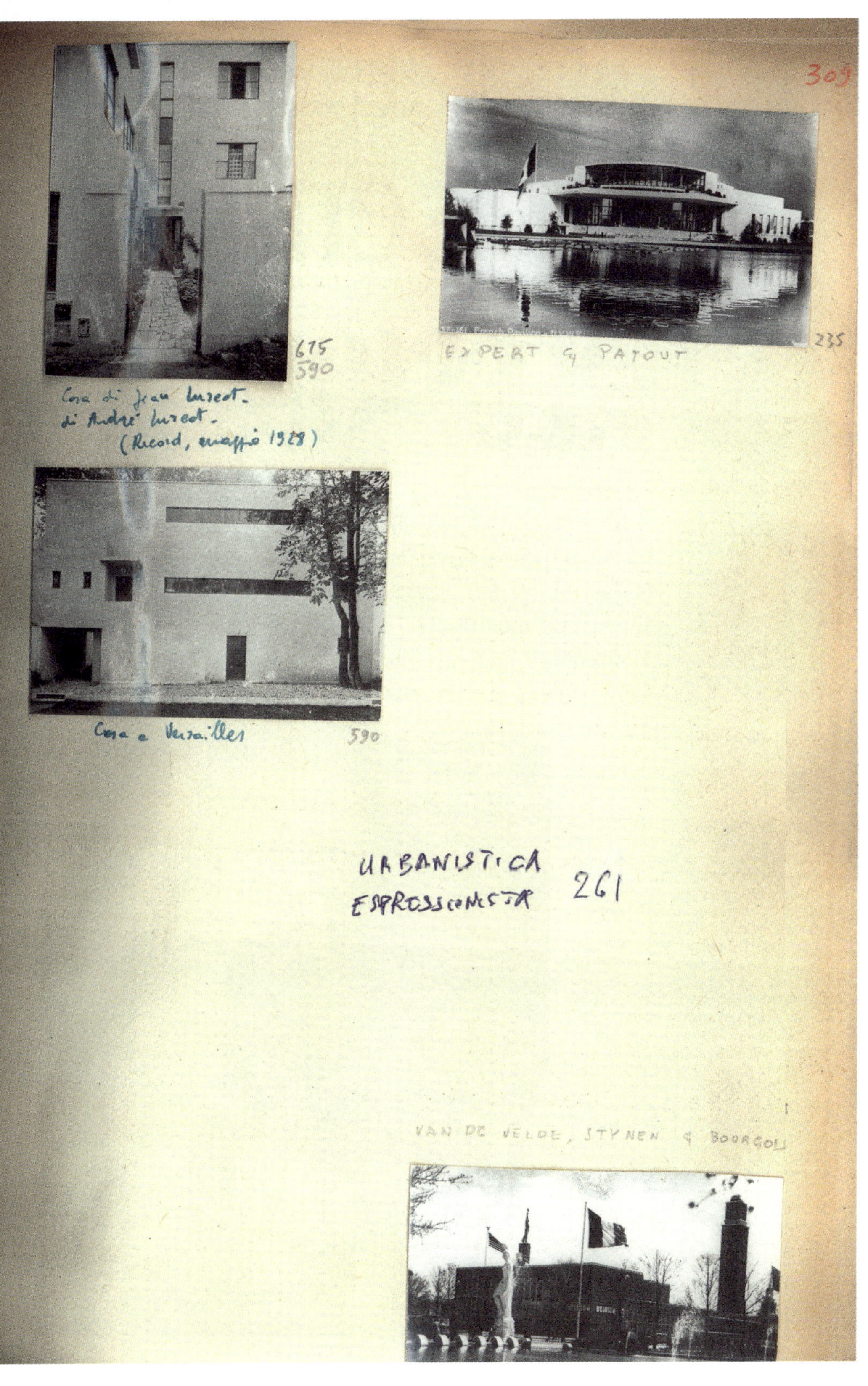
309
675
590
Casa di Jean Lurçat.
di André Lurçat.
(Record, maggio 1928)
EXPERT & PATOUT
235
Casa a Versailles
590
URBANISTICA
ESPRESSIONISTA
261
VAN DE VELDE, STYNEN & BOURGOIS

ARTI

GRANDI EVENTI / LA MOSTRA D'AUTUNNO A PALAZZO GRASSI

Ora e sempre ESPRESSIONISMO

colloquio con Bruno Zevi — di Alessandra Mammì

È LA PRIMA COSA CHE SI VEDRÀ. PRIMA DI PAGARE IL biglietto, prima di varcare l'ingresso, prima di raggiungere i famosi dipinti dell'"Espressionismo tedesco" che Palazzo Grassi mette in mostra dal 7 settembre all'11 gennaio del '98. Un monumento, anzi un simbolo di quel movimento d'arte, di pensiero e di vita che ha scosso l'Europa delle due guerre. Impossibile evitarla: è una torre alta sei metri, che si dilata su tutto il pavimento dell'atrio per raggiungere in altezza il secondo piano del nobile palazzo veneziano. Modello fedelissimo dell'osservatorio astronomico edificato tra il 1919 e il 1923 a Potsdam per permettere ad Albert Einstein di studiare le deviazioni dello spettro solare in base alla teoria della relatività. Rivoluzionaria nella concezione e nella forma almeno quanto era destinata ad esserlo nelle funzioni.

La progettò un genio, Erich Mendelsohn, perché ospitasse le ricerche di un altro genio. Sarà ricostruita fedelmente, in un quinto delle sue originali proporzioni: «Pura materia plasmata da due forze: quella che dell'esterno preme contro la torre e la consuma e quella che dall'interno reagisce». Così la descrive Bruno Zevi che sull'architettura espressionista ha scritto in catalogo un saggio profondo, problematico e soprattutto polemico: contro i falsi giudizi storici, contro le schematizzazioni da sussidiario, contro chi giudica l'Espressionismo un puro movimento d'avanguardia

Movimento di avanguardia? O risposta trasgressiva a ogni regola nell'arte? Ora che a Venezia si celebrano gli artisti tedeschi d'inizio secolo, il grande storico dell'architettura esalta il messaggio espressionista come libertà senza tempo

106

Fig. 5 Reproduction of the article "Ora e sempre Espressionismo: Colloquio con Bruno Zevi," *L'Espresso*, no. 21 (August 1997): 106. The article mentions a 6-meter-high reconstruction of Mendelsohn's Einstein Tower in the Palazzo Grassi in Venice at the 1997–98 exhibition on German expressionism, linked to German Celant's Biennale on the theme "Futuro, presente, passato."

Esempi di architettura espressionista anni '90. A sinistra: l'edificio della National Nederlande a Praga, progetto di Frank Gehry e Vlado Milunic. Sotto: una costruzione firmata da Zvi Hecker. In basso: giardino d'infanzia Lungisland di Günther Behnisch. Nella pagina accanto: la torre Einstein di Mendelsohn, ricostruita a Palazzo Grassi; a sinistra, un bozzetto dell'autore

inizi secolo e in un ultima analisi anche contro i curatori della mostra (Wolf-Dieter Dube e Sthepanie Barron) che nella loro accurata ricognizione hanno deciso di chiudere la grande stagione espressionista al 1924. Errore, dice il nostro più grande storico dell'architettura in questa intervista: l'Espressionismo è vivo e anzi proprio adesso sul finire del millennio celebra il suo trionfo.

Duecentocinquanta opere, venticinque sale, nonché film, foto, documenti: il tutto per raccontare un movimento che secondo il curatore Wolf-Dieter Dube, uno dei più autorevoli studiosi in materia, si chiude inesorabilmente negli anni Venti. Ma lei, professor Zevi, parla di un primo, secondo e perfino terzo Espressionismo, che parte dalla notte dei tempi e giunge fino a noi. Insomma non sembrate molto d'accordo.

«È possibile che il professor Dube abbia ragione per quanto riguarda la pittura. Ma è certo che per l'architettura questo non è vero. L'Espressionismo non muore affatto nel '24. Forse va in letargo ma l'evento inatteso, stupefacente si verifica negli anni Novanta con l'"Action architecture" che approda a una rivoluzione linguistica e al raggiungimento di un obiettivo millenario posto già nelle caverne e nei nuraghi».

Ma che cos'è per lei l'Espressionismo?

«Partiamo da un eterno dilemma etico e linguistico: quello tra il "finito", il perfettamente eseguito a cui nulla può essere aggiunto o sottratto, e il "non finito" che muta e cresce continuamente. Nel primo partito militano i professionisti che progettano secondo regole, ordini, regolamenti. Grandi manager dell'architettura come l'Alberti, Bramante, Bernini o Gropius. Nel secondo i ribelli, i nemici dei dogmi come Brunelleschi, Michelangelo, Borromini, Wright o Mendelsohn. Negli anni dell'Espressionismo propriamente detto questo scontro diventa palese. La ricerca e la cultura architettonica si dividono fra chi come Van Doesburg, capo del De Stijl, elaborava una grammatica cubista che cercava di rifondare un nuovo classicismo su regole geometriche, e

chi come Mendelsohn sfidava la terza dimensione, cercava la profondità materica. Su questo punto le grandi avanguardie si confrontarono a Parigi un giorno del 1914».

Che cosa successe quel giorno?

«Ci fu una riunione fra cubisti francesi, espressionisti tedeschi e futuristi italiani. Si cercò un alleanza, un'intesa, l'elaborazione di un manifesto. Ma tutto ciò rimase lettera morta e non poteva essere altrimenti».

Perché?

«Perché, come ho detto, i cubisti volevano solo dividere lo spazio in lastre bidimensionali per poi ricostruirlo come oggetto quadrimensionale. I futuristi pensavano che bastasse animarlo con elementi cinetici, tipo tapis roulant o ascensori. Solo gli espressionisti ave- ➤

1 Zevi's exploration of expressionism through the idea of degree zero has been given little attention; one exception is Franco De Faveri, "L'espressionismo come "grado zero" dell'architettura," in *Tra passato e future: Assaggi di Teoria dell'architettura*, ed. Yvonne Bezrucka (Trento: Editizione Autem, 1995), 13–40.

2 Bruno Zevi, *The Modern Language of Architecture* (New York: Van Nostrand Reinhold, 1981), 69.

3 Bruno Zevi, *Landscape and the Zero Degree of Architecture Language* (Venezia: Canal & Stamperia editrice, 1999), 371.

4 The other co-directors were Pierre Vago, editor-in-chief of *L'architecture d'aujourd'hui*; the Argentine artist and publisher Jorge Glusberg, who founded the Buenos Aires International Biennal of Architecture; and Julius Posener, who had worked in Mendelsohn's office and was an expert on Poelzig.

5 *Architectural Review* 177, no. 1060 (June 1985). Zevi also republished many of the articles of this issue in his journal *L'architettura*. Peter Blundell Jones, "Commentary on the Submission of a PhD by Publication," related to the submission of the PhD thesis *A Forty Year Encounter with Hans Scharoun* (PhD diss., School of Architecture, The University of Sheffield, 2013), 20. https://etheses.whiterose.ac.uk/5934/1/Peter%20Blundell%20Jones%20thesis.pdf.

6 Zevi, *Landscape and the Zero Degree of Architecture Language*, 420.

7 Peter Blundell Jones, "Hugo Häring and the Search for a Responsive Architecture," *AA Files*, no. 13 (Autumn 1986): 30–43.

8 Paola Décina Lombardi, "Architettura anno zero. Addio incubi di vetro-cemento," *La Stampa* (September 18, 1997), 22.

9 Bruno Zevi, "A Message to the Congrès International d'Architecture Moderne," excerpt reprinted from *Metron*, nos. 31–32 (1949): 11. Bruno Zevi Foundation, Rome, Serie 06, Sottoserie 02, Fascicolo 07.

10 Zevi quotes a response from himself in this passage to those who complimented him on his book in: Zevi, "A Message to the Congrès international d'architecture moderne," 18.

11 Ibid., 11–12.

12 Ibid., 5.

13 The titles of the books are mentioned in English but the years refer to their original publication, which have been translated in English, except for Franco Borsi and Giovanni Klaus König's book: Ulrich Conrads and Hans G. Sperlich, *Phantastische Architektur* (Teufen: Niggli, 1960); Dennis Sharp, *Modern Architecture and Expressionism* (New York: G. Braziller, 1966); Franco Borsi and Giovanni Klaus König, *Architettura dell'espressionismo* (Genoa: Vitali e Ghianda, 1967); Wolfgang Pehnt, *Die Architektur des Expressionismus* (Stuttgart: Hatje, 1973).

14 See Ita Heinze-Greenberg's essay for Zevi's publications on Mendelsohn (endnote 32), published after the earlier biographies on Mendelsohn, heavily controlled by Mendelsohn himself: Ita Heinze-Greenberg, "Heroic Narratives: Bruno Zevi and Eric Mendelsohn," in *Bruno Zevi: History, Criticism and Architecture after World War II*, ed. Matteo Cassani Simonetti and Elena Dellapiana (Milano: FrancoAngeli, 2021), 129–150. As early as 1954, Zevi began to publish about Mendelsohn in *Metron* and in *Cronache di architettura*: Bruno Zevi, "Erich Mendelsohn," *Metron*, nos. 49–50 (1954): 66–84; and Bruno Zevi, "Opere postume di Erich Mendelsohn: Il testament nel tempio," *Cronache di architettura*, no. 2 (1954): 376–381. The first important works are Bruno Zevi, *Erich Mendelsohn: Un ismo per un uomo. Rassegna delle realizzazione di Erich Mendelsohn nel 10° anniversario della morte*, monographic issue of *L'architettura: Cronache et storia*, no. 95 (September 1963); and Bruno Zevi, *Erich Mendelsohn: Opera completa: Architetture e immagini architettoniche, con note biographiche di Louise Mendelsohn* (Milano: Etas Kompass, 1970). For a list of other publications of Zevi on Mendelsohn, see the Fondazione Bruno Zevi website, https: //www.fondazionebrunozevi.it/en/bruno-zevi-publications/.

15 George R. Collins and Adolf K. Placzek, eds., *Modern Architecture Symposium, Columbia University, 1962: Architecture 1918–1928, from the Novembergruppe to the C.I.A.M. (Functionalism and Expressionism): Proceedings*

(New York: Dept. of Art History and Archaeology and the Avery Architectural Library, Columbia University, 1963).

16 "L'architettura espressionista: La IV giornata del convegno di Palazzo Vecchio," *Giornale del mattino*, May 23, 1964. Foundation Zevi.

17 "Architectural Expressionism: A Re-evaluation," AA Symposium, February 5-9, 1980, at Architectural Association in London. Bruno Zevi Foundation, Rome, Serie 07, Fascicolo 32, "1980."

18 Special issue dedicated to the competition "Bando del concorso," *L'architettura: Cronache e storia* 29, no. 12 (December 1979): 675.

19 Antonella Romano, "La Rappresentazione dello spazio architettonico nella didattica di Zevi," in *Bruno Zevi e la didattica dell'architettura*, ed. Pier Ostilio Rossi et al. (Macerata: Quodlibet, 2019), 261-270.

20 Bruno Zevi, *Controstoria e storia dell'architettura* (Rome: Newton & Compton, 1998). On the operative criticism of Zevi, see also Luca Monica, ed., *La critica operative e l'architettura* (Milano: Edizioni Unicopli, 2002).

21 My own translation, from Zevi, *Controstoria e storia dell'architettura*, 1998, 9.

22 Rosemarie Haag Bletter, "Bruno Taut: A Reassessment of Expressionism in Architecture," summary of conference paper, Bruno Zevi Foundation, Rome, Serie 07, Fascicolo 32, "1980." Haag Bletter developed the conference paper and published it as "Expressionism and the New Objectivity," *Art Journal* 43, no. 2 (1983): 108-120.

23 Ibid., 110.

24 Ibid., 119.

25 Bernd Hüppauf, "Das Unzeitgemässe der Avantgarden. Die Zeit, Avantgarden und die Gegenwart," in *Der Blick vom Wolkenkratzer*, ed. Wolfgang Asholt and Walter Fähnders, Avant Garde Critical Studies, 14 (Amsterdam: Rodopi, 2000), 547-581; Vivian Liska, "The Untimeliness of German Expressionism," in *Modernism: A Comparative History of Literatures in European Languages,* vol. 21, ed. Astradur Eysteinsson and Vivian Liska (Amsterdam/Philadelphia: John Benjamins, 2007), 195-206.

26 On Nietzsche's notion of the untimely and revisionist architectural histories in the '60s and '70s, see Wouter Van Acker and Steven Lauritano, "Untimely Teachers: Recovering Postmodernism's Anachronic Pedagogies," *Architectural Theory Review* 28, no. 1 (2024): 1-22.

27 Adrian Sheppard, "The Return of Expressionism and the Architecture of Luigi Moretti," online at McGill University's Institutional repository, May 2016, https: //www.mcgill.ca/architecture/files/architecture/ExpressionismMoretti.pdf.

28 Zevi, *The Modern Language of Architecture*, 68-69.

29 Ibid., 219.

30 On Kahn's concept of "Volume Zero," see Stanford Anderson, "Public Institutions: Louis Kahn and the Reading of Volume Zero," *Journal of Architectural Education* 49, no. 1 (September 1995): 10-21. The speech given at Aspen, Colorado, on June 19, 1972, is reprinted in *Louis I. Kahn, What Will Be Has Always Been: The Words of Louis I. Kahn*, ed. Richard Saul Wurman (New York: Access Press/Rizzoli, 1986), 151.

31 On Kahn's conception of form as Volume Zero, see Amanda Reeser Lawrence, *The Architecture of Influence: The Myth of Originality in the Twentieth Century* (Charlottesville: University of Virginia Press, 2023), 101.

32 Zevi, *The Modern Language of Architecture*, 222.

33 Ibid., 23.

34 Bruno Zevi, "Architecture versus Historic Criticism," RIBA Annual Discourse, London, December 6, 1983, Fondatione Bruno Zevi Serie 07 Fascicolo 35, "1983."

35 Zevi, *The Modern Language of Architecture*, 70.

36 Roland Barthes, *The Neutral: Lecture Course at the Collège de France (1977-1978)*, trans. Rosalind E. Krauss and Denis Hollier (New York: Columbia University Press, 2005), 7.

37 Ibid., 7.

38 For a detailed explanation of Barthes's understanding of the paradigm of meaning and how it excludes other meaning, see Claude Stephane Perrin, *Le neutre et la pensée* (Paris: L'Harmattan, 2009). Thanks to Lyna Bourouiba for this reference.

39 Bruno Zevi, "The Zero Degree of Architectural Writing: A Mirage or a Challenge," *a/mbiente*, special issue, *Criticism in Warsaw* 8 (June 1981). A late transcript of this lecture is republished in Bruno Zevi, "Il 'grado zero' della scrittura architettonica," in Bruno Zevi, *Pretesti di critica architettonica* (Torino: Einaudi, 1983), 273–280.

40 At the CICA meeting in New York in December 1980, a discussion between Zevi, Toshio Nakamura, and Jorge Glusberg on the subject of zero degree in architectural writing, served as a run-up to the Warsaw Congress. See the CICA meeting report "Third Criticism Meeting in New York," Bruno Zevi Foundation, Rome.

41 Roland Barthes, *Writing Degree Zero*, trans. Annette Lavers and Colin Smith (New York: Hill & Wang, 1968), 87.

42 Ibid., 67.

43 On the notion of "regression" in the historiography of the modern movement, including in the writings of Zevi, see Spyros Papapetros, " Architecture and Regression: On the Pre/post/erous Histories of the Modern Movement," *The Cornell Journal of Architecture* 8 (2011): article 22.

44 He showed three paintings by Barthes, as indicated in the last page, "Warsaw-Illustrations," added to the typescript of his lecture "The Zero Degree of Architectural Writing: Mirage or Challenge?," Bruno Zevi Foundation, Rome.

45 Bruno Zevi, *Apprendre à voir l'architecture* (Paris: Les editions de minuit, 1959), 82–84.

46 Zevi explains this in Zevi, *Apprendre à voir l'architecture*, 104–109.

47 Quoted from Juliet Koss, "On the Limits of Empathy," *The Art Bulletin* 88, no.1 (2006): 141.

48 I refer here to the aesthetic philosophy of Robert Vischer and Theodor Lipps, as interpreted by such art historians as August Schmarsow, Alois Riegl, and Wilhelm Worringer. On how this aesthetic theory was essential in expressionism, see Koss, "On the Limits of Empathy."

49 Zevi had already appropriated this view when studying at Harvard's GSD during WWII, through his reading of the work of the English architectural historian Geoffrey Scott (1884–1929). Raul Martinez Martínez, "Bruno Zevi, the Continental European Emissary of Geoffrey Scott's Theories," *The Journal of Architecture*, 24, no. 1 (2019): 27–50.

50 Giorgio Agamben, *The Signature of All Things: On Method* (New York: Zone Books, 2009), chapter 1, "What Is a Paradigm?", 9–32

51 Zevi, *The Modern Language of Architecture*, 61.

52 The exhibition was *Espressionismo Tedesco*, curated by Wolf-Dieter Dube and Stephanie Barron. See Alessandra Mammi, "Grandi eventi / La Mostra d'autunno a Palazzo Grassi: Ora e sempre Espressionismo. Colloquio con Bruno Zevi," *L'Espresso* (21 August 1997), 106–107.

53 Bruno Zevi, "Le Corbusier et le degré zéro de l'écriture architecturale," in *Le Corbusier, voyages, rayonnement international, Les Rencontres de la Fondation Le Corbusier, 6-7 juin 1997* (Paris: UNESCO, 1997), 6.

Zero Degree, Capitalism, and Architecture: Manfredo Tafuri, Bruno Zevi, and the Translation of a Literary Concept into Architecture

Gilles Malzac,
Giulia Tellier

comments by
Andrew Leach

Quaderni rossi

1

Lotte operaie nello sviluppo capitalistico

di Vittorio Foa

Il livello raggiunto dalle lotte sindacali non ha spento, anzi ha ravvivato, lo spirito critico all'interno della organizzazione. La ricerca è sempre aperta, gli interrogativi sono spesso assillanti. Essi investono tutti gli aspetti della esperienza sindacale, i contenuti rivendicativi, le forme della lotta, i metodi di direzione e, più in là, necessariamente, la prospettiva strategica.

Fra i motivi di preoccupazione sta il crescente squilibrio nel movimento. Pur con notevoli eccezioni, il Nord presenta un quadro complessivamente dinamico, lotte sostenute e largamente di tipo nuovo. Nel suo insieme il Sud, pur esso con notevoli eccezioni (miniere sarde, elettrici in Sicilia, scioperi delle autolinee, lotte importanti di fab-

Fig. 1 Cover of *Quaderni Rossi*, no. 1 (1961).

The starting point of our article is the inherent indeterminacy that we perceive in the idea of "degree zero," also called "white" or "neutral writing." These terms, which are all in use to refer to the same thing, are a symptom of this blur. We are not the only ones to question this Barthesian imprecision: it was already challenged in 1954, by the Italian critic and poet Franco Fortini (1917–1994):

> There is nothing worse than unavowed Marxisms and, above all, false Marxisms. One must be profoundly incapable of recognizing that the avant-garde is dead to believe in the zero degree of writing, in non-style, in short, in revolution as a mystical confusion of languages.[1]

Fortini's criticisms of the degree zero, beyond its stylistic and notional content, is closely related to his militant and Marxist position as an intellectual who believes in the importance of praxis and action.

Concepts and theories travel, and the degree zero is no exception. In a chapter of his book *The World, The Text and The Critic*, Edward Said writes about the travel of theory and concepts to new environments (epistemological, disciplinary, geographical, etc.) and suggests that such movements are never unimpeded. This is why the specific problem of what happens to concepts when they move from one place, where controversies are already present, to another is an interesting subject for investigation.

In our investigation on how the degree zero has traveled to become a design tool or a project instrument in the architectural field, our intention is to extend Fortini's critical gaze on the idea's (and term's) political effectiveness, inquiring about the ideological functions it has expressed in specific historical-political situations, and *in fine*, to verify its operativity. To do this, we propose to move from the conversation between Barthes and Fortini toward Bruno Zevi and Manfredo Tafuri, who have both, in different ways, contributed to the traveling of the concept of degree zero to and within architecture.

If we consider that all cultural production is not only historically situated, but also actively constitutive of productive and class relations, then by focusing on the epistemo-critical positions of Zevi and Tafuri, we can furnish a coherent context for their various historical and architectural investigations. Our analysis of Zevi and Tafuri's interpretation of the degree zero as a cultural fragment, including its political use, is informed by their take on the totality of architecture as well as the world system under capitalism.

THE CRISIS OF IDEOLOGY AND THE "PLAN OF CAPITAL" IN ITALY

In the 1950s and 1960s, Italy witnessed the "miracolo economico italiano," a period of strong economic growth. This growth was linked to the unprecedented process of modernization of its industrial production, one of whose results was the reorganization of social relationships in work settings. This is what Mario Tronti, Italian philosopher and a member of the journal *Quaderni Rossi*, called, following Karl Marx, the "Plan of Capital" (Fig. 1).

"The Plan of Capital" is the title of the third chapter of *Workers and Capital* [*Operai e Capitale*], a group of texts and articles written by Tronti for different journals (first *Quaderni Rossi*, then *Classe Operaia*). *Workers and Capital* was published in Italy in 1966. For many, it was a political guideline, embodying what would later be called the thought of "the first Tronti." The idea of a "plan of capital" is that capitalism contains the program of its own development and that this development arises from the fact that integrating the labor class into capitalism is, for its own sake, a necessity. To put it another way, the "plan of capital" arises from the need for capital to make the social labor force, constituted as a class, function *within* production. Thus, Tronti criticizes the ideological roles and functions of trade unions, allied to the reformist Italian left, showing how they participated in implementing this new organization of labor that integrates workers' criticisms. He shows how the bourgeoisie integrated unions and a part of the constitutional left to maintain a capitalist mode of production, that is to say, the production of added value (Fig. 2).

At the time of Tronti's analysis, the Italian Socialist Party (PSI) was gradually abandoning its historical alliance with the Communist Party to intensify its rapprochement with the Christian Democrats. This political change was based on the Italian socialists' belief that a rationally planned and socially sustainable economy can be used as a means of social pressure to improve the welfare of its workers. For this reason, the socialists renounced the rhetoric of class conflict in favor of the reformability of the production system. The operaist movement, opposed to this political choice, produced a virulent critique to the reformist tendencies of the historical left (the unions and the major parties), insisting on the autonomy of the working class, and the primacy of social struggles over capitalist development. Zevi's and Tafuri's careers were influenced by this new geographical and historical reconfiguration of capitalism—and by the new intellectual and political strategies developed to resist it, Zevi expressing reformist needs and Tafuri, revolutionary aspirations.

ZEVI AND TAFURI AS POLITICAL ARCHETYPES: ON ARCHITECTS AND HISTORY WITHIN CAPITALISM

In the series of disputes between Tafuri and Zevi that began in 1954,[3] a major controversy began to unfold around the Michelangelo Architetto exhibition of 1964 at the Palazzo delle Esposizioni in Rome, co-organized by Zevi and Paolo Portoghesi. Tafuri criticized the "tormented iron mesh" of the exhibition and the iconoclastic distortion of the figure of Michelangelo into a "Zevianised" Michelangelo. In a later interview, he presented this exhibition as the feverish and decisive moment that made him favor history over architecture.[4] The exhibition proposed, according to Tafuri, a "poetics of heroic jubilations"[5] to disillusioned and frustrated intellectuals. He condemned the approach of the curators, which he defines in *Theories and History of Architecture* as "operative criticism" and the "projection of a precise poetic direction, anticipated in its structures."[6] For Tafuri, operative criticism represented the intersection between history and the project: an historiographical method oriented toward action, which renounces numerous *verifications* in order to satisfy its own objectives. He believed that this distorted and "operative" history nevertheless failed precisely in the field of concrete action, where it did not produce the expected effects on architectural culture and the project, because it was "incapable of using its dagger in the political struggle."

Tafuri's historical activity (or historical writing) is in itself a critique of architectural ideologies and therefore a political activity that clarifies the institutionally and historically conditioned role of architecture in the perspectives of capitalist *civilization*. For him, there are two opposing histories, one operative and the other critical, both producing divergent strategies: preserving architecture as an *institution* or destroying architecture as an *institution*.

Zevi's selective and operative approach was already well embedded in his book of 1950, *Storia dell'architettura moderna*.[7] At a certain point, for example, Zevi explains the collaboration of progressive architects with the Fascist regime and introduces the figure of the heroic architect. He presents the history of the Italian modern movement under Fascism as a challenge to the dominant system of values and as a personal and individual story of resistance: "a formidable individual struggle, hampered by corrupted and incompetent authorities and by the indifference of the general public; that of a desperately heroic minority whose every civic and social aspiration was undermined."[8] Zevi's vision of architectural heroism under Fascism, largely inspired by his personal history in the Resistance, is a moral heroism and an exaggerated humanism that attempts to reaffirm the function of the architect as an intellectual, and of architecture as a vector of cultural values that is irreducible both to politics and to the new market logics. Tafuri intensely criticized and contested

Fig. 2 Members of the editorial team of *Quaderni Rossi*, 1962, (from left) Mario Tronti, Raniero Panzieri, Gaspare De Caro, and Antonio Negri.

this position. It is interesting to note that, according to Tafuri, many historians (Zevi is not named, but he seems to be targeted) attribute the crisis of modern architecture to political regressions, starting in the 1930s, of which European fascism is an exemplary manifestation, while ignoring the international reorganization of the cycles of capital through the adoption of planning policies. Behind an ideological veil, an operative critique, as defined by Tafuri, masks a historical reality from which it selects certain developments and omits others. This distortion of history means that, instead of realizing that architects have become organizers of the rationalization of the urban machine, some of them persist in pursuing theoretical hypotheses that, for Tafuri, can only end "in self-deception,"[9] in the development of myths, moral and Promethean, that prevent us from seeing the crisis of the ideological function of architecture.

What is more, the mobilization of the figure of the heroic architect responds to a strategic ambition: Zevi suggests that architects should reformulate the principles of progressive architecture, so as to redefine the political orientation of modernism in Italy. For Zevi, architecture, newly redeemed from all compromises and the holder of high social values, now proposes to revive the figure of the committed intellectual invested with a social mission.[10] The modalities of opposition to capitalist contradictions and cycles, even if they are developed on the horizon of a bourgeois culture that cannot be surpassed, still leave room for the poetic intervention of architecture to counterbalance the environment generated by the structural crises of the market. Zevi's heroic rhetoric provides solutions to the crisis in which architecture is immersed, linked to the loss of the intellectual function of the architect in the face of capitalist planning (Fig. 3).

Following the work and criticisms of some well-known operaists in the field of theory whom he met through the journal *Contropiano*, Tafuri questions both the production of architecture as intellectual labor and the new role of architects.[11] According to him, architects, from then on incorporated into the reality of wage labor within capitalism, have changed positions in the social and production process. From anticipators invested with a social mission—a very modernist conception—they became mere organizers of the production cycle. While Tafuri encourages architects to subscribe to this new proletarianization so as to produce a class critique and organize themselves as workers, others, like Zevi, prefer fighting against this institutional disappearance, seeing in the new disciplinary frustration the heroic intellectual challenge to lead against capital.

AL While Tafuri's arguments would from the end of the 1960s foreground the worker and intellectual work within broader historical cycles, at the start of that decade, when still in Rome, as a recent graduate, and a young architect, Tafuri shared this fight with Zevi—only disagreeing (productively, for some years) on the cause of this institutional disappearance. On one hand, the heroic architect, capable of leadership; on the other hand, the architect with the authority and insight to break into the power systems circumscribing the possibilities of that hero.

But this Zevian opposition still functions in terms of bourgeois ideology, obscuring the real reasons for the collapse of previous disciplinary positions, which were instead historically explained by Tafuri.

If we follow Zevi's line of reasoning, architects should pose the conditions of their survival as a reformist alternative. This proposition can be summed up as an attempt to maintain professional symbolic functions by incorporating its contradictions.[12] While the appearance of architecture as a social mission and internal alternative to capital is thus maintained, the real political and economic content of architectural work remains hidden. In contrast to the operaist leitmotiv "dentro e contro" ("in and against"), architects do not seem to be capable of anything other than a "dentro e con"

Fig. 3 Bruno Zevi on the cover of *Domus*, no. 647 (February 1984).

Fig. 4 Manfredo Tafuri on the cover of *Domus*, no. 618 (June 1981).

("within and with") position, which appears to be a sort of historical reformism. At least, this is the hypothesis pursued by some contemporary critics, such as Pier Vittorio Aureli,[13] Jacopo Galimberti,[14] and, in a way, GIZMO.[15] Coming back to Zevi, we can say, from our materialist perspective, that he answered the canonical alternative proposed by Le Corbusier ("Architecture or Revolution?")[16] with a double negation: neither Architecture, nor Revolution - but Reform. Written this way, "history" gets rid of the crises and contradictions that have shaped architectural culture, so as to naturalize an historical narrative oriented toward freedom and social justice. In a very precise and exhaustive way, Tafuri's various studies of the American city, the first Soviet five-year plan, and the social democratic experiments of the Weimar Republic demonstrate the lack of political verification of these reformist experiments.

In this, I believe, the counterpoint is not (or not yet) the Venice projects on the major political systems and their architecture and planning but rather Rome and its development against the Piano Regolatore Generale, in which Tafuri (and another set of protagonists) first formulated an idea not of "in and against" (nor of "within and with") but "against, against, against." The Soviet, American, Viennese, and German cases to which he turned in the 1970s were themselves an historical verification of the structure of a situation that was much closer, and less "historical," in which the idea of architecture and the fate of its institutions was felt as a kind of immediacy.

As an answer to Zevi, Tafuri responds with a critique of ideology applied to the architectural discipline and asserts that a fundamental social transformation is a precondition for the proper effectiveness of architectural ambitions.

While we need to keep in mind that intellectual paths are often marked by ruptures and contradictions, even more so when looking at this path with the hindsight of a few decades, an opposition nevertheless emerges. On the one hand is Zevi's liberal, political, and institutional commitment;[17] on the other, Tafuri's militant and Marxist commitment.[18] These political divergences, even if they cannot sum up the complexity of life experiences, reveal the normative and programmatic aims adopted by the protagonists in their work.

ZEVI'S AND TAFURI'S USES OF "DEGREE ZERO"

The first occurrence of Roland Barthes's third term in Zevi's work is to be found in *Il linguaggio moderno dell'architettura*, published in 1973.[19] In the first French edition of this book (1981), the conclusion is entitled "Prehistory and the degree zero of architecture." Then, during the '90s, Zevi increasingly made use of the concept of degree zero, trying to translate it to architecture. His goal, in doing so, was to "extend all the conquests of the avant-gardes," which can be summarized as a "liberation" of architecture from the classic, authoritarian, academic, and postmodern languages.[20]

As far as Tafuri is concerned, his affiliation with Barthes's concept is the result of a later construction, which can be retraced through the Anglo-Saxon reception of the Italian critic's works.[21] *Opposition* was one of the first journals to make Tafuri's work available in English, but in a broken chronological order. For the members of the editorial committee of the third issue in which we find Tafuri's "L'architecture dans le Boudoir," Tafuri was "a key signifier of European theory" and the paragon of the application of Marxist theory to architecture (Fig. 4).[22]

But the place of critical history, which Tafuri defended, was gradually eclipsed in favor of theoretical essays experimenting with "analogies and transfers of notion between architecture and other cultural and disciplinary fields."[23] Thus, the personal agendas of some of the journal's personalities, starting with one of its editors, Peter Eisenman, easily contributed to bringing together the "Tafurian despair" and various explorations of disciplinary autonomy and literary concepts. A few years later, faced with the "formally regressive"[24] character of postmodernist design and the conservative turn of contemporary American politics, the group around the journal *ReVision* broke out of an architectural theory then dominated by the formalist methods of *Oppositions* and remobilized Tafuri to inject "historical" and "materialist" concerns into debates on the politico-cultural praxis of architects.

An operation I can only imagine he would have welcomed...

The publication of a symposium organized by *ReVision* in 1982, and more particularly a text by Fredric Jameson,[25] would definitively associate Tafuri with Barthes and his degree zero.

For the American reader, *Architecture and Utopia* would always be the touchstone, but Tafuri discusses Barthes and the degree zero at length in his *Theories and History of Architecture* (first edition 1968).

Therein, degree zero comprises one of a set of tools to understand the nature of the avant-garde, in history, and as a precedent for the conditions of the present in which he wrote. Interestingly, he comes at Barthes through the work of Angelo Guglielmo.

In his article, Jameson specifically compares *Architecture and Utopia* (1973) to Theodor Adorno's *Philosophy of Modern Music* (1949) and Barthes's *Writing Degree Zero* (1953). He portrays the three authors as defenders of cultural pessimism, incapable of moving toward a dialectical "third term" that had the potential to break the deadlock in which structuralism and phenomenology seemed to find themselves at the time. Jameson's article, but also, paradoxically, *ReVision*'s separation of the context of Tafuri's writing from the social memory of it, were the pinnacle of the depoliticization enacted upon Tafuri's work. When Tafuri summons Barthes, it is first and foremost to refute any rhetoric that tends to exalt the creative force of the subject in artistic work, or the independence of art from any external influence. Tafuri would rather draw on Barthes's *Mythologies*, or *Critique et verité*, to formulate an ideological critique of architectural culture as an apparatus that transforms historical reality into a naturalized process.[26]

Despite Jameson's misinterpretations[27] of Tafuri, several passages of his text devoted to Barthes helped us understand Zevi's use of the degree zero. Jameson mentions Barthes's conception of the degree zero as a form freed from class belonging and from symbolism. The integration of the problematic of class struggle into their respective work leads Tafuri and Zevi to a different mobilization of Barthes. In his "Historical Project," Tafuri explicitly sets out the terms of the alternative: first, descend into the "magic circle of language" and multiply the metaphors within the architectural text, and second, analyze the external factors of work, the material structures.

VERIFYING OPERATIVITY

If we take up the reformist and continuist theme defended by Zevi and many other intellectuals, such as Jürgen Habermas or Axel Honneth,[28] in the face of the reconfigurations of capitalism, then degree zero, expurgated and transmuted to architecture, perfectly embodies the political perspective of Zevi.[29] Degree zero, "liberated from all servitude to a pre-established state of language,"[30] becomes for Zevi a weapon against artificial symbols, allegories, and classicism.

In this, as you suggest, Tafuri and Zevi would align, though standing on the same patch of discursive ground while facing different, though not opposite, directions.

The idea that one can deploy this concept to strip back layers of artificiality to a kernel of unassailable purpose is crucial—both for the examples (as in this essay) where it takes place and for the demand it makes upon those who use it to have a clear sense of their purpose in the first place.

It is also interesting to note that the degree zero revival at the turn of the 1990s, promulgated by figures such as Zevi, but not exclusively,[31] coincided with a theoretical and political alignment of the discipline with neoliberalism. Rather than assuming that the architectural sphere was being utterly depoliticized in the 1980s, we believe it is more appropriate to think in terms of political repositioning. While this "sullen withdrawal"[32] is not homogeneous in the architectural field, it nonetheless characterizes a significant part of the intellectual production of the period, focused on the research and production of forms without modern utopias.[33] This repositioning goes along with the new organization of labor[34] and the spread of architectural mediation[35] that modify criticism and its proper conditions of production.

In addition, the "post-era," as some have called it, and the way it has been formulated and assimilated with the "end of history" by Francis Fukuyama[36] (which can also be read as the end of politics) also favors interpretations of a degree zero that encourages the development of disciplinary autonomy.[37] Frederic Jameson and Jacques Derrida[38] have hinted at this: if it is the end of history, then what is left is the withdrawal to the strict so-called disciplinary foundations.

In this essay we have tried to verify the political implications of zero degree for architectural history and criticism. The notion of "verifica" is a central concept for Fortini.[39] In *Verifica dei Poteri*[40] he analyzes the place of the literary critic within the framework of the dominant bourgeois culture and the attacks of capitalism and reaffirms the crucial importance of political commitment for poets, writers, and intellectuals. The term "poteri" used by Fortini in tandem with "verifica" thus refers to the subsequent authority that falls to critics and theorists, but also to the material possibilities of action. Therefore, we also ask ourselves: why should we be interested in degree zero today? The different ways it can be understood show that its operativity cannot be determined once and for all. Maybe the answer is to be found within a "verifica dei poteri" of this concept throughout history, from specific points of view. In continuation with this work, there is a second level of verification, as Fortini states: "More than in the pages of historians, verification takes place in the action of the present."[41]

1 We translated this quote from French, into which it was translated by Guido Mattia Gallerani for his paper, "Roland Barthes contesté: Franco Fortini, Pier Paolo Pasolini, Umberto Eco," *Revue belge de philologie et d'histoire* 94, no. 3 (2016): 597–610. The quote comes from Fortini's review of *Le degré zéro de l'écriture,* first published in 1954 in the journal *Lo Spettatore Italiano*, and taken up almost fifty years later, in 1999, for the second opus of *L'ospite ingrato: annuario del Centro Studi Franco Fortini*, no. 2, 267–269. Despite all our efforts, we could not find the original of this review. (All translations are ours unless otherwise noted.)

2 The Italian economy experienced an average rate of growth of GDP of 5.8% per year between 1951 and 1963. Nicholas Crafts and Gianni Toniolo, *Economic Growth in Europe since 1945* (Cambridge: Cambridge University Press, 1996), 428.

3 Manfredo Tafuri mentioned this date in an interview with Luisa Passerini, referring to the beginning of his polemical engagement with Zevi's texts. Manfredo Tafuri and Luisa Passerini, "History as Project: An Interview with Manfredo Tafuri," *ANY: Architecture New York*, nos. 25–26 (2000): 20.

4 Ibid., 31.

5 Manfredo Tafuri, *History of Italian architecture 1944–1985* (London: MIT Press, 1989), 79.

6 Manfredo Tafuri, *Théories et histoire de l'architecture* (Paris: Éditions S.A.D.G, 1976), 189 and 201.

7 Bruno Zevi, *Storia dell'architettura moderna* (Torino: Giulio Einaudi editore, 1950).

8 Bruno Zevi, "Gruppo 7: The Rise and Fall of Italian Rationalism," *Architectural Design* 51, nos. 1–2 (1981): 41–43.

9 Hilde Heynen, *Architecture and Modernity* (London: MIT Press, 1999), 144.

10 Jean-Louis Cohen, *La coupure entre architectes et intellectuels, ou les enseignements de l'italophilie* (Liège: Mardaga, 2015); Marco Biraghi, *L'architetto comme intellettuale* (Torino: Giulio Einaudi editore, 2019).

11 *Contropiano* was founded in 1968 by Alberto Asor Rosa, Antonio Negri, Massimo Cacciari, and Mario Tronti. Intended to be the continuity of *Classe Operaia*, this new journal aimed to publish essays and theory rather than to have any direct political intervention. Tafuri wrote for *Contropiano* and exchanged ideas with the founders of it.

12 Pier Vittorio Aureli, "Recontextualizing Tafuri's Critique of Ideology," *Log*, no. 18 (2010): 89–100.

13 Pier Vittorio Aureli, *The Project of Autonomy: Politics and Architecture Within and Against Capitalism* (New York: Princeton Architectural Press, 2008)

14 Jacopo Galimberti, *Images of Class: Operaismo, Autonomia, and the Visual Arts* (1962–1988) (London: Verso Books, 2020).

15 GIZMO, *Backstage: L'architettura come lavoro concreto* (Milano: FrancoAngeli, 2016).

16 Le Corbusier, *Vers une architecture* (Paris: Éditions Crès, 1923).

17 This civil commitment was reflected in political movements and parties, starting with his militancy in Giustizia e Libertà (1942–1944), during the years of war and Resistance. In 1944 he returned to Rome, where he took part in the anti-fascist struggle in the ranks of the Partito d'Azione. At the end of the war, he worked for the local elections in Rome. From 1951, and for eighteen consecutive years, he was secretary general of the INU (Istituto Nazionale di Urbanistica). In 1966 he joined the central committee of the Partito socialista unificato (Partito socialista italiano (PSI) and Partito socialista democratico italiano (PSDI)), from which he withdrew two years later following the split between PSI and PSDI. In 1987, he was elected to the Chamber of Deputies on the list of the Radical Party, of which he was also president between 1988 and 1991.

18 In 1962, following the publication of the *Piano Regolatore Generale di Roma* and faced with the *centrosinistra*'s programmatic disinterest in land issues (especially during the conflict with Florentino Sullo), Tafuri, then a member of the AUA, decided to join the PSI. In 1964, he became a member of the PSIUP (Partito

socialista italiano unità proletaria). In 1968, following the events of May, Tafuri left the PCI. Andrew Leach, *Choosing History* (Ghent: A&S Books, 2007).

19 1973 was a year of strong social struggles, during which Autonomia "replaced" Operaism. About this historical movement and these changes in class composition, the struggles' goals, and terminological issues, see Steve Wright, *Storming Heaven: Class Composition and Struggle in Italian Autonomist Marxism* (London: Pluto Press, 2017), and also Nanni Ballestrini and Primo Moroni, *L'Orda d'oro. 1968-1977: La grande ondata rivoluzionaria e creativa, politica ed esistenziale* (Milano: Feltrinelli, 1988).

20 In answer to his own question, "How to amplify all the achievements of the avant-garde?," Zevi says that "Barthes, theoretician of 'degree zero,' provides us with an answer: 'In the effort to free us from the literary language, there is another solution: creating a white writing, detached from every duty ... Degree zero writing is basically an indicative writing, if you want, amodal. Its aim is to overcome Literature with a capital L, relying rather on a basic language. Only then the instrument is no longer ideological, becoming closest to silence ... If writing is truly neutral, then Literature is defeated.'" Zevi goes on to "translate: if architectural writing is really neutral, then the architecture of power, classic, authoritarian, academic, postmodern, is defeated." Bruno Zevi, *Paesaggistica e linguaggio, Grado Zero dell'architettura* (Venice: Canal & Stamperia Editrice, 1999), 43.

21 Our own first understandings proved to be initially biased and distorted by this Anglo-Saxon reception, which is still tenacious and "canonical" for a contemporary reading of Tafuri's works. To methodologically deconstruct this approach, to understand its effects as well as its aims, we recommend Diane Ghirardo, "Manfredo Tafuri and Architecture Theory in the U.S., 1970-2000," *Perspecta* 33 (2002): 38-47, and Gail Day, "Manfredo Tafuri, Fredric Jameson and the Contestations of Political Memory," *Historical Materialism* 20, no. 1 (2012): 31-77.

22 Day, "Manfredo Tafuri," 41.

23 Hélène Jannière, *Critique et architecture: Un état des lieux contemporain* (Paris: Editions de La Villette, 2019), 76.

24 Mary McLeod, "Introduction," in *Architecture, Criticism, Ideology*, ed. Joan Ockman (Princeton: Princeton Architectural Press, 1985), 7.

25 Fredric Jameson, "Architecture and Critique of Ideology," in *Architecture, Criticism, Ideology*, ed. Joan Ockman (Princeton: Princeton Architectural Press, 1985).

26 Manfredo Tafuri, *Théories et histoire de l'architecture* (Paris: Editions SADG, 1979), 147 ; Manfredo Tafuri, "The Ashes of Jefferson," in *The Sphere and the Labyrinth* (Cambridge, MA.: MIT Press, 1987), 301-302 ; Manfredo Tafuri, "L'architecture dans le Boudoir," *Oppositions*, no. 3 (1974): 37-62 ; and Jean-Louis Cohen, "'Experimental' Architecture and Radical History," *ANY: Architecture New York*, nos. 25-26 (2000): 42-47.

27 We are talking about a misinterpretation, because a few years later, Jameson re-evaluated his judgement. See Fredric Jameson, "From Metaphor to Allegory," in *Anything*, ed. Cynthia C. Davidson (Cambridge, MA: MIT Press, 2001).

28 Stathis Kouvelakis, *La défaite de la critique: Émergence et domestication de la théorie critique, Horkheimer – Habermas – Honneth* (Paris: Éditions Amsterdam, 2019).

29 Bruno Zevi, "The Seven Myths of Architecture," *Social Research: An International Quarterly* 52, no. 2 (1985): 411-422.

30 Ibid., 411.

31 In the French context, for example, Jean Attali and Dominique Gonzalez Foerster, "Le degré zéro de l'architecture," *L'Architecture d'Aujourd'hui*, no. 336 (2001): 64-67.

32 Reinhold Martin, *Utopia's Ghost, Architecture and Postmodernism, Again* (Minneapolis: University of Minnesota Press, 2010), xiv.

33 Following the example of the articles by Joan Ockman, "Form Without Utopia: Contextualizing Colin Rowe," *Journal of the Society of Architectural Historians*

57, no. 4 (1998): 448–456, and Tafuri, "L'architecture dans le Boudoir," we refer to the architectural production of Peter Eisenman, John Hejduk, Michael Graves, Robert Stern, Robert Venturi, Denise Scott-Brown, and Aldo Rossi.

34 We refer here to themes that will not be developed in this text, but whose main characteristics can be listed: starchitecture, international exports, large national symbolic projects, etc.

35 Marcela Garcia Martinez, "Architects to the Rescue: Exhibitions in the Architectural Gallery Aedes, 2000– 2015," *Dialectic*, no. 4 (2016): 68–76.

36 Francis Fukuyama, "The End of History?," *The National Interest*, no. 16 (1989): 3–18.

37 Gilles Malzac, "La Ruse des Colombes," *Exercice(s) d'architecture*, no. 9 (2020): 90–97.

38 Frederic Jameson, "Reflections in Conclusion to Adorno," in *Aesthetics and Politics* (London: Verso, 1977), 196–213 ; Jacques Derrida, *Spectres de Marx* (Paris: Galilée, 1993). See also Jürgen Habermas, "La Modernité: Un projet inachevé," in *L'époque, la mode, la morale, la passion* (Paris: Éditions du Centre Georges Pompidou, 1987).

39 Franco Fortini, *Verifica dei poteri: Scritti di critica e di istituzioni letterarie* (Milano: Il Saggiatore, 1965).

40 This title refers to the work of the Italian Romantic writer Alessandro Manzoni, *La Rivoluzione Francese del 1789 e la Rivoluzione Italiana del 1859* (Genoa: F. Sanguineti, 1985), a comparative analysis of the French and Italian Revolutions.

41 Fortini, *Verifica dei poteri.*

III

Ways for Research to Be a Form of Know-ledge

253
ARCHITECTURE BEYOND THIRD TERMS AND SPACES: THE CASE FOR PLURALISTIC ARCHITECTURAL METHODOLOGIES
Jorge Mejía Hernández, Klaske Havik
comments by
Christophe Van Gerrewey

269
TYPE AND CLICHÉ: REPETITION RECONSIDERED WITH QUATREMÈRE DE QUINCY'S *DICTIONNAIRE HISTORIQUE DE L'ARCHITECTURE*
Adil Mansure
comments by
Sunil Manghani

281
THE PRESENCE OF MYTH IN CONTEMPORARY LIFE. BRUNO ZEVI AND KENNETH FRAMPTON IN THE FIELD
Lyna Bourouiba
comments by
Joseph Bedford

297
UNCOVERING INVISIBLE EDITORIAL WORK: TRANSLATION AND REPRESENTATION IN THE MAGAZINE *SPAZIO E SOCIETÀ*
B. Beril Kapusuz-Balcı
comments by
Jorge Mejía Hernández

Architecture Beyond Third Terms and Spaces: The Case for Pluralistic Architectural Methodologies

Jorge Mejía Hernández & Klaske Havik

comments by
Christophe Van Gerrewey

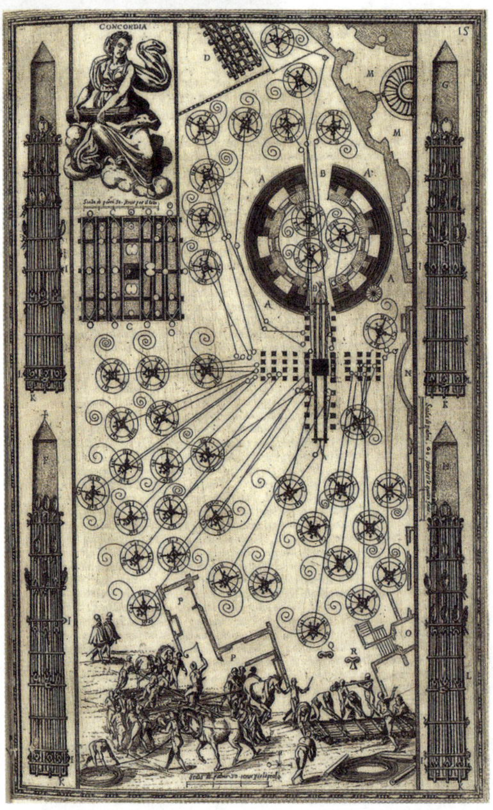

Fig. 1, 2 Plates from Domenico Fontana's *Movement of the Vatican Obelisk,* which Pamela O. Long uses as an example of convergence of "skilled" and "learned."

TRADING ZONES, POLYGLOSSIA, AND DIALECTICS

In *Artisan/Practitioners* and the Rise of the *New Sciences*, the historian Pamela O. Long makes a convincing case for the positive effects of pluralism in the growth and development of knowledge.[1] The extraordinary scientific developments that took place in Europe between 1400 and 1600, she argues, were founded on a notable increase in productive exchanges between the different communities of—in her terms—"the learned" and "the skilled." Fostering those exchanges are what Long refers to as "trading zones," where "the unskilled learned and the skilled practitioners exchanged substantive knowledge" (Fig. 1-2).[2] Similarly, the Russian literary scholar Mikhail Bakhtin argues that in the Middle Ages, Europe was the perfect breeding ground for the emergence of the novel as a literary genre. "A multitude of different languages, cultures and times became available in Europe," he says, "and this became a decisive factor in its life and thought."[3] It was on these international, and interlingual, grounds where a distinct *polyglossia* (the coexistence of different languages, dialects, and jargons in one society or area) emerged. According to Bakhtin, it was through Medieval European polyglossia that new linguistic creations and literary forms originated.

Aware of the productive role that "trading zones" and other forms of productive exchange play in our own work as architects, in this chapter we have chosen to examine the differences that exist between *monism* (the theoretical explanation of everything in terms of one principle) and *pluralism* (the theory that reality consists of two or more independent principles) in the growth and development of architectural knowledge. We will examine how the Hegelian dialectical model of interpretation that is commonly used among "the learned" serves as a point of departure, but is also transformed in Roland Barthes's "writing degree zero" and Edward Soja's "thirdspace."

CVG It is never easy to establish how ingrained ways of thinking are...
Is it really still common to interpret and reason dialectically, particularly in the Hegelian way?
Hasn't Hegel become one of the more unfashionable philosophers?

By doing so, we will try to understand possible ways in which we can productively integrate Barthes's and Soja's dialectical interpretations of reality in professional research and practice, given the renewed interest among architects in the work of both Barthes and Soja. This interest became evident to us in the symposium The Degree Zero of Architectural Writing, where a preliminary version of this chapter was first presented.[4] On the other hand, faced with the provocation to *theorize*, *draw*, and *debate* the "third term," the divergent yet comparable directions in which the two authors elaborate beyond the dialectical model of interpretation emerges as particularly relevant to our professional activity.

The architectural discipline is by nature dilemmatic and therefore favors dialectical interpretations. Common to the everyday work of architects are questions like, Is architectural design an additive or a subtractive practice? Why is it often said that architecture can be learned but not taught? Do architects conceive of built space moving from parts to wholes or from wholes to parts? Is architecture art or technique, science or craft? Does it issue in tangible objects or in void spaces where actions take place? Does the architect's mind proceed analytically or synthetically? And finally, is reflection the basis of architectural practice, or is it the other way around?

If both Barthes and Soja depart from a dialectical interpretation of reality, what does that mean? A laconic definition of the philosophical notion of the Hegelian dialectic describes it as

> an interpretive method, originally used to relate specific entities or events to the absolute idea, in which some assertible proposition (thesis) is necessarily opposed by an equally assertible and

apparently contradictory proposition (antithesis), the mutual contradiction being reconciled on a higher level of truth by a third proposition (synthesis).[5]

Rooted in Plato's discursive (or Socratic) method, in which truth is pursued by exchanging conflicting arguments in dialogue, Hegelian dialectics reconsider the objective of that dialogue altogether, by transcending the pursuit of partial, transient truths and aiming instead to *solve* perceived contradictions. This synthetic resolution takes the form of a monistic "absolute idea," taken for a superior form of thought.[6]

Karl Marx's methodological transformation of Hegelian dialectics into a purported "dialectical materialism" has become foundational to the work of many intellectuals.[7] Marx's interpretation of social life as a zero-sum conflict between necessarily opposing interests and the vision of society he proposed as the "synthetic" unraveling of that conflict have been adapted by influential segments of "the learned" in order to interpret different aspects of reality as necessary oppositions that—from the dialectician's perspective—must be resolved synthetically.

This is the actual problem: the obligation to resolve oppositions, and to move forward... What about Benjamin's "dialectics at a standstill," or Adorno's "negative dialectics," as ways of rescuing and transcending Hegelian models of thought?

How this looks in architecture was made clear by the art historian Ernst Gombrich. In his description of Hegelian determinism in architectural historiography and theory, the architect-as-artist is taken for an exceptional individual, gifted with the unique ability to capture the *spirit* of a time or nation in a work that is basically fated to follow the inexorable *rhythm* of history.[8]

Despite their Marxian foundations, Barthes and Soja take much less reductive or deterministic trajectories than Hegel—thus our claim that they *evolve beyond* the dialectic. Yes, they both base their work on a dialectical mode of interpretation manifestly, as we note below; yet they also *proliferate* within this model—they add elements to it—and therefore erode the elemental basis of Hegel's monism.

To better understand this dual condition in Barthes and Soja, who, on the one hand, remain tethered to a dialectical mode of interpretation, but who, on the other hand, are also able to recognize contradictions and insufficiencies in that model, let us briefly examine a few aspects of their work.

POSITIVE AND NEGATIVE DIALECTICAL SYNTHESES

Barthes's "writing degree zero" can be seen as an attempt to solve the perceived conflict between writing (thesis) and style or language (antithesis) by attaining an elemental form of writing that is uncontaminated by style and can therefore be taken for supra-literary (synthesis). This argument was developed through a series of articles published in the Parisian newspaper *Combat*, edited by the Marxist activist Victor Fay, and later published in book form as *Le Degré zéro de l'écriture* in 1953.[9] Eventually, Barthes's complex, and in many cases contradictory, dialectic interpretation percolated into mainstream architectural discourse in the 1970s. Barthes's use of dialectics is complex and even contradictory for several reasons.

Dialectical dialectics, perhaps? Isn't there something within dialectical thinking that sabotages and rescues it at the same time?

First, he adds nuance to the dialectical understanding of reality, notwithstanding language's inability to fit within the dialectic model, especially given its fundamentally linear and therefore singular nature.[10] Over the course of several decades, Barthes considered several ad hoc appendages to the dialectic, such as "dialectics of 'two terms,'" "'amputated' dialectics," and so on. [11]

These appended versions of the dialectic are proliferative, in the sense that apparent insufficiencies or inconsistencies in Hegelian or Marxist dialectics are dealt with expediently. This, of course, can only mean that the number of elements taken into consideration increases beyond the three terms, *thesis*, *antithesis*, and *synthesis*. How does this look like in practice? Referring to Edgar Morin's "open" dialectics, for instance, Barthes challenges Hegel's belief that conflict is resolved into an "absolute idea." By claiming that "the principle of synthesis in no way extinguishes the principle of antagonism,"[12] he effectively adds a fourth term to conventional dialectics. In other words, even after two opposites have been synthesized into a supposedly third and final understanding, there remains a fourth term—an unresolved (or unresolvable) antagonism.

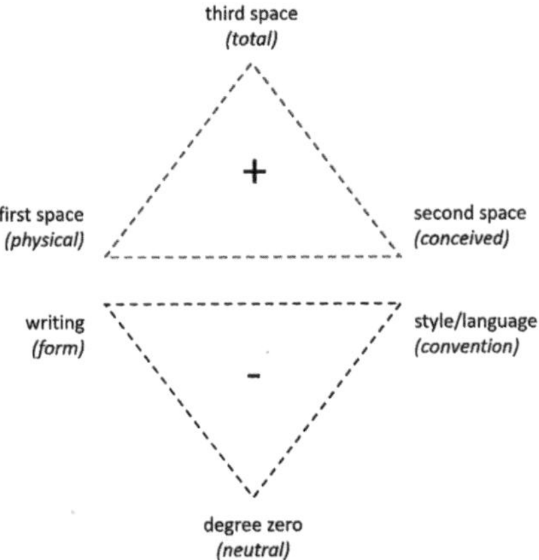

Following a different trajectory, Soja's "thirdspace" is an offshoot of the basic ideas advanced by the French Marxist philosopher and sociologist Henri Lefebvre in *The Production of Space* (Fig. 3).[13] Whereas Lefebvre's dialectic interpretation of the ways in which human beings relate to built space intends to solve the opposites of what he calls "perceived" and "conceived" spaces into a synthetic "lived" space, Soja adapts these terms into a slightly different conflict—that between a perceived "firstspace" and a conceived "secondspace," to be synthesized into a "thirdspace,"

> where everything comes together . . . subjectivity and objectivity, the abstract and the concrete, the real and the imagined, the knowable and the unimaginable, the repetitive and the differential, structure and agency, mind and body, consciousness and the unconscious, the disciplined and the transdisciplinary, everyday life and unending history.[14]

Soja takes the dialectical method of interpretation as a point of departure, as Barthes does, but it soon evolves beyond the mere synthesis of opposites and into a "trialectic"—a term already used by Lefebvre.[15] This evolution is evident in the article "The Socio-Spatial Dialectic," in its confrontation of what Soja sees as an "increasingly rigidifying pattern" in dialectically inspired Marxian spatial analyses. To overcome perceived limitations in the dialectic, Soja appends it via proliferation—the addition of variables in the consideration of a discrete question. In this case (and in his own terms), Soja's "socio-spatial dialectic thus represents a call for the reinclusion of socially produced space in Marxist analysis as something more than an epiphenomenon."[16]

Beyond the quality of Soja's and Barthes's hypotheses, in terms of explanatory power and applicability in real-world conditions, in both cases the synthetic solution to the dialectic interpretation of reality is reconsidered. There is an evident will to see the world from a dialectical perspective, but there is also awareness that additional elements are required to make that interpretation work.

Yes, indeed! So the opposite might be true: not a dialectics at a standstill is needed, but a dialectics that never stops...

Fig. 3 Diagram of Edward Soja's "thirdspace" versus Roland Barthes's "degree zero."

According to Andy Stafford,

> Reality, [Barthes] asserts, might be *"several things at once"*—that is, contradictory, even dialectical—but language is "linear, monadic [*monodique*]." It is this structure of language that prevents the writer from being dialectical in language; for the language of a writer is obliged to list these contradictory realities one after the other, that is, only in serial, not synthetic, fashion. Thus "a writer," asserts Barthes, "can declare the dialectic, but not represent it."[17]

Barthes and Soja take what appear to be divergent directions toward a synthetic resolution. To some extent it is this divergence (and its resonance with the dilemmatic nature of our profession) that encouraged our joint study of these two authors. Faced with the question of architecture as an additive or subtractive practice, for example, Soja attempts a positive or additive synthesis, in which two conflicting interpretations of space merge into an expansive—today one could even say "holistic"—realm, which is deliberately kept indeterminate and therefore open to interpretation. Barthes, on the other hand, advances a negative or even subtractive mode of dialectical interpretation. Rather than bringing two apparently antithetical forms of communication toward a blanket resolution, the choice here is to reduce them into elementality in order to reveal an underlying essence.

Akin to Chinese Taoism and its claims that opposition between the two elemental forces, yin and yang, can be resolved in the passive or receptive principle, Barthes too suggests that perceived dichotomies in language are synthesizable via non-action, emptiness, or negation.[18]

DIALECTIC AND PLURALISTIC APPROACHES IN ARCHITECTURAL DISCOURSE

In architecture, Soja's work has been especially relevant at the scale of city planning, given his work's origins in urban geography and what we might call socio-territorial studies. The historian Yael Allweil, for instance, uses Soja's work to argue for the "social turn" of architecture in recent decades, related in turn to the "spatial turn" in the historiographies of Foucault and Lefebvre.[19] Barthes's influence on architectural research and practice, on the other hand, is eminently theoretical. Mention *Writing Degree Zero* in a group of architects and the discussion usually leads to Manfredo Tafuri's "L'Architecture dans le Boudoir," in which the author says that anyone who wants "to make architecture speak" today "is forced to rely on materials empty of any and all meaning: he is forced to reduce to degree zero all architectonic ideology, all dreams of social function and any utopian residues."[20]

From this succinct mention it is often inferred that Tafuri sought to incorporate Barthes's "degree zero" in architectural theory. But is Tafuri actually referring to Barthes when he talks about architectural "trends that respond to language as a purely technical neutrality, which set themselves against the destruction of language as it is generated by a bureaucratized architecture," or when he talks about "research based on the dissolution of language itself, on the systematic destruction of form that is aimed at the total control of the technological environment"?[21]

Whatever the case, a few fragments from Tafuri should be taken not as exhaustive readings of Barthes but rather as part of a broader postmodern theoretical discourse in which Barthes naturally fits. An influential part of this discourse was brought about amid a pluralistic environment—a "trading zone," to use Long's term. This "trading zone" was the renowned Institute for Architecture and Urban Studies (IAUS) in New York and its journal *Oppositions*—the name itself revealing an obvious dialectical mindset—where Tafuri's "Boudoir" was published.

Illustrative of the journal's dialectical focus are the two well-known editorials, consecutively published, by Mario Gandelsonas and Peter Eisenman, though they do not refer to Barthes directly. In these editorials, first Gandelsonas pits Venturi's neo-realism against Rossi's neo-rationalism and synthesizes them into what he calls neo-functionalism. Then Eisenman followed with his own synthesis, which he calls post-functionalism.[22] Tafuri's interest in Barthes is thus totally in line with

Gandelsonas's and Eisenman's dialectical interpretations, where thesis and antithesis are synthesized into a higher level of understanding, pointing—at least in these three cases—toward architectural *meaning* as synthetic resolution of the *form-versus-function* dilemma.

More consistent and elaborate than Tafuri's use of Barthes, though, is Jorge Silvetti's article "The Beauty of Shadows," also published in *Oppositions*. Silvetti finds it "appropriate to recall Barthes," especially when he talks about the "double, paradoxical nature of architecture":

> There are those who want a text (an art, a painting) without a shadow, without the "dominant ideology"; but this is to want a text without fecundity, without productivity, a sterile text. . . . The text needs its shadows; this shadow is a bit of ideology, a bit of representation, a bit of subject: ghosts, pockets, traces, necessary clouds: subversion must produce its own chiaroscuro.[23]

Silvetti is still able to present architecture in oppositional terms, with text as thesis and *ideology* as antithesis; and yet, he says, merely synthesizing both terms can only result in "sterile text." Therefore, Silvetti proliferates beyond the dialectic by adding other terms (ghosts, clouds, etc.) piecemeal, bit by bit.

Proliferating beyond the dialectic... The ultimate opposition might be the one between language and architecture—after all, for Hegel, architecture was the art form devoid of ideas, and thus of language.

Tacitly or overtly, elements of this same discourse—one that is fundamentally carried out in dialectical terms, even if not referred to Barthes—appear in other writers related to the IAUS (Fig. 4).[24] Kenneth Frampton's *Critical Regionalism*, for example, and even Rem Koolhaas's appeal to surrealism in *Delirious New York*—both active in the IAUS during the late 1970s—frame some of their best-known arguments as conflicts between theses and antitheses, and then try to solve them via imaginative syntheses, be they a renewed version of a "spirit of place" or the use of deliberately elastic terms like "congestion," or "bigness."

However, the pluralistic nature we have attributed to the IAUS would not be complete without alternatives to the pervasive use of Hegelian, Marxist, and, later on, postmodernist forms of dialectical interpretation. We thus come back to Long's and Bakhtin's accounts of the Middle Ages, and ask ourselves to what degree the relevance of the IAUS might owe to the proliferation of diverse viewpoints, within what could also be taken for a vibrant architectural "trading zone."[25]

In alto / Top row, from left to right: Joseph Rykwert, Duarte Cabral de Mello, Isaac Mario Gandelsonas, Kenneth Frampton, Jachim Mantel, Gregory Gale, Thomas Schumacher, Stanford Anderson.
In basso / Bottom row, from left to right: Elizabeth Cromley, Robert Slutzky, William Ellis, Beth Spekter, Emilio Ambasz, Peter Eisenman, Victor Caliandro, Suzanne Frank.

Fig. 4 Members of the IAUS, football team version.
On the shirt is the Vitruvian Man of Cesar Cesariano.

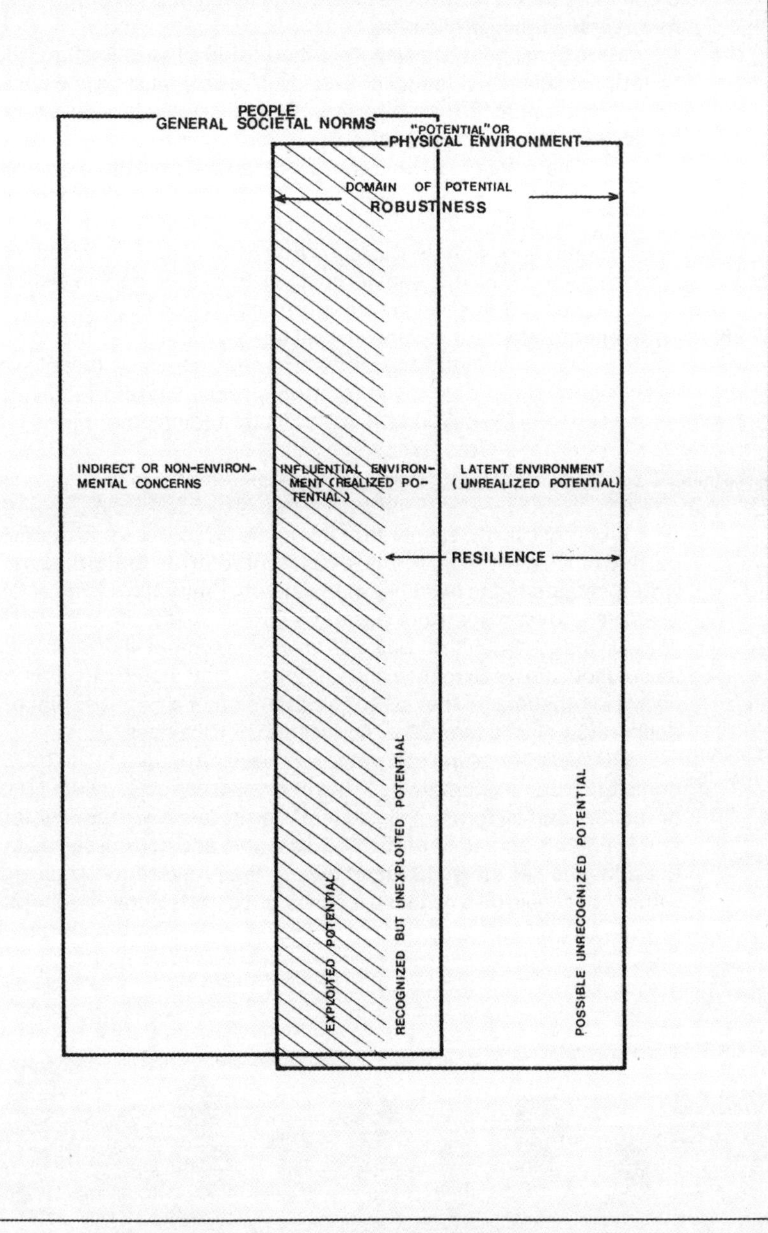

1. Social and physical environments yield influential and latent environments.

Fig. 5 Diagrams included in Stanford Anderson's introduction to *On Streets* (1978).

SYMPATRY, ORDINARY PLANNING, AND PROLIFERATION

Certainly less popular than Tafuri, Koolhaas, Frampton, or Eisenman, the historian Stanford Anderson's work within the IAUS offers a series of methodological alternatives to dialectical methods of interpretation. Anderson's major work within the Institute—the seminal *On Streets*, published in 1978—categorically rejects Hegel's ambition to solve contradiction into "absolute ideas," turning instead towards proliferation and plurality as the means for piecemeal truth-finding (Fig. 5-6).[26] In stark opposition to any form of "class struggle," for instance, in "People in the Physical Environment" Anderson introduces the anti-dialectic ecological notion of *sympatry* to explain the wealth of an ecosystem as the result of coexisting adversarial species—a far cry from the dialectic's antithetical methodology.[27] Furthermore, in the special issue of the Italian journal *Casabella* devoted to the IAUS, published in 1971, Anderson sternly opposes the kind of top-down planning inherent to Marxist dialectical materialist practice, by recognizing the built environment as an artifact that issues from a proliferation of countless individual human actions, at once unforeseen and with unforeseeable results—and none other than F. A. Hayek is cited as the source for such interpretation.[28]

Not one, not two (opposing) actions or voices but an infinite amount of commentaries...

In addition to the similarities that exist between Anderson's sympatry, Bakhtin's polyglossia, and Long's "trading zones," key for the argument we are developing here are the 1968 proceedings of an interdisciplinary conference, *Planning for Diversity and Choice*, edited by Anderson. Among the contributions is "Telos and Technique: Models as Modes of Action," by Marx W. Wartofsky, who unequivocally confronts the reductive determinism built into a dialectic interpretation. Wartofsky, a philosopher of science, proposes instead that we regard ordinary or everyday decision-making processes, carried out by many individual human beings, as a provenly reliable method for both truth-finding and the construction of possible futures. The different "models" we use to build our future, he says,

> characterize the normal process of creating the future, by bringing it down from the scale of cosmic crisis to that of daily and local necessity. I do not think there is a millennial solution to the future; but I do think that the pattern of our ordinary planning and striving prefigures whatever larger structures there are in terms of which long-range creation of the future take place.[29]

Also included in the proceedings is the "Outline of a Pluralistic Theory of Knowledge and Action," by Paul Feyerabend, another philosopher of science, who makes a case for proliferation as the *sine qua non* for the growth and development of knowledge in any field.[30] Feyerabend argues that a better epistemic model than that found in intellectual circles—those communities of "the learned" referred to by Long, where experts claim to have arrived at conclusive truths within a well-defined state of the art—can be found in the court of law. There, a multiplicity of viewpoints—from not only the skilled and learned but also many other individuals who might not quite fit either category—issue in a comprehensive and in many cases original understanding of reality:

> Who does not remember trials where the point of view of the prosecution is supported by the evidence to an extent that makes doubt not only impossible but simply irrational? And who does not remember his surprise at the way in which a clever and resourceful counsel for the defense can develop an alternative interpretation which first provides reasons for seeing the evidence differently and then shows that the alternative is supported by the newly arranged evidence as firmly as was the original view of the prosecution? The starting point of such a

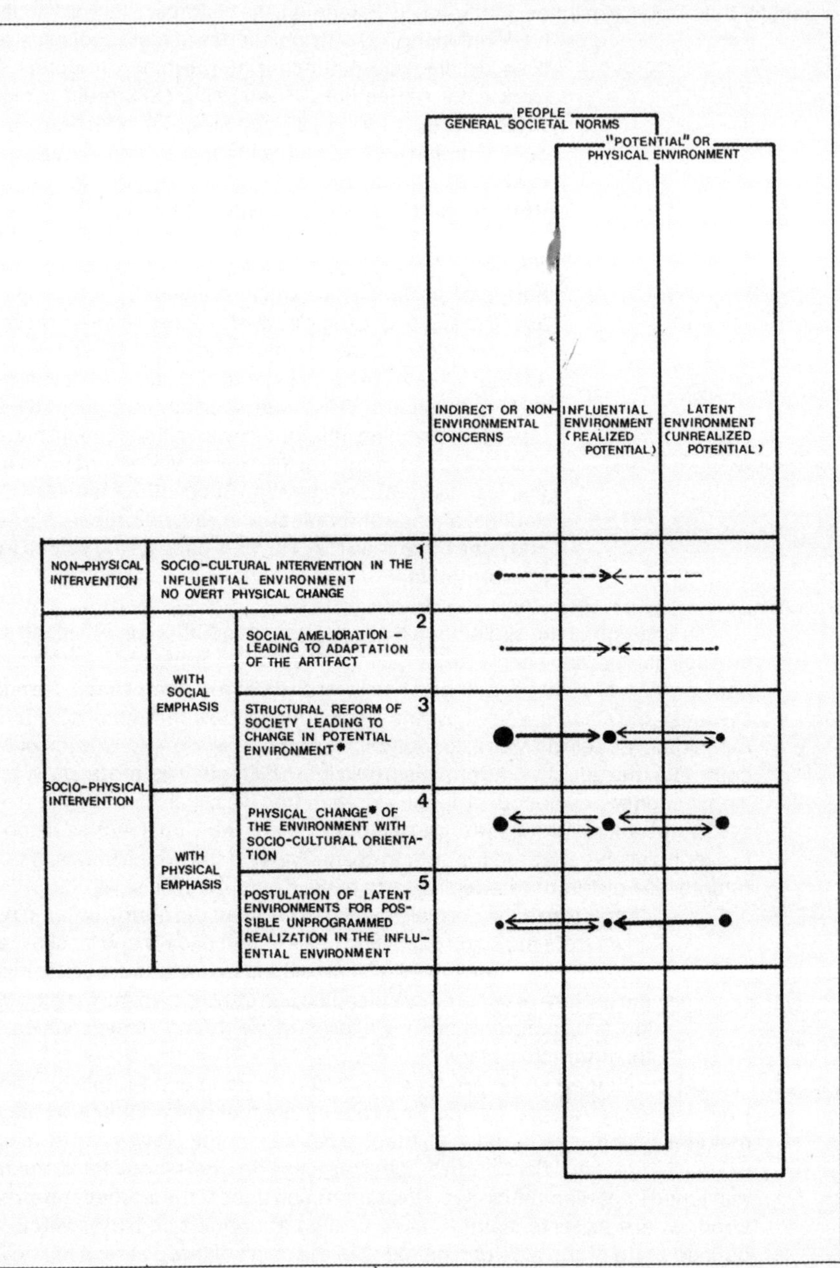

2. Types of planning intervention for change of the influential environment.

Fig. 6 Diagrams included in Stanford Anderson's introduction to *On Streets* (1978).

procedure is always an idea that is inconsistent with the theory to be criticized and that is therefore initially incompatible with evidence of the most convincing kind. But such a foolish and absurd conjecture may make one look at the evidence in a new and different light and may lead to the discovery of facts that are fatal for the "well established" position.[31]

Evidently, the procedure so vividly described by Feyerabend is entirely at odds with the presumption that prosecution and defense represent radically opposite arguments, in the form of theses and antitheses. Instead, he makes clear that

we can increase the strength of experimental refutations by replacing these metaphysical assumptions with scientific theories, that is, by again developing alternatives to the theories under test: decisive refutation is impossible without proliferation. To sum up, proliferation is required both in order to strengthen our tests and in order to bring to light refuting facts that would otherwise remain inaccessible. The progress of science is unthinkable without it.[32]

After this necessarily compact overview of Anderson's distinct voice within the IAUS, it seems useful to look back at where we started. Long's and Bakhtin's histories of scientific and artistic development in the Middle Ages made us aware that, to a large degree, our work recognizes pluralistic "trading zones," or "polyglossia," as fertile grounds for the development and growth of architecture knowledge. Then, Barthes and Soja offered us a clear-cut example of how an eminent instrument of "the learned," known as dialectical interpretation, can in effect be proliferatively "opened" beyond final resolution into monistic synthesis, by addition or by subtraction. This "opening" of the dialectic took place at the IAUS, where Barthes's work was relevant, and where "learned" and "skilled" architects used and offered distinct resources—Marxist and postmodernist dialectics as well as Hayek's, Wartofsky's, and Feyerabend's analyses. Now, we can move on to see to what extent some of these ideas are present in our own work.

PROLIFERATION AT WORK

Some of the questions discussed so far are clearly related to the way we research and teach architecture in disparate settings. The knowledge that emerges in conversation with master's students in a theory seminar is not the same as that which emerges while drawing at the design studio table and is quite different from knowledge that develops among deliberating researchers and practitioners from various disciplines. Barthes's and Soja's evolution beyond the dialectic model of interpretation helps us deal with these differences by prompting us to examine proliferative collaborations between different (e.g., more and less experienced) architects, but also between architects and non-architects alike. Following Long's and Bakhtin's explanations of the conditions that fostered the development of modern science and the appearance of new art forms in the past, we—as practicing architects who also teach at TU Delft—also strive for pluralistic methodologies as means for the growth and development of our knowledge of the built environment.

We employed such a pluralistic methodology for the public lecture series Architectural Positions, held at TU Delft in 2007, which we then developed into a lecture and seminar course within the Master of Architecture curriculum.

Think of The City of the Captive Globe by OMA/Rem Koolhaas: a seemingly neutral grid of positions that can no longer be (dialectically) related to each other or "opposed"—isn't this what is commonly known as postmodernism?

Both instances—lecture series and course—were pluralistic in the sense that they began from the premise that it is not the architectural educator's role to teach students to adopt a single position, as is traditionally the case in master-apprentice forms of architectural education, where students are encouraged to mimic their professor (Fig. 7).

In fact, the lecture series was initially still bound to a Hegelian dialectic model. To address different aspects of architecture (e.g., definitions, perceptions, temporalities, monumentality, image, practice), we encouraged confrontation between two architects with radically different viewpoints, while a third speaker, who introduced the theme, attempted to synthesize both "oppositions." In the session themed "Image," for instance, the architects Michiel Riedijk and Lon Krier developed antithetical arguments, which the Flemish philosopher Lieven De Cauter then tried to make sense of from a philosophical perspective.

The book resulting from the lecture series, *Architectural Positions: Architecture, Modernity and the Public Sphere*,[33] helped us proliferate beyond that simpler form of the dialectic in ways whose relationship to Barthes and Soja is now clear.

Compare to what Botho Strauss wrote in his 1981 book *Paare, Passanten*: "Without dialectic we suddenly think dumber; but that's the way it has to be: get rid of it!"[34]

Rather than synthesizing two opposing postures into a third mediating voice, the book gathers no less than six different arguments around each theme. A fictional "round table" discussion is thus created between an equal number of "learned" or "skilled" architects, each of whom presents a distinct take on each matter.

In the subsequent theory seminars we developed based on this book, students are asked to examine and evaluate the different, sometimes even notably contradictory arguments developed in each chapter. In this way, they come to recognize that reality consists of a number of independent principles and should therefore be examined and evaluated from a number of independent perspectives, including their own. For the current iteration of the lecture series, open to all Master of Architecture students in our department, the book has also served as springboard by which to broaden our knowledge of architectural theory and practice, moving beyond the handful of well-known architects who appear in the book. Our "trading zone" is thus currently expanding to include more, different, equally insightful, albeit perhaps lesser known architects.

Another "trading zone" that grows around our work consists of the different outcomes of the EU-funded COST (European Cooperation in Science & Technology) action called Writing Urban Places (COST actions are innovation-focused interdisciplinary networks).[35] Beginning in 2019, this collaboration grew over the course of four years to include a wide network of researchers of very different ages and professions, from almost every European country. The plurality of geographical and disciplinary backgrounds within the network allowed us to collect numerous theoretical notions by which to speak about the city from contrasting perspectives. A collection of terms and concepts used by network participants, ranging from architecture to visual anthropology, from media studies to literary theory, was issued in 2020 in the collectively authored *Vademecum: 77 Minor Terms for Writing Urban Places* (Fig. 8).

Following that publication, we explored a similarly diverse range of methodological perspectives. A first attempt to collect a database of methods used by

Fig. 7 Michiel Riedijk and Léon Krier in conversation. Photograph of the Positions debate "Image Building and Public Space," 2007, with Lieven De Cauter, Michiel Riedijk and Léon Krier, moderated by Klaske Havik and Tom Avermaete.

network members to analyze and practice within their own disciplines took shape within a digital Padlet platform. A considerable number of methods, complete with concrete assignments for their use, were uploaded on that Padlet—a selection of which resulted in the collectively authored *Repository: 49 Methods and Assignments for Writing Urban Places*.[37]

Yet another publication, *Other Destinations: Translating the Mid-sized European City*, collects a series of contemporary writings that address urban experience in intermediate European cities.[38] A shared interest in literary texts was paired with diverse geographical and linguistic backgrounds. Together we collected, translated, and introduced short, relatively unknown pieces about rather uncharted urban places in Europe.

Toward the end of our collaboration, we began to look beyond the realm of "the learned." Like Barthes, noticing the paradoxical relation that exists between a dialectic reality and a non-dialectical language, we too felt that despite the unquestionable pluralism of the abovementioned collections, ours was still a conversation between scholars. We therefore chose to shift gears, toward non-academic forms of communication, and made several movies that listen and speak to diverse urban publics: two shorts, *The City that Was Not Supposed to be on the Map*, by Büşra Dilaver, Diana Malaj, Elsa Paja, Holly Dale, and Klodiana Millona, and *One Hundred Columns of Skopje*, by Antonio Paoletti.[39] In both shorts, we can clearly perceive some of Soja's "thirdspaces" and Anderson's "many unforeseen human actions leading to equally unforeseeable results" at work—more than just the voices of a few "learned" interpreters. The city of the "skilled" emerges from the voices of a driver, a bookseller, a street musician, and two blacksmiths, among others.

THE RATE OF CHANGE

It is indeed possible to productively integrate Barthes's and Soja's evolved dialectics in current architectural research and practice. The thoughts and experiences related above describe one of the many possible ways in which architects can deal with the different dilemmas of our profession. Our work as researchers and teachers of architecture relies on multiple, independent viewpoints. In that sense, it resonates with the few aspects we have singled out from both Barthes's and Soja's work. Recall the former's ad hoc dialectical categories, or his recognition of language's non-dialectical nature, or Soja's critique of Marxian interpretations of space, for example. Like them, we inevitably remain tethered to a number of heartfelt beliefs. And yet, also like them, we also seem capable of recognizing when some of our ideas start failing us.

In this essay, we interrogated a few aspects of the dialectical method of interpretation, as part of those ideas and beliefs. Why does this method recur among "the learned"? As we've seen with Barthes and Soja, it might have something to do with a quest for certainty—always comforting, certainly gratifying.

And yet: dialectics is also the absence of certainty, since every idea is confronted with its opposite, which can be equally true.

Fig. 8 The three Writing Urban Places books: *Vademecum: 77 Minor Terms for Writing Urban Places*, *Repository: 49 Methods and Assignments for Writing Urban Places*, and *Other Destinations: Translating the Mid-sized European City*.

Besides, the mere presumption of a singular, higher truth about something automatically generates the need for an interpreter capable of revealing that truth. Feyerabend explains:

> The restrictions that the guardians of knowledge—be they scientists or philosophers—want to impose upon us are usually defined . . . by what some rather clever men have arrived at after long study and patient investigation. They merit serious attention. But these restrictions, this concentration upon a narrow domain of theories indicates also that the scientists have come to the end of their rope, that they can no longer think of any decisive objection (or of any decisive reason for defending an alternative) and that they have therefore, for the time being, agreed to accept a single point of view to the exclusion of everything else. Of course, the situation is hardly ever presented in this way. Instead of admitting that their ingenuity has given out and that they are no longer able to advance knowledge, scientists are usually in the habit of saying that they have finally arrived at the truth.[40]

It is not difficult to draw a parallel between these scientists' and philosophers' "truth" and one of the many syntheses that result from dialectical interpretations of reality. Evidence of the operative limitations of dialectic interpretation in real-world conditions invites us to wonder what would actually happen if we ever achieved a genuine "degree zero" of anything, or if we managed to reach a bona fide "thirdspace."

Perhaps one plausible answer to this question, among many possible answers, lies in our earlier mention of Barthes's interest in Taoism, especially when we recall that the doctrine of fundamental inaction attributed to Lao Tzu is based on an even older understanding, where the two elemental forces of yin and yang are already recognized.[41] But rather than aiming for any form of definitive resolution, positive or negative, in pluralistic and fundamentally open works like the *I Ching* (also known as the *Book of Changes*), these forces are allowed to group and regroup themselves proliferatively, first into elements and further into a diversity of situations in permanent, unavoidable, and yet always gradual change.[42]

By acknowledging this difference—on the one hand, seeing the world as a system of necessary oppositions and the ambition to achieve their resolution into a single principle, and on the other, seeing the world as the proliferation of an enormous amount of objects and events in constant change—we are able to recognize that different forms of dialectical interpretation "merit serious attention," as Feyerabend acknowledged that the work of scientists and philosophers did. But we are also able to recognize that it is possible to think and practice architecture beyond third terms and spaces and to work instead to generate pluralistic "trading zones," as the means for the piecemeal growth and development of architectural knowledge.

1 Pamela O. Long, *Artisan/Practitioners and the Rise of the New Sciences, 1400-1600* (Corvallis: Oregon State University Press, 2011).

2 Ibid., 8. Long takes the notion of "trading zone" from Peter Galison, as noted on pages 94 and 156. Cf. Jorge Mejía Hernández and Cathelijne Nuijsink, "Architecture as Exchange: Framing the Architecture Competition as a Contact Zone," *Footprint* 26 (Spring/Summer 2020): 1-6, which develops the similar notion of a "contact zone" taken from Mary Louise Pratt, "Arts of the Contact Zone," *Profession* (1991): 33-40.

3 Mikhail Bakhtin, *The Dialogic Imagination* (Austin: University of Texas Press, 1981), 11.

4 The Zero Degree of Architectural Writing: Theorizing, Drawing, and Debating the "Third Term," symposium, Brussels, November 2-3, 2022, https://zerodegreesymposium.wordpress.com/ (accessed March 20, 2024).

5 "Hegelian Dialectic," in *Random House Unabridged Dictionary*, 2023. See also "Hegel's Dialectics," in *Stanford Encyclopedia of Philosophy*, https://plato.stanford.edu/entries/hegel-dialectics/ (accessed September 21, 2023).

6 Cf. David P. Goldman, "Right-Hegel Meets Left-Hegel," *Tablet Magazine*, September 18, 2024, https://www.tabletmag.com/sections/arts-letters/articles/odd-couple-at-the-end-of-history.

7 For example, K. Michael Hays notes how Tafuri's work, "profoundly marked by his philosophical position within the *dialectic materialist* approach, has been developed by means of modern theoretical concepts drawn from French and Italian structuralism." Introduction to Manfredo Tafuri, "L'architecture dans le Boudoir: The Language of Criticism and the Criticism of Language," in *Oppositions Reader*, ed. K. Michael Hays (New York: Princeton Architectural Press, 1998), 291.

8 Ernst Gombrich, "Hegel and Art History," in *On the Methodology of Architectural History*, ed. Demetri Porphyrios, special issue, *Architectural Design* 51, nos. 6-7 (1981): 3-9.

9 Roland Barthes, *Le degré zéro de l'écriture* (Paris: Editions du Seuil, 1953); in English: *Writing Degree Zero*, trans. Annette Leavers and Colin Smith (London: Jonathan Cape, 1967).

10 Andy Stafford, "Roland Barthes Dialectician? In the Final Instance?" *Barthes Studies* 3 (2017): 97-120.

11 Ibid., 100-101, 103-105.

12 Stafford (ibid.) refers to Barthes's "Brecht, Marx et l'histoire" on 106n37.

13 Honri Lefebvre, *The Production of Space*, trans. Donald Nicholson-Smith (Oxford: Blackwell, 1991).

14 Edward W. Soja, *Thirdspace* (Oxford: Blackwell, 1996), 57.

15 Ibid., 53-82 (chapter 2, "The Trialectics of Spatiality").

16 Edward Soja, "The Socio-Spatial Dialectic," *Annals of the Association of American Geographers* 70, no. 2 (June 1980), 207-225.

17 Stafford, "Roland Barthes Dialectician?," 107.

18 For Barthes's interest in Taoism, see Lucy O'Meara, *Roland Barthes at the Collège de France* (Liverpool: Liverpool University Press, 2012), esp. chapter 4, "Japonisme and Minimal Existence in the Cours," 118-162.

19 Yael Allweil, "Beyond the Spatial Turn: Architectural History and the Intersection of the Social Sciences and Built Form," in *Proceedings of Spaces of History / Histories of Space: Emerging Approaches to the Study of the Built Environment*, April 30-May 1, 2010 (Berkeley: University of California, 2010), 1-9.

20 Tafuri, "L'architecture dans le Boudoir," 292. Originally published in *Oppositions* 3 (May 1974): 37-62.

21 Ibid. Tafuri also cites Barthes's "Critiques et verité," in 296n9.

22 Mario Gandelsonas, "Neo-Functionalism," in *Oppositions Reader*, ed. K. Michael Hayes (New York: Princeton Architectural Press, 1998), 7. Originally published in *Oppositions* 5 (Summer 1976): 4-5; Peter Eisenman, "Post- Functionalism," in *Oppositions Reader*, ed. K. Michael Hayes (New York: Princeton Architectural Press, 1998), 9. Originally published in *Oppositions* 6 (Fall 1976): 4-7.

23 Jorge Silvetti, "The Beauty of Shadows," in *Oppositions Reader*, ed. K. Michael Hayes (New York: Princeton Architectural Press, 1998), 387. Originally published in *Oppositions* 9 (Summer 1977): 262.

24 Among those who mention Barthes are two more authors in *Oppositions Reader*, ed. K. Michael Hayes (New York: Princeton Architectural Press, 1998): William Elis, "Type and Context in Urbanism," 225–252, and Hajime Yatsuka, "Architecture in the Urban Desert," 253–287. Their relevance for our argument is marginal, though.

25 Suzanne Frank, *IAUS, The Institute for Architecture and Urban Studies: An Insider's Memoire* (Bloomington: Author House, 2011).

26 Stanford Anderson, ed., *On Streets* (Cambridge / London: The MIT Press, 1986 (1978)).

27 Stanford Anderson, "People in the Physical Environment: The Urban Ecology of Streets," in ibid., 1–11.

28 Stanford Anderson, "L'ambiente come artefatto: Considerazione metodologiche / Environment as Artifact: Methodological Considerations," *Casabella* 35, nos. 359–360 (1971): 71–77.

29 Marx Wartofsky, "Telos and Technique: Models as Modes of Action," in *Planning for Diversity and Choice: Possible Futures and Their Relations to the Man-Controlled Environment*, ed. Stanford Anderson (Cambridge: The MIT Press, 1968, 260).

30 Feyerabend was Anderson's teacher at UC Berkeley in the fall of 1958, as noted in Stanford Anderson, "Architecture and Tradition that Isn't Trad, Dad," in *The History, Theory and Criticism of Architecture*, ed. Marcus Whiffen (Cambridge: The MIT Press, 1965), 77n15. This relationship is explored extensively in Jorge Mejía Hernández, *Transactions; or Architecture as a System of Research Programs* (PhD dissertation, TU Delft, 2018).

31 Paul K. Feyerabend, "Outline of a Pluralistic Theory of Knowledge and Action," in *Planning for Diversity and Choice*, 278.

32 Ibid., 283.

33 Tom Avermaete, Klaske Havik, & Hans Teerds, eds., *Architectural Positions: Architecture, Modernity and the Public Sphere* (Amsterdam: SUN Publishers, 2009).

34 Botho Strauss, *Couples, Passersby*, trans. Roslyn Theobald (Evanston: Hydra Books/Northwestern University Press, 1996), 69.

35 Writing Urban Places, COST Action CA18126, website at https://writingurbanplaces.eu/ (accessed 3/20/2024).

36 Klaske Havik, Svava Riesto, Henriette Steiner, and Kris Pint, eds., *Vademecum: 77 Minor Terms for Writing Urban Places* (Rotterdam: Nai010 Publishers, 2020), https:/writingurbanplaces.eu/vademecum-77-minor- terms-for-writing-urban-places/.

37 Carlos Machado e Moura, Dalia Milián Bernal, Esteban Restrepo Restrepo, Klaske Havik, and Lorin Niculae, eds., *Repository: 49 Methods and Assignments for Writing Urban Places* (Rotterdam: Nai010 Publishers, 2023), https://writingurbanplaces.eu/repository-49-methods-and-assignments-for-writing-urban-places/.

38 Michael G. Kelly, Jorge Mejía Hernández, Sonja Novak, and Giuseppe Resta, eds., *Other Destinations: Translating the Mid-sized European City* (Osijek: Faculty of Humanities and Social Sciences, J. J. Strossmayer University of Osijek, 2023), https://writingurbanplaces.eu/other-destinations.

39 Since 2023, when they were first screened in Delft, both movies have been shown internationally at many specialized festivals and public events.

40 Feyerabend, "Outline of a Pluralistic Theory," 279.

41 Lao Tzu, *The Tao Te Ching*, trans. James Legge (Oxford: The Clarendon Press, 1891).

42 *The I Ching, or Book of Changes: The Richard Wilhelm Translation*, trans. Cary Baynes (New York: Pantheon Books, 1950). In the book, the two fundamental principles, yin and yang, are assembled as continuous or broken lines, first into trios (elements) that in turn combine into hexads or sextets (situations). The graduality of change refers to the way one hexagram mutates into another, via declination of one or more (but very seldomly of all) lines.

Type and Cliché: Repetition Reconsidered with Quatremère de Quincy's *Dictionnaire Historique de l'Architecture*

Adil Mansure

comments by
Sunil Manghani

Fig. 1 Repairing a stereotype matrix, Leipzig, 1953.

Type in architectural theories from the 18th century onward has been a crucial tool for surveying global architectural variety and tracking repetition, continuity, and change in the discipline.[1] Whereas discourses on types have focused on so-called architectural exemplars, paying much heed to questions of origins, architect's intentions, and what ought and ought not to change with time in design procedures, little have the modus operandi of type been considered: repetition itself. What is at stake here is less the physical features of drawings, forms, or buildings and more the enduring practices by which they are imagined and (re)invented. Other than the mimesis of nature championed by many an architectural theorist, we might ask, what about involuntary repetition in design procedures? What about habits and tendencies of inhabiting spaces, from the street up, as it were, in 19th-century Europe? What if the logic or means of circulation of an idea (rather than its inherent value) dictates its repetition? What about the influence of persistent recurring architectural images in wide circulation? How to tell such repetitions apart from the presumed durability of architectural exemplars? To consider the various dynamics of repetition itself, we shall need to look outside architectural theory, especially to language studies, where the material means of propagation have not been overlooked. Studying repetition through the linguistic concept of the cliché will illuminate some of the marginal but significant dynamics of repetition at work—which, as we shall see, architectural types are not immune to.

In literary studies, a cliché is often considered to be an undesirable form of repetition. A metaphor originating in the mechanical and repetitive inscriptions of the movable typeface, to the point of its becoming worn out—referring in language usage to the repetition of a phrase, idiom, or concept to the point of almost nullified meaning—clichés are usually dismissed as inferior linguistic phenomena used with little thought, expression, or effort. They are linguistic formulations and visual associations taken at face value, which spread under the surface of what is lexically and socially valued. But repeat and spread they do! Despite being widely considered trite, everybody uses them. Lacking origins or authors, and often coming to mind involuntarily, clichés belong to everyone. Gaining momenta of use, they consolidate and repeat even further, beyond "rhyme or reason," as it were, and in contexts far beyond their original. Accruing meaning through ample repetition, however, clichés encode various dimensions of human experience, especially those that are difficult to otherwise codify. Thus their futility, ironically, often results in a residual economy of utility. They are the shared linguistic and behavioral substrate of a society, perhaps even what Roland Barthes calls the "degree zero" of language: the inevitable mass behavioral means, norms, and scaffolds of our shared social formations.[2]

An anchor of this essay shall be one of the progenitors of the theory of architectural types, Quatremère de Quincy, especially via his 1832 *Dictionnaire Historique de l'Architecture*.[3] Despite the fact that he provides ample analogies equating architecture to language—and analysts of his theory have modeled the diffusion of architectural ideas and elements in time akin to the epidemiology of language—much prior work on both Quatremère and architectural types has overemphasized semiotics at the cost of the material means and infrastructures of information dissemination—in both oral and print cultures.[4] As we shall see, the molds, casts, reliefs and other residues of print culture as well as popular language usage prompt much un-programmatic repetition, which, arguably, feeds back *meaningfully* into language proper. The mid-18th-century book type that Quatremère sought to write—a dictionary—contends inevitably with this: with not only explaining institutionally ascribed rules and word meanings to a wide readership but also comprehensively including meanings that consolidate from the habits, accidental mimetics, and mass behavioral evolutions of popular language usage. As we shall see, the forces of repetition that become evident by studying cliché are precisely what the *Dictionnaire* illuminates to be at work with architecture too. Exploring the means and modes of repetition itself, we shall see just how intertwined the exemplary and the everyday, canon and convention, and type and cliché can be.

FROM ENCYCLOPEDIA TO DICTIONARY

The *Encyclopédie, ou dictionnaire raisonné des sciences, des arts et des métiers*, edited by Denis Diderot and Jean le Rond d'Alembert and published between 1751 and 1772, was a multi-authored compendium of knowledge from various realms that spanned numerous volumes.[5] Consumed by increasingly literate societies in France and widely translated across Europe, this book type contributed not only to the systematization of knowledge but also its secularization and democratization. Another consonant project of much importance and influence was the *Encyclopédie méthodique par ordre des matières*, produced between 1782 and 1832, during which over 200 volumes were published, each a topical expansion of an alphabetical dictionary entry, written by an invited expert. With numerous writers involved, commensurability between knowledge realms became key. It was Quatremère who contributed the three volumes on Architecture between 1788 and 1825. His 1832 *Dictionnaire historique de l'Architecture* would borrow much from the *Encyclopédie*: the multivolume format, its alphabetical organization, and its branching out structure of information.[6] Despite the fact that dictionaries were designed to make knowledge appeal to a wide audience, aspects of Quatremère's book, paradoxically, also harbor Royalist and conservative Catholic sympathies, which become especially evident in the canons or genealogies of knowledge given preferential treatment (such as Greek antiquity).[7] To be comprehensive, however, encyclopedias and dictionaries need to flatten hierarchies and include material outside their authors' preferred canons, and moreover, by the 19th century, to do so from across the globe.[8] So Quatremère's *Dictionnaire* emerges, from the very outset, amidst the incongruous tasks of the treatise-like teaching of exemplary architectural canons but simultaneously making architectural knowledge commensurable to and consumable by a wide readership.

TYPE

Such conundrums, as we shall see, become evident in the various ways Quatremère discusses "type" in the *Dictionnaire*. In the initial definition, type refers not to the functional uses of a building (hospital, library, etc.) but rather to a set of qualities or its "character," which, as per Quatremère, ought to develop from an architect appropriately "imitating" nature such that not images of nature's objects or elements are "copied" but its "systems" or orders of relations are inherited and recreated in subsequent architectural inventions.[9] Imitation, claims Quatremère, operates through allegory.[10] The Greek temple being an "imitation" of the wooden carpentered hut—nature's most primordial expression in Greece—is one such instance in the *Dictionnaire*, where the hut is the "type" of the temple. Here, proportion is the key modus operandi of an analog or system of relations carrying from one building to the next. Quatremère insists on these relations being non-visual and in fact steadfastly expresses his concerns about the rampant mechanical "copying" of visual architectural elements occurring without necessarily grasping the underlying idea and structure of what is being copied.[11] A copy to him has no moral value. He contrasts the precision of a copy (or model) with the vagueness of a type, the latter affording much room for inventiveness.[12] In a successful "imitation" of a type, an architect ought not only to conserve its *typical* values but also thoughtfully reinvent some of its most significant tropes. Whereas Quatremère's contemporaries such as Jean-Nicolas-Louis Durand analyzed the evolution of building typologies visually by making comparative matrices of floor plan diagrams, a type for Quatremère was to be purely intellectual and only analogically detectable and reproducible.[13]

For many prior architectural theorists, imitation via types spotlighted the heredity of architectural objects, for example, Abbé Laugier and his seeking architectural origins in carpentry. Incidentally, the frontispiece of his *Essai sur l'architecture* was also one of the earliest printed images in architectural books. By comparison, origins were less clear in Quatremère's case: even though the Greek temple was the favored system, he also included Egyptian cave temples (the originary types of which were hollowed-out stone buildings) and East-Asian structures (the originary types of which were tents). Such multiple origins have led scholars such as Sylvia Lavin to point out just how socially and historically contingent architecture is in Quatremère's theory of cultural history, and therefore how similar to language it is.[14] The epigenetic nature of architectural knowledge, like linguistic material, is an affordance of Quatremère's theory that implicitly diminishes authorship, and thereby makes for an expansive historical framework. The forms of language that, over time, become authorless—with both type and cliché—form precisely a kind of *degree zero* substrate, which repetition both ensues from and reinforces. The above-discussed affinity for vagueness and the non-visual only make them more amenable to epigenesis.

With many a global architectural genealogy becoming known in Europe in the 19th century, the burden of understanding the intellectual lineage and context of a type for its subsequent imitation is placed by Quatremère on the discerning architect. The *Dictionnaire* here straddles a contradiction: in addition to championing the idea of type founded on non-visual analogy and vagueness, his tomes also address the contrary notion of type as the inadvertent physical replication of both text and image. Apropos the latter, from *epi typon* or "bas-reliefs of varying projections"; to *entypos* or "hollowing [sunk carving] as applied to figures, either in molded or cast works, or thrust in a hole in the earth, or formed in a bronze or plaster mold"; to *ectypos*, "a production made from a hollow mold, from which one extracts the sample which has been impressed"; to *prostypos* or the "figure which stands out against a flat background, or what is known as raised relief"—the aspect of material being pressed down to leave an impression appears to amply be on the sculptor Quatremère's mind.[15] At the print house, there is something sculptural about typography even. His dictionary entry "type," both etymologically and discursively, begins with: "'Type' comes from the Greek word 'typos,' a word which expresses by general acceptance (and thus is applicable to many nuances or varieties of the same idea) what one means by model, matrix, imprint, mold, figure in relief or in bas-relief."[16] As Leandro Madrazo's retracing further clarifies, "*type* derives from the Greek *typos*, which in turn comes from the Indo-European word *typto*, that meant 'to beat, to hit, to mark."[17] A bas-relief—characterized by Quatremère as a "speaking picture"[18]—even if carved or molded for a specific project, would usually have afterlives, change hands, and cast other copies for use beyond its original. The labor and mechanical infrastructure of a mold (textual or pictorial), evident especially in the depth of its inscription, determines not only the starkness or weight of the shadows the protrusions cast, but also how many copies it can cast as it wears down with use. Such material—and even sculptural aspects of "type"—though overshadowed by its chiefly allegorical use by Quatremère's interpreters, pervade the *Dictionnaire*. Type itself appears to be not about language writ large, but about its material means of dissemination. The physics of pressure and the psychological impact of impressions stand thoroughly muddled in several *Dictionnaire* definitions.

This all affects even the most non-material of entities in the *Dictionnaire*: an "idea," for example, the epitome of intellection, is for Quatremère also "all that impresses the exterior senses," as "one speaks of *grasping and retaining the images of corporeal beings*" (emphasis not added).[19] He even claims that "idea and image are metaphysically synonymous."[20] Another instance of the importance of physical replication is evident in the entry "character:" this presumably qualitative attribute is also described as "to engrave", "to imprint."[21] And an "imprint" in turn is discussed as the "impact that an idea leaves behind." Just think of the literal typefaces reused for numerous dictionary entries as Quatremère scatters and scrambles "idea," "image," "character," and "engrave" throughout various dictionary articles. The *Dictionnaire* perhaps marks an 18th-century shift in how memory is itself construed: less so allegorically and rather deeply conditioned by the repeat appearances of common inscriptions and imagery. Typefaces or molds produced for an architectural edifice similarly accrue memorability, meaning, and commensurability not only because of their original or inherent qualities, but in a parallel manner, and perhaps even more crucially, because of both their casting blocks and cast impressions appearing in wide circulation. How can any procedure of architectural ideation be unaffected by this shared material strata? We might even consider this very matter of the *degree zero of architecture* to be a mass psychological effect of material repetition.

DEPLOYING TYPES

Such repetition, however, is not what most 19th-century architectural theorists observed in types. They pursued in types not only a model of architectural history but also a canonical repertoire of architectural motifs for a Neoclassicist to draw from. Architectural typologies, especially those visualized, provided architects with attributes and patterns of repetition in a legible epistemological format, which they might project into future designs. Hence also perhaps the popularity of Durand's diagrams of architectural plan typologies, as they were easy to draw from and with.[22] Such impetuses of using types and their consequent effects have been well-characterized by Micha Bandini:

> [I]f type is the end-product of a reductive process, the form which results cannot be seen as a mere model but must be regarded as the internal structure of a principle which includes not only all the formal manifestations from which it has been derived but any future elaborations developed from it.[23]

If upheld as desirable forms of repetition, types could be instrumentalized to discount the complexity of mass human behavior in vastly expanded disciplines and cityscapes, and partake in a kind of *prediction modeling*: a forced reduction of the scope of architectural-historical consideration, and the bracketing away of uncertainty and variability in an ecology of ample repetition. Indeed, architectural history and practice could emerge through reflexive, recursive, and cyclical loops.[24] The material aspects of repetition discussed above are not among such impetuses of modeling architectural history.

CLICHÉ: RECONSIDERING REPETITION ITSELF

Having observed terms pertinent to print culture populate the *Dictionnaire*, let us now consider *repetition* with *cliché* and its effects as discussed in literary theory and philosophy; because, as we shall see, these are precisely what are amiss in theories of architectural types and largely underappreciated in most *Dictionnaire* articles. As Michel de Certeau has shown us, everyday life, subject to the dynamics of collective activity in larger and more urban societies since the 19th century, becomes invariably more complex.[25] There comes an increase in the use of language not only because of bigger bureaucracy and the complex organization of large urban populations, but also because of increased socialization and talking, which don't quite fit the communicative programs, rules, and grammars of institutional linguistics. On the one hand, talking shapes us by our use of common verbiage, but on the other hand, mass participation also shapes language itself as increasingly dynamic and unstable. In cities, it is not just the institutional types and power structures that shape space, but significantly, everyday repetitive acts of walking, gathering, and talking—in de Certeau's terms, "tactics"—which parallel or even resist those structures.[26] In common parlance, words mutate, attributed meanings drift, and tone and tenor dictate much. Indeed, as Lorraine Daston points out, by the publication of the 1740 edition of the *Académie française*, language usage had reigned supreme over reason, and all hope had been abandoned for rules with invariable principles of use.[27] How our common linguistic, behavioral, and social substrates come to be is anything but formulaic (as also discussed above with the diffusion of architectural ideas). This, however, is by no means to suggest that all is chaos outside the academies. Amidst instabilities and fluxes, repetitions occur, norms emerge, and both linguistic and social forms are attained—other than institutionally.

Clichés are one site of these coalescences. In *Beckett and Authority: The Uses of Cliché*, Elizabeth Barry, drawing on Gilles Deleuze and Félix Guattari, discusses clichés as exhibiting a "molar" tendency in language, or its predisposition to "organize into fixed forms."[28] These molar thought formations, unlike their "molecular" counterparts, cannot be easily deconstructed or their formational procedures easily explained.[29] Clichés are precisely such formulations: even though they originate as metaphors in some original context, having become memorable and in wide circulation, they are easily reproduced in various other contexts, even when not semantically apposite. There is much ambiguity about *what* they mean, *how* they come to mean, and indeed their very *means* of repetition. Many a stock phrase, idiom, and rhyming couplet are recited verbatim, sometimes simply because of their aurality and prosody. For example, alliterations and rhymes may pattern idioms as catchy, yielding both rhythm and cadence. For instance, repetition "dime a dozen!" Clichés are usually authorless or the link to their origins is hardly consequential. They often come to mind involuntarily and can persist despite our best efforts to not use them.

In their pervasiveness and ubiquity, however, clichés acquire certain roles in language. Ruth Amossy, in *Cliché in the Reading Process*, discusses some. For example, when we say "fair and square" or "white as snow," we transport linguistic form but not meaning between various contexts. These idioms thus exhibit an "intertextuality."[30] In print, claims Amossy, a cliché "orients and models reading," and it "helps the reader get his bearings and models his attitude and expectations along familiar horizons."[31] Through their familiarity, clichés provide a baseline or stratum—a degree-zero horizon—upon which further linguistic and social stratification occur. Crucially, they do so precisely because they are not the semiotic focus of attention. And this has other implications: an effect of encountering repetition as with cliché, as Amossy puts it, is witnessing *déjà vu*.[32] That is, the familiarity of ordinary repeated phraseology, of words that we utter yet are not ours, evokes an eeriness in us. As using cliché makes strange *usuality* itself, we confront just how much of even our most thoughtfully produced language is drawn from shared social horizons, and indeed, how we are collectively and socially immersed in language.[33]

Some of these features of cliché are best brought forth by artists who craft with repetition. The playwright Samuel Beckett, for example, uses trite idioms or strings of clichéd utterances in his prose in almost identical episodes. In his *Krapp's Last Tape*, for example, a one-man show about a 69-year-old man reflecting on his younger self, "spool" recurs as an enervated yet persistent utterance. We find joy with Krapp's amusement in its phonetic qualities but also reflect on its polysemy and the very mechanisms of repetition as he recoils through both the mechanical contraption of the tape recorder on stage and his own memories—that is, in both celluloid and cerebral recollection. On stage, Krapp ages and wears out "spool" itself, putting on display and catalyzing longue durée linguistic and social processes.[34] Each repeated utterance in Beckett's play parallels language itself being hollowed out—just like a print head or even a coin losing its metallic pronouncement. We confront here the very material media of language—including the human mouth and mind—and their "wear and tear," as it were. This worn-out language vitally persists in circulation, and artfully so with Beckett. The word and phenomenon of spooling both pattern the performance, and precisely because of its hollowed-out semantic basis, provide metered or temporal anchors about which slight differences in narrative repetition can be tracked. Similitude—not exact sameness—breeds much difference, we are amused and surprised to find. The prediction modeling discussed above with architectural types is in contrast here to an entropy of sorts, to the unpredictability of modern life, despite the escalating typicality of its constituent parts.

REPETITION AND ARCHITECTURE

But such phenomena are not of language alone: molar formations (in the Deleuzian sense discussed above) resulting out of habits of using, inhabiting, and designing spaces; the intertextuality—or rather inter-contextuality—of building components; and the smooth absorption and commensurability of common modules—which is also accompanied by the odd familiarity of typical components and tropes—are all features of architecture too. If clichés occur in the marginalia of language nevertheless feeding back into language proper, such is also the case with architecture. As Walter Benjamin argues, architecture is always engaged with in a state of distraction.[35] That is, regardless of whether our focus may be on a building or artifact, other architectural objects are nevertheless formational parts of our urban experience. Out of the corner of our eyes, a "speaking picture" may summon, faded copies included. And causes for retaining it in memory might have much to do with how much one encounters it in circulation, even if peripherally. Incidentally, Quatremère acknowledges the substantial material presence of hieroglyphs that are common but redundant or with inscriptions that are no longer pertinent.[36] Such familiar tropes are nevertheless recalled and put to use by a "distracted" designer—which only further augments their momentum of use. Is this not inherently evocative of an unfamiliar familiarity and unrehearsed repetition akin to that of using cliché? And are we not similarly at home in but also estranged by both language and architecture?

The *Dictionnaire* does indeed capture some of this. Let us consider one final dictionary entry, "conventionality," where molar formations that repeat, similarity and difference, and the complexities of belonging to and producing in a collective are all manifest.[37] Recall that Greek temples are "conventional" for Quatremère because their designers ought not to lose the genealogical thread to the wooden hut, their originary "type." One "imitates" and works up from typical elements (columns, capitals, pediments), to select orders or characters of space (Doric, Ionic, and Corinthian architectural orders), to the evolutionary state of a petrified wooden trabeated hut, and ultimately, to the vague, un-imaged, and ideal hut itself.[38] The persistence of a type is here effectively an artistic achievement arrived at by working up levels or strata of conventionality.[39] This is effectively the above-discussed kind of predictable modeling of history via ideal channels of imitation. However, other than such ideal strata that must be worked up, temples can be "conventional" also because several genera exist in an un-stratified and indiscrete horizon of ample repetition. That is, the commonality of columns, bas-reliefs, and other parts—even in contexts where they are not entirely apposite—makes the temple itself commensurable—which is why even an *undistracted* architect might favor it. The sheer availability of a mold, the accessibility to labor, and such other material aspects may only augment the commonality of use.

How then can any architectural aspect be qualified as solely imitative? How to distinguish the virtues of familiarity and commonality from the compositional beauty resulting from imitating nature? Such conundrums of repetition become especially evident in Quatremère's discussion of the contrasting concept-pair of "principles" and "rules." Whereas "principles are origins [of a system of imitation], rules are the consequences," he claims.[40] Much like in language, rules in architecture are "composite in nature," "derive from more than one source," and "relate to varied ends."[41] Four categories of rules are provided in the *Dictionnaire*, with the third category including customs, examples, and grammars; and the final including habits and prejudices.[42] These latter two categories fit especially well what Daston calls *thin rules:* "They are unencumbered by examples and exceptions; they do not traffic in specifics; they float above context." Furthermore, she claims, "they eschew commentary and have no need of hermeneutics."[43] In architecture, such rules are precisely what may emerge from the above-discussed repetition in both psychological and material registers. The result or mix is especially hard to dissect. Architectural discourses through the early modern period have taken note that conventions coalesce through such rules; for example, Claude Perrault's observation of the "customary" uses of architectural orders.[44] By the 18th century, the habits and customs of society layering patterns and customs of use upon the rules and principles set forth by institutions becomes even more evident.[45] That conventionality results from sum totals and averages is well-reflected in Quatremère's latter two categories of rules. Eventually, he describes "convention" itself as a "happy mean."[46] This statistical concept, even if a metaphor, captures the sheer momentum of repetition by the masses, the recognizability of its patterns, and ultimately, the resulting democratization of information that the inclusion of various architectural means or averages in a dictionary bring. And indeed, where else than a dictionary might such *means* be manifest?

As to the question of how might we distinguish type from cliché? Where they differ most significantly is the preemptive judgement conferred upon them: whereas certain types have been widely accepted and canonized in architectural discourses, clichés have generally come to be devalued and considered trite, trivial, and hackneyed. If, however, such judgement is momentarily left aside, it becomes evident how undifferentiated they can be in their means of repetition and propagation. To analyze cliché is itself to foreground not the visual features of drawings, forms, or buildings, but rather the authorless and obscure practices by which the former are repeatedly reborn. To analyze cliché, thus, is to inevitably perform a reversal of judgement, bring forth that which was mere background, and retrieve architectural histories that were previously relegated to the margin. In doing so, we may bring forth the even broader historical contexts and common horizons from which utility and futility, noise and message, and type and cliché emerge.

SM Quatremère's theory of "type" invites thoughts on the *mark* and the *trace*, where the tension between presence and absence destabilizes the very notion of origin. A type, much like Derrida's *trace*, resists being pinned down as either fully present or absent; it is always already caught in a network of relations.[47] The idea of the Greek temple as an "imitation" of the wooden hut exemplifies this logic: the hut as origin is both invoked and displaced, existing as a spectral presence that haunts the temple without fully manifesting in it. Quatremère's type aligns with Derrida's *différance*—an origin deferred; iterable yet never fully recoverable.

The intertwining of *idea* and *image* in Quatremère's lexicon further complicates this genealogy. If an "idea" is synonymous with an "image," as claimed, then we can consider both to operate as per W.J.T. Mitchell's (1986) proposed "family of images"—a system of *relations* where no single image can claim primacy or autonomy.[48] For Mitchell, images are not static objects but dynamic entities, defined by their interaction with other images, contexts, and media. Similarly, type functions less as an isolated archetype and more as a generative matrix, an imprint whose value lies in its capacity for reinvention.

Between the material and the conceptual—between the mold and its casting, the image and its iteration— the interplay highlights a critical tension in Quatremère's thought. The type is both a mark and a trace: it bears the pressure of its historical and material conditions while gesturing toward an idea that exceeds them. What Derrida might call the "arche-writing" of architecture thus unfolds as an epigenetic process, where repetition, rather than eroding meaning, becomes its very substrate.

We might evoke Roland Barthes's triad: *text*, *texture*, and *textile*, as worked through in "From Work to Text."[49] Barthes contrasts the closed objecthood of a "work" with the interwoven, processual nature of a "text," wherein meaning emerges through interaction and interpretation. Quatremère's type, then, like Barthes's text, is *textile* (to suggest both material and action, as in "projectile")—a weave of analogies, histories, and forms that resists being reduced to a singular essence. Its texture lies in its repetitions and variations, its capacity to be "read" differently in each new context.This invites us to see the work of type as a social practice, conditioned by collective memory and shaped by the contingencies of culture.

It is fruitful to *take a walk* amidst the dynamics of repetition and circulation in Michel de Certeau's notion of "tactics"— the everyday acts of resistance and reinterpretation that subtly shape the structures of language and space. If architectural types and linguistic "clichés" operate within these shared horizons, they emerge not as static artifacts but as iterative processes that *gain* meaning through their use and reuse.

Here, then, lies the degree zero of architecture: not a pure origin but a shared network of traces—inscriptions, imprints, and systems of relation—that condition the architect's work. To grasp the type is not merely to conserve its typical values but to acknowledge the iterative play of idea and image, text and textile, presence and absence, material and conceptual, that defines its essence. It is through this social and material practice—oscillating between type and cliché—that architecture, like language, achieves its enduring force. (And if Barthes might consider cliché "myth," then let us not forget the work of the reader of myth).

What if we abandon the privileging of type as a foundational concept altogether and instead embrace the cliché (its moveable type) as a more radical mode of understanding architecture? Clichés, unlike types, embody the unrefined collective labor of repetition, reshaping meaning through use rather than idealized origins. Might the so-called "triviality" of the cliché be reconceived as an egalitarian principle—a way of foregrounding architecture s entanglement with mass culture, unregulated patterns, and the wear-and-tear of everyday life? Such a turn would shift focus from the architect's individual mastery to the anonymous, generative force of the collective—a force that Quatremère's type, for all its richness, resists fully acknowledging.

1 There has been renewed interest in types since the second half of the 20th century, of which some relevant writings include: Anthony Vidler, "The Third Typology," *Oppositions* 7 (Winter 1976): 1-4; Anthony Vidler, "The Idea of Type: The Transformation of the Academic Ideal, 1750-1830," *Oppositions* 8 (1977): 95-115; Giulio Carlo Argan, "On the Typology of Architecture," trans. Joseph Rykwert, *Architectural Design* 33 (1963): 564-65; and Werner Oechslin, "Premises for the Resumption of the Discussion of Typology," *Assemblage* 1, no. 1 (1986): 37-53; And more recently: Leandro Madrazo, "The Concept of Type in Architecture: An Inquiry into the Nature of Architectural Form" (PhD diss. no. 11115, ETH Zürich, 1995); Sam Jacoby, "Typal and Typological Reasoning: A Diagrammatic Practice of Architecture," *The Journal of Architecture* 20, no. 6 (2015): 938-61. The titles that focus on Quatremère de Quincy specifically include: Sylvia Lavin, *Quatremère de Quincy and the Invention of a Modern Language* (Cambridge, MA: MIT Press, 1992); Vittoria Di Palma, "Architecture, Environment and Emotion: Quatremère de Quincy and the Concept of Character," *AA Files*, no. 47 (2002): 45-56.

2 See Roland Barthes, *Writing Degree Zero*, trans. Annette Lavers and Colin Smith (New York: Hill and Wang, 1968): 5. As the editors of this volume have kindly pointed out, Barthes discusses repetition with the idea of stereotype (if not with cliché or types explicitly), which literary authors such as Ruth Amossy have taken up and discussed in parallel with cliché. See Ruth Amossy and Anne Herschberg Pierrot, *Stéréotypes et Clichés-3e Éd.: Langue, Discours, Société* (Paris: Nathan, 1997).

3 Samir Younés's translation of the two volumes is the main source document: (Antoine- Chrysostome) Quatremère de Quincy, *The True, the Fictive, and the Real: The Historical Dictionary of Architecture of Quatremere de Quincy*, trans. Samir Younés (London: A. Papadakis, 1999).

4 The analogy of the spread of linguistic material to epidemiology is from Dan Sperber, *Explaining Culture: A Naturalistic Approach* (Blackwell Publishing, 1996): 57-58; and Dan Sperber, "Anthropology and Psychology: Towards an Epidemiology of Representations," *Man (London)* 20, no. 1 (1985): 73-89.

5 Denis Diderot and Jean Le Rond d'Alembert, *Encyclopédie, ou Dictionnaire raisonné des sciences, des arts et des métiers, par une société de gens de lettres*, 17 vols (Paris: André Le Breton, Laurent Duran, Antoine-Claude Briasson, Michel-Antoine David, 1751-72).

6 The respective final volumes of the *Encyclopédie* and the *Dictionnaire* are completed roughly at the same time, in 1825, even though the latter is published seven years later. Vidler, "The Idea of Type," 114.

7 Some of his actions even necessitate him seeking exile in Germany during the French Revolution. He nevertheless ends up back in Paris by 1800, as the permanent secretary of the Académie des Beaux-Arts by 1816. See the chronology provided by Samir Younés in de Quincy, *The True, the Fictive, and the Real...*, 54.

8 Anthony Vidler discusses how dictionaries needed to provide "the semblance of completeness and all the apparent eclecticism of their [diverse readers'] needs." See Anthony Vidler's introduction to Quatremère's article "Type," translated and reprinted in *Oppositions* 8 (1977): 147-148.

9 de Quincy, *The True, the Fictive, and the Real...*, 125.

10 Ibid., 147-8.

11 Ibid., 125. In such a case of "copying," he called the copied motif or object the "model."

12 He claims, "All is precise and given when it comes to the model, while all is more or less vague when it comes to the type." Ibid., 254.

13 A case in point is the frontispiece of Durand's 1809 book *Précis des leçons d'architecture données à l'École royale polytechnique*.

14 Lavin, *Quatremère de Quincy and the Invention of a Modern Language*.

15 de Quincy, *The True, the Fictive, and the Real...*, 254.

16 Ibid.

17 Madrazo, *The Concept of Type in Architecture...*, 28; see also Vidler, "The Idea of Type...," 99.

18 Lavin, *Quatremère de Quincy and the Invention of a Modern Language*, 115.

19 de Quincy, *The True, the Fictive, and the Real...*, 173.

20 Ibid., 172.

21 Ibid., 103. See also Di Palma's discussion of "character" as she describes the explicit link to typography and print media. Di Palma, "Architecture, Environment and Emotion...," 45.

22 Durand's represented models of architectural evolution mirror those of natural historians such as George Cuvier, especially the latter's taxonomies and evolutionary diagrams. This in the hope of providing architecture with scientific bases outside the field. For a discussion of types versus typologies, see Jacoby, "Typal and Typological Reasoning...," 949.

23 Micha Bandini, "Typology as a Form of Convention," *AA Files*, no. 6 (1984): 73-82; 75.

24 Vidler, "The Idea of Type...," 107.

25 Michel de Certeau, *The Practice of Everyday Life*, trans. Steven Randall (Berkeley, Los Angeles, and London: University of California Press, 1984).

26 Ibid., Parts I and III especially.

27 Lorraine Daston, *Rules: A Short History of What We Live By* (Princeton, NJ: Princeton University Press, 2022), 200.

28 In the context of Beckett's work. Elizabeth Barry, *Beckett and Authority: The Uses of Cliché* (London: Palgrave Macmillan, 2006), 1.

29 Deleuze and Guattari explain "man" as a molar construct, as a standard, emerging as typical through history. "There is no becoming-man," they claim, "because man is the molar entity par excellence, whereas becomings are molecular." Gilles Deleuze and Félix Guattari, *A Thousand Plateaus: Capitalism and Schizophrenia* (Minneapolis: University of Minnesota Press, 1987), 292.

30 Ruth Amossy, "The Cliché in the Reading Process," trans. Terese Lyons, *SubStance* 11, no. 2 (1982): 34-45; 37.

31 Ibid., 36-38. An important voice of the feedback loops between text and orality is Walter J. Ong, who points out that modern print culture is prone to reproduce precisely the most common oral phraseology, thus only setting up for further repetition, both written and oral. See Walter J. Ong, *Orality and Literacy: The Technologizing of the Word* (London and New York: Routledge, 1982), 9, 34.

32 Amossy, "The Cliché in the Reading Process," 34, 38.

33 Barry discusses cliché as making hidden appeals to us, as us being compelled to and even interpellated into society by language. See Barry, *Beckett and Authority*, 4.

34 Barry reflects well on the affordances of tape: "Mix[ing] it all up' and changing 'the natural order' might in fact make this registration better equate to the working of real memory, but both artistry and memory itself are doomed to falsify one's past life". Ibid., 121.

35 Walter Benjamin, "Walter Benjamin: Selected Writings, 1935-1938," in *The Work of Art in the Age of Its Technological Reproducibility*, ed. Michael W. Jennings and Howard Eiland, vol. 3 (Cambridge, MA: The Belknap Press of Harvard University Press, 2002), 119-121.

36 Di Palma, "Architecture, Environment and Emotion...," 55.

37 In a contrast to molar repetition and aligning with the molecular, Antoine Picon discusses Laugier's hut as an assemblage that is easy to deconstruct and whose process of composition is transparent. Quatremère, on the other hand, leaves whole the object to observe in its broader context. See Antoine Picon, "The Freestanding Column in Eighteenth-Century Religious Architecture," in *Things That Talk. Object Lessons from Art and Science*, ed. Lorraine Daston (New York: Zone Books, 2004), 88.

38 de Quincy, *The True, the Fictive, and the Real...*, 124. The conventional elements discussed are composite architectural orders (Corinthian, Tuscan, etc.), pediments in interiors, and engaged columns and pilasters.

39 Ibid., 125.

40 Ibid., 222.

41 Ibid.

42 Ibid., 222–225.

43 Daston, *Rules: A Short History of What We Live By*, 93.

44 Claude Perrault, *Ordonnance for the Five Kinds of Columns after the Method of the Ancients*, trans. Indra Kagis McEwen (Santa Monica, CA: Getty Publications, 1996), 51. Perrault discusses the five orders and their associated systems of proportion to originate not only from the ideal human body but to carry through customary uses that create a further probability of repetition. In the book's introduction, Alberto Pérez-Gómez especially draws out the dissociation of proportion from the human body. See pages 15 and 21.

45 Daston, *Rules: A Short History of What We Live By*, 6, 46–47.

46 de Quincy, *The True, the Fictive, and the Real...* Quatremère's mean seeks a balance between "too great a severity of reasoning" and "too great a complacency of imagination" in creative endeavors of imitation.

47 Jacques Derrida, *Of Grammatology*, trans. Gayatri Chakravorty Spivak (Baltimore: Johns Hopkins University Press, 1976).

48 W.J.T. Mitchell, *Iconology: Image, Text, Ideology* (Chicago: University of Chicago Press, 1986).

49 Roland Barthes, *Image Music Text*, trans. Stephen Heath (London: Fontana Press, 1977).

The Presence of Myth in Contemporary Life. Bruno Zevi and Kenneth Frampton in the Field

Lyna Bourouiba

comments by
Joseph Bedford

AN INTERNATIONAL QUARTERLY
OF THE SOCIAL SCIENCES

VOLUME 52, NUMBER 2
SUMMER 1985

Fig. 1 Cover of the event publication.

In 1984 in New York, from October 11 to 13, the conference *The Presence of Myth in Contemporary Life*, organized by Dore Ashton, an art historian and critic, and Matti Megged, a novelist and professor of comparative literature,[1] was held at the Graduate Faculty of the New School and The Cooper Union for the Advancement of Science and Art. The conference comprised twenty-five talks, divided into six sessions. The cast was impressive. All the speakers were widely respected in their fields of expertise: literature, philosophy, political philosophy, art, music, human and social sciences—such as political science, psychiatry, and theology—anthropology, ethnology, history, semiology, and architecture. Most were Americans or worked in the United States, some were from France, Japan, Poland, England, and Greece, and the event ended with a screening of the 1982 film *The Path of the Dead Indians* by the anthropologist Michel Perrin and the ethnologist Jean Arlaud.[2]

Bruno Zevi and Kenneth Frampton represented the field of architecture as both historians and architecture critics. In the early 1980s, at the time of the conference, Zevi was still an established intellectual figure, but he was no longer a leading one. He had lost much intellectual authority, first in Italy, then more generally in Europe and the United States. One of the reasons for this decline was the success of the ideological and political positions of his counterpart Manfredo Tafuri. By the end of the 1960s, and in particular with the publication in 1973 of his book *The Modern Language of Architecture*,[3] Zevi's work reflected an interest in linguistics; he brought language and architecture together as a way out of the postmodern crisis. From then on, and especially in the 1980s, Zevi repeatedly used the idea of a "degree zero of architectural writing," which he borrowed from Roland Barthes's book *Writing Degree Zero*.[4] He exploited the concept to renew his ways of expressing the ethical and political ambitions that underpinned his fight against postmodernism. He also viewed it as a method for architects to overcome the postmodern ideological and stylistic impasse. In a literal analogy between literature and architecture, Zevi attributes to degree zero—that form of (architectural) writing devoid of any external meaning, free from the weight of language and style—the capacity to transcend the conflictual relationship between the popular and the literary in the history of language—or architecture. These reflections received little credit from his colleagues who held dominant intellectual positions at the time, such as Frampton. For a 2018 publication, Peter Eisenman, who worked with Frampton at the Institute for Architecture and Urban Studies (IAUS)—a teaching, research, and exhibition center that was "already a legend in its own time"[5]—commented on their relationship to Zevi:

> Still, at that time it was difficult for us to understand Zevi's work, we were more attached by Manfredo Tafuri's ideas . . . Another reason why there could be no natural relationship even if it could have been, it was because Zevi supported organic architecture, F. L. Wright, which we considered nostalgic, whereas he [Zevi] had no interest in post-structuralism, which was our bible.[6]

This chapter examines both Zevi's lecture at the conference and the ensuing debate with Frampton that began with Frampton's response as session chair, because together, the lecture and the debate encapsulate the intellectual positions and discursive strategies Zevi adopted at this specific period in his career. Indeed, as he moved from a position of dominance to one of diminished influence in the world of ideas, he began to argue ardently and unequivocally in favor of an architectural degree zero. Drawing upon the sociologist Pierre Bourdieu's theory of the field, this article examines the relationship between Zevi's loss of symbolic power and his determination to advocate for a degree zero in architecture.[7] It proposes that the practice of architectural history, theory, and criticism can be considered as a *field*—a space of highly competitive relations within which all the players vie for positions (social and symbolic) and position-takings (intellectual and discursive).[8]

JB Another figure who brought Bourdieu's work to bear on architecture is Garry Stevens, in a number of articles on architectural education and specifically in his book *The Favored Circle*.[9] And more broadly, the approach taken in this paper reminds me of the sociology of the profession developed by Magali Sarfatti Larson in her book *Behind the Postmodern Facade*.[10]

To analyze what is at stake for Zevi in the notion of degree zero, this article investigates how an idea, its mode of enunciation, and the symbolic place of its enunciator —in relation to the other agents in the field—are intertwined.

A lot rests on this word "intertwined." While the idea of degree zero is being traced here as it moves from Barthes to Zevi and through Eisenman and Frampton, there is equal concern for the context within which it moves, notably the cresting of the fortunes of postmodern architecture and the aging of a historian feeling his influence diminish. While the shadow of Bourdieu's work cast across the paper might lead to a reduction of truth to power, or a reduction of culture to an economy of private interests, it is wise to hold both ideas and the social context within which those ideas move in balance and conceive of them as intertwined. Yet what does a concept like intertwining tell us about the underlying conflict in methodological approaches in architectural history? Does it tell us something about how they are intertwined? And what do we learn about the relationship between ideas and contexts? Or does the word serve primarily to displace the conflict between ideas and contexts in the methodology of architectural history from the scope of the paper's analytic concerns?

THE DIALECTIC OF DISTINCTION

At the conference on October 12, the morning session, Visual and Performing Arts, moderated by Dore Ashton, featured Zevi, the American composer Earle Brown, and the American painters Paul Rotterdam and Timothy Clark. Frampton and the Anglo-American sculptor William Tucker chaired the panel. Zevi spoke first, with a text entitled "The Seven Myths of Architecture." Probably to align with the conference topic, Zevi drew not on *Writing Degree Zero*, as he usually did, but on another of Barthes's books, *Mythologies*, published in 1957,[11] in which Barthes observes society through a wide range of social and cultural practices, including contemporary myths and their ideological effects. The notion of a degree zero, and an explicit reference to *Writing Degree Zero*, recurs sporadically in *Mythologies*, in a parallel between myth and language, between myth and writing. Literature is reaffirmed as a "mythical system"[12] against which degree zero acts as an overthrowing tactic. Degree zero, says Barthes, is a "subversion of writing"[13] that seeks to escape the normative framework circumscribed by Literature, a bourgeois myth that governs language and its conventions. It is this same bourgeois myth that Barthes sets out to qualify and disqualify, since what he intends to do, in writing the book, is to "give a detailed account of the mystification that transforms petty-bourgeois culture into universal nature," beyond providing "an ideological critique of the language of so-called mass culture."[14] In *Mythologies*, as in his earlier *Writing Degree Zero*, seeking the degree zero is driven by a desire for justice. With a degree zero, Barthes seeks to combat the bourgeois myth of Literature, refusing to abandon the struggle by relying on formalism. The idea stands its ground while paradoxically being itself what Barthes calls "a mythology of literary language."[15]

Once we understand how Barthes articulates the notions of degree zero and myth, Zevi's argument for this conference paper appears clear. To pursue his already well-established plea for a degree zero in architecture, he decides to distinguish valuable architectural myths from illegitimate architectural myths, rather than to fight myth in general—architecture naturally feeds on myth, says Zevi, and he uses birth, quest, love, and death as examples, but he specifically targets the bourgeois myth. The myth of an architectural degree zero is a valiant one, despite its utopian and unattainable nature. It reflects what architects must aim for to reach "justice and accuracy."[16] For Zevi, postmodernism is a debilitating myth because of its authoritarian and illusory character. It represents an "old myth" that makes architects repeat "old mistakes."[17]

More generally, and for the sake of this distinctive approach, Zevi lists books and their authors with whom he agrees or disagrees, chosen because they all preach in favor of certain architectural myths, seven in general. Starting in the mid-nineteenth century, he cites ten authors, including himself (Zevi's critical activity is almost always an opportunity for self-promotion). Listing these authors allows him to answer a question he does not explicitly state: what are the myths around which architecture revolves? Within a dialectic of distinction,[18] he classifies those myths into two categories: one to advocate and the other to incriminate. However, Zevi does not consider these architectural theories—those that are valid in his eyes—as absolutes, not even his own. They would have been no more than "compensation"[19] for a shaky and unsatisfactory situation. Indeed, "the real struggle is between order (or orders) and freedom."[20] The only way to win it is for architecture to reach a state of Barthesian degree zero that would satisfy "a concrete need for environmental and architectural quality, the true myth of today."[21] These are the last words of his presentation.

INVESTIGATING THE DISPUTE

Zevi's paper was published twice, first in 1985, in a special issue of the journal *Social Research*,[22] and then in 1986, in the "Myth and the Arts" section of the booklet of papers from the event (Fig. 1).[23] The nature of another contribution to that section, authored by Frampton, is significant. Despite its seemingly innocuous title, "Presence of Myth,"[24] the essay is not an opinion on architectural myths but an updated transcript of his speech as session chair. Instead of considering the proposals of the other speakers, as might have been expected of his role, Frampton used his speaking time to respond to Zevi's paper, entering into a dispute with Zevi. What did that dispute mean for Frampton, or in Luc Boltanski's terms, how does this dispute testify to divergent "qualification[s] of reality"?[25]

Frampton's critique is long, skillful, and severe, yet tactful. It seeks to demonstrate to the audience the extent of his disagreement with Zevi's position-taking. Frampton highlights a recurring complaint made by those who qualify Zevi's approach. His way of conceiving the world—and within it, architecture as a cultural field—is restrictive. His vision is a caricature of reality, dividing it. It makes Zevi adopt stark oppositions and disregard certain elements when it suits him.

Frampton's own writings are themselves prone to stark oppositions, as is the common trope of thinkers of crisis as he is. One thinks of the stark historical oppositions he suggested in his text "Industrialization and the Crises in Architecture,", in which he draws from Hannah Arendt's reading of the crisis in phenomenology to mark a stark opposition between the technical and the esthetic that began to emerge in the nineteenth century with the split between the École Polytechnique and the École des Beaux-Arts.[26] That kind of stark division has been the basis by which Frampton has carved up history on two sides of a crisis in his subsequent work, and it is what, arguably, has made him a "critical historian" in a manner not too dissimilar to Zevi.

In other words, he makes use of a distinctive dialectic. Based on this argument, Frampton nuances Zevi's opinions to prove that his own world is not polarized and thus that in his own vision of reality, everything must be balanced. To demonstrate this ethical divergence and to assert his position in the field, he depolarizes Zevi's cherished conception of classicism on which Zevi built his critical history. There would be not one classicism but at least two: a liberating classical tradition and a nostalgic one. Frampton associates the former with such figures as Henri Labrouste, Gunnar Asplund, Ludwig Mies van der Rohe, Le Corbusier, and Guiseppe Terragni. He assigns the nostalgic tradition to Charles Garnier, Daniel Burnham, Albert Speer, and Henry Bacon. In completing Zevi's thought, Frampton highlights its incompleteness. From within the classical tradition, Frampton intends also retain its honorable intentions and results and, to prove it, Frampton lends himself to the same distinctive exercise as Zevi, while underlining the paradoxical nature of his approach—that of playing the very game he critiques.[27]

Later in his essay, Frampton ventures into Zevi's "flirtation"[28] with the degree zero. He seeks to reveal Zevi's infidelity to Barthes's text by demonstrating how Zevi's distorted conception of the classical tradition skews his understanding and use of the notion. In other words, his dual conception of the world warps his reading of the text.

It is curious that Frampton would critique Zevi for warping his reading of the text; this sounds akin to the criticism that Tafuri had of Zevi's historical work more generally. For Tafuri, in effect, he felt that Zevi cooked the books too much, and read history according to a presentist agenda that did not allow the past its own due and did not allow it to teach us anything or change how we think in the present. I say it is curious because four years later "History, Theory and Criticism: Operative Writing in a Post-Modern Period," delivered at the 76th Annual Meeting of the Association of Collegiate Schools of Architecture in 1988, he would distance himself from Tafuri's side of this methodological debate and embrace the notion of operative history as something that described his own approach.

According to Frampton, Barthes maintained a distance from the classical tradition, a "respect for the classic."[29] He then imagines what an architectural degree zero might be. He links the concept to a classical but subversive architectural tradition with minimal expressions, as in the projects by Adolf Loos, Mies van der Rohe,[30] or Aldo Rossi. Frampton's architectural translation of the degree zero thus focuses on forms and their reduced expressions. Through his affiliation with the IAUS, where the writings of Barthes and the reference to the degree zero are mostly relayed by Eisenman,[31] Frampton was familiar with the idea and could manipulate it. In the 1980s, for example, he explored the critical positions of a series of post-World War II Japanese architects, such as Kazuo Shinohara, Kazunari Sakamoto, Toyo Ito, and Hiromi Fujii. He published a monograph on Fujii, who was intellectually close to Eisenman, structuralism, and the degree zero.[32] In his text "Building Degree Zero: Megalopolitan Reality and Japanese Critical Practice,"[33] Frampton uses the concept in the title to refer to these architects's commitment to conceiving an architecture that would address the traumas caused by destruction, modernization, and Western imperialism.

Fig. 2 Zevi expressed his feelings regarding postmodernism at the CICA session of the XVII Congress of the International Union of Architects in Montreal.

PUBLICATION AS A SPACE OF POSITION-TAKING

Zevi did not respond to Frampton during the conference but instead used the editorial process that followed the event to continue the debate publicly. In 1987, he allowed himself the right to reply in an editorial in his journal *L'architettura: Cronache e storia*. The title, "Reply to Kenneth Frampton: There Is No Liberating Classicism,"[34] immediately foreshadows the content of the article. The form of the response is equally efficient. Zevi lists the points that Frampton raises, quoting him, and then responds to those points. He agrees with some of the substantive elements but not with those that specifically attack his approach. Zevi's response to this is categorical only, rather than demonstrative; he asserts his position without any argument. He states that "a liberating classicism doesn't exist"[35] and that "symmetry, too, can be called progressive at certain points. It can be said but knowing that from prehistory to the present it has never been."[36] He continues by saying that he prefers the discomfort of his incisive positions to the intellectual cowardice of Frampton. In this editorial, as in his presentation at the conference, Zevi deliberately caricatures a thought by establishing concepts that he immediately opposes against each other: order against freedom, void against space, symmetry against asymmetry. His arguments are divisive because they belong to a political rhetoric. This is his discursive way to "take a place... on a chessboard of more or less valorized 'classifying-and-classified' postures."[37] Those who know his work well might identify this as Zevian style, characterized by a specific rhythm and substance and by his provocation, stubbornness, and dominance. All speakers improve and adapt the style, the phrasing, the tone, and the silence of their discourse. It is the hallmark of those who not only want to say something to others but desire to be heard by them. But in this game for a place on the architectural-media chessboard, Zevi seems to fall into his own trap. He prefers to be heard rather than to refine what he wants to say, opting for the discursive mode of politics. If making a speech means "wearing a linguistic mask,"[38] Zevi conceals his language with unambiguous assertions, systematic provocations, and excessive repetitions of the same ideas. His style seems to stifle the meaning of his words. While he has made the degree zero his hobbyhorse, he does not appear to apply his reflections to the modalities of his discourse, since, again in the words of Barthes, "style is almost always an alibi, designed to evade the deep motivations" (Fig. 2).[39]

Paradoxically, Zevi seems flattered by Kenneth Frampton's not-so-eulogistic text, apparently proud to publish it. He even declared it "excellent."[40] Indeed, Frampton's critique is a sign of consideration for Zevi and an opportunity by which to reopen the debate. In the dominating position that Zevi occupied in the 1980s in the world of ideas, the period in which the conference took form, forging alliances was essential for him to continue to exist in the field beyond his previous contributions to the field. Entering into a game of publication and response is also strategic. While stating publicly that his moral alignment with Frampton outweighs their disagreements, he indirectly benefits from Frampton's high symbolic capital. Frampton was in his fifties at the time. He had been involved for more than ten years in prestigious teaching establishments and was renowned for his commitment to the practice of architectural history, theory, and criticism. In the early 1980s, three events strengthened his reputation and his power to act in the field. In 1980, he published his first book, *Modern Architecture: A Critical History*,[41] an anthology of modern architecture that remains a reference today. The same year, he asserted his position on postmodernism by leaving the curatorial committee of the first international architecture exhibition of the Venice Biennale, *The Presence of the Past*. Then, in 1983, he published "Towards a Critical Regionalism: Six Points for an Architecture of Resistance,"[42] a text whose role in architectural theory and criticism has been and remains undeniable to this day.[43] Just as Zevi was losing recognition in the field in the 1980s, Frampton was experiencing the opposite dynamic, able to assert his legitimacy and reinforce his authority.

A GAME OF PROXIMITY AND DISSIMILARITY

The disagreements and asymmetries of power between Frampton and Zevi may have fostered a sense of rivalry on Zevi's part.

One thinks also of Bruno Latour's method of analysis, which might be said to be similar to Bourdieu's insofar as it also assumes that the networks (or fields) of power that advance or impair an idea are more real, or at least ultimately more important to history, than the idea itself.

While such a dynamic did exist, it is better understood through the ideological proximity of the two men. Intellectual positions in the architectural field at the time tended to be polarized: those who aligned themselves with postmodernism versus those who resisted it. On both sides, and particularly in the resistance camp, particularisms emerged that broadened the debate. But despite these specificities, which enable us to distinguish the approaches of Zevi and Frampton, for example, both Zevi and Frampton placed themselves, and are still so placed, on the same side, that of a continuity of modernity that advocates not a formal return to the past but rather a reinvention of it (Fig. 3). In 1983, in an article following the annual speech of the Royal Institute for British Architects (RIBA), the two men were introduced as part of the same struggle: "In many respects it was appropriate that Zevi should follow on 12 months after Kenneth Frampton's 1982 discourse to reinforce the message that modern architecture is very far from dead."[44]

When positions in the field are similar, agents can form alliances rather than compete for the same seat, or they can choose to reinforce their specificities. Zevi's republication of Frampton's text appears as a strategy of alliance from Zevi toward Frampton and, above all, from Zevi toward the sub-field of modernism. Beyond a desire to affiliate with the position Frampton took, the strategy attests to Zevi's ambition to assert his particularism within the field and ensure he is not confused with anyone else. The tactic seems relevant given the competitive dynamics of the field and Zevi's mission to remain part of it. It allows him to reassert himself as an ally of Frampton, an agent with high capital, in their common struggle against postmodernism. It also gives him the means to position himself as a unique, somehow irreplaceable character whose ideas are close to those of his ally but also diverge in certain respects (Fig. 4–5). In other words, Zevi plays a controlled game of proximity and dissimilarity to designate both his cobelligerents and his uniqueness at the same time and to continue to exist in the field in a specific way. His distinctive dialectic also seems to respond to the distinctive logics of the field, by which players are organized hierarchically according to their effective and symbolic positions in the social space.

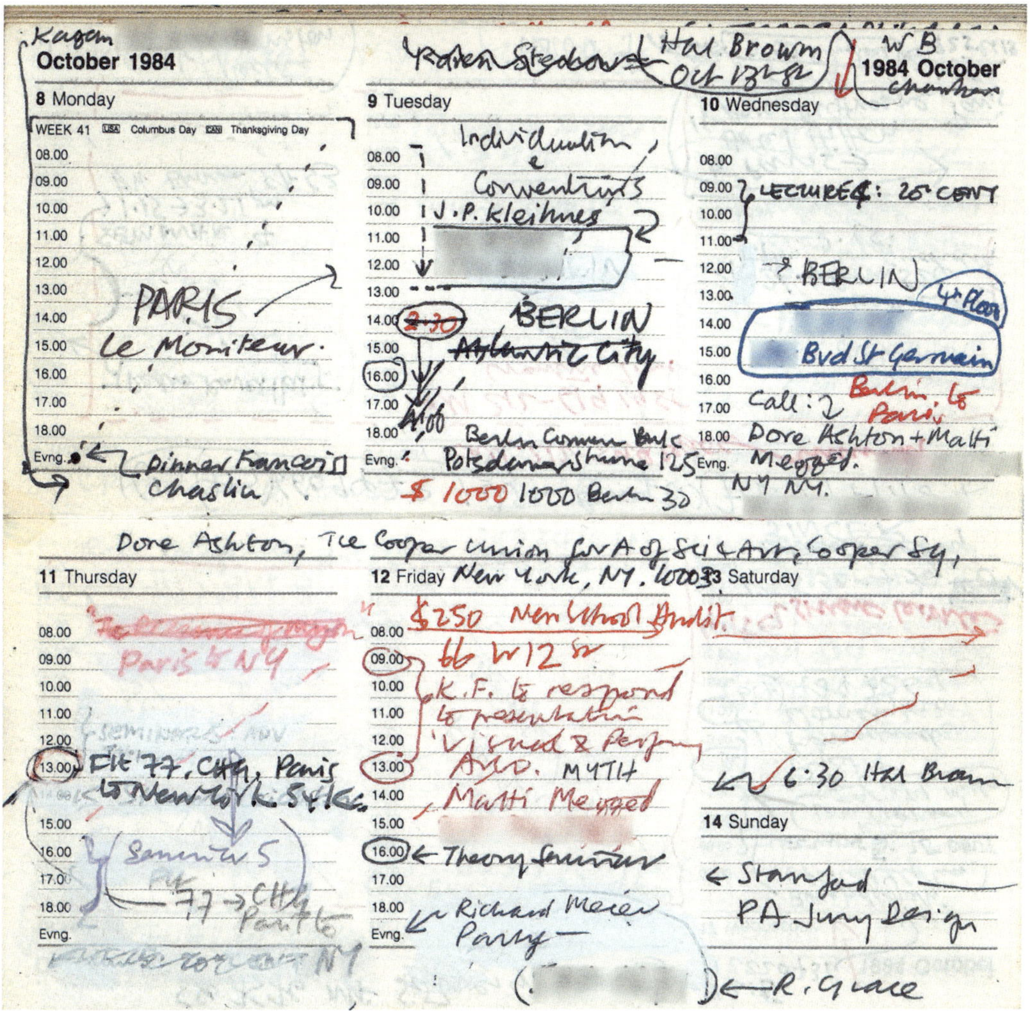

Fig. 3 A testimony to a practice of architectural history embedded in a globalized world, this episode is documented in Kenneth Frampton's 1984 agenda, which places his participation in the conference *The Presence of Myth in Contemporary Life* between a trip to Paris and Berlin and a party organized by Richard Meier.

ARCHITECTS FIND A NEW BULGARITY

Who is spreading 'architectural Aids'? Who threw the book at Bruno Zevi? Edinburgh architect Mark Cousins was in Sofia, Bulgaria, to watch the old guard take on the avant-garde.

The notion that Bulgaria should become the new world forum for the architectural avant-garde is an ambitious, if somewhat far-fetched, idea. The Bulgarians, however, have spent the last 10 years struggling to achieve this goal through the auspices of the World Biennale of Architecture. Vast sums of money have already been spent by the none-too-prosperous Bulgarian Government to help establish the Biennale as a regular event and in 1987 its credibility was enhanced by the creation of two rather nebulous organisations: the International Academy of Architecture (IAA) and the International Forum for Young Architects, both of which operate from a restored monastery some miles south of Sofia. The IAA includes an impressive list of architectural worthies from around the world, including Foster, Meier, van Eyck, Correa, Erskine, Niemeyer et al. There are obvious parallels with the UIA but no formal links exist at present.

Trafficking magazines

The Bulgarian Union of Architects instigated the above programme in an attempt to add some much needed glamour to the distinctly drab and insular world to which the Soviet Bloc consigned itself after the Second World War. The legacy of the Iron Curtain has been to effectively isolate East from West and thwart any constructive cross-fertilisation of ideas and information. Concerned critical debate was forced underground and relied on illicit magazines which were smuggled in from the West, eagerly photocopied or bootlegged, and distributed within a small group of cognoscenti. Informed discussion was therefore limited to theoretical treatises which were quickly outdated. Today the situation is not quite so restricted but the perennial problem of hard currency still means that only the major public libraries can purchase the best foreign magazines.

Entitled 'Interarch '89', this was the fifth consecutive Biennale and was held in the new wing of the National Palace of Culture in Sofia.

Exhibitions included 'Three Austrian Architects—Peichel, Holzbauer and Reiner', 'Roman Architects: 1930-1980' and a retrospective exhibition of the Soviet architect/artist Yakov Chernikov. This last exhibition is due in London, probably April 1990, at the RIBA Gallery and comprises some 660 works which form only a tiny percentage of the 70 000 items scattered among various archives and collections. The parallels with Kandinsky, Klee and other Bauhaus tutors are self-evident but the work also allows a striking comparison with contemporary figures such as Tschumi and Hadid. Chernikov has often been pigeon-holed as a Muscovite Constructivist, but this exhibition illustrates the expansive breadth of his inventive and artistic genius—a talent which embraces the didactic simplicity of line and plane to the Piranesian complexities of his most inventive forms.

In stark contrast with this, the bulk of the exhibits in the main International Open Exhibition were simply dismissed by Bruno Zevi because they 'do not mean anything, do not convey anything'. Even the Bulgarian president of the Academy, Georgi Stoilov, admitted that 90 per cent of the exhibits were the work of 'self-satisfied pragmatists' with no sense of the poetic and little imagination. The four Grand Prix prize-winners, however, were as follows: the Public Library by Teodoro Gonzales de Leon and Francisco Serrano, Mexico; the Hiroshima Museum of Contemporary Art by Kisho Kurokawa, Japan; the reconstruction of several small towns by Peter Olekov, Bulgaria; and the Teplice House of Culture by Karel Hubacek, Czechoslovakia. There were no British entries.

The guest speakers were an eclectic grouping of the familiar and the foreign, with the British representatives undoubtedly rescuing the Biennale from slipping into the insipid. Dr Catherine Cooke gave a scholarly explanation of Chernikov's philosophy and working methodology, while Dennis Sharp dissected some recent examples of Nicholas Grimshaw's new-found maturity.

Designer pyramid

Some of the Eastern Bloc speakers used the opportunity to present their erudition and expand their idiosyncratic and highly abstruse theoretical diatribes. Others simply mumbled diplomatic platitudes and soporific musings. The debate only really came alive on the penultimate day when Charles Jencks made a joke at the expense of Le Corbusier and dismissed I.M. Pei as the 'Yves St Laurent of architecture', a mere design label.

The principal target of his eloquent attack was, of course, the pyramid at the Louvre which he castigated as 'semantically a catastrophe and historically a blasphemy'. Harry Seidler of Australia decided that Jencks was a fraud and made the facile accusation that in his promotion of Post-Modernism Jencks was in fact spreading 'architectural Aids around the world'.

The second fracas flared up during the debate on 'Deconstructivism' when Peter Cook lost his patience with the staccato delivery of Bruno Zevi who continually quoted from the catalogue for the MOMA show at New York as the avowed manifesto of this new sensibility within architecture. Cook made a highly personal and thoughtful analysis of each of the Gang of Seven which ended with the catalogue being thrown to the floor.

The stated aims of the Biennale to unite the fragmented world of architectural discourse are unquestionably noble, but the organisers must weed out any complacency. As a jamboree for the Soviet Bloc architects wearied by the wheels of bureaucracy, it is a much-needed morale-booster. ■

Mark Cousins is an architect/designer currently working with Campbell & Arnott Architects, Edinburgh.

Cook: Let's be frank, Bruno.

Zevi: I want my MOMA.

Fig. 4 Mark Cousins's critical report of *Interach 89*, 5th World Biennale of Architecture in Sofia. The article testifies to Zevi's discursive strategy of repeating the same ideas or references, this time not degree zero but the 1988 Moma exhibition *Deconstructivist Architecture*. It also exposes the general provocative discursive mode used by the agents acting in the field of architectural history, theory, and criticism.

LOGICS OF THE FIELD

Considering architectural history, theory, and criticism as a field allows ideas to appear as more than the sole product of thought expressed in a certain way and in a specific historical, geographical, political, economic, and social context. The authors's need to enter and remain in the competitive space of the field shapes their content and form.

The question is, how much does the field shape ideas? Does it does so to such a degree that we might say it determines them? Or does it lightly refract their path? It always seems easier for the historian to emphasize context because it is what can be documented with empirical evidence, and because history, especially since the twentieth century, has moved away from the Hegelian legacy that once dominated historical thought and become much more of an empirical science. On this point I am indebted to Lynn Hunt's excellent book *Writing History in the Global Era*.[45] But how would one tell a history in which ideas and truth did have their own reality, or perhaps their own power? What methods would we use to speak of the past in a way in which the life of ideas animated our historical narratives? I say all this because ultimately this book and all the essays in it were drawn together by an idea, the idea of degree zero, and one wonders if throughout the book, our own sense of history embedded within our reigning historical methods prevent us from truly examining that idea as much in its own terms than in terms of the many social histories within which it was intertwined.

Zevi's indefatigable invitation to see the degree zero as the only way out of the postmodern architectural crisis lasted almost thirty years without being renewed. His peers who occupied symbolically and effectively dominant positions in the field, such as Frampton at this conference and many of those who studied his work posthumously, quickly discredited Zevi's proposal. However, given Zevi's symbolic downgrading at that time, I argue that this plea cannot simply be understood as a hollow idea tirelessly repeated or as an unsuccessful reflexive method that he misused. After having acted as an intellectual leader in post-Fascist Italy, after having been a dominant figure, he makes a plea that more importantly appears to be a response to the field in which he had to distinctively re-take his position to continue to occupy any position. If we also consider Zevi's plea as a strategy to maintain himself in the social space of the practice of architectural history, theory, and criticism, it appears that the distinctive logic of the field, which organizes both the promotion of its agents and their rejection, must also be questioned: "Is the context stronger than the concept?"[46]

CATTEDRA DI STORIA DELL'ARCHITETTURA
FACOLTÀ DI ARCHITETTURA
UNIVERSITÀ DI ROMA

PROF. DOTT. BRUNO ZEVI ARCHITETTO

"L'ARCHITETTURA - CRONACHE E STORIA" - VIA NOMENTANA, 150 - TEL. 8380481

00162 ROMA August 27, 1981

Prof. Kenneth Frampton
The Institute for Architecture and Urban Studies
Eight West Fortieth Street
New York, N.Y. 10018

Dear Kenneth Frampton,

It was a great pleasure to receive your letter of August 5. I am very sorry of the misunderstanding between you and Jorge Glusberg on the Warsaw Congress. It was a splendid experience, because the meetings organized by CICA were attended by a very large public. In fact, they were the most successful manifestation of the Congress.

Thank you very much for the time you spent on the manuscript by Andrea Dean. I am sure that she will try to satisfy your requirements as much as possible. I must say that I am rather hostile to the idea of a biographical photo-essay, as I believe that this should be a book on an architectural approach to architecture, and not on a person. But, again, Miss Dean will meet the Rizzoli people and will decide. In anycase, I am very grateful to you for your attention and your appreciation.

I did not know about our being coupled together, and with Aldo van Eyck, as "enemies" of Charles Jencks. I am proud to be with you and Aldo. In Warsaw, Jencks was very much on the defensive. He almost criticized "post-modernism". I have the impression that he is dominated more by its success than by what he believes in.

Here is my book-review, published in "L'Espresso", March 22, 1981. You can do whatever you like with it, and if you think useful to have it translated in part or in toto, you are free to do it.

I must say that I am not fully satisfied with this book-review. Your "Modern Architecture - A Critical History" deserves much more than that. I have been reading other reviews of your book. And none I find really good. This depends on the fact that it is a rather difficult book, especially for its structure. My attempt was to demonstrate its importance in spite, or because of, the authors and the works you have chosen not to mention. And there is a full agreement on the conclusions.

I look forward to the special issue of AD dedicated to you. You certainly deserve it. In my magazine "L'architettura", I have often quoted your ideas and positions as exemplary.

Thanks again,

Most friendly,

Bruno Zevi

Fig. 5 Zevi and Frampton are part of the same team. In this letter, Zevi refers to Charles Jencks's allusion to an "old guard" represented by Zevi, Frampton, Vittorio Gregotti, and Aldo van Eyck, who defends a "degree zero of architecture." See Jencks, "La bataille des étiquettes. Modernisme tardif contre postmodernisme," in *Nouveaux plaisirs d'architectures : Les pluralismes de la création en Europe et aux États-Unis depuis 1968 vus à travers les collections du Deutsches Architekturmuseum de Francfort* (Paris: Centre Georges Pompidou, 1985), 27.

Fig. 6 *L'architettura* magazine reports on the CICA's fourth International Meeting while eating Aldo Rossi's Teatro del Mondo to illustrate its fight against postmodernism. At this conference, Bruno Zevi organized a session titled 'The Zero Degree of Architectural Writing: Mirage or Challenge?' Frampton was invited to be one of the panelists with Jorge Glusberg, but only Glusberg took that role (see Fig. 5.).

1 Megged's identification as novelist and professor of comparative literature is printed in the event program, and in biographical indexes, he is generally presented as an author and professor. Although he has sometimes worked as a critic, poet, translator, and scientific editor, his main areas of expertise are art and literature.

2 The original French title is *Le chemin des indiens morts*. All translations are mine unless otherwise indicated.

3 Bruno Zevi, *Il linguaggio moderno dell'architettura: Guida al codice anticlassico* (Turin: Giulio Einaudi, 1973).

4 Roland Barthes, *Le degré zéro de l'écriture* (Paris: Seuil, 1953).

5 Kim Forster, *Building Institution: The Institute for Architecture and Urban Studies*, New York 1967-1985 (Bielefeld: Transcript Verlag, 2024), 7.

6 Peter Eisenman, "Peter Eisenman on Bruno Zevi," in *Zevi's Architects: History and Counter-History of Italian Architecture 1944-2000*, ed. Pippo Ciorra and Jean-Louis Cohen (Macerata Roma: Quodlibet, 2018), 139.

7 For Pierre Bourdieu, the field is an analytical tool. It reveals the rules that organize social human relationships within specific domains such as religion, literature, politics, or science. This approach echoes in several of his works, such as *La Distinction: Critique sociale du jugement* (Paris: Ed. de Minuit, 1979) and *Les règles de l'art: Genèse et structure du champ littéraire* (Paris: Seuil, 1992). In 2022, *Microcosmes: Théorie des champs* (Paris: Raisons d'Agir), a book dedicated to the notion of field that Bourdieu had planned but never completed, was finally published.

8 In architectural history, Helene Lipstadt has studied Bourdieu's work to define architecture as a field of cultural production: "Can 'Art Professions' Be Bourdieuean Fields of Cultural Production? The Case of The Architecture Competition," *Cultural Studies* 17, nos. 3-4 (2010): 390-418; "Theorizing the Competition: The Sociology of Pierre Bourdieu as a Challenge to Architectural History," *Thresholds* 21 (2000): 23-36; and "Sociology: Bourdieu's Bequest," *Journal of the Society of Architectural Historians*, 64, no. 4 (2005): 433-436.

9 Garry Stevens, *The Favored Circle: The Social Foundations of Architectural Distinction* (Cambridge Mass.: MIT Press, 2002).

10 Magali Sarfatti Larson, *Behind the Postmodern Facade: Architectural Change in Late Twentieth-Century America* (California: University of California Press, 1993).

11 Roland Barthes, *Mythologies* (Paris: Seuil, 1957).

12 Ibid., 208.

13 Ibid.

14 Ibid., 7.

15 Ibid., 208.

16 This is inspired by Marielle Macé's passage: "I'm convinced that the task of qualifying these forms, describing them accurately and treating them with justice (treating them with respect, but also with anger when we want to change something), is a responsibility that is truly shared by literature and the social sciences (which in this sense are both 'sciences of style')," in *Styles: Critique de nos formes de vie* (Paris: Gallimard, 2016), 14.

17 "Our culture seems to be based on old myth and on the repetition of old mistakes," writes Zevi, in "The Seven Myths of Architecture," *Social Research* 52, no. 2 (1985): 416.

18 I owe this title to Annie Ernaux, who writes about Pierre Bourdieu's book *La Distinction: Critique sociale du jugement* in her chapter "La distinction, œuvre totale et revolutionnaire," in *Pierre Bourdieu: L'insoumission en héritage*, ed. Edouard Louis (Paris: puf, 2013), 26.

19 Zevi, "The Seven Myths," 416.

20 Iibd.

21 Ibid., 422.

22 Ibid.

23 I only have the summary of the "Myth and the Arts" section, which appar-

ently corresponded to the conference session, and Zevi's contribution. I found these documents in Zevi's archives. The rest of the booklet has been cut out. Zevi tended not to keep the contributions of others at this kind of event, a symbolic act that shows his propensity to look at himself in reference to others: at himself in the field.

24 Kenneth Frampton, "Presence of Myth: Intervention and Commentary by Kenneth Frampton, 1984," in the Kenneth Frampton archives, CCA, Montreal, AP197.S1.SS9.004, *Kenneth Frampton texts, articles and notes*, MO-Z, 1967-2015.

25 That's how sociologist Luc Boltanski describes the scenes of dispute he studies. Marielle Macé explains it in a lecture about his book *De la critique: Précis de sociologie de l'émancipation* (Paris: Gallimard, 2009): "The intention was, and I quote again: 'to take seriously this constant anxiety about what is and what is worth, and which manifests itself vigorously in scenes of dispute.' Because what are we disputing? We're disputing what Boltanski called the qualification of reality, in other words, the definition of what is in situations where it counts and where it matters." Macé, "De la Critique (2009) de Boltanski," Conference at the Bibliotheque nationale de France (BnF), Cycle la petite bibliotheque des sciences sociales, March 09, 2017, by BnF, YouTube, 01:12:35, https://www.youtube.com/watch?v=uoSOpijghyE, at 00:21:33.

26 Kenneth Frampton, "Industrialization and the Crises in Architecture," in *Oppositions*, no. 1 (September 1973), 57-82.

27 Frampton, "Presence of Myth," 6: "Although this is admittedly a rather odd taxonomic distinction, it does nonetheless suggest the oversimplifies nature of Zevi's 'classic equals fascist' argument."

28 Ibid., 5. "I would like to conclude with a few ~~comments~~ remarks about Zevi's ~~preoccupation~~ flirtation with the idea of an 'architecture degree zero'." The quotation is taken from a draft before the text was published. The erasures are retained to show how and where Frampton chose to clarify his thoughts.

29 Ibid. "This concept (misappropriated I think one might say from Roland Barthes' Writing Degree Zero of 1953, since it does not seem to share Barthes's respect for the classic) may be ~~revealingly~~ critically evaluated."

30 Ibid., 2. "I liked Zevi's use of the term 'zero degree' architecture and I will attempt, somewhat later, to address myself a consideration of what a truly 'zero degree' architecture might be. Theo Van Doesburg's, "16 points of a New Plastic Architecture," was obviously an attempt at a totally new beginning, related to the organic tradition of the Gothic Revival, although there were other 'zero degree' figures who were tied more closely to the western classical tradition line; figures such as Adolf Loos and Mies Van der Rohe who were surely as commited to a zero degree architecture reduced expression, as any other pioneer modernist."

31 When naming its journal *Oppositions*, the IAUS refers to Barthes's degree zero. The title has a double meaning: it can be understood as an "opposition" but also as a "0 position." The concept also appears in pedagogy. In 1982, Eisenman invited his students to read an article by Susan Sontag dealing with the degree zero. They would have to replace the word *literature* with *architecture* and Barthes's name with his own to understand his approach to the discipline. See Peter Eisenman, "Transcript of a Class or Group Discussion," 1982, IAUS archives, CCA, Montreal, AP057.S4.SS2, 057-2004-013 T, ARCH153850, D2-7, 19.

32 Kenneth Frampton, ed., *The Architecture of Hiromi Fujii* (New York: Rizzoli, 1987).

33 Frampton, "Building Degree Zero: Megalopolitan Reality and Japanese Critical Practice," Kenneth Frampton archives, CCA, Montreal, AP197.S1.SS9.001, Kenneth Frampton texts, articles and notes, A-Z, 1964-1990.

34 Bruno Zevi, "Riposta a Kenneth Frampton: non c'è un classicismo liberatorio," *L'architettura: Cronache e storia* 33, no. 2 (1987): 82-83.

35 Zevi, "Riposta a Kenneth Frampton," 83.

36 Ibid.

37 Macé, *Styles*, 121.

38 Roland Barthes, *Comment vivre ensemble: Cours et séminaires au Collège de France* (1976-1977) (Paris: Seuil, 2002), 193.

39 Barthes, *Mythologies*, 102.

40 Zevi, "Riposta a Kenneth Frampton," 83. "Kenneth has written an excellent essay that we are reproducing on the facing page." The editorial summary was translated by the editors into English, German, French, and Spanish.

41 Kenneth Frampton, *Modern Architecture: A Critical History* (London: Thames and Hudson, 1980).

42 Kenneth Frampton, "Towards a Critical Regionalism: Six Points for an Architecture of Resistance," in *The Anti-Aesthetic: Essays on Postmodern Culture*, ed. Hal Foster (Washington: Bay Press, 1983).

43 See *OASE*'s 103rd issue (2019), *Critical Regionalism Revisited*, ed. Tom Avermaete, Veronique Patteeuw, Lea-Catherine Szacka and Hans Teerds. More recently: Stylianos Giamarelos, *Resisting Postmodern Architecture: Critical Regionalism before Globalisation* (London: UCL Press, 2022). https://doi.org/10.2307/j.ctv1v090hv.

44 Ian Latham, "Instructive Intentions," *Building Design* (1983): 2.

45 Lynn Hunt, *Writing History in the Global Era* (New York: W. W. Norton & Company, 2014).

46 In the song "La Belle et le Bad Boy," MC Solaar repeats the phrase "the context is stronger than the concept" and emphasizes how social and gender dynamics model the life of a bad boy. MC Solaar, "La Belle et le Bad Boy," *Cinquième as*, 2001.

Uncovering Invisible Editorial Work: Translation and Representation in the Magazine *Spazio e Società*

B. Beril Kapusuz-Balcı

comments by
Jorge Mejía Hernández

In 1988, architectural theorist Christian Norberg-Schulz published, "La Terza Alternativa," an essay on the architectural practice and intellectual position of the Italian architect, planner, writer and educator Giancarlo De Carlo. He identifies De Carlo as a unique figure who represents "the third alternative"

JMH Upon his election in 1992, Bill Clinton's advisory team started using the term "third way" to describe yet another iteration of the age-old political ambition to syncretize socialist governance with the unhindered exchange of goods and services. Several years later, a group of European politicians, including Gerhard Schröder and Tony Blair, rose to prominence by claiming that their "Third Way" and "Neue Mitte" programs constituted unprecedented syntheses of time-tested policies. For more than a decade, politicians across the globe profited from such syncretic claims, campaigning as so-called "social democrats" while promising to keep their countries open to free trade. The unavoidable vagueness that characterized third way platforms made it possible for politicians as diverse as Muamar Gaddafi, Wim Kok, Juan Manuel Santos, and Helen Clark to converge around the use of the term and its many possible interpretations.

that transcends both modern and postmodern architectural approaches.[1] He believed that this "third position," while not encompassing all of De Carlo's architectural practice, is evident in the exchange of ideas and continuous research conducted through the International Laboratory of Architecture and Urban Design (ILAUD) and the magazine *Spazio e Società: Rivista internazionale di architettura e urbanistica (S&S)*. Norberg-Schulz observes that these forums, shaped by De Carlo's vision of architecture, were fundamentally different from other architectural institutions and publications of the 1970s in Italy.

Drawing upon the third position posed by Norberg-Schulz, De Carlo's "third way" of writing, communicating, and representing architecture can be traced back through his teaching and editorial practices developed in the late 1970s and early 1980s. In an era of "oppositions"[2] and zero positions, *S&S* appeared as a complex editorial space capable of enabling other positions to emerge. The magazine featured a diverse range of content, including essays, interviews, theoretical reflections, and case studies, focusing on topics such as the role of architecture in shaping social spaces, the relationship between built environments and their users, and the political implications of urban design. De Carlo's editorial direction fostered a dialogue between architecture and other disciplines, making *S&S* a key publication for architects, urbanists, and theorists interested in the socio-political dimensions of space. During his presentation of the *S&S* in 1980 at the National Gallery of Modern Art in Rome, De Carlo declared, on behalf of the magazine's editorial team,[3] that they "refused to accord to architecture a superstructural status" and "rejected the principle of autonomy of architecture," defining architecture as "heteronomous" by nature.[4] Initially, this heteronomy, called for social engagement and forms of participation through an emphasis on the "Greater Number," a central theme associated with Team X, of which De Carlo was a member, advocating for more human-centric and socially responsible approaches to architecture and urban planning. The concept underscored the idea that architectural and urban design should prioritize the needs and desires of the general population rather than a select elite. The magazine defended the heteronomy of architecture through an interdisciplinary and international approach, with a focus on the organization and form of physical space in its various scales and geographies.[5] In this sense, *S&S* understood architectural heteronomy as deeply embedded within and intrinsically interwoven into society, everyday life, and the city.

Assuming a non-academic position, *S&S* also aimed to communicate through a comprehensible language, demystify architectural writing, and avoid "verbal terrorism,"

Another example of third way politics was the program of the Greek Prime Minister Costas Simitis, who governed between 1996 and 2004. His former party, the Panhellenic Socialist Movement (PASOK), founded by Andreas Papandreou, went from having more than 40 percent of the vote in 2009, to less than 5 percent in 2016. The term "Pasokification" thus refers to a steep decline in a political party's success, especially regarding the fate of third way politics across the globe after 2010. "Pasokification" is seen as evidence that, in the opinion of voters, the promise of a renewed and

Fig. 1 Giancarlo De Carlo and Giuliana Baracco, Milan, 1964.
Fig. 2 Peter Prangnell with Aldo van Eyck, Toronto, 1968.

productive balance between freedom and order has not been achieved. The decline of third way politics since the 2010s has actually reinvigorated the contending arguments those campaigns intended to address. The promised balance has therefore turned into the opposite: a growing polarization, which explains the notable success since 2010 of politicians who use the age-old argument known as "populism" in a variety of contexts.

as De Carlo called it.[6] Shifting the focus from the objects of architecture to the social and material processes of the built environment (including territory, landscape cities, buildings, urban interiors, and infrastructure), *S&S* assigned more space to visual materials than to other more conventional architectural drawings, such as plans and sections. Lushly illustrated, *S&S* reassigned the power of the architectural photograph from sterile photographs of buildings that lack evidence of human use or occupation to a form of critical photography that built on direct experience of space and participation. As this Italian "rivista" was packed with vivid pictures and appealing illustrations, *S&S* flirted with the formats of popular media and fashion magazines, an editorial choice that might have been informed by the influence and contribution of Alison Smithson and Peter Smithson.[7]

Although *S&S* was referred to as an initiative of De Carlo, archival research allows a comprehensive view of *S&S* and the various actors and interactions enhancing De Carlo's initiative, like members of Team X.[8] This chapter focuses on overlooked actors behind the scenes, Giuliana Baracco and Peter Prangnell in particular, and how they communicated internally on the journal's distinctive content and form. Baracco (Fig. 1) was a driving force within the editorial ecology of *S&S* and De Carlo's lifelong partner and Prangnell (Fig. 2) was a British architect and educator who had been part of De Carlo's international network since the 1960s[9] and was a frequent contributor of *S&S*, with texts and photo essays. Through their close collaboration (which would turn into a sincere friendship in the following years), De Carlo, Baracco, and Prangnell sought to create a neutral verbal-visual language. From their ongoing correspondence it becomes evident how uniquely effective their collaboration was in translating and representing Prangnell's ideas on architecture.

This paper argues that Baracco's and Prangnell's contributions were essential in establishing what is described here as the development of a "third term," or "degree zero," of writing and representation. Through their roles in *S&S*—Baracco's "verbal" role through rewriting and translations, and Prangnell's visual role through his controversial photographic series—as I will argue, they sought to implement a degree zero in print, a representation of text and photographs that was clearly communicated and centered on the vocabularies and practicalities of human experience. Although neither Baracco, De Carlo, nor any other member of the editorial team explicitly used Barthes's concept of "writing degree zero," this chapter introduces and mobilizes this notion to articulate the editorial project's unique approach to architectural discourse and representation.

TRANSLATION: DEMYSTIFYING ARCHITECTURAL WRITING

Baracco, originally a translator, assumed the position of editor-in-chief of *S&S* from its second issue, published in April 1978, until the magazine's ninety-second and final issue of October–December 2000. As a non-architect, Baracco's interests extended to "other" forms of architecture within the city and everyday life. Since De Carlo was the visible and acknowledged spokesperson of the magazine, Baracco's essential and active role in the editorial process remained "backstage," first becoming evident in a series of interviews conducted by scholars interested in the history of *S&S* after the magazine's conclusion and prior to her passing in 2003.[10] Baracco's significant role in De Carlo's career needs to be equally highlighted.[11] In this role she made use of her proficiency in English and her deep engagement with literature, particularly Anglo-Saxon culture.[12] Despite her unfeatured presence, her frame of mind "spoke little but said significant things,"[13] and, De Carlo himself never failed to mention her pivotal role. Through her editorial practice and engagement in defining *S&S* as architectural medium, she sought to establish a channel by which space or environment could conversationally speak to society.[14]

Baracco holds significance here for two primary reasons. First, her "disinterested" perspective as a non-architect played a pivotal role in the way she organized materials for publication, which included translated many text by foreign contributors into Italian. Second, her meticulous, almost artisanal approach to assembling materials from contributors entailed intensive correspondence with them. Her editorial work involved not only editing and compiling but also, in many cases, substantially rewriting texts, or "simplifying," as she called it.[15] Reflecting on the editorial process of *S&S*, Baracco emphasized the importance she placed on clear and comprehensible communication through texts:

> I simplified them. What we wanted to communicate had to be comprehensible at once and perfectly clear. All that took up much time. Then, I kept in contact with the contributors; I had a very close rapport with some. But I must say that a fundamental role in the practical everyday conduct of the work was simply being a point of reference for all the contributors, orienting and co-ordinating.[16]

And while translating is always to some extent a "betrayal," as in the old Italian saying "Traduttore, traditore," her editorial work fundamentally contributed to a pursuit of a "degree zero of writing" by demystifying the architectural language of the journal's contributors.

Indeed, Baracco was trying to avoid the deep theoretical and academic tone "stranded in the shallows of architecture."[17] She was interested in the social dimension of the discussions that "mean something to people."

Populism is a political instrument that describes any given society as being comprised of two clear-cut contending factions: one being a purported majority, nebulously referred to as "the people" (collective) or "the common man" (individual); and the other being an equally ambiguous minority described as an "elite." Based on said explanation, politicians who use populism as an instrument claim to act on behalf of the former by protecting them from the latter, who are made responsible for one or more particularly incensing real or perceived problems, failures, or threats. Since its appearance in the late nineteenth century the term has been used broadly and vaguely, with both positive and negative connotations.

She notes that the editorial board was "fanatical about being able to understand everything, being as clear as possible," explaining why she had to continually rewrite to simplify the texts. Following a deep argument with Baracco and considering previous feedback from the readers, De Carlo wrote a letter to one Italian contributor in which he boldly declares the aims and ambitions of *S&S*, giving a detailed commentary on the texts expected:

> [W]e want to show that you can talk about architecture without using the jargon of (Italian) architecture, and that means freeing ourselves from the *mystificatory and terrorist threats that this jargon contains.*[18]

Baracco and De Carlo, while warning contributors of obscurity within architectural jargon, explicitly intended to cultivate an appropriate vocabulary to facilitate "more meaningful and flexible communication."[19] They advised against including notes that might disrupt a reader's focus on the main argument and recommended that authors explain references to other authors or events to ensure clarity. The contributors were also encouraged to include a glossary to clarify rarely used or complex terms whenever they appeared in the text. These intensive contacts with the authors made up a significant part of the editorial processes, over the whole publication life of *S&S*.

REPRESENTATION: REINVENTING ARCHITECTURAL PHOTOGRAPHS

The selective collection of valuable photographic materials gathered in De Carlo's archives resonates directly with the visual approach of *S&S* and his ambition to attain a degree zero in architectural publications. His archives include photographs that document his architectural projects throughout their life cycles, their users, and the ever-changing surrounding landscape. This collection illustrates his disinterest in both the timeless, sterile photographs typically associated with modern architecture and the typological photographs often employed by the Italian Rationalists. Photographs in the archive were mostly taken by renowned Italian photographers, including Giorgio Casali, Gabriele Basilico, Mimmo Jodice, and Antonio Garbasso, who specialized in "reportage photography." This archival content provides insights into De Carlo's interest in photography, by which he documented and interpretated his participatory environments over time.[20] The contributions to *S&S* from Team X members Herman Herzberger, Aldo van Eyck, Alison Smithson, and Peter Smithson were instrumental in defining the magazine's unique aesthetic, as they adeptly combined written content with striking images of people interacting with architectural spaces. Through such photographs and the photography of Pragnell, *S&S* reflected on how architectural space is used and appropriated by society.

S&S obeyed the strict rule that photographs should not be published without including people, according to Franco Mancuso, a Venetian architect and professor of urbanism, because people were considered the accurate measure of a building's success.[21] Authors were often asked to provide "better" and more recent photographs that conveyed the character of the territory and illustrated the relationships between buildings and their urban context. De Carlo and Baracco urged contributors to provide visual interpretations of the environments they discussed, which required the authors to actively participate in producing the material for publication. Since *S&S* did not commission photographers, they trusted the authors to provide "up-to-date material, meaning a series of photographs on [their] most recent experience with exhaustive enough captions as descriptions and comments."[22]

Prangnell, a faithful contributor to *S&S*, was invited by De Carlo to write critical reviews on architecture. A distinguished architect and educator, Prangnell held influential academic positions at leading institutions in the UK, USA, and Canada. His relationship with De Carlo began in the mid-1960s, when he was teaching at Columbia University. Prangnell invited De Carlo to participate in a series of seminars, in which Prangnell developed a humanist critique of modern architecture.[23] Prangnell's most significant academic role was as chair of the Department of Architecture at the University of Toronto from 1968 to 1976, where he was pivotal in shaping the student-centered program. Under his leadership, the department became a center for progressive architectural education, fostering interdisciplinary approaches, including the use of photography as a pedagogical tool, and promoting critical engagement with contemporary issues in architecture and urbanism.[24] In the years that followed, in alignment with *S&S*'s international character, De Carlo sought Prangnell's contributions to the magazine, where he represented a Canadian affiliation. Prangnell often referred to himself as an outsider in both academic and practical architectural contexts. The satirical texts he wrote for *S&S* were deliberately crafted in a non-academic voice, further reflecting this experimental approach. Prangnell's non-representational method of photography was evident in the speculative photographic sequences and portfolios accompanying his articles. From his distinctive intellectual position, he contributed unconventional photographic representations that may be regarded as a form of writing. The visual content of *S&S*, which emphasized human relevance, was further enriched by Prangnell's object-oriented approach, offering an alternative perspective to the magazine's photographic language (Fig. 3).

Prangnell was a dedicated and loyal contributor to *S&S*, with articles published in sixteen issues over two decades, from 1980 to 2000. His photo essays, featuring his own photography, complemented his critical reviews and held a significant status

Fig. 3. Cover of *Spazio e Società*, no. 12 (December 1980).

within the magazine. De Carlo praised these contributions for their ability to engage a broader audience and enhance the publication's appeal. Prangnell's writing was speculative and polemic, and was mainly published in the magazine's section titled "Congetture," or "Speculations." He offered both *S&S* and its readers an alternative way of writing about the built environment by translating architectural ideas into photographic illustrations of themes and objects of everyday life and human relevance. He also reviewed canonical architectural projects through actual photographs of the buildings and adding critical notes based on his most recent "conversations" with them. His interest in how we inhabit architecture and the routines of everyday life appear to intersect with Baracco's ideas, which might explain her enthusiasm for translating Prangnell's pieces into Italian (Fig. 4).

For Prangnell, objects, and by extension architectural objects, were "inanimate constructions that support us in our everyday life" that possessed a "friendly" condition by which their agency and intentionality were communicated to their user. According to him, "buildings as friendly objects" "activate their responses of practical need and associational participation." At a certain point, he says, "[t]he importance of the friendly object is that it manifests human relevance."[25] In his view, human and non-human communication relies on issues of familiarity, practicality, and materiality. Prangnell's conception of buildings as friendly objects rejected the sort of analysis of abstract architectural space that is rooted in art theory. He emphasized that space aligns with the non-human elements it contains, serving as a volume for human use.

Prangnell's concept of the "friendly object" emerged from his pedagogical experiments at Columbia in the mid-1960s and later, while designing the curriculum at the University of Toronto's Department of Architecture in 1967. He prioritized the social dimension in architecture and explored architectural representation beyond its traditions. His students were asked "to look at relatively mundane things about the city, to record them and to analyze how they provided a built counterform to certain fundamental activities."[26] His concern was to shift the focus from abstract space to everyday objects and habits, to demystify the design process, and to "unveil" communication between the built environment and the users.[27]

His photographic work held as much significance as his written contributions in breaking down hierarchies of meaning and form. Prangnell's "photo essays" offered content that held intrinsic value. His architectural critique, nurtured by the nature of his translation and representation of friendly objects, carved out a space opened by Baracco and De Carlo that distinctly redefined the role that architectural photography played in *S&S*. Prangnell took photographs that were synchronized with and specific to each of his reviews published in *S&S*. This approach aligned with the editors' initial objective, which was to have contributors use accurate and contextually relevant photographs of the architectural subjects discussed in their articles. Most of Prangnell's photographs were taken specifically to illustrate each of his reviews. In addition to human figures and natural or urban landscapes, they captured infrastructural and architectural components and furniture. His photographic narratives were accompanied by textual voice-overs in captions, meticulously translated by Baracco, which enhanced the readers' understanding of his architectural vision. Prangnell's enthusiasm for each review he submitted to Baracco and De Carlo is evident in his numerous letters, which meticulously addressed every photograph and caption in great detail.

One of those enthusiastic contributions, Prangnell's second review for *S&S*, was on Pierre Chareau's Maison de Verre (1928–1932). This came eleven years after Kenneth Frampton's article on the building was published in *Perspecta*, to which Prangnell directly refers, particularly highlighting Frampton's significant use of photography. Frampton's article included seventy-four photographs of the Maison de Verre, the result of four years of documentation, which he did with the help of his friends. Prangnell's piece, too, is quite long—eleven pages. His photographs narrate everyday life in the house, focusing on different responses from the objects, such as the separatory glass screens, as they occupied the space with their users.

Although his review recalls the way in which Frampton's article was illustrated, Prangnell himself was the photographer, and the captions address not only the objects within the building but also his own immediate experience and bodily relation with(in) the space. Prangnell's photographs were originally in color, unlike Frampton's black-and-whites. However, due to the publishing policies of *S&S*, Prangnell produced black-and-white scans of the photographs, which were "not as comprehensive as he would have liked,"[29] perhaps implying that he would rather have color involved in his compositions to avoid the code of timeless, black-and-white images that illustrated Frampton's articles (Fig. 5). Prangnell was in search of a different narration of this space that had already been thoroughly documented and was frequently represented.

The editorial work *S&S* invested in narrating architecture through photo essays aligned with what Jorge Otero-Pailos describes as a process of "interpretations" that render architecture as "cultural work."[30] In contrast to theory, *interpretation* attributes intellectual agency to multiple media without any hierarchy. Otero-Pailos writes, "One could say that there is no mother tongue to architectural communication," and he mentions the photo essay as one of the many forms of interpretation and communication.[31] Prangnell sought to unravel the unique associations triggered by novel and unfamiliar forms, and he did so, for example, by juxtaposing modern ventilation mechanisms with traditional windows and curtains (Fig. 6). In a manner akin to Frampton's documentary approach, which Otero-Pailos describes as the "pursuit of a more authentic experience of architecture through architectural photography,"[32] Prangnell's distinctive photographic techniques reformulated the documentation of architectural space. To give voice to the objects in the framed space, as in the case of moving bidet and glass panels, he used techniques such as a "long exposure," by means of which he could portray objects in "conversation" with the space and himself (Fig. 7-8). Prangnel claims that "each object tells us something of its maker and our relation to him. It can, by its condition, tell us something of its relation to other users. It can, also by its condition, suggest something of the attitude that is expected of us."[33] Yet the iconic and aesthetic photographs of the house celebrated through Frampton's earlier work were reinvented in unpretentious and appealing photographs of Prangnell's collection of friendly objects.

EPILOGUE

Spazio e Società's approach to visual elements in architecture, particularly the use of photography, was a defining feature as it evolved into a bilingual magazine with a neutral language.

Derived from the Latin term for "spreading," "propaganda" describes a particular way of communicating a program or agenda. While other forms of communication try to persuade or convince by appealing to people's reasoning, propaganda uses slogans, images, manifestos, and other condensed media in order to target their emotions. Given its apparent simplicity, especially when compared to complex and contradictory forms of communication, those who find advantage in communicating via propaganda (e.g. populist politicians) frequently, present their ambitions as elemental, natural, or neutral.

Despite criticisms from Italian academic circles, the magazine continued to make extensive use of photographs, especially documentary ones, and photographic narrations were purposefully accompanied by generous captions, which demonstrated again the core ambition of *S&S* to convey the social dimension of architecture and the material relations of space.

Through its visual and verbal language, *S&S* engaged with diverse intellectual perspectives. Architects and urban planners like Herzberger, Van Eyck, and the Smithsons all made significant contributions to *S&S*, including through their photography. These contributions shaped the magazine's humanist and ethnographic lens and defined its distinct appearance in the Italian architectural publication scene.

The productive collaboration and profound bond between the parallel, albeit different, minds of Baracco and Prangnell was unveiled and acknowledged through a hundred letters over sixteen articles.[34] Their disinterested attitude toward the disciplinary paradigms of architecture and interest in the other quotidian forms of language gave way to unique speculative and performative forms of architectural writing. In the magazine's editorial workplace, the goal of exchanges in the culture of writing and photography was to establish a zero degree in architectural publishing through a particular focus on human relevance with objects, spaces, places, and familiarity derived from everyday life. Yet the non-academic and speculative writing and interpretative use of photographs helped form the idiosyncratic position of *S&S* as a journal willing to communicate to the broader public. The negotiated character of architectural knowledge in multiple modes deserves further attention in the writing of alternative histories, to trace the complex relationships at play and to re-capture the stories of "other" actors and allow them to be heard.

Milan, March 4, 1981

Dear Mr. Prangnell,

The truant picture is safely in our hands, and your article (stimulating as usual) has already been translated.A few things presented some difficulties due to a language gap between English and Italian. The N.K.Smith's quotation about the Johnson Wax building, for exemple, was all based on the word understanding which in Italian could only be translated intesa, which has none of the standing meaning which Smith uses. So, to avoid clumsy attempts at conveying the idea, we preferred to cut off the whole paragraph in the Italian version. Also the Nantucket "widows on their walks" get lost, because the "widow's walks" in Italian are simply called "altane", which is a beautiful word but unfortunately has nothing to do with widows or with walks.

Two weeks ago I sent you two copies of number 12 with your "Maison de Verre" piece: hope you liked it. And what about the next? N.13, with your "Villa Savoye" will come out in June, and n.14 in October, but we have to go in print before the August holidays: which means that we should get at least the text by the end of April. Do you think you can make it? Please let us know something.

All best wishes

Prof. Peter Prangnell
52 Playter Boulevard
Toronto
Ontario M4K 2W3

Fig. 4 Letters from Giuliana Baracco to Peter Prangnell (4 March 1981; 26 March 1981).

Milan, March 26th, 1981

Dear Peter,

I am glad you liked the way we published your article and I can tell you that our readers love your witty approach and acute observation, so that I feel compelled to push you into writing the other five pieces. I also give you a strict deadline for the first one (Mackintosh or Kelmscott): the end of April for the text and the 20th of May for the illustrations (for these we may give you some help, if you need it).

All best wishes,

Dear Peter,

Of course your Villa Savoye will appear on n.13. It wasn't mentioned in "Nel prossimo numero" only because we were not sure, at that time, to get it.

As to the "widows' walks", both the photograph and the reference in the text are certainly included: what gets lost (I was not very clear in my letter) is only the "widows on their walks..." which I liked and has to be simply replaced by "le altane...". I also find the "altane" very poetic: there are lots of them in Italy, even in ugly Milan, though it is difficult to notice them in the jumble of the present cityscape. Also a poem by a Milanese poet mentions "le altane lombarde...".

I hope you'll be able to write and send in time your fourth article: our readers are becoming addicted to your pieces and I fear withdrawal symptoms if they do not find one in n.14

Best regards.

Prof. Peter Prangnell
52 Playter Boulevard
Toronto, Ontario, M4K 2W3

School of Architecture

6600 Washington, #306
St. Louis, Mo 63130

October 6, 1980

Dear Giancarlo,

I have just sent off two packages to you, one with the photographs and captions of the Maison de Verre and the other with a copy of the manuscript with the photos keyed in. Sorry they're a bit behind schedule, but it was the mail strike in Canada that did it!

The photographs are not as comprehensive as I would have liked - I took most of the pictures in colour and I don't think they transpose so well as these which are from b. & w. negatives. If you think it is a problem, let me know - perhaps we could use some of the pictures from Ken Frampton's article in Perspecta (though I'd rather not). I am, however, particularly pleased with photo #12 and hope that you can give it plenty of space! It's the one with the moving bidet!

The manuscript is unchanged except that I've had to delete the reference to "Persians" and "Marathon" (page 4, para 2, last sentence). I've searched everywhere but cannot find the reference I want - so I have to believe that I remember it from a movie!

What do you think about the captions? I tried to make them read on their own but, with less than comprehensive pictures, it doesn't seem to be a very accurate summary of the argument. Do you think it might be better to lift pieces from the text? Or simply key them in to the text?

Friends in Toronto are having difficulty getting copies of Spazio e Societa. They've been ordered through Ballenford Architectural Books, 98 Scollard Street, Toronto, Ontario M5R 1G2. The people at Ballenford say they're having difficulties with the U.S.A. distributor. They would very much like to deal with your publisher directly. They are a very good architectural bookstore and cover all of Canada and some of the U.S.A. Will you do something for them? They are trying to get a number of copies of no. 8 (the Van Eyck one) and promise a substantial order for later ones - nos. 11, 12 & 13 in particular!

With best wishes
Peter

Giancarlo De Carlo
Editor: Spazio e Societa
via Mascheroni 18
20145 Milan

P.S: I almost forgot - and it's important - can you add a footnote after the title to the effect that "I am grateful to Antoine Grumbach and the "Friends of the Maison de Verre" for allowing me to take photographs (and inconvenience them) in 1977" ?

Washington University
Campus Box 1079
St. Louis, Missouri 63130
(314) 889-6200

Fig. 5 Letter from Peter Prangnell to Giancarlo De Carlo (6 October 1980).

velatura di una barca per farla procedere sotto vento. La nostra energia regola e controlla la casa, modificandone le risposte a una data situazione in modo che le nostre esigenze – vale a dire le nostre ambizioni e aspirazioni – vengano soddisfatte. E, proprio come uno strumento, la casa mette a nostra disposizione la possibilità di realizzare.

Forse, anziché «rozza», è più corretto dire che una casa normale è *dilettantesca*; e allora possiamo dire che la Maison de Verre è *professionale* (come è giusto che sia, visto che è stata fatta da architetti). Esperienza e abilità tecnica sono confluite nella sua realizzazione, portandola a un livello di esecuzione superiore a qualunque altra casa che io conosca. È uno stradivario di casa! E, se una casa normale si può regolare, la Maison de Verre si può *accordare*. Forse è una differenza piccola, ma per me implica la possibilità di un coinvolgimento emotivo e psicologico importante.

La musica può essere sublime;

4 La ventilazione del soggiorno è controllata da una serie di persiane regolabili girando la ruota. Manovrare questo meccanismo, mettere in moto il sistema di ingranaggi, manovelle e leve, è emozionante come azionare una chiusa. Per un momento, nell'immaginazione, ci si avvicina a forze potenti, al di là di noi.

5 Questa modesta tendina trasforma il sole. Grazie a loro, il sole attenua la sua forza inflessibile. La tendina diventa un nostro intermediario – attraverso di lei, manovrandola, arriviamo più vicini al sole. («Casa El Greco»)

4 *Ventilation for the living room is controlled through a bank of louvers which may be adjusted by turning the wheel. Operating this mechanism, setting in motion the system of gears, cranks and levers, is as impressive as working sluices or locks – momentarily, in our imagination, we can be connected to powerful forces beyond us. It is as if we can be «taken out of ourselves».*

5 *This modest curtain transforms the sun, just as the awnings do (photo 3). By them, the sun loses something of its relentless single-mindedness! They are our agents and, by our dealings with them, we may come closer to the sun. (The «El Greco House»).*

58

Fig. 6. (Left) Excerpt from Peter Prangnell's Maison de Verre article with "still" ventilation. (Peter Pragnell's black-and-white digital scan of the original slide).
(Right) Unpublished photograph of Maison de Verre with ventilation-system, 1977.

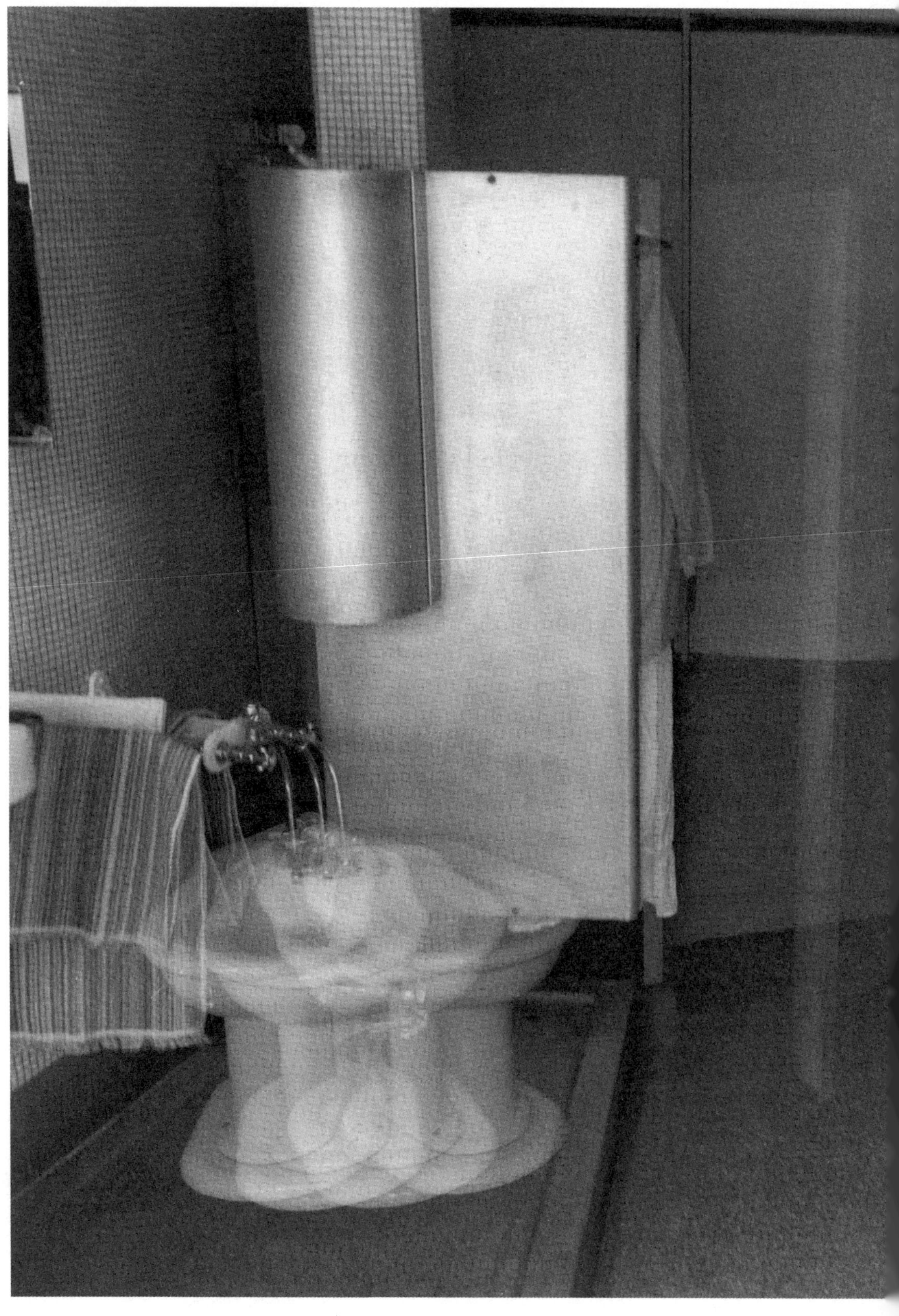

Fig. 7 Photograph of Maison de Verre with the moving bidet, 1977.

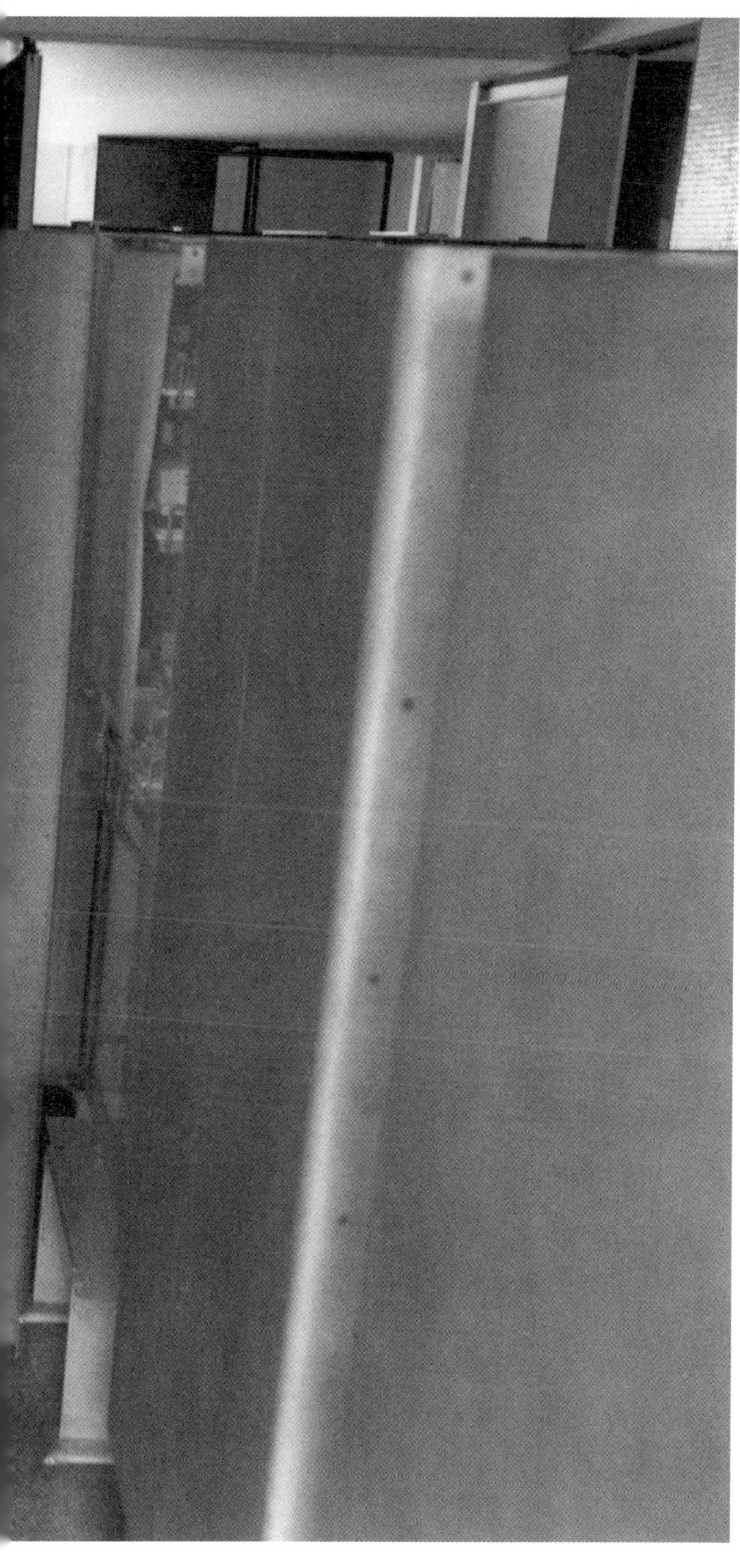

Fig. 8 The photograph of Maison de Verre with moving glass screens, 1977.

1 Norberg-Schulz's ideas greatly influenced De Carlo, and he participated in and lectured at ILAUD several times. Another figure, Lamberto Rossi, the author and editor of the book in which Norberg- Schulz's article appeared, was also affiliated with De Carlo and ILAUD. As a young architect from Rome, his appearance in ILAUD in Urbino in 1978-79 would be continued later with his collaboration with De Carlo in Milan and led to Rossi's extensive work on him. Christian Norberg-Schulz, "La Terza Alternativa" in *Giancarlo De Carlo: Architetture* (Milano: Arnoldo Mondadori Editore, 1988), 17.

2 Hanno Weber from Washington University School of Architecture found the magazine to be "neither totally biased nor uncommitted to a position" in comparison with its counterparts, *Oppositions* and *Architectural Association Quarterly*. Weber to De Carlo (17 April 1978), 037247, Spazio e Societa-cor/02/01, Fondo Giancarlo De Carlo (FGDC), Archivio Progetti (AP), Universita IUAV di Venezia (IUAV), Venice.

3 Under the direction of Giancarlo De Carlo, Baracco was the coordinator of the editorial team of Italian architects and academics Giovanni Galli, Gaddo Morpurgo, and Daniele Pini (former assistant of De Carlo during his teaching years at Iuav); Giovanni Galli was responsible for the graphic design and layout.

4 Francesco Samassa, ed., *Spazio e Società: Una sezione longitudinale sulla rivista* (Santarcangelo di Romagna: Maggioli Editore, 2000), 38.

5 Ibid., 41.

6 Ibid.

7 The Italian word "rivista" is commonly translated in English as "magazine," yet many *riviste di architettura* are considered now to be academic journals. Given the large audience and its particular visual approach, we speak here of *S&S* in terms of a magazine. *Domus*, *Casabella*, *Lotus International*, *Paramero*, and *Controspazio* were its contemporaries from the 1970s to the 1980s, and formed an important part of the architectural discourse in Italy, each contributing in distinct ways to debates on modernism, postmodernism, and the role of architecture in shaping society. While some, like *Domus* and *Casabella*, had broader international followings, others, like *Controspazio* and *Parametro*, were more specialized but still influential in Italy's architectural scene.

8 During archival research conducted by the author as a part of her postdoctoral research, primary sources were identified in the Giancarlo De Carlo Fonds at IUAV University of Venice. The sub-folder dedicated to *S&S* reveals a rich collection of materials illuminating the magazine's dynamic intellectual and material process. The *S&S* sub-folder, organized and transferred to the Archivio Progetti (Projects Archive) under Francesco Samassa's supervision, contains a substantial collection of correspondence. These letters involve Director Giancarlo De Carlo, the editorial team, and contributing authors. The correspondence, especially between De Carlo, Giuliana Baracco, and the contributors, offers valuable insights into background processes previously obscured. The Archivio Giancarlo De Carlo is online at https://www-archive.iuav.it/ARCHIVIO-P/ARCHIVIO/collezioni/De- Carlo-G/index.htm.

9 The international network brought Prangnell and Team X members, including De Carlo, together in the '60s through the international seminars Prangnell organized at Columbia School of Architecture. Tony Schuman, "Form and Counterform: Architecture in a Non-Heroic Age," *Journal of Architectural Education* 35, no. 1 (1981): 2–4. https://doi.org/10.2307/1424573.

10 As a part of the scholarship on the histories of architectural publications, significant studies focus on the editorial ecology of *S&S*. See, for example, Francesco Samassa and Giuliana Baracco, "On the Backstage," in Francesco Samassa, ed., *Spazio e Società: Una sezione longitudinale sulla rivista* (Santarcangelo di Romagna: Maggioli Editore, 2000); Franco Buncuga, *Conversazioni con Giancarlo De Carlo: Architettura e libertà* (Milano: Eleuthera, 2000); Isabella Daidone, *Giancarlo De Carlo: Gli editoriali di Spazio e Società* (Rome: Gangemi Editore spa, 2018).

11 *Women Writing Architecture*, an open-access and ever-growing annotated

bibliography of architectural texts written by women, and *Women Writing Architecture: Female Experiences of the Built 1700–1900*, a project that unveils women's contributions to the architectural sphere through writing and editing," are worthy of attention for the voice and visibility they give to women figures and their texts remained out of the canon. Both are online: https://womenwritingarchitecture.org/ and https://wowa.arch.ethz.ch/.

12 A few of the many of her translations: Nicolaus Pevsner, *I pionieri del movimento moderno da William Morris a Walter Gropius* (1945); Frank Lloyd Wright, *Architettura e democrazia* (1945); Serge Chermayeff and Christopher Alexander, *Spazio di relazione e spazio privato : verso una nuova architettura umanistica* (1968); Lewis Mumford, *Verso nuove citta per l'America* (1969); Kevin Lynch, *Il tempo dello spazio* (1977).

13 Daidone, *Giancarlo De Carlo*. The quote, "parlava poco ma diceva delle cose significative," is translated by the author from Daidone's interview with Alberto Cecchetto, professor of urbanism at IUAV University of Venice, who was a colleague of De Carlo.

14 Buncuga, *Conversazioni con Giancarlo De Carlo: architettura e libertà.*

15 Samassa, *Spazio e Società*, 12.

16 Ibid.

17 Ibid., 10.

18 Ibid., 29 (emphasis mine).

19 Ibid.

20 In his comprehensive research into De Carlo's participatory approach in architecture, with a specific focus on his Matteotti Village housing Project, Alberto Franchini addresses De Carlo's collaboration with Basilico for the photographs of the project to be published in Casabella. The visual narrations represented the users' diverse forms of dwelling and everyday life practices through photographic reportages of the households. Alberto Franchini, *Il Villaggio Matteotti a Terni: Giancarlo De Carlo e l'abitare collettivo* (Roma: L'Erma di Bretschneider, 2020).

21 Daidone, *Giancarlo De Carlo*, 216.

22 De Carlo to Colin Ward (30 June 1978), 037247, Spazio e Societa-cor/01, FGDC, AP, IUAV, Venice.

23 Tony Schuman, "Form and Counterform: Architecture in a Non-Heroic Age," *Journal of Architectural Education* 35, no. 1 (1981): 2–4. https://doi.org/10.2307/1424573.

24 Peter Prangnell, *Work in Progress 1973–1975, Department of Architecture Catalogue* (Toronto: University of Toronto Press, 1977). See also Beatriz Colomina, Ignacio G. Galán, Evangelos Kotsioris, and Anna-Maria Meister, eds., *Radical Pedagogies* (Cambridge: MIT Press, 2022), 38.

25 Peter Prangnell, "The Friendly Object," *Harvard Educational Review*, special issue, *Architecture and Education* 39, no. 4 (1969): 36–41.

26 Max Bond and Paul Broches, "Social Content in Teaching and Design: Max Bond Interviewed by Paul Broches," *Journal of Architectural Education* 35, no. 1 (2014): 51.

27 Prangnell emphasized the efficacy of incorporating photography and cameras due to their familiarity among students, as opposed to the unfamiliarity of drafting pens. He explained, "Building upon this familiarity, we instructed each student to create a visual essay that captured how people utilized a specific location within the city." These photo essays were then presented in the form of diptychs or sequences. Peter Prangnell, *Arch. Ed.* (Toronto: PP Ink, 2009), 15.

28 Kenneth Frampton, "Maison de verre," *Perspecta* 77 (1969): 128.

29 Prangnell to De Carlo (6 October 1980), 037344, Spazio e Societa -cor/01/082, Fondo Giancarlo De Carlo (FGDC), Archivio Progetti (AP), Universita IUAV di Venezia (IUAV), Venice.

30 Jorge Otero-Pailos, *Architecture's Historical Turn: Phenomenology and the Rise of the Postmodern* (Minneapolis: University of Minnesota Press, 2013), 6–7.

31 Ibid., 6–7.

32 Ibid., 203.

33 Prangnell, "The Friendly Object," 36.

34 Following Prangnell's passing in January 2023, I reached out to his long-time partner, the architect Anthony Belcher, having learned about him through Prangnell's letters. He generously shared a significant collection of Prangnell's materials. In our conversations, Belcher fondly recalled Prangnell's passionate contributions to *S&S* and his extensive correspondence with Baracco. In our conversation in March 2023, Belcher noted that "Peter cherished the way Giuliana translated his articles, and she once confided that among all the authors she worked with for *S&S*, translating his was the most enjoyable."

51
GROUND ZERO
Thomas Daniell
comments by
Matthew Mullane

75
THE SIGNIFICANCE OF THE GENERAL FORM: REFLECTIONS ON THE DEGREE ZERO
Martin Steinmann
introduced and edited by
Irina Davidovici
translated by
Duncan Brown
comments by
Carla Frick-Cloupet

93
BUILDING ON CONVERSATIONS WITH ÉRIC LAPIERRE
Lyna Bourouiba,
Carla Frick-Cloupet
comments by
Victoire Chancel

109
THE RIGHT TO ARCHITECTURE
Geert Bekaert
translated and introduced by
Christophe Van Gerrewey
comments by
Pierre Chabard

121
DEGREE ZERO REVISITED. A LOOK BACK ON SWISS ARCHITECTURE AT THE TURN OF THE TWENTY-FIRST CENTURY
Irina Davidovici
comments by
Thomas Daniell

137
NOTES ON ARCHITECTURE, BARTHES'S ZERO DEGREE, AND AI IMAGING
Sunil Manghani
comments by
Adil Mansure

155
BORROMINI '67
Andrew Leach
comments by
Gilles Malzac,
Giulia Tellier

171
AT THE MARGINS: CHOMSKY, PALLADIO, AND THE COMPUTER
Pablo Miranda Carranza
comments by
B. Beril Kapusuz-Balcı

187
GAUGING TSCHUMI'S POINT ZERO: WEAVING AND WRITING AN ARCHITECTURAL TEXT WITH DERRIDA, BARTHES, AND BATAILLE
Ole W. Fischer
comments by
Pablo Miranda Carranza

215
EXPRESSIONIST ZEROING. ANACHRONISM IN BRUNO ZEVI'S PARADIGMATIC COUNTER-HISTORIES
Wouter Van Acker
comments by
Irina Davidovici

237
ZERO DEGREE, CAPITALISM, AND ARCHITECTURE: MANFREDO TAFURI, BRUNO ZEVI, AND THE TRANSLATION OF A LITERARY CONCEPT INTO ARCHITECTURE
Gilles Malzac,
Giulia Tellier
comments by
Andrew Leach

253
ARCHITECTURE BEYOND THIRD TERMS AND SPACES: THE CASE FOR PLURALISTIC ARCHITECTURAL METHODOLOGIES
Jorge Mejía Hernández,
Klaske Havik
comments by
Christophe Van Gerrewey

269
TYPE AND CLICHÉ: REPETITION RECONSIDERED WITH QUATREMÈRE DE QUINCY'S *DICTIONNAIRE HISTORIQUE DE L'ARCHITECTURE*
Adil Mansure
comments by
Sunil Manghani

281
THE PRESENCE OF MYTH IN CONTEMPORARY LIFE. BRUNO ZEVI AND KENNETH FRAMPTON IN THE FIELD
Lyna Bourouiba
comments by
Joseph Bedford

297
UNCOVERING INVISIBLE EDITORIAL WORK: TRANSLATION AND REPRESENTATION IN THE MAGAZINE *SPAZIO E SOCIETÀ*
B. Beril Kapusuz-Balcı
comments by
Jorge Mejía Hernández

Degree Zero in Architecture

Form, Value, Authorship

INTRODUCTION

Fig. 2, 3 Courtesy of Moniek E. Bucquoye personal archives.

Fig. 4 Photographer unknown. Source: "Is now the age of neo-and non-creation...?", *Shinkenchiku*, no. 55 (1980): 200.

Fig. 5–11 Courtesy of Yuri Fujii, Fujii Architects Studio.

Fig. 12 © OMA.

Fig. 13–16 Courtesy of Lars Lerup.

Fig. 17 Embroidery by Anne-Laure Iger.

Fig. 18 Design by Lyna Bourouiba.

Fig. 19 Photograph by Lyna Bourouiba.

GROUND ZERO

Fig. 1 Courtesy of Toho Studios.

Fig. 2 © Universal History Archive / Getty Images.

Fig. 3 Photograph by Takeo Ishimatsu. Courtesy of Oita Art Museum.

Fig. 4 Courtesy of Akiharu Meiji Fujikura.

Fig. 5 Source: *Bijutsu Techō* special issue "Contemporary Images,"14, no. 203 (April 1962).

Fig. 6 © James Martin/CNET.

Fig. 7 Courtesy of Casey Mack/ Popular Architecture.

Fig. 8 Source: *Shinkenchiku*, 30, no. 4, April 1955.

Fig. 9 Source: *Kenchiku*, no. 106 (July 1969).

Fig. 10, 11 Courtesy of Tange Associates.

Fig. 12–15 Courtesy of Sei'ichi Shirai Architectural Institute.

THE SIGNIFICIANCE OF THE GENERAL FORM

Fig. 1 Courtesy of Diener & Diener © Diener & Diener.

Fig. 2 Photograph by Wolfgang Siol. Courtesy of Stiftung Hochschule für Gestaltung Ulm © HfG-Archiv.

Fig. 4 © Sigfried Giedion, gta Archiv.

Fig. 5 Source: Thillmann, W. (2015 . *Perfektes Design: Thonet Nr. 14* (Bielefeld: Kerber Verlag, 2015 , 55.

Fig. 6 Photograph by Marius Gravot. © FLC / ADAGP.

BUILDING ON CONVERSATIONS WITH ÉRIC LAPIERRE

Fig. 1 Source: Verveling, Sint-Amandsberg, Art Paper Edition, collection *Gallery Magazine*, no. 1, 2020.

Fig. 2 Photograph by Rodolphe Escher. © Rodolphe Escher.

Fig. 3 Photograph by Christophe Mahout, model by Éric Lapierre Expérience. © Christophe Mahout© Éric Lapierre Expérience.

Fig. 4 Photograph by Filip Dujardin. © Filip Dujardin

Fig. 5 Photograph by Hélène Binet and Christophe Mahout. © Hélène Binet and Christophe Mahout.

Fig. 6 Photograph by Éric Lapierre, plan by Éric Lapierre Expérience. © Éric Lapierre © Éric Lapierre Expérience.

THE RIGHT TO ARCHITECTURE

Fig. 2, 3 © OMA.

DEGREE ZERO REVISITED

Fig. 1, 2, 3, 4, 6 Photograph by Heinrich Helfenstein.

NOTES ON ARCHITECTURE

Fig. 1 Source: gallica.bnf.fr, Bibliothèque Nationale de France.

Fig. 2 © Sunil Manghani, 2024.

Fig. 4 © Victor Burgin.

Fig. 5 Courtesy of the artist Ian Dawson.

Fig. 6 Courtesy of Kunsterisches Museum.

Fig. 7 Courtesy of Rijksmuseum Amsgterdam.

Fig. 8 © Sunil Manghani 2024.

BORROMINI '67

Fig. 2 Photograph by Marcello Fagiolo.

Fig. 5 Photograph by Wladimir Piliawskij.

Fig. 6 Photograph by Christian Norberg-Schulz.

Fig. 7 Photograph by the author of *Studi sul Borromini*

Fig. 8 Photograph by Andrea Busiri Vici.

Fig. 2, 4 , 5, 6, 8 Source: *Studi sul Borromini*, vol. 1.

AT THE MARGINS

Fig. 1, 9 © Massachusetts Institute of Technology.

Fig. 5 Photograph by Margherita Spiluttini.

Fig. 6 Source: Noam Chomsky, *Syntactic Structures*, 19.

Fig. 8 Source: George Stiny and James Gips, *Shape Grammars and the Generative Specification of Painting and Sculpture*, in IFIP Congress (1971): 19.

EXPRESSIONIST ZEROING

Fig. 1–4 Courtesy of Bruno Zevi Foundation.

Fig. 1 Source: *L'architettura: Cronache e Storia*, 29: 12 (December 1979): 700-701.

ZERO DEGREE, CAPITALISM, AND ARCHITECTURE

Fig. 2 Courtesy of Centro Studio Piero Gobetti.

ARCHITECTURE BEYOND THIRD TERMS & SPACES

Fig. 1, 2 Source: Domenico Fontana, *Della trasportatione dell'obelisco vaticano et delle fabriche di nostro signore Papa Sisto V* (Rome: Appresso Domenico Basa, 1590), 14 and 19.

Fig. 3 © Jorge Mejia, 2024.

Fig. 4 Source: *Casabolla*, nos. 359-360 (December 1971): 101.

Fig. 5, 6 Source: Stanford Anderson, *On Streets* (Cambridge / London: The MIT Press, 1986 (1978), 6 and 8.

TYPE AND CLICHÉ

Fig. 1 Photograph by Roger Rössing & Renate Rössing. Source: Deutsche Fotothek.

THE PRESENCE OF MYTH

Fig. 1 Source: *Social Research*, 52, no. 2 (1985).

Fig. 2 Source: "Reuniones y Conferencias de la CICA," journal unknown. Courtesy of Bruno Zevi Foundation.

Fig. 3, 5 Courtesy of Canadian Centre for Architecture, Kenneth Frampton fonds, Gift of Kenneth Frampton.

Fig. 4 Source: *Architect Journal*, no. 19 (July 1989), 15.

Fig. 6 Source: *L'architettura*, cronache e storia, no. 10 (1981).

UNCOVERING INVISIBLE EDITORIAL WORK

Fig. 1 Source: 066021, Portraits of GDC, Fondo Giancarlo De Carlo (FGDC). Courtesy of Archivio Progetti, Universita Iuav di Venezia.

Fig. 2 Source: http://peterprangnell.com/reflection%3A_the_U_of_T_years_2.html

Fig. 4, 5 Source: 037344, Spazio e Società-cor/01/082, FGDC. Courtesy of Archivio Progetti, Universita Iuav di Venezia.

Fig. 6 (Left) Photograph by Peter Prangnell. Courtesy of Anthony Belcher.

Fig. 6 (Right) Source: *Spazio e Società*, no. 12 (December 1980): 58.

JB Joseph Bedford is associate professor of history and theory at Virginia Tech. He holds a PhD from Princeton University, architecture degrees from the University of Cambridge and The Cooper Union, and is the founding editor of the *Architecture Exchange*, a platform for theoretical exchange in architecture.

GB Geert Bekaert (1928–2016) was a Belgian architecture critic, theoretician, and historian, who published more than 1,000 articles and texts, in magazines, newspapers, books, and journals. He was professor at TU Eindhoven and KU Leuven, and editor of *Archis*. His archives and his library are located at Ghent University.

LB Lyna Bourouiba is an architect and PhD candidate in the Faculty of Architecture La Cambre Horta of the Université libre de Bruxelles. She is a member of the research collective Bureau FL5.2. Her research focuses on the transcultural history of the idea of an architectural degree zero within the social space of the practice of architectural history, theory, and criticism, portrayed as a means of domination through knowledge

PC Pierre Chabard is an architect, critic, and historian of architecture and urbanism. He is currently associate professor of history and theory at the École Nationale Supérieure d'Architecture de Paris-La Villette. An author and editor of various books and a founding member of the French journal *Criticat* (2008–18), he now runs the Éditions de la Villette.

VC Victoire Chancel is an architect and a PhD candidate at the Université libre de Bruxelles. After practicing and teaching in Marseille (ENSAM), she moved to Brussels, where she co-founded the office l'*ÉQUIPE*. At the same time, she continues exploring the relationship between built form and image through publications, cultural projects, and collective practice, notably with Bureau FL5.2.

TD Thomas Daniell is professor of architectural history, theory, and criticism at Kyoto University Japan. His publications include *FOBA: Buildings* (Princeton Architectural Press, 2005), *After the Crash: Architecture in Post-Bubble Japan* (Princeton Architectural Press, 2008), *Houses and Gardens of Kyoto* (Tuttle, 2010), *Kiyoshi Sey Takeyama + Amorphe* (Equal Books, 2011), Kansai 6 (Equal Books, 2011), and *An Anatomy of Influence* (AA Publications, 2018).

ID Irina Davidovici is an architect, historian, and the Director of the gta Archive at ETH Zurich. Among numerous other publications, Davidovici is the author of *Forms of Practice. German-Swiss Architecture 1980–2000* (gta, 2012 and 2018) and *The Autonomy of Theory: Ticino Architecture and Its Critical Reception* (gta, 2024).

OWF Ole W. Fischer serves as professor of history and theory of architecture and design at the Stuttgart State Academy of Art and Design. His research interests range from late nineteenth-century style reform, to the critique of modern architecture during the 1960s, '70s, and '80s, to contemporary issues.

CFC Carla Frick-Cloupet is studio director for the Y1 at EPFL Architecture. She is a scientific collaborator at the Hortence Laboratory of the Université libre de Bruxelles. She defended her PhD thesis in 2023 on contemporary architecture and its links with analytic philosophy. In 2023 she founded the office *L'ÉQUIPE* in Brussels where she practices architecture mainly for cultural institutions on the Brussels scene.

KH Klaske Havik is professor of methods of analysis and imagination at TU Delft and chair of the European network *Writing Urban Places*. Her publications include *Urban Literacy* (nai010, 2014) and the edited volumes *Architectural Positions* (Sun, 2009) and *Writingplace* (nai010, 2016). She was editor of *OASE* and initiated the *Writingplace Journal for Architecture and Literature*.

BBKB B. Beril Kapusuz-Balcı is assistant professor in the Gazi University Department of Architecture, specializing in architectural theory, urban history, architectural exhibitions, publications, and photography. She earned her PhD in 2018 and conducted postdoctoral research at Iuav University of Venice, focusing on ecological pedagogies of photography in architectural education.

AL Andrew Leach is professor of architectural history. He held the Wallace Fellowship at Harvard's Villa I Tatti in 2018. Among his books are *What is Architectural History?* (Polity, 2010) and *The Baroque in Architectural Culture, 1880–1980* (2015, edited with Maarten Delbeke and John Macarthur).

GM Gilles Malzac is an architect and associate professor at ENSA Lyon. After 10 years working in architectural agencies (Fernandez & Serres, Boris Bouchet) and as a liberal practitioner, he started a PhD at Paris Malaquais in 2019. His research focuses on the historical mediations between architectural and urban forms, and the emergent forces of capitalism.

SM Sunil Manghani is Professor of Theory, Practice, and Critique at the University of Southampton and a research fellow of The Alan Turing Institute. He is managing editor of *Theory, Culture & Society*, and co-editor of *Journal of Visual Art Practice*. His books include *Image Studies* (Routledge, 2013), *Zero Degree Seeing* (Edinburgh University Press, 2019), and *Farewell to Visual Studies* (Penn State University Press, 2015).

AM Adil Mansure is a PhD student working on maritime indigenous histories of technology, architecture, and the environment. Adil has held the *H. Allen Brooks Traveling Fellowship*, co-edited the volume *Finding San Carlino* (Routledge, 2019), and has taught at various schools in North America. He holds degrees from Yale, Cambridge, and Mumbai universities.

JMH Jorge Mejía Hernández graduated as an architect in Colombia, and earned his PhD at TU Delft, where he currently researches and teaches. His dissertation *Transactions; or Architecture as a System of Research Programs* advances a methodological framework to examine the individual and social rationales that determine the growth and development of architectural knowledge.

PMC Pablo Miranda Carranza is senior lecturer at Lund University's Department of Architecture and the Built Environment. His research focuses on the history of technology in architecture and its influence on practices and discourses. He is currently studying the use of computer models in urban planning, funded by the Swedish Research Council.

MM Matthew Mullane is assistant professor of the history and theory of architecture at Radboud University. His book *World Observation: Empire, Architecture, and the Global Archive of Itō Chūta* (University of Pittsburgh Press, 2025) offers an alternative origin for global architectural history in nineteenth-century Japan.

MS Martin Steinmann (1942–2022) was a Swiss historian, theoretician, and critic of architecture, and professor emeritus at EPFL Lausanne. As editor of the journal *Archithese* (1980–1986) and *Faces*, he published many thematic issues and landmark essays that articulated theoretical frameworks for Swiss architecture since the 1970s.

GT Giulia Tellier graduated in 2018 as an architect. After working three years for Atelier Construire, founded by Patrick Bouchain, she started a PhD in 2022 at Paris Malaquais. Her research focuses on architectural labor under financial capitalism. She is a member of GRAPE: Groupe de Recherche et d'Action sur la Production de l'Espace.

WVA Wouter Van Acker is an engineer-architect and associate professor in the Faculty of Architecture of the Université libre de Bruxelles. He is co-editor of several journal issues and volumes including *Architecture and Ugliness* (Bloomsbury, 2020), *Intermediality in Architecture* (for *Clara*, 2024), and *Untimely Teachers* (for *Architectural Theory Review*, 2024).

CVG Christophe Van Gerrewey is the author of, most recently, *Something Completely Different: Architecture in Belgium* (MIT Press, 2024). He is editor of the architecture journal *OASE* and of the art journal *De Witte Raaf*, and was professor of architecture theory at EPFL Lausanne from 2015 to 2024.

This edited volume is the outcome of an international symposium realized as part of the FNRS-funded research project "Bruno Zevi and Degree Zero of Architectural Writing" (2020-2024), hosted by the Faculty of Architecture La Cambre-Horta of the Université Libre de Bruxelles (ULB) and its research center Hortence.

The publication was made possible with the financial support of the Fund for Scientific Research (F.R.S.-FNRS) through grant no. 40027867, as well as the Fondation Universitaire, the Fonds David et Alice Van Buuren, and the Fondation Jaumotte-Demoulin. Additional funding was provided by the Université Libre de Bruxelles, its Faculty of Architecture La Cambre-Horta, and Hortence.

Both the symposium and this volume were made possible thanks to the contributions of many people, who collaborated generously in various ways. The editors would like to warmly thank the scientific committee for their active participation in the selection of abstracts following the call for papers, and their contributions to the symposium: Paola Ardizzola (Gdansk University of Technology), Joseph Bedford (Virginia Tech), Pierre Chabard (ENSA Paris La Villette), Thomas Daniell (Kyoto University), Irina Davidovici (ETH Zurich), Andrew Leach (Queensland University of Technology), and Sunil Manghani (University of Southampton). We thank all the authors for their patient work and all the contributors to the symposium: Matthew Allen, Andrea Canclini, Andrea Alberto Dutto, Michael Mossman, Alberto Petracchin, and Francesca Privitera. We are also grateful to all those who accepted our invitation to write a series of short reflections on the chapters.

We would also like to thank Carol Rossius and Isabelle Wargnies from the administrative staff of the Faculty of Architecture La Cambre-Horta of the ULB for coordinating the room logistics; Caroline Rosiers from the cafeteria for coffee and her eternal enthusiasm; the team of Arpaije and the restaurant L'Architecte for the catering and the sweetness; and Cécile Stas for her immeasurable help and efficiency in managing the budget and organizing the accommodation of the speakers and catering. We also thank Axel Wlody and Anne-Laure Iger for the layout of the booklet. Thanks to Pippo Ciora, Antonino Saggio, and Alessandra Muntoni for their contributions to an online seminar on Bruno Zevi and the zero degree of architectural writing in 2021; and to the Academia Belgica in Rome (Sabine Van Sprang, Angie Vandycke, Charles Bossu) for hosting this event which was finally cancelled because of the COVID pandemic.

We are particularly grateful to Lenore Hietkamp for bringing her editorial precision and precious advice to this book project. Warm thanks to Lee Gilette for his careful reviews during the copy-editing process and to Duncan Brown for the translation of Martin Steinman's typescript. For the images, we thank Alessandra Chiappini and the Foundation Bruno Zevi, and the Canadian Center for Architecture for their generous welcome and for providing the scans. We particularly thank Yuri Fujii, Hiromi Fujii's daughter and collaborator, and Lars Lerup for their generosity and for allowing us to publish so many beautiful drawings and photographs. A special thought goes to Moniek Bucquoye, who recently passed away, and who shared all her memories of the CICA with us, as well as some of the materials published in the book. Last in the process, Clémentine Léon and Gautier Scerra of Service Local have gone far beyond what is traditionally expected in designing an academic book. By deeply engaging with the content of the manuscript, they have truly given a graphic form to this book that resonates with the editorial positioning regarding authorship. Robert Stürzl and Anne König of Spector Books deserve our warm thanks for their critical insights on the mock-up, which substantially contributed to the material quality of this publication.

A special thanks to our colleagues Anne-Laure Iger, Quentin Nicolaï, and Alice Paris for re-reading some chapters and for their continued help, support and advice during the editorial process; and to the Bureau FL5.2 for being that precious collaborative space. We feel indebted to the members of the supervisory committee of Lyna Bourouiba's PhD for their engagement in this research project: Jean-Didier Bergilez, Pierre Chabard, and Andrew Leach. A final thought goes to Marielle Macé and Roland Barthes, whose writings provide an unfailing spark of thought.

Degree Zero
in Architecture
Form, Value, Authorship

Edited by
Lyna Bourouiba, Wouter Van Acker

Graphic design
Service Local
Clémentine Léon, Gautier Scerra
Typeface
EB Trainer Grotesk
Image correction
Oleksii Novikov
Copyediting
Lenore Hietkamp, Lee Gillette
Proofreading
Anne König
Printing and binding
Westermann Druck Zwickau GmbH
Published by
Spector Books
Verlagsgesellschaft mbH
Harkortstraße 10
04107 Leipzig
www.spectorbooks.com

Distributed by
Germany, Austria: GVA,
Gemeinsame Verlagsauslieferung
Göttingen GmbH&Co. KG,
www.gva-verlage.de
Switzerland: AVA
Verlagsauslieferung AG,
www.ava.ch
France, Belgium: Interart Paris,
www.interart.fr
UK: Central Books Ltd,
www.centralbooks.com
USA, Canada, Central and South
America, Africa: ARTBOOK/D.A.P.,
www.artbook.com
Japan: twelvebooks,
www.twelve-books.com
South Korea: The Book Society,
www.thebooksociety.org
Australia, New Zealand:
Perimeter Distribution,
www.perimeterdistribution.com

First edition: 2026
Printed in the EU

ISBN 978-3-95905-905-3 DZ